Y0-BEE-765

REWEAVING THE WEB OF LIFE

Book design and layout by Nina Huizinga
Cover design by Barbara Benton
Cover photograph by JEB
Photography by JEB, Diana J. M. Davies/Insight and Dorothy Marder as credited with each photograph.

Library of Congress Number: 82-81879
ISBN: 0-86571-017-1 Hardbound
0-86571-016-3 Paperbound

Printed in the United States

New Society Publishers is a collective of Movement for a New Society, a network of small groups working for fundamental social change through nonviolent action.

This book has been reviewed by the Southwest Regional Service Collective of Movement for a New Society (MNS), acting as the representatives of the MNS Network. It has our sponsorship as a valuable piece of literature, with perspectives worthy of consideration and discussion. The opinions stated herein do not necessarily represent agreed-upon positions of either the Southwest Regional Service Collective or the MNS Network as a whole.

Reweaving The Web of Life

Feminism and Nonviolence

Edited by Pam McAllister

New Society Publishers

This anthology has a life of its own but many friends gave it shape and spirit. Nina Huizinga was my right hand and heart-sister during this project. Her tireless work on all aspects of the book's creation has been invaluable. I am also deeply indebted to the other members and friends of New Society Publishers who stood by the book through thick and thin: Matt Becker, Paul Lieberman, Alice Maes, Max!, Suzanna Tvede Jones, David Albert and Ellen Sawislak. In addition, I wish to thank the people who worked on production: Heather McDonald, Stewart J. Thomas, Karen Dorsky, Lysbeth Bori, Cheong Soon Wah, Anneke van Os, Herb Ettel, Kathy Spaar and Joan Nikelsky.

Barbara Deming, whose work and life have influenced the imaginations and hearts of so many of us, brought healing and inspired courage at the most crucial moment and breathed life into the anthology once more.

I thank the Racism Task Force for its part in shaping the landscape of this book and Marion McNaughton, Nancy Brigham and Robert McClellan for offering their skills at facilitating several meetings.

I thank Canadian friend Taylor for his varied expressions of support, Jerry Kyle, the curator of the Swarthmore College Peace Collection, for opening up a whole new world to me, Diane Clancy for her sincere perserverance and Loreine Kendrick, the unwitting matchmaker who sparked the meeting from which this book was born and, by a strange turn of fate, became the roommate who was there with encouraging words at the project's end.

Most of all, I thank all the generous, patient and creative contributors to this anthology, a network of new friends, whose correspondence and work have enriched my life and given me the strength to help in reweaving the web of life.

Grateful acknowledgment is made for permission to reprint previously published and copyrighted articles and material from the following sources:

"I Am A Dangerous Woman," by Joan Cavanagh. By permission of the author.

"Patriarchy: A State of War," by Barbara Zanotti, first published in *Peacework, Feminism: The Hope for a Future,* Peacework, AFSC.

"Patriarchy Is A Killer: What People Concerned About Peace and Justice Should Know," by Donna Warnock, from the War Resister's League's Organizer Manual, 1981.

"Women, Peace and Power," by Jo Vellacott, from the 1981 Rachel Cadbury Lecture sponsored by the Friends General Conference.

"A Song for Gorgons," by Barbara Deming. By permission of the author.

"Feminism and Disobedience: Conversations with Barbara Deming," by Mab Segrest, first published in *Feminary: A Feminist Journal for the South,* Volume XI No. 1 & 2.

"Ida B. Wells: Free Speech and Black Struggle," by Rosemarie Freeney-Harding. "Free Speech" is a chapter in Rosemarie's M.A. thesis on Ida B. Wells for Goddard College's Graduate School. She received support for the research and writing through a grant from the Center for the American Woman and Politics at the Eagleton Institute of Rutgers University.

"Jessie Daniel Ames: Grass-Roots Anti-Lynching Campaign," by Jacquelyn Dowd Hall, first published in *Southern Exposure,* 1977.

"Fannie Lou Hamer: Baptism By Fire," by Susan Kling, this excerpt reprinted from *Fannie Lou Hamer: A Biography* published by Women for Racial and Economic Equality, 1979.

"We Started From Opposite Ends of the Spectrum," by Cynthia Washington, first published in *Southern Exposure,* 1977.

"Women's Consciousness and the Southern Black Movement," by Sara Evans, first published in *Southern Exposure,* 1977.

"More Power Than We Want," by Bruce Kokopeli and George Lakey, first published in *Win* magazine, July 29, 1976.

"Only Justice Can Stop A Curse," copyright ©1982 by Alice Walker. First published in *Motor Jones,* Sept./Oct., 1982.

"Foolish Notion," by Holly Near. Words and music by Holly Near, recorded on *Fire in the Rain* (Redwood Records 402), © 1980 Hereford Music. All rights reserved. Used by permission.

"Cop Tales," by Grace Paley first published in *Seven Days,* April, 1980.

"Breaking the Racism Barrier: White Anti-Racism Work," by Donna Landerman was excerpted from "White Anti-Racism Work" by Donna Landerman and Mary McAtee, available from the YWCA, 135 Broad Street, Hartford, Conn., 06105. An expanded version of Donna's essay also appeared in *Aegis: Magazine on Ending Violence Against Women,* 1982.

"Women and the Draft," by Karen Lindsey first published in *Second Wave,* 1979.

"The Army Will Make A 'Man' Out of You," by Helen Michalowski, first published in *WIN,* March 1, 1980.

"Uneasy Borders," by Valerie Miner appears under the title "Maple Leaf Or Beaver," in the novel, *Movement,* by Valerie Miner, The Crossing Press, 1982.

"Macho Obstacles to Peace," by Ann Davidon first published in the *Bulletin of the Atomic Scientists,* June, 1977.

"Daughters, I Love You," by Linda Hogan used by permission of the author. These poems will be published by Women's Research Center, Loretto Heights College, Denver, Colorado.

"Message to the Next Civilization," by Joan Baez, from World Federalist Association, 1011 Arlington Blvd., Suite W-219, Arlington, VA 22209, © Joan C. Baez.

In the article by Barbara Zanotti, the lines from "Natural Resources" are reprinted from *The Dream Of a Common Language, Poems 1974-1977,* by Adrienne Rich, with the permission of W.W. Norton & Company, Inc. Copyright © 1978 by W.W. Norton & Company, Inc.

In the article by Erika Duncan, "The Lure of the Death Culture," the section of the poem, "Prelude to a New Fin-de-Siecle," by David Gascoyne is reprinted with his permission. In the same article, the section of the poem, "Beauty and the Beast," from *Beginning with 0* by Olga Broumas published by and copyrighted by Yale University Press is reprinted with the permission of Yale University Press.

In the article by Betsy Wright, "Sunpower/Moonpower/Transformation," the words to the song "God Bless the Grass," by Malvina Reynolds are reprinted with permission from Schroder Music Company, 2027 Parker Street, Berkeley, California, 94704.

Contents

PART II

"the passion to make and make again
where such unmaking reigns"—Adrienne Rich

Introduction

The "Strength" card in my Tarot deck depicts, not a warrior going off to battle with his armor and his mighty sword, but a woman stroking a lion.

The woman has not slain the lion nor maced it, nor netted it, nor has she put on it a muzzle or a leash. And though the lion clearly has teeth and long sharp claws, the woman is not hiding, nor has she sought a protector, nor has she grown muscles. She doesn't appear to be talking to the lion, nor flattering it, nor tossing it fresh meat to distract its hungry jaws.

The woman on the "Strength" card wears a flowing white dress and a garland of flowers. With one hand she cups the lion's jaws, with the other she caresses its nose. The lion on the card has big yellow eyes and a long red tongue curling out of its mouth. One paw is lifted and the mane falls in thick red curls across its broad torso. The woman. The lion. Together they depict strength.

* * * * *

The books on the shelf above my desk depict the dual nature of my primary research. One half of the shelf is stacked with books about rape, books about battery, wife abuse, feminist analyses of pornography, psychological and sociological studies of aggression. Half way across the shelf they meet the other side of my life—books about Gandhi, nonviolence, the history of pacifists and Quakers and peace movement activists, books by Barbara Deming and Martin Luther King, Jr.

* * * * *

Several years ago I toured ten southern cities, stayed in women's collectives and led community meetings to hear what kind of violence the women were facing and what solutions they were finding. Two experiences on my tour stand out as most intense, memorable and rewarding for me. The one was my week visiting Barbara Deming and Jane Gapen in the Florida Keys. I had read Barbara's books in college and most of my understanding of nonviolence was a direct result of her writing. She had eventually become my mentor: I would send her my work and she would send me encouragement. Through her I had come to understand the vital link between feminism and nonviolence. She embraces the whole spectrum of life with unfragmented concern—from love for the Great White Heron who haunts the quiet canal in front of her house and concern for the endangered snails in a Florida stream, to concern about the global implications of the military maneuvers at Key West and the urgency of offering asylum to a battered neighbor.

The week spent with her was the realization of a dream. It was another world, this simple life in a tropical climate: the avocado trees and lizards; the slow, long quiet of the steamy nights; Jane's easy talk and Barbara's intense listening. In the evenings I listened by candlelight to Barbara's stories of her experiences during the Civil Rights days. Her thin arms gestured, palms up in challenge to the hardened hearts encountered on those long, dry walks for peace. Her hands crossed at her heart in a gesture of empathy. Her fist clenched at her stomach in a gesture of outrage. I thought then of other young sisters in ages before us listening to the wise women who told their stories by campfire, casting long shadows with boney, storytelling hands. And in these night listenings, I began to understand more about Barbara's vision of nonviolence and feminism, her determined belief in the wisdom of "clinging to the truth."

Three days after I left the Keys, I visited a women's collective in northern rural Florida. These women had armed themselves, slept with pistols beneath their pillows and talked freely about the significance of women becoming willing, able, and prepared to use guns for self defense. "I think that a woman owes it to herself and the rest of womankind to shoot to kill a rapist," explained one woman who expressed the consensus among her housemates. "And I say that every battered wife owes it to herself and every other woman on the face of the earth to defend herself. If that means running and hiding, that's okay. If that means pulling a .38 on the dude because the cops aren't going to get there first, then that's okay too."

They took me to the police range where they practiced and gave me one lesson in how to shoot. I remember that afternoon as one of the most satisfying I'd spent in months—standing beneath a sunny, vividly blue sky with six women absolutely committed to the "I'm-not-a-victim-anymore" spirit. When

Annie put a real pistol in my hand and showed me how to load and shoot it, I wasn't the least bit afraid or unsure. I ringed the bull's eye with all but two of the bullets! The women rewarded me with hugs and hearty shoulder slaps. "Well, so much for aimlessness," said Sue in her Mississippi drawl. "McAllister, you're a natural killer!" shouted Maryanne, congratulating me with her version of a compliment. And I loved these women with all my heart. I felt one in the spirit with these fine sisters—in their rage and their solid commitment to resistance and in their boisterous laughter—even though I couldn't affirm their adopting the patriarchy's answer-to-everything (threat of death).

How do I explain that I was so at home with both radical pacifists and with the gun-toting women? How do I reconcile these two apparently contradictory experiences, both of which touched my heart and changed my life?

* * * * *

Feminist nonviolence is the process/strategy/philosophy which makes sense of both my rage and my vision of the world I want to live in. For me, means and ends need to be consistent. I do not believe I can endorse the patriarchy's notion of blood-and-guts power in my day-to-day confrontations and, at the same time, be taken seriously when I speak of a futuristic ideal which exalts wisdom, sensitivity, fairness and compassion as basic requirements in running the affairs of the world. A new world, the world I long for, cannot be built with the tools, psychology, belief system of the old. It will be born of the changes encoded in the details of our lives as we are living them now. The fabric of the new society will be made of nothing more or less than the threads woven in today's interactions.

The peculiar strength of nonviolence comes from the dual nature of its approach—the offering of respect and concern on the one hand and of defiance and stubborn noncooperation with injustice on the other. Put into the feminist perspective, nonviolence is the merging of our uncompromising rage at the patriarchy's brutal destructiveness with a refusal to adopt it's ways—a refusal to give in to despair or hate or to let men off the hook by making them the "Other" as they have made those they fear "Others." Together, these seemingly contradictory impulses (to rage against yet refuse to destroy) combine to create a "strength" worthy of nothing less than revolution—true revolution, not just a shuffle of death-wielding power. But one impulse without the other only keeps us mired in the patriarchy's mess. We will never outlive our rage: it cannot be assuaged by revenge. Our rage is fed by the collective flames of women martyred centuries before us, of women moaning in their bedrooms and the back alleys this very hour. To focus on rage alone will exhaust our strength, forge our energy into a tool of the patriarchy's death-lure, force us to concede allegiance to the path of violence and destruction. On the other hand, compassion without rage renders us impotent, seduces us into watered-down humanism, stifles our good energy. Without rage we settle for slow change, feel thankful for tidbits of autonomy tossed our way, ask for something mediocre like "equality." It is with our rage we defy the male supremacists, find the courage to risk resistance. And it is with our intimate connection to the life-force which pulses through our own veins that we insist there is another way to be. By combining our rage with compassion, we live the revolution every day.

Voices expressing both defiance and no-nonsense goodwill, hiss-scream-sing from this anthology. There are over fifty contributors to this book. We come from many perspectives, all parts of the United States, and cover a wide range of age and experience. Some of us are professional poets, writers, teachers, used to capturing our passion on paper. Others of us are not polished writers and are sharing our recorded observations perhaps for the first time. Almost all of us are dedicated activists, committed to working for social change.

There are enough variations in our perspectives to render this anthology a "dialogue," though it is, as was intended, primarily a dialogue among people who want to pursue the revolutionary implications of combining nonviolence and feminism. Some of us come most strongly from a feminist background, focusing our attention on fighting for the rights of women, Blacks, gays and may have long ago shunned involvement with the largely male-led peace movement activities. Others of us come more from a pacifist perspective and are still struggling with all the implications of feminism. Some of the contributors believe that women are biologically or spiritually attuned to a gentler impulse than are men. Others reject this as a dangerous notion. Some, while committed to resisting war, nuclear energy, and the draft, would see no contradiction in using physical force for self defense. Others would. Some desire an egalitarian world where men and women would live harmoniously; others have lost patience with this ideal. In spite of the variations, almost all of the contributors embrace both feminism and nonviolence in a way which transforms both, and the differences only add complexity and value to the pattern we weave. And, with few exceptions, we agree that to be nonviolent means, first of all, for women, to love ourselves, or, as Andrea Dworkin has said, to refuse to be a victim anywhere for friend or foe; and that it is imperative that we be as committed to resisting the institutions which perpetuate the violence of racial prejudice, unfair distribution of wealth and opportunities, and heterosexist privilege as we are to resisting war, rape, and nuclear power.

There are three essays in this anthology which qualify as exceptions in the dialogue. The first is the inclusion of Jo Vellacott, a Canadian woman in a line-up of otherwise all U.S. based writers. This book was intended to be limited to the writings of U.S. feminists with the hope that perhaps another volume would follow which would include articles by feminists from other countries. But when this extraordinary essay came our way, we decided to make an exception. We welcome Jo to this anthology.

The second exception is Barbara Reynold's "Sailing Into Test Waters." In this narrative, Barbara draws some conclusions to her own experience which will leave feminist readers gasping. But it is included here because Barbara's experience is women's history and exemplifies the struggle of women in the traditional, male scheme of things, both in the family and in the peace movement. It is an important story for feminists to hear especially as we begin to take for granted the value of woman-bonding and the networks we have to sustain us today. We welcome Barbara to this anthology.

Finally, the third exception is the essay "More Power Than We Want" written by two men, Bruce Kokopeli and George Lakey, in an otherwise all female anthology. In addition to the fact that this is an especially fine essay, it is included here to remind us that there are a few men who are struggling, in their own way, to defeat the patriarchy and who understand the innate destructiveness of the artificial, masculine paradigm created as a tool for the patriarchy. Bruce and George are welcomed to this anthology.

There is one thing probably all of the contributors have in common and that is dissatisfaction with the words at our disposal. We are not alone in this discontent nor in our inability to come up with any better words. Barbara Deming put her finger on the problem when she wrote, "If people doubt that there is power in nonviolence, I am afraid that it is due in part to the fact that those of us who believe in it have yet to find for ourselves an adequate vocabulary. The leaflets we pass out tend to speak too easily about love and truth. . . The words do describe our method in a kind of shorthand. But who can read the shorthand?''[1]

While the word "pacifist" sounds too much like its antithesis "passivity," the word "nonviolence" is similarly confused. It is often used incorrectly, by both its advocates and by the wider, unconvinced population, to mean any event or time when physical violence is not employed. In this way, sipping eggnog might be considered a "nonviolent action." This, of course, is far from the correct use of the word, that being the identification of a specific method of struggle, a particular way of transforming relationships.

In addition to this confusion, "nonviolence" is a sadly self-limiting and inadequate expression, camouflaging the true nature, scope and power of the strategy/philosophy to which it refers. How often have we heard a panel described as having both angry revolutionaries *and* pacifists (as though pacifists were *not* angry revolutionaries) or a demonstration described as nonviolent *but* spirited. And if "nonviolence" sounds limp to some, to others it serves to underscore violence. In *Thinking Like a Woman,* Leah Fritz suggested that "...the word 'nonviolence' has a violent ring in our ears. It suggests that violence is some kind of a norm, whereas for thousands of years it has been quite an eccentric quality in half the human population."[2] And Catherine Reid, an activist, writer from Vermont, has written, "I am often frustrated by the term nonviolence as it seems to convey false assumptions of submission, passivity. 'Not violent' is only a fraction of its definition. Gandhi's term 'satyagraha' seems much more useful. It means truth force. 'Force' implies a more assertive, positive stand than does nonviolence—that we rely on the strength of truth rather than on physical force." This anthology, which uses "pacifism" and "nonviolence" interchangeably, will do little to advance a new vocabulary, though it should dispel the confusion of nonviolence with the dreaded passivity. These essays echo Gandhi's statement, "It is better to resist oppression by violent means than to submit, but it is best of all to resist by nonviolent means."

Several writers have chosen to use spelling variations in place of "woman" and "women." This, as Jane Meyerding has written in explanation, is not to express rejection of men but to emphasize the basic feminist belief that "womyn's liberation requires us to develop our identities according to our own realities and our own values. Even if the word 'woman' had nothing whatsoever to do, originally, with the word 'man,' it is historically true that womyn have been identified and have identified ourselves by male perspectives. Removing the words 'man' and 'men' from the words 'womon' and 'womyn' is, for me, an easy, effective way to emphasize my womon-identification. I do so in order to remind myself, to help myself resist the tendency to revert to the old, easy, familiar ways of thinking which excluded womyn's realities from 'man's' experience."

This book is structured in two parts. The first part deals primarily with theory. The writers explore various ideas about the revolutionary implications of combining feminism and nonviolence and address such issues as masculinity and war, women's commitment to peace, patriarchal power and feminist resistance, sexism in the peace movement and feminist distrust of traditional nonviolence theory. In the second part of the book the writers generally show how feminism and nonviolence apply to specific areas of struggle: tax resistance, anti-war and anti-nuke work, self defense, animal rights, personal relationships, anti-racism work.

The title, *Reweaving the Web of Life: Feminism and Nonviolence*, comes from Catherine Reid's essay which captured a recurring theme in the writing and artwork found throughout the anthology—images of spinning, weaving and mending the fine and vulnerable connections that are our beauty and our survival.

This anthology is a beginning. It is the first substantial collection of writings by feminists who embrace radical nonviolence and, as such, it serves two immediate needs. The first is our need to find each other, to read each other's work, to see ourselves as a cohesive, viable community of women primarily, women with a unique political vision and a lot to offer. This volume represents process; it motivated many of the writers published here to formulate expressions of their life experiences, their experiments with the "complicated truth," their raw theories, questions, hopes.

The second primary function of this book is to become a visible reminder to the larger feminist community that a dialogue on women's use of violence or nonviolence is very much a worthwhile dialogue, not one to be scorned as suspicious. To that end, this first volume of writings by feminists who embrace a nonviolent perspective will hopefully give us a foundation for the future discussion of that perspective which is often, in the feminist community, dismissed as trivial or the equivalent of passivity.

This book is a potential tool, as well, for peace movement activists who have for too long ignored the violence at their own doorstep, that violence and threat of violence aimed at women on a day-to-day basis. As this book is incorporated into the body of "peace movement literature," there will be less excuse for such blatant sexism.

Here, then, is something brand new, a first in our body of literature, a promise of dialogues to come. And while the book is new, the idea is old, as old as the "Strength" card in the Tarot deck. And it is something of power, perhaps of more power than any of us could imagine, although it has been glimpsed in our collective dreams. Barbara Deming has written, "I have had the dream that women would at last be the ones to truly experiment with nonviolent struggle, discover its full force." Indeed, it is the conviction of most of those in this anthology, that nonviolence and feminism together hold the key to the revolution which would end the patriarchy and reweave, mend the web of life. And so we go—spinning, weaving, mending.

The Power Of Wimyn

In the Middle Ages, millions of wimyn were burned to death because they were a threat to Church and State authority. What was their challenge, their power, their threat?

My picture, "The Power of Wimyn," portrays some of the special powers wimyn have. The wimyn in my picture are weaving tapestries of their lives. Into the pattern they weave the leaf, symbol of the healing power of wimyn; the labrys, symbol of wimyn's fighting spirit and a tool used in early matriarchal societies; the moon and stars, symbols of wimyn's spirituality; the snake, originally a positive symbol of life and death. Another image in the tapestry is of a womyn giving birth. She is a squatting, groaning, powerful goddess of early Aztec culture. She is the nurturing, creative power of wimyn.

The weavers are young, middle-aged and old—the maiden, mother and crone images of witchcraft. They are proud, strong, young and old, Black and white manifestations of the goddess. THEY ARE WIMYN WHO LOVE THEMSELVES.

—Judy Costello

Part I

"I have had the dream that women
would at last be the ones
to truly experiment with nonviolent struggle,
discover its full force."

—Barbara Deming

Joan Cavanagh
I Am a Dangerous Woman

The contributors to this anthology are dangerous people; dangerous, that is, to the system of male supremacy and all its grotesque manifestations.

Watch the hands. There's the danger. They take away, obstruct, refuse to build the walls and bombs and jails. And then they give, stretch out, open, gesture a return, offer not rejection but solace. Hands holding guns are less confusing. Hands holding guns are less dangerous in the long run.

The voice in this poem is the feminist-pacifist voice confronting the system of male domination with both defiance of the masculine paradigm and insistence that men understand that "our lives are bound together." The poem is not structured, as one might be tempted to structure such a poem, in two parts—the first voicing the poet's rage, the second voicing her concern. Instead, Joan weaves the two into one voice. She writes, "I will not share one square foot of this earth with you/while you're hell-bent on destruction,/But neither will I deny that we are of the same earth,/Born of the same Mother."

Joan Cavanagh wrote this poem in the spring of 1976 when she lived at Jonah House, a resistance community in Baltimore. She had been active in the late sixties and early seventies in the United Farm Workers' Union and in resistance to the United States' war against Indochina. During that time she was frequently arrested and served many jail sentences for acts of civil disobedience.

A growing awareness of feminism as a revolutionary force led her to move to New Haven, Connecticut in 1977, seeking to make connections in her life between her resistance to the nuclear arms race and her understanding of its roots in a system whose values, structures and actions are deeply oppressive and increasingly threatening to the lives of women.

Joan, now 27, is a member of the Steering Committee of the New Haven Feminist Union which has task forces on reproductive freedom, nuclear weapons and nuclear power, and violence against women. She is a "Founding Mother" of the two-year-old Anti-Nuclear Task Force (also known as SONG, Spinsters Opposed to Nuclear Genocide), which makes connections between violence against women and the nuclear arms race through education, public speaking, direct action and civil disobedience.

I am a dangerous woman
Carrying neither bombs nor babies
Flowers nor molotov cocktails.
I confound all your reason, theory, realism
Because I will neither lie in your ditches
Nor dig your ditches for you
Nor join in your armed struggle
For bigger and better ditches.
I will not walk with you nor walk for you,
I won't live with you
And I won't die for you,
But neither will I try to deny you
Your right to live and die.
I will not share one square foot of this earth with you
While you're hell-bent on destruction,
But neither will I deny that we are of the same earth,
Born of the same Mother.
I will not permit
You to bind my life to yours
But I will tell you that our lives
Are bound together
And I will demand
That you live as though you understand
This one salient fact.

I am a dangerous woman
Because I will tell you, sir,
Whether you are concerned or not,
Masculinity has made of this world a living hell,
A furnace burning away at hope, love, faith, and justice,
A furnace of My Lais, Hiroshimas, Dachaus.
A furnace which burns the babies
You tell us we must make.
Masculinity made "femininity,"

Made the eyes of our women go dark and cold,
Sent our sons—yes sir, *our* sons—
To war,
Made our children go hungry,
Made our mothers whores,
Made our bombs, our bullets, our "Food for Peace,"
Our definitive solutions and first-strike policies.
Masculinity broke women and men on its knee,
Took away our futures,
Made our hopes, fears, thoughts and good instincts
"Irrelevant to the larger struggle,"
And made human survival beyond the year 2000
An open question.

I am a dangerous woman
Because I will say all this
Lying neither to you nor with you
Neither trusting nor despising you.
I am dangerous because
I won't give up or shut up,
Or put up with your version of reality.
You have conspired to sell my life quite cheaply,
And I am especially dangerous
Because I will never forgive nor forget
Or ever conspire
To sell your life in return.

Jane Meyerding

Reclaiming Nonviolence: some thoughts for feminist womyn who used to be nonviolent, and vice versa

Many of us have been challenged by both our feminist and our pacifist sisters. Embracing our feminist friends—whose rage and woman-loving joy we share—we're told, "I don't consider myself nonviolent anymore." We turn to embrace our pacifist friends—whose urgency and passion for life we share—and are met with condescending sympathy, "Oh yes, I used to be into feminism too."

Jane Meyerding directly addresses both sets of colleagues in this essay, showing how the fine threads of both feminism and pacifism are best woven into one sturdy, rainbow-splendored web. After a defense made with exquisite care, she affirms her belief that there can be no truly radical movement for social change without the empowerment of women and that the most radical changes are possible only through nonviolence.

Jane is serious about experimenting with "the complicated truth" through her feminist pacifism and this has led, at times, to unique confrontations. On June 13th, 1978, she and BettyJohanna committed civil disobedience in the Seattle office of Save Our Moral Ethics (SOME), the group sponsoring an initiative which would have removed protection for lesbians and gay men from the Seattle civil rights ordinance. "We disrupted SOME's campaign by entering their office and pouring blood (our own and friends') on initiative petitions and financial records. We were arrested. At our trial in July, we chose to let our statement speak for us. We served 18 days in jail, which totally changed the next few years of our lives because of our continuing involvements with the lives and struggles of the other womyn we met there.

"Our action was part of our on-going experiment in integrating radical feminism and radical pacifism. SOME's existence and purpose, we believe, were very much connected with other aspects of increasing repression against poor people, womyn, people of color, etc. We were concerned about the appealingly populist appearance some of these reactionary movements take and we believe it is important to expose and clarify what these movements are really all about—not to let them grow in 'decent' obscurity. By acting very clearly and personally as human individuals rather than nameless, faceless 'social forces' or 'political masses,' we hoped to speak to the fears of those who feel drawn (by their fears) to these reactionary movements."

This was not the first experience with civil disobedience in which Jane was involved. In 1970 she was one of eight people who destroyed draft records and files of the U.S. Attorney and attempted to remove files from the FBI office in Rochester, NY. She served 10 months of a 12 month sentence for this. In 1976, Jane helped start Out and About, *a Seattle monthly lesbian-feminist newsletter for which she typed, did paste-up, collated, folded and wrote for five years.*

She writes, "I live with my mother, which many people think is the strangest thing about me—but they don't know my mother! I am a vegetarian for moral and ethical reasons (briefly stated: I like animals) and a non-aligned anarchist. Feel free to describe me simply as 'Jane, daughter of Esther.' I want to acknowledge that BettyJohanna gave me spiritual and editorial support in the writing of this essay."

> *In my view, any commitment to nonviolence which is real, which is authentic, must begin in the recognition of the forms and degrees of violence perpetrated against women by the gender class men. Any analysis of violence, or any commitment to act against it, that does not begin there is hollow, meaningless—a sham which will have, as its direct consequence, the perpetuation of our servitude. In my view, any male apostle of so-called nonviolence who is not committed, body and soul, to ending the violence against us is not trustworthy. . . . He is someone to whom our lives are invisible.*
>
> *(Andrea Dworkin, "Redefining Nonviolence," 1975)*

Is a commitment to radical feminism incompatible with nonviolence? I believe, to the contrary, that the analyses which underlie feminism and nonviolence greatly illuminate and complement one another. On the other hand, I certainly can understand why many womyn who have become radical feminists have found it necessary to *un*become members of nonviolence groups, movements, and/or communities.

Anger is the reason most frequently cited by feminists for their inability to remain advocates of nonviolence. As we become able to see and understand the immensity and intensity of womyn's oppression in patriarchal societies, it is true: there are times when our anger overwhelms our analytical commitment to nonviolence. But I don't think anger is the primary reason we feel a conflict between nonviolence and radical feminism.

The inability or unwillingness of men to change is another

reason often given by feminists who no longer consider themselves nonviolent. And again, it is true: on the whole, nonviolent men have not been eager to study or accept feminist analysis nor to make the changes in their lives and work which a commitment to feminism would demand. Womyn in nonviolence groups have enjoyed no special advantage in their work for reforms within these groups in sexist language, sexist divisions of labor, womon-hating attitudes, etc. But again, I do not think the unwillingness of nonviolent men to change is the major cause of anti-nonviolence feelings among formerly nonviolent feminists.

Some womyn who are able to remain in mixed (male/female) nonviolence groups may believe that radical feminism is "divisive" in insisting that all men acknowledge their responsibility for the oppression of womyn. It is proof of how basic sexism is in this culture that many of us who are willing to accept the statement "all whites are responsible for the violence done to people of color by racism" remain unwilling to accept the fact that all men are responsible for the violence done to womyn by sexism. Clearly, a radical feminist analysis, such as Andrea Dworkin's quoted above, is no more incompatible with nonviolence than is an anti-racism analysis. The wall of defensiveness radical feminists meet when trying to communicate their ideas to the majority of people in nonviolence groups certainly doesn't make feminists feel welcome in those groups.

Most basically, however, I think the reason many of us radical feminists find it necessary to turn away from nonviolence is our acceptance of—our failure to challenge—traditional limitations on nonviolence theory and practice. Our experiences of nonviolent actions may have led us to form some unfortunately simplistic assumptions:

Q: How do you go about being a nonviolent activist? A: You join a group doing nonviolent action.

Q: What is nonviolent action? A: Civil disobedience (preferably mass and on TV) against war, the military, nuclear power, segregation (formerly), or (occasionally) racism.

Although there have been a few shining exceptions, most nonviolent feminists have felt bound by these traditional boundaries of nonviolence and thus have been unable to act on their feminism. What a contradiction!—involvement in nonviolent activism can prevent us from taking action to oppose violence against womyn. Within the limits of traditionally defined nonviolence, feminism has been forced to be inactive;

feminism becomes something you talk about, merely a theory you try to integrate into nonviolence rhetoric.

Womyn's acceptance of the traditional limits of nonviolence has worked against feminism and feminists in two ways: Womyn who have remained inside the nonviolent "mainstream" have been forced to compromise their feminism (i.e., have been unable to follow feminist analysis to its roots and thus have been severely limited in their ability to act on their feminist beliefs). And womyn who have insisted on getting to the roots of feminist analysis (i.e., "radical" feminists) and acting out of this analysis have necessarily believed themselves to be thinking and working beyond the potential of nonviolence theory and practice. Accepting the traditional limits of nonviolence, radical feminists have felt compelled to abandon the ideas and ideals of nonviolence *in toto*, with little attempt even to salvage from their own study and experiences those aspects of nonviolence which might be of great practical value in their work with womyn.

Traditional nonviolence has suffered from a tendency to perceive the various forms and expressions of violence as having a hierarchical relationship with one another: this violence is more important than that violence. (Hence the tendency toward a series of single-issue mass "movements" which, being single-issue, can aim only at reform rather than radical social change.) This "rating" of issues has been with us for a long time:

> *I remember the first Peacemaker conference I ever attended—in 1960. . . . the question as to whether or not pacifists should take part in civil-rights actions began to be discussed. Many pacifists who were present said that we shouldn't. Because there were so few of us and disarmament was such a pressing priority, they were afraid that we would dissipate our energies. I remember one man making the point: 'If we all blow up, it's not going to matter whether we blow up integrated or segregated.' That fight was for later. . . . What did seem obvious to a lot of pacifists then was that a black man who professed belief in nonviolence was inconsistent in his thought, was fooling himself that he was nonviolent unless he came out against war. . . . But it* wasn't *obvious to a lot of pacifists that* they *were inconsistent in their nonviolence if they didn't act against racism.*
>
> *(Barbara Deming, "On Anger,"* Liberation, *Nov. 1971)*

Today, we still are likely to see either anti-war or anti-nuke work as the "obvious" priority for nonviolent activists, with specifically feminist issues relegated to that level of the issues-hierarchy labeled "for later."

An important part of feminism, for me, is the rejection of hierarchies wherever they develop. We have to make a lot of choices in our lives, and many of those choices are hard ones. No matter how tempting it is to "go with the flow" or "take the path of least resistance," however, it is never consistent with feminism to make a decision on the basis of a "given" hierarchy of values. There is no such thing as a "moral majority"—not even a moral majority of pacifists—that holds a monopoly on Truth and in relation to whom we can confidently measure the "correctness" of our choices. To quote Joanna Russ:

> *All the issues are related. Now nobody can deal with all the issues—there isn't energy and time. But we can deal with 'our' issues (the ones that affect us immediately) in a way that relates them to all the others.*
>
> *I think that we had better, because otherwise we're bound to fail. And... that's fine, if what you really want is* to be right.
>
> *But not if you want to change things.*
>
> *(Joanna Russ,* Out and About, *Jan. 1981)*

The first step for radical feminists committed to nonviolence must be to realize that we are not required to "prove" to the other nonviolent activists before we begin our work that work against the oppression of womyn is "more important" than work against war, any more than we must "prove" to feminist advocates of violence that nonviolence is the only valid method for political work.

I believe it is time for nonviolent feminists to stop concentrating on "integrating feminism into nonviolence" and start working at integrating specific ideas from nonviolence theory into feminist theory and practice. We need to reexamine our understanding of nonviolence, rejecting those aspects of traditional nonviolence which are irrelevant or inconsistent with feminism and *reclaiming* those aspects which belong in our lives and our work.

Integrating nonviolence into feminism requires us to really believe that the personal is political and there is no dividing line between them, no hierarchy of which is more important. This is necessary because from the beginning of history, no method of hiding, disguising, excusing, or rationalizing violence has ever been as successful as the trivialization of violence against womyn. And this violence has been trivialized precisely by the creation of the dichotomy between personal and political, with "political" defined as important and male, and "personal" defined as unimportant and female.

Empowerment

Briefly, the two aspects of nonviolence theory which I find most essential for feminism are: 1) the concepts of power and empowerment, and 2) the unique ability of nonviolence to simultaneously accept and reject—to acknowledge and connect us with that which is valuable in a person at the same time as it resists and challenges that person's oppressive attitudes or behavior.

According to nonviolence theory, power is not a characteristic owned by any individual, but rather a dynamic which is present in every relationship. This analysis allows us to see that every living person—even the most bitterly oppressed—does have some measure of power, if only the power to not cooperate in oppressive situations. We can call this form of inalienable power "personal power" to distinguish it from the many forms of "power-over-others" and to indicate its most important characteristic: it is power which arises from an individual's decision to assume control of one or more aspects of her own life.

Empowerment is the process by which people realize their personal power. Although an individual may enter into this empowering process accidentally (i.e., simply as a result of a combination of circumstances), the process can also be facilitated by one person for another. The study and practice of nonviolent techniques can help us help others toward empowerment. When empowerment is consciously chosen rather than coincidental, nonviolence training can help keep clear the differences between personal power and power-over-another.

The effects of empowerment are multiple. For the individual, the realization of personal power in relation to one aspect of life easily leads to a general re-evaluation of capacities for creating and choosing alternatives which are neither oppressed nor oppressing. The empowerment of previously disempowered individuals thus has a ripple effect on society, because the norm for empowered individuals or groups becomes change rather than stasis. An increase of power through nonviolent empowerment of individuals has a crucially different effect on society than a shift in power distribution caused by, for example, the violent overthrow of a government. In contrast to violent methods of social change which tend to concentrate and centralize power, the newly realized power activated by nonviolent empowerment is "personalized"—autonomous and decentralized. Thus nonviolent empowerment, in addition to its effect on the specific situation of the empowered individual, also represents a broad-based challenge to the "powers-that-be," the position-holders in the hierarchy of power-over-others.

The nonviolent concepts of power and empowerment are especially well suited to womyn, and therefore to feminist work, for several reasons related to our position and history in patriarchal society. As womyn, we traditionally have been oppressed by "private" structures such as "the family" and marriage, as well as by sexism, racism, classism, etc., institutionalized in such "public" structures as the church and state. Much of our oppression has been experienced (and reinforced) through interpersonal relationships, including our relationships with acquaintances, co-workers, and strangers (e.g., people we pass on the street) as well as through our closer relationships with family members, friends, lovers, etc. Although lack of attention to sexism has prevented traditional nonviolence theory from addressing this "personal" political reality of womyn's oppression, the theory of empowerment has great potential as a means by which womyn might become able to resist oppression institutionalized within "private" structures. Feminism's need for empowerment theory is emphasized by the fact that many womyn's "personal" relationships are destructive either for the womyn themselves (e.g., the relationship between an abused wife and her husband) or for others (e.g., the relationship between an abused child and her mother). In terms of long-range tactics, we should remember that a womon who is empowered to choose to leave or change an abusive "personal" situation will be better able (more powerful) to join in resistance to, for example, an abusive welfare system, than will be a womon who is helped out of an abusive situation with no increase in personal power.

Another reason nonviolence theories of power and empowerment are particularly suited to womyn is that nonviolent empowerment does not depend on one's possession of or control over tools such as weapons, muscular strength, or specialized knowledge. Thus nonviolence is a method of change and liberation accessible to all womyn.

Throughout history there are many examples of womyn's attempts at self-empowerment. Many of these attempts have been distorted, of course, into disguised forms of "power-over" as womyn use their personal power for self-protection in oppressive situations (e.g., womyn who "get ahead" through sexual flattery or favors; who manipulate their husbands through systematic nagging, whining, silences, and other such behavior management techniques; who guilt-trip their children, etc.). Even these distorted attempts at empowerment are a hopeful sign in that they show womyn's gut-level comprehension of power as inherent in relationships rather than in individuals.

When we look for examples of womyn's *overt* self-empowerment, we run into the usual problem: our history as womyn has been hidden and is as yet only partially rediscovered.[1] It is clear, however, that men consistently have invaded and taken over with their technology those areas where the traditional powers of womyn have been seen as threatening to male/patriarchal control (e.g., pregnancy and child-bearing, child-rearing and housework, the production of food and clothing, etc.). One major effect of these male-identified technological take-overs has been to de-value womyn's skills and powers—and empowerment. As feminist, womon-identified advocates of nonviolence, we must help womyn *respect* the personal power which many womyn now use in disrespectful, ultimately self-destructive ways.

Australian feminist Janna Thompson, writing about the apparent conflict between womyn with "traditional values" (e.g., lives centering on family life, nurturance, "personal" relationships) and politically active feminist womyn, urges feminists to help womyn with traditional values see "that their values and priorities, properly understood, are human values and priorities which may be realized and fought for in ways they haven't anticipated." Feminism can help womyn respect their own power. Nonviolence can help them use their power effectively in a way which maintains that respect and extends it to others.

"The Complicated Truth"

The second aspect of nonviolence which I believe vital for feminists has been expressed by Barbara Deming: "...if the complicated truth is that many oppressors are also oppressed—nonviolent confrontation is the only confrontation that allows us to respond realistically to such complexity. In this form of struggle we address ourselves both to that which we refuse to accept from others and that which we have in common with them—however much or little that may be."

It may not be true that womyn are "naturally" less prone to violence than men are. (I am not yet ready to believe men are "naturally"—inevitably—violent.) In any case, it is historically true that womyn have been less actively violent and have received far less training and encouragement in violence than men have—and I think we can use that historical distinction to the advantage of all people if we help womyn learn to discard their traditional passivity without adopting traditionally male violence. The vast majority of womyn have loved at least one man in their lives—father, brother, lover, son—and thus are in a particularly good position to understand the "complicated truth" of oppression and violence in this society and to welcome a method of change which allows them to maintain a humane relationship with those they must resist and confront.

Nonviolence is especially crucial for feminists as a means by which we can speak to non-feminist and anti-feminist womyn. And the need for such communication has never been more desperate. Writing about the anti-choice "right to life" movement, Diedre English says (in *Mother Jones*, Feb./March 1981): "The very existence of such a movement represents a deep crisis in the community of women. The female subculture has actually divided into two camps: feminist and anti-feminist. It is the worst nightmare of the women's movement come true. . . . It is as if, at the height of the civil rights movement, a large percentage of blacks had suddenly organized to say: 'Wait a minute. We don't want equal rights. We like things just the way they are.' "

It is not true, of course, that the womyn to whom English refers literally "like things just the way they are." Rather, they would like things to be the way they *were supposed to be*—back before the new wave of feminism disrupted the traditional agreements about sociosexual roles and rules, back in the "good ol' days" when womyn were universally assured of their right to expect certain compensations for acceptance of sexist oppression (e.g. financial security in return for the sexual/domestic service contract of marriage). No matter that compensation is not the same as justice/equality/freedom, or that these expectations were often unmet (*always* unmet, for certain groups of especially disadvantaged womyn). At times we all prefer the fantasy of secure dependence (the traditional feminine role) to the—often unsought—opportunity for insecure independence. Anti-feminist womyn are afraid to give up the privileges doled out by patriarchy, because they have no sense of their own ability (power) to achieve and maintain secure, meaningful lives for themselves and their children—especially, perhaps, for their daughters.

Because of its dual accepting/resisting nature (because it

allows us to acknowledge our commonalities as womyn without requiring us to ignore or deny our differences), nonviolence offers a way to establish relationships with anti-feminist womyn which will benefit both sides of this unfortunate schism. Anti-feminists can learn about empowerment, learn to respect and depend on their own power and thus begin to lose the fear which binds them to oppressive situations and relationships and divides them from us. As for feminists, many of us have a great deal to learn from closer, more conscious and less pre-judgmental connections with non-feminist and anti-feminist womyn. We must learn, realistically, the kinds of options and the forms of support womyn from all backgrounds and experiences need in order for radical change to become a real possibility in their own lives.

The more we learn about each other and about how our experiences as womyn cross boundaries of race, class, and age, the more we will understand also about how those boundaries have kept us apart and made our experiences differ. The more we learn about "the complicated truth" of womyn's lives—womyn on the streets and in the jails, as well as in the factories, offices, schools, and homes—the more accurately we will be able to focus our power on the roots common to all forms of violence and oppression in this society.

The broad or long-term effects of womyn's empowerment are impossible to predict, but exciting to speculate about. Although womyn have been called this country's "biggest minority" (i.e., largest disempowered group), our position and role in this society certainly have been far different from those of other "minorities." We have been far more radically disunited than other oppressed classes, and our survival mechanisms traditionally have constituted a major (perhaps *the* major) block of support for the status quo. Just think of all the womyn who supported Kissinger's egomania during the Vietnam war. Think of all the file clerks, dish washers, floor scrubbers, childcare workers (moms and otherwise), sex partners, ego massagers, etc., etc., who "service" and maintain the top brass of the Pentagon. Nor should examples be drawn only from the military. As a typist in a major university, I see daily proof that not even "good" institutions in this society are free from violence in its many forms. And have you taken a look at the movie industry lately? Or the industry of religion? Behind every traditionally successful man in this death-dealing culture, there is a small army of traditionally supportive womyn who survive by making his success possible.

But there is another side to that coin. Empowered womyn—womyn with realistic alternatives and the power to make free choices—are much more likely to be radical, in the real meaning of that word, than men are.

There have always been fewer womyn than men in the forefront of U.S. struggles for change—the feminist movements, of course, excepted. And that, I think, is not only because womyn weren't allowed up front (though it's true we've always had to fight to be there); nor is it only because we had to stay home with the kids (we've taken them along, when necessary). I think most womyn, deep down, have recognized the limitations of traditional male struggles—whether in the form of wars or of "movements." We have wept and we have cheered, we've gone to work in the factories and halls. And yet these struggles always remain, for most womyn, to a greater or lesser degree, a matter of "the boys" and their "toys." No large mass of men has ever been interested in truly radical change, because radical change would require them to fight against their own interests as men.

I believe, therefore, that there can be no truly radical movement for social change without the empowerment of womyn. As a corollary, I also believe that the most radical changes are possible only through nonviolence. Violent changes are, in effect, limited to the sphere of technology; they are simply power shifts or power reversals which cannot even pretend to attempt the abolition of hierarchical (i.e., oppressive) practices. Violences can be an effective method for *reform*, but it cannot effect radical change.

Given these two beliefs, it is clear that radical feminists literally cannot do without nonviolence, and that nonviolent advocates of radical social change must accept feminism as essential. I am convinced it is crucial for radical feminists to reclaim nonviolence as the method and tactics most appropriate to womyn's current situation and most consistent with our long-range goals.

Barbara Zanotti
Patriarchy: A State of War

"It is no accident that patriarchy relates history as the history of war—that is precisely their history." In this essay, Barbara dares us to name the enemy—patriarchy.

Barbara writes out of her conviction that the danger of nuclear war and growing militarism is deeply linked to institutionalized male dominance, and that the violence in women's lives is intimately connected with the violence of war. She challenges us to examine our own non-participation in the decisions which affect our lives and says that our task is nothing less than "shifting the weight of the world."

"I wrote this essay because I love life and because I believe a human world can be created. At this point, it really seems necessary to struggle generously to preserve and enhance life, not just for ourselves, but for the whole human family. It seems to me that the reality of devastation is very near."

Barbara lives and works in Cambridge, Mass. and studies issues of feminism, war, and peace at Harvard Divinity School where she has worked with Mary Daly. Barbara was formerly the Boston coordinator of Mobilization for Survival. She has four children ages nine through sixteen.

Why weren't we prepared for this?—the imminence of nuclear holocaust; the final silencing of life; the brutal extinction of the planet. Surely there have been substantial clues throughout history. Male supremacy. Wars. Witch-burning. Male religious myths. Weapons of increased destructive capacity. Institutionalized greed. The enslavement of half the human race. Centuries of violence.

Why weren't we prepared for this? We have lived with violence so long. We have lived under the rule of the fathers so long. Violence and patriarchy: mirror images. An ethic of destruction as normative. Diminished love for life, a numbing to real events as the final consequence. We are not even prepared.

Mary Daly, in *Gyn/Ecology: The Metaethics of Radical*

Feminism, writes: "The rulers of patriarchy—males with power—wage an unceasing war against life itself. Since female energy is essentially biophilic, the female spirit/body is the primary target in the perpetual war of aggression against life. Women must understand that the female self is the enemy under fire from the patriarchy." She further writes that "clearly the primary and essential object of aggression is not the opposing military force. The members of the opposing team play the same war games and share the same values. The secret bond that binds the warriors together is the violation of women, acted out physically and constantly replayed on the level of language and shared fantasies."

We needn't look far for evidence to support her theory. Recall the US Army basic training jingle: "This is my rifle (slaps rifle). This is my gun (slaps crotch). One is for killing; the other for fun." The language of war is the language of gynocide. Misogynist obscenities are used to train fighters and intensify feelings of violence. War provides men with a context to act out their hatred of women and to embody their ancient warrior myths. War is rape.

In the male world of war, toughness is the most highly prized virtue. Some even speak of the "hairy chest syndrome." The man who recommends violence does not endanger his reputation for wisdom, but a man who suggests negotiation becomes known as soft, as willing to settle for less. To be repelled by mass murder is to be irresponsible. It is to refuse the phallic celebration. It is to be feminine, to be a "dove." It means walking out of the club of bureaucratic machismo. It is no accident that patriachy relates history as the history of war—that is precisely their history. In remembering their battles, the fathers recall the deep experience of their own violent proclivities and relive the euphoria of those ultimate moments of male bonding.

The history of wars speaks volumes about national will in a patriarchal culture. Wars are nothing short of rituals of organized killing presided over by men deemed "the best." The fact is—they are. They have absorbed in the most complete way the violent character of their own ethos. These are the men who design missiles and technologies as extensions of themselves. These are the men ready to annihilate whole societies. These are the men honored as heroes with steel minds, resolute wills, insatiable drives for excellence, who are capable of planning demonic acts in a detached, non-emotional way. These are hollow men, capable of little but violence.

It is significant that during and after the accident at Three Mile Island, women were more concerned about danger than men; women knew that they were being lied to about the real-life effects of nuclear technology. Women were resistant to the repeated declarations of male decision-makers that everything was under control, that there was nothing to be alarmed about, that nuclear engineers could solve any difficulties. Women felt the lies.

Women know and feel the lies that maintain nuclear technology because we have been lied to before. We are the victims of patriarchal lies. We know the deceit that grounds patriarchal colonization of women. We know, feel and intuit that deception forms the very character of male rule.

Women are the first victims of the patriarchal state of war:

Violence to our bodies: A woman is raped every three minutes. A woman is battered every eighteen seconds. Women are physically threatened by a frightening social climate structured in male might. Women are depicted in pornography as objects to be beaten, whipped, chained and conquered. The myth prevails that women like it.

Violence to our hearts: The positing of male comradeship as the model of human relationships. The systematic separation of women's culture. The erasure of women's history. The sanctifying of the heterosexual norm with its limited understanding of the giving and receiving of affection and its arrogant reinforcement of male privilege and female vulnerability.

Violence to our spirit: The dismemberment of the goddess and the enthronement of the male god. The ripping away of women from a life in tune with natural patterns and rhythm of the universe. The ongoing patriarchal work of rendering women unconscious to ourselves.

Violence to our work: The exploitation and devaluation of women's labor. The relegation of women to supportive, maintenance roles. The deliberate structuring of women's economic dependence.

Under patriarchy, women are the enemy. This is a war across time and space, the real history of the ages.

In this extreme situation, confronted by the patriarchy in its multiple institutional forms, what can women do? We can name the enemy: patriarchy. We can break from deadly possession by the fathers. We can move from docility, passivity and silence to liberation, courage and speech. We can name ourselves, cherish ourselves, courageously take up our lives. We can refuse to sell our bodies and refuse to sell our minds. We can claim freedom from false loyalties. We can bond with other women and ignite the roaring fire of female friendship.

This much we have learned from our living: life begets life. Life for women, life for the earth, the very survival of the planet is found only outside the patriarchy; beyond their sad and shallow definitions; beyond their dead and static knowing; beyond their amnesia; beyond their impotence; beyond their wars—wars which unmask the fear, insecurity and powerlessness that form the very base of patriarchal rule.

To end the state of war, to halt the momentum toward death, passion for life must flourish. Women are the bearers of lifeloving energy. Ours is the task of deepening that passion for life and separating from all that threatens life, all that diminishes life; becoming who we are as women; telling/living the truth of our lives; shifting the weight of the world.

Will such measures put an end to war? What we already know is that centuries of other means have failed. In the name of peace, war is waged, weapons are developed, lives are lost. And though there are testimonies announced, treaties signed, declarations stated, pronouncements issued, still the battles go on. The patriarchy remains intact. Women are not free. Nothing changes.

This time the revolution must go all the way.

In the words of the poet:

> This is what I am: *watching the spider*
> *rebuild—"patiently," they say,*
>
> *but I recognize in her*
> *impatience—my own—*
>
> *the passion to make and make again*
> *where such unmaking reigns*
>
> *the refusal to be a victim*
> we have lived with violence so long

(Adrienne Rich, "Natural Resources")

Donna Warnock
Patriarchy Is a Killer: What People Concerned About Peace and Justice Should Know

This essay is written for pacifists. It is a challenge expressed in terms so bold even the most reluctant can't miss the point. "If the peace movement is to make nonviolent revolution, it must commit itself to overthrowing Patriarchy... (W)e must dismantle the mental weaponry as well as the miltary."

The mental weaponry Donna addresses here includes the rape mentality, masculinity, mechanistic thinking, and other institutions the Patriarchy uses to maintain its death-wielding power.

Donna is a writer, speaker, organizer and the coordinator of the Program on Feminism and Nonviolence at War Resisters League/West (85 Carl Street, San Francisco, CA 94117). Before coming to WRL, she was with Feminist Resources on Energy and Ecology in Syracuse, NY. She is the author of Nuclear Power and Civil Liberties: Can We Have Both? *(Citizens Energy Project, Wash., DC, 1979). In 1980 Donna was an organizer for the Women's Pentagon Action and is continuing to work on similar political events in the San Francisco area.*

An earlier version of the following paper appeared in the War Resisters League's Organizer Manual *(1981) and a condensed version of it was read at the War Resisters League's Feminism and Militarism Conference in the spring of 1981.*

Every three minutes a woman is beaten by her male partner—a man who often claims to love her. Every five minutes a woman is raped, and they call that "making love" too. And every ten minutes a little girl is molested, sometimes by a relative, perhaps her own father. The violence mounts. "Every few seconds in America a woman is slapped, slugged, punched, chopped, slashed, choked, kicked, raped, sodomized, mutilated, or murdered. She loses an eye, a kidney, a baby, a life. That's a fact," writes Ann Jones in *Take Back the Night.*[1] "And if the statistics are anywhere near right, at least one of every four women reading this paragraph will feel that fact through firsthand experience."

That these tragedies are so overlooked and unappreciated as

the horrible acts of war they are is testimony to how much damage has already been done in the hearts and minds of the people. Andrea Dworkin writes in "Remembering the Witches," "(T)hey think of us today what the Inquisitors thought of us yesterday." She goes on to quote the witchhunters, "Carnal lust. . .is in women insatiable."[2] We "asked for it." We "wanted it." We "*loved* it." They try to drum it into our brains: *The victim is to blame.* Nowhere are we safe. "(T)he world, even a girl's neighborhood, becomes a mined field," writes the poet Susan Griffin.[3] The fear of rape keeps us prisoners in our own homes. Still there is no security: Over half of all rapes involve break-ins.

Numerous studies confirm that rapists are, for the most part, "normal" men. And more and more normal men are becoming rapists. Rape is the most frequently committed and fastest growing violent crime in America. Increasingly it incorporates other acts of violence against women, as virility and violence become more closely linked in the pornographic masculine model.

"Pornography," writes Adrienne Rich, "is relentless in its message, which is the message of the master to the slave: *This is what you are; this is what I can do to you.*"[4] Violence against women[5] has proliferated in pornography. Magazines as common as *Playboy, Penthouse, Oui* and *Hustler* feature pain-filled scenes; women handcuffed, gagged, whipped, beaten, hanging from chains, sucking guns, having their fingernails pierced. Porn shops sell the really hard core and specialty publications like *Bondage,* in which women have torches or knives held to their breasts or vaginas, and worse. Theatres across the country attract eager crowds with the film *Snuff,* which purportedly shows the *actual murder and butchering* of one of its actresses. In the final scene, the Director reaches into the victim's abdomen and waves her insides high above his head in orgastic delight. "*Snuff* forced us to stop turning the other way each time we passed an X-rated movie house," wrote Beverly LaBelle who saw the film and reported on it in *Take Back the Night.*

Military Virility

While films like *Snuff* "entertain" male viewers, the military has offered hands-on experience. Veteran Richard Hale reports that on the way to Vietnam troops were told, "There's a lot of loose ass over there men, and they just love GI dick. And best of all, they are only Gooks, so if you get tired of them, you can cram a grenade up their cunt and 'waste' them.''[6] Many soldiers seized the opportunity; stories of wartime atrocities abound. ''This is my rifle,'' the troops chant, ''This is my gun,'' they slap their crotches; ''One is for killing, the other's for fun.'' Four-hundred thousand Bengali women were systematically raped by Pakistani soldiers; how many women have our boys raped? After all, women have been bounty in every war.

Misogyny[7] and homophobia[8] are basic components in military indoctrination. ''When you want to create a solidary [sic] group of male killers,'' goes the Marine philosophy, ''you kill 'the woman' in them.''

In a society where each man is trained to equate violence with vivility, it follows that public policy, dominated as it is by males, will also adopt such a posture. In 1957, for example, Henry Kissinger told Congress that the U.S. would be ''emasculating itself'' by not providing military funds for Angola.

''War is simply an extension of the colonial policy of the subjugation of the female culture and 'weaker' male cultures, i.e., 'weaker' national cultures,'' Barbara Burris and others pointed out in ''The Fourth World Manifesto.''[9] Men have been conditioned to respond with patriotic bellicosity at the suggestion that a foreign military target is somehow effeminate. And so ''Fuck Iran!'' became a slogan of the times during the Iranian hostage episode. This kind of merger of violence and lewdity permeates military thinking even in the highest echelons of government. After President Johnson ordered North Vietnam PT boat bases and oil depots bombed, he bragged to a reporter, ''I didn't just screw Ho Chi Minh. I cut his pecker off.''

The logical extension of this lascivious violence is articulated on a plaque which hangs on the wall of the Syracuse Research Corporation, a private ''think tank'' with large military contracts. Illustrated with a missile in flight, the inscription reads:

I LOVE YOU BECAUSE:
--Your sensors glow in the dark
--Your sidelobes swing in the breeze
--Your hair looks like clutter
--Your multipath quivers
--Your reaction time is superb
--Your missile has thrust; it accurately hones in on its target
--The fuse ignites, the warhead goes;
SWEET OBLIVION!

If a missile launching can be sexually fantasized by leading militarists as "sweet oblivion," it follows that total annihilation would be the ultimate orgasm. And they'd claim they did it for our welfare. Patriarchy has turned our worst nightmare into a frightening possibility.

Because the socialized violence of "masculinity" has been widely accepted as normal, indeed cultivated, the illness it has produced has been treated with increased dosages. The nuclear arms race itself is an example of violent, spiraling male chauvinism: Though the United States can destroy the USSR fifty times over, and that country can only destroy us twenty times over, and, in any case, no country can be destroyed more than once, the U.S. continues competition for competition's sake. It is preoccupied with size and power. We need to be more potent in order to feel more secure, the argument goes. We want to stay on top, don't we? But the ultimate effect of chauvinist behavior is increased vulnerability, and so the vicious cycle is perpetuated. Such is life under Patriarchy.[10]

It's a Man's World

> *Patriarchy is the power of the fathers: a familial-social ideological, political system in which men—by force, direct pressure, or through ritual, tradition, law and language, customs, etiquette, education, and the division of labor, determine what part women shall or shall not play, and in which the female is everywhere subsumed under the male. It does not necessarily imply that no woman has power or that all women in a given culture may not have certain powers. . . .*
>
> *The power of the fathers has been difficult to grasp because it permeates everything, even the language in which we try to describe it. It is diffuse and concrete; symbolic and literal; universal, and expressed with local variations which obscure its universality.*
>
> —Adrienne Rich, *Of Woman Born*[11]

Patriarchy is a society which worships the masculine identity, granting power and privilege to those who reflect and respect the socially-determined masculine sex role. The cliche, "It's a man's world" provides an apt description. In fact, the word "Patriarchy" is derived from the Latin "pater," which means "to own." That's it in a nutshell: Under Patriarchy men are entitled to everything. It follows that Patriarchy is inherently violent because it thrives on captured prey.

The underpinning of Patriarchal philosophy and science is the absolute separation of mind and matter (or spirit and body). The former is identified as "male," and deemed superior while the latter is called "female" and deemed inferior.[12] On one side is posited rationality, objectivity, aggression, order, dominance; on the other is intuition ("irrationality"), emotionalism, passivity, chaos, submission. This artificial male/female polarity exists throughout man's[13] value system and sets a pattern for domination in Patriarchal society.

Thus man has come to deify "rational" thought, also known as mechanistic thinking, in which each component of a problem to be solved is analyzed independently, mechanistically, isolated from its environment. Ecological and human consequences are overlooked. Emotion is absent. Feminists Nina Swaim and Susan Koen explain in their *Handbook for Women on the Nuclear Mentality:*

> *When the intellect and the dominating, controlling, aggressive tendencies within each individual are defined as the most valuable parts of their being, and those same attributes are emphasized in the political and economic arena, the result is a society characterized by violence, exploitation, a reverence for the scientific as absolute, and a systematic 'rape' of nature for man's enjoyment. This result is patriarchy.*
>
> *When the patriarchal paradigm becomes operational on the economic and political level, and the exploitation of nature for the sake of technological advancement and profit becomes the* modus operandi *of society, we find ourselves in the interlocking horror story of the nuclear mentality. This mentality is a belief system, an ideology, that would foster the use of destructive technology in order to sustain the expansion and domination which characterizes capitalist patriarchy.*[14]

Mechanistic thinking was originally a way for men to conquer the mysteries of nature. But to conquer nature, they had to conquer women. Pre-Patriarchal cultures believed that, because women alone brought forth life, women therefore held the secrets of nature and the keys to wisdom. To counter such notions, the Catholic Church imposed the Divine Doctrine that the male had dominion over creation. There was tremendous opposition to this idea; it was seen as unnatural. This blasphemous opposition outraged the Church leaders and, more importantly, threatened their power. Consequently, between the fourteenth and seventeenth centuries, they attacked women with brute force: *Somewhere between one and nine million women were burned as witches during the Inquisition.* Two villages were left with only one woman in each.

Times have changed. Women are no longer burned at the stake. We have been allowed to enter the public sphere previously denied us. While the high incidence of rape and wife beating should be sufficient to raise serious questions about the current state of women's liberation, we feminists are nonetheless repeatedly asked to exclude these so-called "exceptional" acts of violence and instead be grateful for the improvements in the day-to-day lives of "average" women in this "advanced" country. "You've come a long way, *baby,*" we're told.

Let's get rid of this notion that the only women whose status counts are the so-called "average" ones, that is, those from the white middle class. Indeed, if we look at the women whose ancestors were on this land before colonization, we find that witchburning has a contemporary parallel in the sterilization of Native American women in the United States. The National Center for Health Statistics estimates that *25 percent of all Native American women have been sterilized—many of them involuntarily.* There is one tribe in Oklahoma in which *all* of the full-blooded women have been sterilized. The implications of sterilizing Native American women should be seen in full. It is anti-woman. It is racism and genocide. It represents an attempt, like the witchhunts, to kill a culture which challenges the anti-nature bias of Christian theology.

And that's not the only remnant of feudalism women face today.

A Man's Home is His Castle

The saying that every man, regardless of social position, can be king in his own home does far more than hark back to a romanticized notion of the days of old. It reveals the truth about the social structure we have adopted. It is significant that the word "family" is derived from "famel," meaning "slave," and that the United Nations has declared marriage a "slavery-like practice."

Wives are viewed under U.S. law as their husbands' property in marriage, with few rights of their own. Sex is among the legal requirement, but love and affection are *not.* And marital rape is legal in all but a few states. Courts have further held that husbands are entitled to free domestic services. Freedom of domicile is denied married women in most places in the United States; that is, a woman must live with her husband where he chooses or be guilty of abandonment under the law, which could result in the loss of child custody, possessions and other financial entitlements such as alimony. This holds true even if it is actually the husband who relocates. If a husband wants his wife to live with him she must, or risk forfeiting her marital privileges.

Until recently, a woman's title indicated her marital status. If unwed, a woman is ridiculed as an "old maid," "spinster," or worst of all, "lesbian." And pity the poor widow! Again language is our teacher: The word "widow" is from the Sanskrit; it means "empty."[15] Similarly, if a woman bears no children, she is considered "barren." Families are what give meaning to a woman's life according to Patriarchal dictate.

Under Patriarchy, every woman's identity is linked to that of a man through the institutions of monogamy, marriage, motherhood and enforced heterosexuality. These institutions are maintained through rigorous promotion, reinforced by legal sanctions and social pressures which punish their transgressors. These are important interrelated components of the Patriarchal structure, for together they maintain patrilineage, the primary power base of the fathers.

Whereas agrarian cultures benefitted from large extended families where women had relatively more support and dignity, the nuclear family has been promoted by today's capitalist leaders because it benefits them politically and financially. When nuclear families form the base of a social structure they divide the society into small, easily-controlled and relatively powerless units which provide a ready vehicle for the perpetuation of hierarchy and domination and the expansion of consumption.

The Good Life

Values based on the idealized middle class life are promoted not because they're idyllic, but because there's power and profit in them for the men who run this country. Women are exploited as consumers, with 75% of corporate advertising aimed at us. These ads are designed to destroy our self-images, to deceive us into thinking that "The Good Life" is a product of American industry. They rob us of our individuality, defining us instead by our possessions and social status. They script us as sex objects and housewives. The media standards set for women are especially damaging to those of us who come from the lower income brackets. We are made to feel like failures when our economic status prohibits achievement of the middle class ideal. The damage has taken its toll in high rates of alcoholism, drug addiction, mental problems and suicide among women.[16] So much for the myth about pedestals.

The truth is that "The servant role of women is critical for the expansion of consumption in the modern economy," as economist John Kenneth Galbraith points out. The housewife market, with its endless array of energy-intensive appliances and ecologically disastrous cleaning agents, has become Big Business. But despite and, ironically, because of these so-called "labor-saving" devices, the woman at home with one child spends, on the average, more than eighty hours a week on household chores, according to the U.S. Women's Bureau.

Women with jobs outside the home work a double shift. Which brings us to yet another middle class myth; namely, that we only work for "pin money." We work because we have to. Yet women are considered the "surplus labor force," the expendable ones. And if conservative political leaders have their way in eliminating workplace affirmative action programs, things will get much worse. Right now fully-employed women make only sixty percent as much as our male counterparts. Women of color make only fifty percent as much as white men. The fifteen million women who head families do it with less than half the income of male heads of households. It is no wonder, then, that women comprise two-thirds of the 25 million people living below poverty. Households headed by women increased fifty percent in the 1970s, and almost one-third of them are below the poverty level (compared to 12% of the population as a whole). Fifty-one percent of the Black female-headed households are below the poverty level. Mothers' economic problems are compounded by lack of childcare facilities, fathers who refuse their childcare responsibilities and welfare regulations which encourage paternal abandonment.

Sexual Politics and Peace

The battlefield in the war against women is in the workplace, on the streets, in our homes, in our most intimate relationships. It is physical and psychological, visited upon us by others and internalized within ourselves. It crosses class and racial boundaries, compounding other oppressions. It is manifested in atomic power development and ecological destruction. The mentality that builds nuclear weapons is the same one that rapes women and destroys the natural environment. No political philosophy or strategy for peace can be complete without addressing sexual politics.

If the peace movement is to be successful in putting an end to war, it must work to eliminate the sex-role system which is killing us all by rewarding dominating aggressive behavior in men.

If the peace movement is to be consistent in its opposition to violence, it must address violence against women.

If the peace movement is truly committed to social justice, it must join the movement for women's liberation.

If the peace movement is to make nonviolent revolution, it must commit itself to overthrowing Patriarchy.

Feminism and Nonviolence

The power of Patriarchy is such that to see through it requires a special kind of vision, a consciousness of the most "ordinary" experience. To understand it requires "thinking across boundaries," as Mary Daly says. To overcome it demands the reinvention of revolution. This consciousness, this vision, this experience, this understanding, this revolutionary politic is feminism.

While the feminist movement has not overtly defined itself as nonviolent, by opposing oppressive institutions of domination, by employing nonviolent tactics, by pioneering in non-hierarchical structures, by formulating principles and identifying visions of harmony and liberation, it has become, I believe, the most powerful force for nonviolent revolution in practice.

The principles of feminism and nonviolence are remarkably similar. Both uphold the rights of all individuals in society to dignity, justice and freedom. Both understand that the revolution is not a before and after affair in which one group of men exchanges weapons and privileges with another, but instead measure revolutionary progress in terms of collective consciousness practiced in present tense. This consciousness challenges the polarized belief system which defines aggression as good and submission as bad, which fosters dominance and stifles nurturance, which glorifies mechanism and suppresses sensitivity. Feminism and nonviolence place ecological laws in social perspective: both understand that social strength depends on social diversity. Both agree that everything is connected, every act has repercussions. The political-economic apparatus, the social structure, the eco-system, the production system, the military-industrial complex, the moral and psychological health of a people are all part of a continuum. Exploitation at any point along the way affects it all. Both feminism and nonviolence see that power, in its healthy form, comes from the strength and sensitivity of this wholistic understanding and leads naturally to the cooperative and nurturing behavior necessary for harmonious existence. Both feminism and nonviolence oppose power which is exploitive or manipulative. Competition and dehumanizing objectification of individuals are seen as forms of domination and aggression and precursors or components of physical violence.

Despite major theoretical commonalities, feminists are not necessarily nonviolent, and nonviolent activists are not necessarily feminist. This merger is our challenge. We are saying that feminism is crucial to pacifism, for we must dismantle the mental weaponry as well as the military. For us, nonviolence is a logical extension of feminism. To call ourselves feminist pacifists is to use neither as an adjective, but to integrate both. We are talking about a philosophy of its own. We are experiencing a leap in consciousness, and we are recognizing that it is revolutionary.

Diana J. M. Davies/Insight

Fannie Lou Hamer, dedicated worker for voter registration in the South.

Jo Vellacott
Women, Peace & Power

Jo Vellacott takes off her worldly spectacles in this essay, and looks at the words "women," "peace" and "power" with her Quaker eyes. What she sees has great relevance for feminist advocates of nonviolence, especially her development of Ursula Franklin's idea that violence is "resourcelessness" and her analysis of the lessons we should learn from the experiences of Britain's suffragists.

Jo was born and brought up in England before the second World War. Though early influenced by a Quaker teacher, she gave up wrestling with the question of pacifism in 1939 to make munitions and became an air engine mechanic and later an Air Engineer Officer. She writes, "I never did kid myself that I was not killing people when I made anti-tank mines or serviced training planes. Nor was I able to depersonalize the enemy I helped to kill; I knew they were people, and the cheering when German plane and crew were shot down chilled me."

Eventually Jo went to South Africa to teach, married a South African, had two children, moved back to England because of the racial situation, had another child and came to Canada when her husband took a commission in the Canadian Air Force as a doctor.

"In part, it was the Vietnam war which brought me back and began to open my closed spirit again," she writes. "One of the ways in which my spirit was touched first was by the ring of truth in the protest songs I heard on the radio—Phil Ochs, Pete Seeger, Joan Baez.

"A lot of things happened to me in the early sixties, nearly all of them good, though there was a lot of pain at the time. I began a long struggle back to a sense of self-worth. I went to graduate school, we joined Quakers, we acknowledged the need for professional help and sought it and were lucky in what we found. Our children weathered the storm and grew up beautifully. One of them now has two children of her own and my grandchildren fill me with hope, as well as with the terrible urgency of the need for the world to turn itself around before it is too late.

"I've done a lot of things rather late in life—in fact, my symbol seems to be the tortoise—and there are some things I regret about that. I got my last degree in 1975 when I was already aware that degrees weren't really important; my marriage didn't end until 1976, to the improved happiness of both of us; my first book, Bertrand Russell and the Pacifists in the First World War *(St. Martin's Press) was published in 1981.*

"I am now taking time to write about the British woman suffragist, peace activist, founding member of the Women's International League for Peace and Freedom whose life I have been researching for a number of years. Her name was Catherine E. Marshall, not to be confused with the American Catherine Marshall.

"In all this talk of writing, studying, and giving courses, I hope it has somehow come through that what really matters to me is people. I deplore what hierarchical structures do to people, but I find that it is not necessary to let them dominate the situation to the extent of inhibiting a real exchange. Good things continue to happen."

The following essay was first delivered as the 1981 Rachel Cadbury lecture, sponsored by Friends General Conference and given in 1981 in Greensboro, North Carolina.

Women, peace and power. I have let these three words joggle around at the back of my head, hoping that they would fall neatly into place, with clear relationships established between them. This did not exactly happen. When I first brought them forward—"Women," "Peace," and "Power"—and put on my glasses to look at them, I found that the word "peace" in juxtaposition with the word "women" is seen to take on a sickly flat greyish-pink colour, very innocuous and ineffective. The word "power" on the other hand, turns black and scarlet, threatening and sinful, by association with women. When I moved the word "women" off to stand by itself, a peculiar ill-shapen question mark hung over it. And as for the words "peace" and "power," when I tried putting them together in my mind's eye, they behaved like two rather dreadful little magnetized toy dogs I once saw, who jumped around always to sniff suspiciously at each other's rear ends and refused to meet each other face to face, or to walk side by side.

Fortunately, after a short time I found that the problem lay in the spectacles I was using. These were the spectacles of the world, worldly spectacles, made up of the values to which we are constantly exposed and the attitudes we meet all the time. I took them off, and looked with my would-be Quaker eyes. What I saw was very different, though I know only too well that my vision is far from perfect and not wholly free from distortion.

Let me tell you what I plan to do. The concept of power turns out to be central, and I must begin by talking about it: the meaning of power, the source of power, the use of power. Then I will speak of peace. Of women, I shall be talking throughout, because I shall be talking about people; towards the end I shall speak of some things which are perhaps particular to women in the people/peace/power dynamic.

What is power? The world tells me that money is power, that weapons are power, that a dictator is a powerful man, that my boss has power over me, that men have more power than women. From this it seems that power is exercised through violence, that indeed the potential for physical, economic and psychological violence is almost the definition of power. There is a lovely and profoundly important phrase used by George Fox, the founder of the Society of Friends, "This I know experimentally," and what I have to say now, of this definition of power as violence, is that "This I know experimentally to be untrue."

Last year the small peace studies group of which I was a member struggled to define violence and nonviolence. I spoke with Ursula Franklin, a Canadian Friend of great warmth and wisdom and a professor in the Engineering Department at the University of Toronto; she told me that the same problem had recently exercised her mind and suggested that the definition of violence that had finally come to seem most satisfactory to her was "resourcelessness." At first, I did not even understand what she meant—violence is resourcelessness?—but the more I have thought about it the more depth I see in it. I urge you too to turn it over in your minds.

I have been trying this definition out on various scenarios, and have been startled by what I have found. I am a member of an oppressed minority; I have no way of making you listen to me; I turn to terrorism. I am a dictator, yet I cannot force you to think as I want you to; I fling you in jail, starve your children, torture you. I am a woman in a conventional authoritarian marriage situation; I feel helpless and inferior and powerless against my husband's constant undermining; so I in turn undermine him, manipulate him, make him look foolish in the eyes of his children. Or I am a child unable to prevent her parents' constant quarrelling and to defend herself against her mother's sudden outbursts of rage, I smash something precious and run away, or I take to thieving, or I may even kill myself. Or I am the President of the United States; with all the force at my command I know of no way to make sure that the developing countries—especially the oil-rich nations—will dance to my tune; so I turn to the use of food as a political weapon, as well as building ever more armaments. Violence is resourcelessness.

I have an anecdote to illustrate the other side of this coin; the power and resourcefulness of nonviolence. Several years ago a group of Canadian Indians came from all across the country to the nation's capital in Ottawa, with a strong felt need to represent the injustices and the aspirations of their people. By the time they arrived in Ottawa their numbers, as far as I remember, were somewhere between one and two hundred. Their advance planning was excellent and at dusk they seized and occupied without difficulty an empty building in wasteland under one of the river bridges, intending to declare it to be their embassy. The leaders had a strong commitment to nonviolence, and had not allowed any one to bring arms. The police, unfortunately, were incredibly tense about the whole situtation, knowing the caravan was coming but knowing nothing of their plans; you might have thought the invasion of the Russian army was expected rather than the advent of two hundred Canadian citizens. Fortunately, the building they occupied was not in the jurisdiction of the Mounties, but in that of the Ottawa city police, who acted with considerable restraint. However, restraint or not, it was naturally not long before armed squad cars were stationed about a hundred yards away on the road overlooking the occupied building, with searchlights and guns trained on the entrance. At this time the phone and services to the building were disconnected. Suddenly the Indians lost their feeling of victory and began instead to feel themselves trapped, without resources; and of course their sincere desire for nonviolence overlay for almost every one of them a lifetime of violent treatment and generally of violent response. They could see no means of communicating their objectives; they expected to be rushed; they believed that any one of them who stepped out might be shot or jumped. Some began to talk of the need, after all, for the breaking of heads.

Travelling with the caravan was a woman who had had experience in nonviolent response. It was given to her (and what a gift—most of us would not want it) to approach the council of Indian leaders and to ask if they would like her to go out to speak with the people up there on the road, invisible behind their searchlights and supposedly with their fingers on the triggers of their guns. It is a nice example of a situation where the fact of being a woman was a special qualification for service in a mission of peace; the leaders recognized this and she opened the door and walked out into the blinding searchlights. The police, as it turned out, were as relieved to have the potentially violent impasse broken as were the Indians. Negotiations were begun, phone service was restored, friends were permitted to bring food in, the government commission which owned the building was persuaded to overlook the squatting ambassadors, whose experiment continued for some time with some limited successes and some bitter failures.

The story illustrates vividly for me the identity between resourcelessness and violence, and between nonviolence, resourcefulness and power.

The second thing I want to do with the word "resourcelessness" and its opposite, "resourcefulness," is to share with you the pleasure I found when I realized that they have as their root the word "source." We cannot think constructively about power without considering its source. There are a number of components to the kind of power of which we should speak; the source is central to them all. Probably all of you here are familiar with the tension that can exist between nonviolence training and nonviolence as a way of life. Nonviolence training is a useful adjunct to a nonviolent life, and it is generally a preferable alternative method for civil action than is violence. But it is only a method and can be used as a strategy by people with no commitment to a way of life informed by nonviolence.

The people whom I know who live a truly nonviolent life are in touch with the source of power, call it what you will; the Light, the seed, God, the holy spirit. Many others of us find this wellspring when we need it, and lose it again, find it and lose it, find it and lose it. Regrettably, I am one of the latter. When I have something very difficult to face that I know I can't cope with, then I turn desperately to the source. One of the things I find most infuriating about myself is that I often let the contact go when the emergency is over and flounder along without it for months on end when my everyday existence could be transformed by it. It is as if I opened the blinds in my house for only an occasional hour when—for example—I had an important visitor, or a cable arrived, or I had to sweep up some broken glass; and afterwards allowed the blinds to fall closed again. So that for ninety percent of the time I bumble around, do my housework in semi-darkness, strain my eyes trying to read and can scarcely discern the features of those to whom I talk. More than anything I want to learn to live in the Light. So I think, anyway, but in fact I perhaps don't altogether want to take the demands involved, don't want to see all the dust in my life.

People reach the source of power through a variety of means. For me, and I will state this without lengthy comment, the route lies through meditation, the silent Meeting for Worship, and time allowed for renewal. For others there are, I am sure, many different routes. It is not given to me to live under a constant sense of guidance, and I envy those who do. In recent years, on two or three occasions, when I have needed it and sought it, power has been given to me: and then its authenticity has been unquestionable—but only as long as I stayed close to the wellspring.

So much for the personal source of power. What are the other components of this kind of power? What do we do with it? How can we pool and increase our power?

Coming at it from a different angle, let us look at the good old Quaker phrase about seeking that of God in every person. Sometimes we tend to downgrade the expression, using it as if recognizing that of God in others was a pious exercise by which we grudgingly admit that there must be some good in every one, however awful they are. I don't need to tell you that that wasn't the way George Fox used the expression. He sought God first in himself; then he reached out to help people become aware of the Light within themselves; and then together Friends learnt to respond to and build on the godly in themselves and others. Fox spoke always of that of God in humanity as power; and, I repeat, he began with himself. We are challenged to consciousness, and to the use of God's power within ourselves.

All of this can become horribly inconvenient. How often have we all said, "Oh, I couldn't do that—I'd like to help but—I'm no good at fundraising—I wouldn't know how to act in a prison—I can't possibly speak in public—that needs someone with more patience than I have—I can't write—I'm all thumbs—I never understand politics—I can't take minutes—I knew it was wrong, but I can't argue with people."

Power does not come from focussing in this way on our disabilities. Power is more likely to come by just going ahead and doing the thing in which we fear our inadequacy. In instances where this really is inappropriate, we can contribute whatever we do have and can build on this. At times this means we have to put ourselves forward, to say, "I'd like to have a shot at designing a poster for this," or "May I come along with your deputation in order to learn how it's done?" We also have to help each other to develop power. This readiness to trust in our own capacities is stressed by Adam Curle, the former professor of Peace Studies at Bradford University (England), who has remarkably combined university work, writing, and involvement in practical conflict resolution in places like Biafra, Northern Ireland and Zimbabwe.

That of God in every person is no respecter of sexes, and, although we Quakers occasionally forget this, no respecter of sects either. Men must learn to work with women, women with men, and Quakers—in my view—must become more willing humbly to see that of God in non-Quakers and work with it.

How much of power is lost by labelling and by role definition. Quakers have always known this, but we had better not be smug about it; when the present women's movement began and consciousness was raised, it was surprising how many beams we found in our own eyes—and I am sure we have still not got rid of all of them.

My example comes from the peace movement of the first world war, and one of the human beings involved is Bertrand Russell. The other is Catherine Marshall, a woman of immense ability as a political organizer. My purpose is to illustrate how tragically role definition can hamper effectiveness—and what miserv it can cause.

Towards the end of 1915, Catherine Marshall began to work for the No-Conscription Fellowship. Throughout the next year, against an everdarkening backdrop, and while one by one the young male leaders went off to prison, she did wonders for the Fellowship. Working alongside her was Bertrand Russell, who indeed came into the organization at her instigation and served something like an apprenticeship to her in the art of political pressure, while making his own great contributions in his campaign for negotiated peace, and perhaps more unexpectedly—as I have shown—as a peacemaker among peacemakers. By the end of 1916, the Fellowship's chairman was in prison, and so was the other young man who had served for a few months as acting chairman. Russell, overage for the draft, and Marshall, as a woman, were among the few leaders left. In an end-of-the-year election, in which both Russell and Marshall were among the candidates, Russell, understandably, was elected acting chairman; Marshall continued as acting honorary secretary. Both he and she were committed anti-authoritarians, opposed to hierarchies, anti-sexist, and agreed on all major points of policy and principle (there were serious divisive issues at the time); above all, both were devoted to the cause. Yet within a few months they were almost unable to work together. What happened? They had fallen inadvertently into a working relationship which was stereotyped both by sex roles and by hierarchical roles. Marshall tried desperately to do the things she saw as appropriate to a subordinate and to a woman in a man's organization. Russell—with marked ambivalence—expected her to remind him of all the things he had to do, and resented her nagging. She began grossly overworking, faultfinding and internalizing self-blame. He became more and more convinced that he was a hopeless administrator—which was originally nonsense but ultimately could have become a self-fulfilling prophecy. When she burst out in criticism of what she saw as a particular example of his inefficiency, he would suddenly step up on his pedestal of status and say, "You really must not write me letters such as the one I got from you this morning. If I did not realize that you are so tired as to be hardly responsible, I should be seriously annoyed."

I have greatly oversimplified the process, but what is plain is that what had been an excellent team while they were working side by side became unworkable when they accepted positions within a hierarchy, positions which threw them back unconsciously into certain roles. The points I am making are three. Firstly, there was a serious wastage of power, with both Russell and Marshall failing to make their best possible contributions. Secondly, acceptance of sex-roles played a major part in this, despite the commitment of both, at a conscious level, to equality. Thirdly, and this may be inseparable from the second, acceptance of an hierarchical order in place of one based on the contribution of each according to ability and the needs of the cause, compounded the problem.

You may remember at the beginning of this talk I mentioned the cozy pink image of "women-and-peace": I am sure you all recognized the traditional view of peacemaking as an appropriate role for a well-behaved woman, wholly passive, passively holy. And peace is the lady in white, the absence of war, the absence of conflict, the absence of any kind of trouble. Instead, of course, we must adopt a definition of peace that is positive and challenging. Whether we speak of peace on a personal level, a family level, within our organizations, nationally or internationally, we must recognize that true peace exists only where all can be reasonably free of fear, and have opportunity for the exercise of body, mind and spirit. A stable situation is not necessarily a peaceful one; injustice, exploitation and discrimination are incompatible with real peace; and so a peace-directed person may be the one on whom it is laid to rock the boat, challenge the system—perhaps accepting in return unpopularity, false witness and various kinds of danger or unpleasantness.

Speaking of challenging the system, I had a letter recently from a young friend of mine. On the outside of the envelope she had written a quotation from Marcuse: "The success of the system is to make unthinkable the possibility of alternatives." It was no surprise when I read the letter to find that Martha was tangling with the established order. A little bit my heart bled for her; it is rough to be so clear-sighted that you see the exploitativeness that other people have come to accept—and, as I had expected, it was not that Martha was being exploited, it was that she was being asked to contribute in a routine fashion to what she saw as the exploitation of others. Very shortly my heart stopped bleeding and sang instead; here is a young woman of clear vision, great courage, and a commitment to seeking for the wisdom with which to work for change. In addition, I know her to be a real seeker after spiritual as well as social and political truth.

I spoke earlier of the difficulties created in a working relationship by the hierarchical structure. Now I want to take this into a much broader context.

We are often perplexed about where to focus our energies; a common conflict within an individual and between groups is what is seen as a matter of priorities. Should we work for peace? for justice? for the E.R.A.? for human rights? for ecology? against the draft? for disarmament? I think if we look closely at these most important areas, the conflict of interest will melt away. No one of these will make real progress without the others; they may even all be one cause.

To help explain what I mean, I am going to back up a little bit—about sixty-five years to be precise, but that *is* only a little bit to a historian. What follows is not just another historical example, though it is that, but is, in addition, the history of an important truth about the women's movement, of which I think we have lost sight.

In Britain before the first World War, as we all know, there was a militant suffragette campaign provocative of mounting official violence and itself using increasingly violent methods. What is far less well known is that there was also a longstanding nonviolent campaign which continued its activities through all the crucial years and which turns out, on closer examination, to have been remarkably efficient and far-reaching, and was, as I have found out, startlingly effective. In my opinion, there is no question but that this organization played by far the larger part in the gaining of the vote (which was coming whether or not the war took place). Their activities do not concern us here, but their principles are of great interest.

The women who were active in this so-called non-militant

organization (the National Union of Women's Suffrage Societies) found themselves, by 1910, beset on both sides by arguments based on force. On the one side, those who were opposed to granting the franchise to women said, loudly and often, that women could not vote because they could not fight, and government rested ultimately on the sanction of force. In other words, when it came right down to it, might was right, and women didn't have might.

On the other side, there were the Pankhursts and their followers, accusing the non-militants of lack of commitment, of cowardice, of half-heartedness and of disloyalty because they would not shout down political speakers, burn buildings, plant bombs and resort to physical violence. Those who were shouting into the non-militants' left ears began to sound singularly like those who were shouting into their right ears.

Being so beleaguered, the women of the National Union were forced to think out, on the one hand, what there was besides force as a basis of government, and, on the other hand, why they chose to stick to methods of nonviolent political pressure—in the face, I may say, of what sometimes must have seemed extreme provocation—and incidentally, why they adhered to democratic forms within their own organization.

The argument that some of the leaders of the non-militants developed from principle and from conviction was simple, and later turned out to be all-embracing. Human government must be based on something more advanced than the right of the physically stronger to push the weaker around; clearly, so it seemed to them, representative institutions had been developed as a substitute for the politics of force, and to make room for the exercise of other qualities of the human will, mind and spirit. Hence it was fit and proper that room should be made for the exercise within the political system of woman's qualities—both those that she shared with men, such as brain power, and what she might have of qualities particular to her half of the human race. And when the militants used violence to press their case, it seemed to the non-militants that they were just lending support to the "might is right" argument of the anti-suffragists.

What happened when war broke out was interesting. Emmeline and Christabel Pankhurst converted easily and instantly from militancy to militarism and turned their talents to the making of recruiting speeches and, as the war went on, to campaigning against bolshevism, pacifism and industrial disaffection. Many of their attractive, high-spirited and rebellious young followers were, I feel sure, among the thousands of young women who joined one or another organization and went off to help the war effort. Just as the militant suffrage campaign received attention at the expense of the non-militants' work, so it is this section of the women's movement which has found its way into those few history books which have as much as discovered the existence of women.

A large number of the non-militants (and you must understand that I am generalizing in both cases), reacted very differently to the outbreak of war. The full development and logical consequence of all their soul-searching on the subject of physical force suddenly became apparent; there was no blinding flash of illumination—it was more as if they now had to deal with the whole of the iceberg, which they had long known was there. They found themselves with a principle and deep convictions that were manifestly as applicable to the international situation as they were to the national. War was a denial on a cataclysmic scale of the only basis on which the vote for women could be claimed; that society rested on some higher principle than that of force. For those to whom this was clear, work for peace was so obviously inseparable from the women's suffrage question that it seemed completely within the terms of reference of the suffragist organization to make this its focus, and direct its work towards education for peace.

I wish I could report that they succeeded in carrying the National Union with them; unfortunately, for a variety of reasons, this did not happen. Perhaps if they had, the course of history would have been so changed that we would all know about it now. However, to cut a long story short, these British women found their views reflected in the minds of thoughtful women suffragists all over the world, not least in the United States, of course. The result was the women's conference held at The Hague in 1915, at which the Women's International League for Peace and Freedom was founded.

My primary intent in this long historical exegesis has been to emphasize the unity of different aspects of the struggle; I think the women of 1915 had a true vision when they maintained that the case for women's rights (if "rights" is an appropriate word) is not separable from the issue of peace, war and international order. We may need to be reminded that the women's peace movement was nurtured from the start by the women's suffrage movement—and vice versa. Secondly, and this brings me back again to the word "power," means cannot be separated from ends. The line between legitimate militancy and coercion is often a fine one; we need constantly to refer back to the source—or, if you prefer it in traditional terms, to ask God's guidance—to make sure we are using methods which are not at variance with our purpose—or God's purpose. Does this restrict the methods available to us? In one sense, of course it does. More strikingly, it expands them—if we really believe in the resourcefulness of nonviolence.

Thirdly—and I am going to throw this major issue in front of you without developing it at length—what are we working towards, as women and men, and as humans committed to sexual equality? Is the exisiting structure of society compatible with sexual equality? Were those who argued that the basis of society was force perhaps right after all? In a militaristic society women are indeed biologically disadvantaged. Some feminists who recognize this hold that the answer is for women to overcome the biological disadvantage, by technological means if necessary, and to be as strong and ruthless as the most powerful of men. If there is another way, and we surely must believe that there is, we must face the fact that we are talking about working for a most radical change in society, not for some little adjustments that will enable us to compete on more equal terms within the existing system.

Elise Boulding's great imaginative survey of women through time, *The Underside of History,* suggests that in a nonviolent world women are indeed marvellously advantaged. She suggests, too, that the times when women have enjoyed freedom and equality (not dominance) have been generally free from war, minimally hierarchical, without intense food shortages, and without authoritarian family structures and rigid sexual mores. I do not think she supposes that these all result from women having a larger say in affairs; they may more probably be the preconditions of true liberation for women, and by the same token, of true liberation for men. So if what you choose to work for is disarmament, ecology, conflict resolution, draft resistance—welcome to the women's movement!

I came in on some splendid mixed metaphors; I will go out on one that I think is not mixed at all and is almost thematic to the whole of my talk. Indeed, I'm not sure it is a metaphor at all. In this time of fear of energy shortages, we speak often of power of resources, of being without resources, of lack of energy, of nonrenewable resources and so on and on. The analogy is clear; let us not forget that we have available to us the greatest renewable source of power, perhaps the only one which is increased the more we use it.

Barbara Deming
A Song for Gorgons

Barbara Deming is quoted widely throughout this book, and rightly so. Her daily life and her work exemplify the attention to detail, the passion and the commitment required of the nonviolent feminist. She is a friend, a "learn-together," a wise-woman-witch, a role model to younger feminists around the globe. For too long her soft, deep voice has sung a lonely song, persistently intertwining the two strands of feminism and nonviolence into one convincing melody. With this anthology she is joined by a fine full-voiced chorus at last.

Barbara has published six books: Prison Notes *(1966),* Running Away From Myself: A Dream Portrait of America Drawn From the Films of The 40's *(1969),* Revolution and Equilibrium *(1971),* Wash Us and Comb Us *(Stories) (1972),* We Cannot Live Without Our Lives *(1974) and* Remembering Who We Are *(1981).*

Barbara, now in her mid-sixties, believes that, because it is often those whom we love who oppress us, it is only by "further inventing nonviolence" that we will find the heart to wage our struggle boldly enough. For women, nonviolence requires that we refuse the roles that have been assigned us and, in effect, "go on strike" against the patriarchy's elaborate two-fold lie: that women belong to men and that women and men are essentially different in nature. By our actions we must convey the truth that men are not our masters but our brothers. Barbara believes too that, though it is very important to establish our right *to self defense through violence, to reply to violence with violence can be a desperate, even a passive act that indicates the acceptance of the oppressor's vision.*

In the following poem, Barbara celebrates the rage of the gorgons, the snakey-haired sisters of Greek mythology who were said to turn beholders to stone. To Barbara, the gorgons are, "those very untidy women who don't hold back any of the truths they experience" and she urges us to embrace our gorgon rage: "We women become our *natural selves as we allow ourselves to* be *gorgons—to acknowledge the anger we feel at what has been asked of us, done to us." Reclaimed by Barbara's pen, the "slandered wrath" of the gorgons becomes healing energy which has the power to turn us all to flesh and blood, not stone as the patriarchs have falsely claimed. (Barbara thanks Grace Shinell whose work appeared in the Goddess Issue of* Heresies *for the spelling of "ssister" used in this poem.)*

Listen carefully to Barbara's song. It brings healing.

Gorgons, unruly gorgons,
With eyes that start, with curls that hiss—

Once
I listened to the fathers' lies,
Took their false advice:
I mustn't look at you, I'd turn to
Stone.

But now I meet your clear furious stare and
It is my natural self that I become.
Yes, as I dare to name your fury
Mine—
Long asleep,
Writhing awake.

Ssisters, ssisters—of course they dread us.
Theirs is the kingdom
But it is built upon lies and more lies.
The truth-hissing wide-open-eyed rude
Glare of our faces—
If there were enough of us—
Could show their powers and their glories
To be what they merely are and
Bring their death-dealing kingdom
Down.

This is a song for gorgons—
Whose dreaded glances in fact can bless.
The men who would be gods we turn
Not to stone but to mortal flesh and blood and bone.
If we could stare them into accepting this,
The world could live at peace.

I sing this song for those with eyes that start,

With curls that hiss.
Our slandered wrath is our truth, and—
If we honor this—
Can deal not death but healing.

I sing: *Our* will be done!

I sing: Their kingdom *wane!*

Diana J. M. Davies/Insight

Barbara Deming

Mab Segrest

Feminism and Disobedience: Conversations with Barbara Deming

At the southernmost tip of the United States, in a little cottage nearly submerged under a sea of avocado, banana and papaya leaves, live Barbara Deming and artist/poet Jane Gapen. It is a peaceable kingdom raging fierce, a mecca for radical feminists, a place for storytelling and healing and witchly conjurings of ways to transform the patriarchy. In the following interview, Mab Segrest has captured some of the magic of meeting Barbara Deming and some of the wisdom of Barbara's deep thinking and active listening.

Mab has written: "My visit to Barbara was important because she too, as a nonviolent resister in/to the South, experienced that same potent blend of oppressions and made the kind of moral choices about whose side she was on that seem totally relevant to my life as a Southern lesbian in the 1980's."

Mab grew up in Alabama in the 1950's, in Tuskegee, at a time of intensifying civil rights struggles. She is still trying to sort through the connections between racism, misogyny and homophobia in Southern culture. Mab is a member of the collective of Feminary: A Feminist Journal for the South *in which this interview first appeared.*

Our trip to talk with Barbara Deming had the makings of a lesbian-feminist journey. We got a map of the Eastern US at an Exxon station in Fayetteville, North Carolina, and there it was: Sugarloaf Key, Florida. Completely South. At the bottom of the world. In two days, we would be there.

Climbing into Minnie Bruce's Volkswagen the first week in March, we entered a strange time warp. The next two days we traveled through spring into summer. Minnie Bruce reported that spring traveled north 30 miles each day. We were going 1000 miles south, accelerating the season change, like speeding up a projector. I had spent the weekend before we left snowed in—under ten inches—fretting about a shrinking woodpile. The first morning of the trip, near Charleston, I took off my sweater. At Savannah, shoes went. On St. Simons Island where we stopped to search out the plantation where Fanny Kemble had lived—her antebellum diaries record her horror at the slavery on her husband's rice plantation—I changed to shorts. (We did not find where Fanny Kemble had lived; the only plaques marked battles—the Revolution, 1812, the Civil War.)

If we traveled forward with the seasons, we went back years. Leaves on the trees, first butterflies, a first spider web: memories gushed of spring in Alabama where we both grew up. We were barefooted with nostalgia for old swimming holes from the sudden burst of Florida heat.

It was a pilgrimage of sorts. We both went wanting things. I, to talk with a lesbian almost twice my age, who had not only survived but kept growing, entering civil rights and peace movements in her forties, lesbian feminism in her fifties, with an integrity I admired. I had read *Prison Notes* the year before at the recommendation of a friend. The book is Barbara's account of her time in jail in Albany, Georgia, where she had been arrested with civil rights and peace demonstrators on a march to Cuba. She explained and illustrated their nonviolent tactics—neither to cooperate with the oppressors nor deny their humanity. In her picture of southern sheriffs, policemen, townspeople, I saw familiar faces. People I grew up with, and lived my early years with in an ambivalence of caring and disgust. In her sympathetic yet uncompromising picture of their bigotry, I felt a wholeness. It struck me with relief. I wanted to explore with her the connection between that experience—the powerful experience, for whites and Blacks, northerners and southerners, of the Sixties in the South—and her present lesbian-feminism. It occurred to me that if I felt such relief at an analysis that did not deny the humanity of white southerners (me), that perhaps women should likewise not deny the humanity of men. As a white, lesbian, feminist, southern woman, the analogy struck at the heart of my experience—however much I resisted its implications, its tendency to deny me immediate female superiority and easy answers.

Minnie Bruce, though also moved by *Prison Notes*, had her own agenda, I felt. It was important for me that Barbara had lived as a lesbian her whole life. She had never married. She had come out in public in her fifties; me in my twenties. Yet I had a strongly atavistic feeling: I could have lived her life. Minnie Bruce, on the other hand, had married, had had two children, come out, been divorced, and lost her children. Minnie Bruce and I both grew up in small Alabama towns in the 1950's. We share many of the same resonances. But I felt since I met her she had lived much of her life as a "flower of southern womanhood." Properly married. Beautiful children. My life, I had lived as a weed. A jimson weed. But as we drove down and she told me again of how she had lost her children, of how cousins and aunts and mother had written letters of disapproval when she had most needed support, I saw that Minnie Bruce's journey out of where we grew up had been as difficult as mine. She talked of being perplexed over her relationship with her sons, via long-distance phone calls and seasonal trips to Kentucky, perplexed about their acceptance of aggression, violence, and war, perplexed about her own desire for a violent response by women to male violence. So we read each other parts of Barbara's books as we drove down, sorting through her words and our lives, stopping to run and meditate and eat seafood and quickly visit the Everglades.

Then off the tip of Florida. First a long drive through swamps, over a bridge to the sudden view of the ocean that still hits me in the pit of my stomach every time. Then down the Keys in darkness. Clear skys, familiar constellations. Further and further down. By 11:30 pm, we were there.

Barbara and Jane live on a canal, in a small open house half a block from the water. Exotic plants fill their yard: coconuts, papayas, banana trees. Minnie Bruce and I settled in their tiny guest house—for me, like Girl Scout camp; for her, like "Push," her great aunt's south Alabama farm, where she visited summers as a girl. We all agreed to rest and do our own work the next morning, then meet over lunch to start our talks. I have arranged the following "conversations" from six hours of tapes. Barbara edited and added to her part—wanting to make it more precise. For as she wrote to us, "The tape recorder did make me nervous, hard as I tried not to be. And I too often couldn't find my words." Minnie Bruce Pratt did a good bit of the transcription.

First Conversation: dropping into deeper struggle

Minnie Bruce: We are interested in your tranformations, your changes—from civil rights and peace activist to feminist. You've spoken of feminism "erupting" in people's lives. When did feminism erupt in you?

Barbara: When I read Kate Millett's *Sexual Politics*. I had been a lesbian since I was sixteen. For a number of years I refused to accept this identity—telling myself, "When I grow up, I will grow up into marriage." But I slowly grew up into believing that it was right for me to be what I am. I think my struggle to hold to my pride in myself as a lesbian could be called a feminist struggle. So in one sense I could say that I'd been waging a feminist struggle most of my life. But I'd been making it with the disadvantage of not fully knowing how legitimate it was to make it. I was in this insane position of feeling more and more strongly, "It is right to be what I am;" of making a certain passage in which I came to know that I wasn't perverse—that *marrying* would be the perverse thing for me to do. And yet—so many of the people to whom I granted authority then—the great male geniuses whose writings I devoured—I was aware that almost without exception they would have named me ill. So I was really a bit insane for all those years—one part of my mind having to be split off from another part. Then when I read *Sexual Politics*—it at once validated all I'd been struggling toward. And now I still saw these men as geniuses; but I could also see that I had a right to think of them as crippled, though geniuses.

Mab: When did you first become political?

Barbara: In 1960 I met some of the people in the Committee for Nonviolent Action (CNVA)—and immediately began to involve myself deeply in the actions they were taking. I had never before wanted to identify myself with any political group, because politics had always meant for me naming this group of people or that group of people "the enemy"—to whom no allegiance at all is due, denying the complexity of human nature. I had begun to read Gandhi, and the politics he taught did not deny this complexity. But it never occurred to me that there were any people in this U.S. who had this same nonviolent vision. I assumed that if they existed I would have read about them in *The New York Times*. The people in the CNVA, you may remember, were the people who swam out to nuclear submarines and climbed onto them in protest, who walked across this country and across Europe to Moscow, urging the people of each country to demand unilateral disarmament. We began to take our disarmament walks through the South, and as there were Black people among us, these walks became walks against racism, too. And I took part in some of the actions led by Black groups—SCLC (Southern Christian Leadership Conference) and SNCC (Student Nonviolent Coordinating Committee). The actions in Birmingham, for example. I began to have more and more faith in what nonviolent action could accomplish—if it were bold enough. When the war against the Vietnamese escalated, the CNVA sent a small team to Saigon to protest the war where it was actually happening, and I took part in that action. I was thinking of volunteering to join one of the groups that destroyed draft files.

Then a turning in my life occurred. While it was taking place I had the painful feeling that I was dropping out of the struggle. But I came slowly to recognize that I was in fact falling into the struggle at a deeper level. And falling into a deeper understanding of what politics is all about. I'd decided against taking the draft file action, because I wasn't in equilibrium enough to take it. My life with the woman I'd been living with for fifteen years had broken up, because she was in love now with another woman. Not long after, I fell in love with Jane. We'd met in college, and had strong feelings for one another—but neither of us at that time had known how the other felt. Then we'd met again years later and become at once deep friends. Now Jane's marriage had broken up. I'd visited. Our old feelings for one another had revived, and this time we'd named them. We decided to live together. But Jane's ex-husband then decided to challenge her fitness as a mother. For a number of months the struggle to help her keep her two children required all our energies. I won't, on tape, go into the details. She did keep them— by keeping the fight out of the courts, and by our paying what amounted to ransom. But it was a scary and exhausting fight. And an utterly lonely one. This was the summer and fall of 1969. The women's movement was already building again, but we were in North Carolina where Jane had been living—not in touch with it, though I can remember day-dreaming that strong women were there to counsel with us and stand by us. We moved North finally—into a house we'd found for the four of us. Shaken by that fight we'd been in. Shaken, too, by the fact that the war against the Vietnamese was still escalating—in spite of all the public protest against it. Our protests didn't seem to be having any effect. Of course in retrospect—as Dave Dellinger's book, *More Power Than We Know*, makes clear—we were having a very real effect. But at the time, it didn't feel like it. I wrote a poem that winter that began, "I lie at the bottom of my spirit's well."

But if it was a very painful time, it was a time of revelations for me, too. I began to recognize that the powers-that-be that were waging that abominable war—presuming to have the right to determine how the Vietnamese had better lead their lives or else!—they were the same powers that had backed up Jane's ex-husband when he presumed to have the right to say how *she* should lead *her* life, or else! I hadn't—during those months—dropped out of my struggle against these powers. I had been engaged in the same struggle—but at closer range. I began to understand what the patriarchy is, with much help of course from the books I was reading now, written by women who understood it before I did.

* * *

The first afternoon after talking we go swimming. Mangrove trees grow at the edge of clear, blue-green water. A great white heron glides in the shadows. Jane, who swims out with fins and mask, reports that angel fish and a large eel live in the reef. Barbara tells us that she wore a whistle while swimming to signal for help if there were shark attacks—until she learned that bright metal attracts them. The bottom is coral, chalk-colored and jagged, so we wade and swim in tennis shoes.

Second Conversation: "clinging to truth"

Mab: How do you see your philosophy of nonviolence applying to feminism?

Barbara: Gandhi's word for nonviolent action, "satyagraha," translates as "clinging to the truth." The patriarchy is so clearly founded on lies and more lies that that definition of struggle makes even more sense to me now than before. Though the words "clinging to the truth" are not quite adequate, are they? They would seem to imply that we know the whole truth. And women are very aware now that we have to *learn* to use our own eyes, to refuse just to see what we're told to see. So we have to try to speak the truth as we think we see it at each moment (speak it with acts as well as words)—but be aware always that if we keep looking and looking for ourselves, we'll keep seeing more clearly, seeing new truths. If we fixate on any one truth we've found and say "Here is ALL the truth," we'll never move as far as we have to move. And we have to keep listening to ourselves in many different ways. Not just to what our minds tell us but to what our bodies tell us. Not shutting out any voice that rises up in us, even if it seems to be contradicted by some other voice in us. Listening to everything we have to say to ourselves (and also to one another) and trusting that we'll come to see how it all fits together. Not being afraid to seem untidy in the process.

The image of the gorgons has more and more meaning for me—those very untidy women who don't hold back any of the truths they experience. The patriarchs, of course, name gorgons violent. I see them now as healers. The patriarchs try to teach us that their glances turn one to stone. They actually turn one not to stone but to flesh and blood. And that's what alarms men. For men want to be treated as gods. Gorgons see through this. We women become *our* natural selves as we allow ourselves to *be* gorgons—to acknowledge the anger we feel at what has been asked of us, done to us. And men can be forced to become *their* natural selves if we stare right through their pretenses.

I'd say the primary lie invented by the patriarchy is the lie that Jane's ex-husband was trying to insist upon: the lie that women (and children) belong to men, are their property. He didn't want the care of the children, actually, as I've explained off tape; but he wanted to retain *power* over them and over Jane. I think this lie, that one can own another person, must have been invented by men centuries ago before they knew that they were natural fathers. They must have been jealous of the fact that women gave birth—seen children as extensions of the selves of the women; seen themselves as simply ceasing to be when they died, while women continued to be, through their offspring. So they invented the lie of ownership, of purchase. The first purchase was the purchase of women. They owned the women, they said; and so they owned her children—and now *they* had heirs; *they* couldn't die.

At a certain point, of course, they discovered that they, too, played a part in the birth of children. And at this point you'd think they might have calmed down and accepted their given human nature. And seen no more need for lies. But I guess by then they were hooked on lying. I guess the lie of ownership is an intoxicant. Now they invented a further lie: the lie that they were the *only* true biological parent. The wombs of women were simply the plots of earth in which they planted their so-called "seed." (The supposedly scientific term "semen" still contains this lie.) And they invented the lie that the source of the universe itself was male; all creative energy was male—God was "Father." Women could be vessels of this male energy, but were nothing in themselves. The only way to become a "real woman" was to attach yourself to a man.

And they keep inventing more and more lies. Because lies are intoxicating but they'll never satisfy you, so they have to keep inventing more and more of them. For example, they have invented (have "given birth to") the "corporation." Look at the pretense in that word—derived from the word for "body", which a "corporation" very simply isn't. Alice Malloy in the "Future Visions" issue of *Country Women* has proposed that we develop the vocabulary required to undermine in court the concept that a corporation is a person under the law. I think it's a brilliant suggestion which women should follow up. And of course men's most horrendous invention of all has been war—and now it's nuclear war, total war. It's hard for me to understand how they could be willing to invent such weapons. And the only way I can almost understand it is in terms of their psychopathic jealousy of us. It's as though they were asserting: "Women may give birth, but we can give death. We are master of *that*." And so this felt need of theirs to find identities they can call superior to ours has brought us finally to this time in which we have to fear not only for our own lives but for the life of the planet itself.

And all the while no need for their jealousy. If they'd only calm down and let this truth finally touch them: Women and men are both able to be parents. (Not that I believe that it's only by becoming parents that we become a part of the life that goes on after we die.) The two sexes—we are in our human natures essentially alike.

To my dismay, some women would deny this likeness—in fact some of the most brilliant women among us, like Mary Daly, whom I would name a genius, her books great gifts to us. But she appears to have decided that men are hopeless, that they are, in fact, just what I've been describing them as—psychopathically afraid of being and essentially barren. It scares me that more and more women are coming to feel this way—to feel that men as an entire gender are hopeless. I agree deeply with what Andrea Dworkin wrote in *Heresies 6:* that the idea of biological superiority and biological determinism is "the world's most dangerous and deadly idea" and if we embrace it, "we become carriers of the disease we must cure."

I have to admit that I know what it feels like to sometimes wish that men just didn't exist. Especially when I think of the very real possibility that they will destroy the planet. And I ask myself in panic: have we time, have we time in which to bring about the changes I very much believe we can bring about if we have time enough, if we have time enough—but do we?

And I think that for a while it's necessary to separate off from men to one degree or another (each of us I think has to determine for her own self to what degree). Because we can't come into our own powers, can't recover from the lie that we've come to half-believe in spite of ourselves—the lie that the male principle is the only creative principle—can't do this while in their very demanding presences.

Men invented the lie that we women only exist if they give us life, but actually they invented this lie out of fear that if they're not in possession of us *they* don't exist. So when we separate off from them, this ancient fear of theirs flares up. It's a necessary move we make, but they will always name it a violence—an attempt to kill them off. If only they realized! But for some peculiar reason they don't seem able to imagine how painful it is for us to have to sometimes wish that they simply weren't there. I believe that the only way we can get where we have to go is by never refusing to face the truth of our feelings as they rise up in us—even when we wish it weren't the truth. So we have to admit to the truth that we sometimes wish even our own fathers, sons, brothers, lovers were not there. But, this truth exists alongside another truth: the truth that this wish causes us anguish.

In the kitchen, off tape, I was talking with Minnie Bruce about my father's death. Years ago now. It was on a weekend in the country and he'd been working outside with a pick and shovel—making a new garden plot. And he'd had a heart attack and fallen there in the loose dirt. We'd called a rescue squad and they were trying to bring him back to life, but—couldn't. I was half-lying on the ground next to him, with my arms around his body. And I realized—this was the first time in my life that I had felt able to really touch my father's body. I was holding hard to it—with my love—and with my grief. And my grief was partly that my father, whom I loved, was dying. But it was also that I knew already that his death would allow me to feel freer. I was mourning that this had to be so. It's a grief that it's hard for me to speak of. That the only time I would feel free to touch him without feeling threatened by his power over me was when he lay dead—it's unbearable to me. And I think there can hardly be a woman who hasn't felt a comparable grief. So it's an oversimplification to speak the truth that we sometimes wish men dead—unless we also speak the truth which is perhaps even harder to face (as we try to find our own powers, to be our own women): the truth that this wish is unbearable to us. It rends us.

* * *

We all meet in the kitchen over preparation for supper. We talk about our families, our work, the anti-Klan rallies.

Third Conversation: men, anger, change

Mab: I would like to talk some about analogies between the civil rights movement and the women's movement. The connection makes it harder for me to believe in automatic female superiority, to believe in men as hopeless. I've been on the other side of that. I have been a white person in the South, and I have been part of a movement which changed society for the better. White people in the South would not have done it if Black people hadn't started. If I'm going to say, "Men are completely inhuman," then I have to say, "White people are completely inhuman. . ." And that's not my sense of myself. If I have to say that as a white Southerner I have changed because of what Black people and other white people have done, I have also to allow that men can change because of what women are doing. It wouldn't have occurred to white Southerners in power to do anything about segregation, it just wouldn't have occurred . . . I wondered, in terms or your being in both movements, what you thought.

Barbara: Well what you have just said speaks altogether for me though I'm a white *Northerner*.

Minnie Bruce: How are men going to change? The meeting between two people, where one opposes the other, is the point of change. But I don't want to have the personal contact, I don't want to do it.

Barbara: I, too, choose more and more to be with women, less and less with men. We've taken this space and in it we're finding ourselves. But I think there's a deep difference between affirming this as a necessity for a time and making the metaphysical statement that for all time to come men are fated to be what they are now under patriarchy.

Mab: I have a quite ambivalent reaction to lesbian-feminism. I feel on one hand, it's given me back my life. But I also feel that much of what I hear, or perhaps much of what I want to believe, is lying about the complexity of truth. To say, "We as women are right, they as men are wrong" is an absolute way. There's all this talk about women and nature, but men are part of nature too.

Barbara: Yes. (Emphatic nod.)

Minnie Bruce: When people talk about not giving men our energies—I agree with that. Which throws me into a terrible ambivalence about my sons. But it costs a huge amount of energy to deny your own feelings. To hold your own feelings in check. We spent a lot of time talking about that and our lesbianism this morning off tape. But if those feelings we are denying are the fact we have affection and love for males—even if they are remote, even if we no longer can show it, even if we choose no longer to have them in our lives—we can spend as much energy denying that we still have feelings for them. It cost us something to deny that.

Barbara: Yes. I think that's a vital point—one that some women haven't yet realized because they're in such fear of where that acknowledgement might take them. Fear that it might take them right back into the same old pattern.

Minnie Bruce: Yes, but it's also a double fear. I'm afraid to admit to myself that I still have these feeling of affection and a desire to be close. But I'm also afraid to let my anger out because I'm afraid of what will happen to me. I spend a lot of energy containing my anger as well as my longing.

Barbara: Yes, I too have been very afraid of my anger. But I think that if we can begin to free ourselves of the lie we've accepted about what it is to be an angry woman—a gorgon—if we can begin to believe in our anger as a healing force, then our own belief in it as that will cause men to begin to experience it in a different way. And our danger from them will decrease. In fact, I think the reason that men are so very violent is that they know, deep in themselves, that they're acting out a lie, and so they're furious. You can't be happy living a lie, and so they're furious at being caught up in the lie. But they don't know how to break out of it, so they just go further into it.

Minnie Bruce: And they blame women for it. They're trapped and they say women are the reasons they're trapped. So instead of changing themselves, they attack women.

Barbara: But although it's a fury that makes them turn on us, and a fury that could even escalate into their blowing up the planet—although it's something we have to dread—I feel we mustn't be hypnotized by this dread. We have to look at the flip side of the coin, which is that they're in a rage because they are acting out a lie—which means that in some deep part of themselves they want to be delivered from it, are homesick for the truth. So their fury gives us reason to fear; but it also gives us reason to hope. If we can remember that.

Minnie Bruce: But they have to deliver themselves. The lie is that we could save them. Virgin Mary. Mother. That we could save them and that we could damn them. And we can do neither. They have to be able to deliver themselves. Just as men can't save us, they can't come and take us off the rock that we're chained to.

* * *

Lunchtime, Minnie Bruce and I drive down to Key West, 20 miles away, to complete the trip South. We wander down the streets of Old Key West. In each sidewalk cafe sit imitation Hemingways, mustached and tanned young men. Occasionally they sip gin out of glasses. Their eyes do not focus. They clench their jaws. We lunch on the concrete dock, watching birds dive and ships leave the harbor.

Fourth Conversation: civil disobedience

Mab: What about civil disobedience? Should women begin to commit civil disobedience as we did in the civil rights struggle and in the anti-war struggle?

Barbara: I've been told that NOW (National Organization for Women) women have talked about committing civil disobedience to get the Equal Rights Amendment passed. And I was thrilled by this. Back in the Vietnam war years Women Strike for Peace talked once of doing this—of just filling the jails until the war was stopped. The Jeanette Rankin Brigade was originally to be a civil disobedience brigade. But then they pulled back from it. And I was heartbroken that they did. I think it could have made a deep difference.

I have to say very quickly, though, that from the very beginning the present feminist movement has been committing acts of disobedience. Some of these acts have been acts comparable to the acts taken in the Sixties. As when we disrupt beauty contests. Or spray paint on some billboard that insults or threatens us. Or destroy the ads outside of movie theatres showing *Snuff*. But we haven't just looked to the actions of the

Sixties and asked ourselves what can we do that's comparable for the cause of women. We've taken many actions that never landed us in jail but involved other kinds of risks—breaking unwritten laws often rather than laws actually on the books. We've risked jobs, risked abuse, risked divorce, the loss of children, risked various forms of retaliation.

Take even the founding of consciousness-raising groups, one of our first actions, and to me they are the basic building blocks of our movement. This action certainly broke an unwritten law: women are not supposed to bond together in this way and to reveal family secrets, talk openly with one another about our oppression at the hands of men. We're supposed to keep quiet about it when we've been beaten, supposed to keep quiet about it when we're raped. Or sexually harrassed at work. We've been breaking all these injunctions. We're refusing to pretend any longer that what's happening to us isn't really happening.

I read some weeks ago in *New Women's Times* (a feminist newspaper from Rochester, NY) of an action I thought beautiful. *The Story of O* was being shown at, I think, the University of Rochester. A group of feminists went into the theatre, and from their seats began openly to express their feeling about the movie. They didn't get thrown into jail for this. But the men in the audience were furious; some men even became very threatening, and the campus police did nothing to protect the women. The show was stopped, I think.

I think we can find way after way of taking this kind of action—just speaking out in public the truth of our feeling about something that's taking place. (Jane did it just very spontaneously one day at a showing of *One Flew Over the Cuckoo's Nest*—at the end of the film, as we were walking down the aisle, she just raised her voice a little and began to talk about how the film slandered women.)

There may well be times when we'll have to speak out so loudly that we'll be arrested for disturbing the peace. But if we say to ourselves, "This won't be a good enough action unless we end up in jail"—this would be ridiculous, and very limiting.

Mab: Yes, I have also thought that the kind of planned confrontation that was taking place in the South, say, in the Sixties with civil rights, wouldn't be effective for women. There you had Black people in a region controlled by white people, but you were trying to get the majority of people outside of the South to bring legal pressure on the South to change, which to a certain extent is what happened. But with women you don't have that analogy of people-in-power-outside-of-women who are going to come in and make the men do something different. You have women going to jail where there are male jailkeepers and male courts and everything else. It seems pretty dangerous. Minnie Bruce asked me awhile back, when we first planned this issue of *Feminary,* why more women weren't doing civil disobedience around women's issues. I thought, "Well, we probably would be killed. There wouldn't be that much public opinion to keep us from getting slaughtered."

Barbara: Yes, it would certainly be easy to get ourselves into situations where we'd be much too vulnerable. Of course one can say already there is retaliation against us. The incidence of rape is mounting, for example, and I don't think that's just coincidence.

But—about the civil rights days: this whole country is racist, so it isn't exactly—is it?—that there was a structure that wasn't racist on which one could depend for help. Though there was the pretense in many official quarters of being all for full rights for Blacks—and that gave some leverage. (Also of course, the kind of disruptions that were taking place made business as usual impossible, and business wanted to move again.) There's the pretense among many patriarchs, too, that they want *women* to be free. So haven't we a comparable leverage? And of course the same leverage of disruption that we could cause.

But yes, we could get hurt. The militant women's suffrage fighters got hurt—as we can read in *Shoulder to Shoulder* and *Jailed for Freedom.* Some women were left invalids. If we engaged again in confrontation actions (nonviolent ones, I mean)—when you said just now, "We'd be slaughtered" something in me panicked and agreed; but—I don't really think we'd be in greater danger than people in the Black nonviolent struggle have been.

And of course—whether or not we're engaged in struggle—we are being hurt right now. And badly. Raped, battered. A daily war is waged against us. We're refusing to pretend any longer that this isn't so.

If more women aren't taking the kind of action that was taken in the Sixties, I think it's because another kind of action seems to us imperative right now. It's a time of renaming everything—renaming the behavior of men toward us, our own behavior, and our own powers, too-long-denied powers. As I've said, we break no written law when we refuse to see God as male. Or declare that pornography does us violence. (Of course if we try to invoke the law of the land to protect us against that violence—or any other—we're likely to be countersued for our presumption, charged with "malicious prosecution." That's a whole other story.)

We're also inventing ways to end our ancient isolation from one another. Many of the acts of disobedience we are taking now we take necessarily alone—or alone at critical moments. For the struggle is the root struggle now. It takes place very often within the home. We've been isolated in these homes, but are beginning now to break out of that isolation—to form systems of support. The circles of supportive women I longed for so during the custody struggle—we're bringing those circles into being.

And it's a time above all, perhaps, in which—within these circles—we're learning to be able to imagine a different future. There's a very beautiful passage in Susan Griffin's *Rape: The Power of Consciousness*. Here: "Now we desire a world in which rape could not be imagined and could never be. We desire nothing less than this. . . I know this world we see the edges of is real. And because we see this world, we can make it be." I believe this last sentence with all my soul.

In the Sixties in the Black nonviolent movement they spoke of the Beloved Community we would bring into being. I took part in actions in which I experienced very strongly the power of holding this in my mind. Felt it sometimes almost as a magic power—on our walks through the South, most especially. Could see it acting on the minds of those who'd accost us; know it brought us safely through some very dangerous situations. I've spoken of some of these experiences off tape—of seeing their faces change, seeing them almost wake up out of a threatening posture. In these past years, as I've made myself look squarely at all that men have done to women—to my dismay, I've often lost my hold on this vision of what is possible. Shocked out of it. I do recover it. And I don't just recover it; it is now stronger for me. Except that I have to say that I still find it harder to hold to. Griffin speaks of it as a taste in the mouth. She writes, "What does the inside of my mouth feel like when even the memory of rape has vanished . . . who are we when we are finally safe with our own kind? Our kind. . ." We *are* one kind—women and men. And that world *is* possible. When more and more of us find we can believe it, and can hold to that belief, then perhaps we'll be able to release all our anger at them without fear.

* * *

Before the last conversation, I realize that I am disappointed.

I want to hear more about Barbara's life as a lesbian. I tell Minnie Bruce, and she says, "But underneath the moral discipline, there is a Parisian sensibility." We decide to ask Barbara more about her lesbianism. She talks first, at her request, off tape.

Fifth Conversation: "You can't throw the truth away."

Mab: I was interested in discussing more of your personal history, biography, out of my need to know lesbians' lives and what they've been like. I feel I know your public life very well from 1960 on, and I was struck by how, in a lot of your writings, there is a kind of public voice. Even for private experiences. I'm interested that you're working on an autobiographical novel. I'd like to hear more of what your life has been like all the way through.

Barbara: Explain a little more what you mean by "public voice."

Mab: The focus was the development of ideas that came out of experiences with other people—out of acting with them. Out of being jailed. Out of going to Vietnam. But when you started writing those letters to your Black friend Ray, in Alabama, about your being lesbian, that tone was different. You were dealing with your own feelings about yourself rather than explaining a more generalized analysis of the way the world is.

Minnie Bruce: You said you were a lesbian when you were sixteen, and there were years of struggling with that. I guess from having read your writings I feel that there's that gap in your personal history that I'm interested in, because I feel there's a gap in my personal history too. Because I didn't know my own feelings. I'm interested in knowing what other people went through in figuring that out about themselves.

Barbara: The difficulty is with speaking to this on tape for possible publication. This was one of the difficulties of coming out. For years I had wanted to be out. The deepest part of me wanted to be—especially with people I cared about. But if you reveal yourself as a lesbian, you expose other people too.

Mab: How are you doing it in your book? How are you dealing with that problem?

Barbara: That's one reason I'm writing it slowly. Because I have to again and again grapple with that problem. I've dealt with it by sometimes slightly altering things. So I call it a novel. I try not to ever not speak the essential truth of any situation, but I'll change things just enough so that it wouldn't hurt another person.

Minnie Bruce: When you say hurt, do you mean reveal their identity?

Barbara: Right. And then I have to ask myself: At this point in history would they mind? Sometimes to answer that question can take a long time. The further I get into the book, the less anxious I become about that.

Mab: Sometimes it's bitter to have to protect people from your love.

Minnie Bruce: Would you be willing to tell the story about the wastepaper basket?

Barbara: Sure—but how does that. . . ?

Minnie Bruce: Well, because we've talked about telling the truth in all of its complexity—not saying something isn't truth if it is truth. Not trying to get rid of it.

Barbara: Yes. Back in my twenties (which was in the 1930s) I was keeping a journal, and I wrote in the journal, "I am a lesbian; I must face this truth." Then rereading my journal a few days later, I thought, "Gosh, I shouldn't have that down here in black and white. Someone might read it." So I took my scissors and cut out that sentence and tossed it in the wastepaper basket. Perhaps half an hour later, as I was moving around the room, I glanced down and there, glaring up at me most conspicuously from the wasepaper basket, was this cut-out sentence. And I remember that it hit me: you can't throw truths away. If you try to throw them away, you get into worse trouble than the trouble you were trying to escape.

* * *

The last evening before we leave, we all read our poetry. Minnie Bruce, Barbara and I read ethereal lyrics, full of the night sky. Jane recites from her "Paean of Hate"—fury, expletive, invective, her rage at men. The air clears, as after a thunderstorm. Barbara leans forward, arms on corduroy pants, hair swinging to one side—lanky, sexy, unguarded, elegant. Somewhere a door opens. I have what I came for.

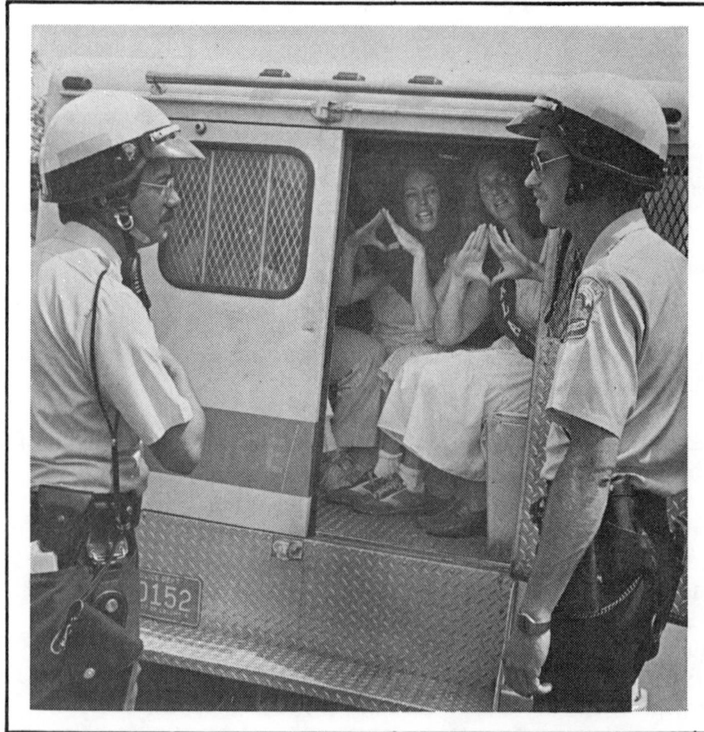

JEB

Members of The Congressional Union make the international sign for women, an alternative power gesture to the phallic raised fist, from a paddy wagon after a Women's Equality Day (pro-ERA) demonstration, August 26, 1981. The twenty-one women were arrested for chaining themselves to the White House fence.

Ellen Bass
Our Stunning Harvest

This poem is a dance. It begins with bent backs, strained necks, arms wrapped tight around torsos. As it evolves we see the heads thrown back, mouths open and singing, bare feet stomping the earth, arms thrown wide in embrace.

This poem is a sustained wail. It catches in the throat of the reader. The pain is never abandoned even as it is transcended in the final healing vision.

This poem is the color of blood, the color of death, the color of hope and healing. It is the color of rape and the color of bombs, the color of little girls' sneakers and of baby blankets.

Part III of this poem should be copied and sent to all the government officials and the pentagon officials and the nuclear power plant officials. It should be memorized and droned by wise old women, acted out on street corners by troops of wandering minstrels, sung by choruses of chest-beating, angry, women-loving women. It should be crooned the way Holly Near tearfully croons over and over, "No, no don't melt into one,/No, no, no, no don't melt into one."

Ellen Bass is the author of four books of poetry, the most recent of which, For Earthly Survival, *won the 1980 Elliston Book Award. She co-edited* No More Masks! An Anthology of Poems by Women *and her work has appeared in many literary, feminist, and survival-oriented journals and anthologies. Presently, she is completing a new collection of poems,* If We Gather, *and is editing an anthology of stories and poems by survivors of child sexual abuse,* I Never Told Anyone.

Ellen lives in Santa Cruz, California with her husband, Alan Nelson, and daughter, Saraswati Bass Nelson, where she writes and teaches "Writing About Our Lives" workshops for women.

I. She recognizes miner's lettuce
nibbles its round leaf.
Her father asks *Do you know*
not to eat the other plants?
and she nods solemnly.

We have taught her not to swallow pits
of cherries or olives.
She spits them out bald
and repeats *Could make a child sick.*
And walking, when we hear a car
she runs to the side of the road
stands, stationary, until it passes.
But how do I protect her
from men who rape children?
from poison in the air?
from nuclear holocaust?

I walk this road—oak trees, eucalyptus
blackberry bushes in white flower
the hard green fruit pushing out behind the blossoms—
the first time I have walked here alone
since that day almost two years ago
when I carried her in my belly,
the morning before her birth.
It was dustier then, drought
the smell of hot clay and stillness
in the tall Queen Anne's lace.
Today the breeze is cool.
But the dread, the urgency
etch my pleasure like acid.

I clean house, shove socks and shirts
in the washer, speed through the grocery,
type, fold, staple—
but what good are dishes stacked in the cupboard,
peaches and avocadoes in the basket, envelopes
stamped in the dark mailbox?

At night I lie in bed imagining what I will do if attacked—
alone, I could run

or fight
but with her—in the stroller, holding my hand
on this country road?
A mother bird flutters and distracts.
She risks her life, but the babies are protected.
I could not even protect her.
She is too small to run. If I whispered *run*
she would not go. And if I tried to carry her
we would be overcome. I could not fight with her
not far from help. I am prey.
With her as hostage
I am blackmailed.
And if I am not enough? if they want her too?

My husband sleeps by my side
his regular sleep breath. I
lean closer, try to absorb
the calm. But the possibilities do not stop.
I don't let them. I keep trying scenarios,
get as far as convincing the rapist to let me take her to a neighbor
then rushing into the house, locking him out.
But he may not even speak English
I sober myself, and besides. . .

I am sick in the night, sick the next day.
My stomach won't digest food, it runs through me
foul, waste.
By noon I fall asleep, she sleeps in the crook of my arm.
We sleep for hours. For these few hours
we are safe.
I know we have been safe
afterward.

II. Yesterday I read they tried to kill Dr. Rosalie Bertell,

a nun who researched radiation-caused cancer. Here,
the resource center for nonviolence is shot up,
tires slashed.

My husband is limiting his practice
so he can work against nuclear destruction.
He says *We may be in danger, you know.*
If the steering on the car ever feels funny
pull right over.
He's had the lug nuts loosened before.

But we both know that is not the greatest danger.
Radiation from Lovecreek, Churchrock, Rocky Flats,
Three Mile Island, West Valley, Hanford—
we live near the San Andreas Fault—
an earthquake
and the Diablo Canyon plant
could kill millions—
and bombs, Trident, the draft beginning again.
Who are these madmen
whose lives are so barren, so desperate
they love nothing?

What will it take to make them change?
What will it take?

What will it take to make *me* change?
I still use plastic bags from Dow Chemical.
When am I
going to stop?

I ask my friend. She smiles.
Polyvinylchloride poisons your food she says.

What do you do with your lettuce? I ask.

Glass jars, or a pot with a lid.

I smile.
I have a pot with a lid.

What good will one woman never again using plastic bags do
in the face of tons of plutonium, recombinant DNA
a hundred thousand rapists?
What good does it do that I feed my daughter organic rice
purple beets, never sugar?
What good that I march with other women
and we yell *WOMEN UNITED*
WILL NEVER BE DEFEATED
banshees into the night?

These things will not save my daughter.
I know. I know that.
But unless I do them
she will not be saved

and I want to save her.
Oh Mother of us all, I am a mother too
I want to save her.

III. I want to talk to the president.
I want to go with other mothers
and meet with the president.
And I want mothers from Russia there.
And the head of Russia.
And Chinese mothers
and the head of China
and mothers from Saudi Arabia and Japan and South Africa
and all the heads of state and the families of the heads of state
and the children, all the children of the mothers.

I want a meeting.

I want to ask the president, *Is there nothing*
precious to you?

And when the president explains how it's the
Russians, I want the Russian women to say *We don't*
want war. I want all the women to scream *We don't want war, we,*
the people, do not want war.

And I want the president to admit he wants war,
he wants power and money and war more
than he wants the lives of his children.
I want to see him turn to his children and tell them
they will not live, that
no one will live,
that with one computer error all life on this planet can be
annihilated, that two men could go mad and push one button
in a silo, in a plane, that these men do go mad,
the men with access to the buttons go mad all the time,
are replaced, that one
might not be replaced soon enough.

I want each head of state to tell his children what will happen
if any country sends a thermonuclear bomb.
I want each head of state, with his own tongue, to tell his children
how the computers of the other country would pick up the signal,
how they would fire back, how the bombs would hit.
I want each president and prime minister and king
to tell his children how firestorms would burn, vaporizing people,
animals, plants, and then as days passed,
how the millions would die of radiation sickness,
their skin sloughing off, the nausea, hair falling out,
hemorrhage, infection, no hospitals, no clean water,
the stench of dead and decaying bodies, bacteria and virus rampant,

insects rampant, and the radiation ticking, ticking
as millions more die over the next years, leukemia, cancer,
and no hope
for the future, birth deformity, stillbirth, miscarriage, sterility,
millions and billions.

I want them to watch the faces of their children.
I want them to watch their eyes pale
the flecks of light fading,
and when their children ask *Why?*
I want them to point to the other heads of state
and the others to point back
and I want the mothers screaming.
I want the mothers of the children of the heads of state screaming.
I want them to scream until their voices are hoarse whispers
raw as the bloody rising of the sun, I want them to hiss
How dare you?
How dare you?
Kill them yourself, then.
Kill them here, now, with your own hands.
Kill all these children, clench
your hands around their necks, crunch their spines.
Kill one
two, three, kill hundreds. If you are going to kill
then kill.

I want to see the faces of the president, the premier, the prime
minister, the chancellor, the king.
I want to see their faces tremble.
I want to see them tremble like a still lake under wind.
I want to see them weep.

I must be crazy myself.
My mother is an optimist. She believes in a survival instinct.

She has read the statistics, knows
plutonium is poison for 500,000 years.
But she does not think of these things.
It depresses her, she says.

I say she is naive.
But I write poems in which presidents and premiers weep
at the voices of raging mothers. I write
they weep.
I must be crazy. I am crazy.
And I want this meeting like a crazy woman wants.

I want to go myself.
I want my daughter to ride her four-wheeled horse around the carpeted room
fast, steering with her red sneakered feet through
        potted plants and filing cabinets,
precise, dauntless.
I want her spirit to inspire us.
I don't want to hear about numbers.
I don't want to hear one number about how many bombs or how much money
or dates or megatons or anything else.
I want to hear *No more.*
I want to hear *My child will not be murdered.*
My child will live.

I want to dance victorious, to dance and dance
ring around the rosie, with no one falling down.
No ashes, no ashes.
I want no ashes from my child's tender head.
I want to dance. I want to sing. I want to kiss all the heads of state,
all the mothers, every child.
I want to kiss them all and dance the hora, dance the mazurka,
        the waltz, the tribal dances, bare feet on red clay
                                                  on white sand
                                                  on black earth.

dancing, kissing, singing
dancing, dancing until our legs are strong
our arms strong, our thighs, lungs, bellies strong,
until our voices are loud, clear, and vibrate with the wind
until we ride the wind
until we ride home, with the wind, flying, flying
laughing, kissing, singing, cackling, our children
tucked under our wings, safe.
Safe. We are safe. We are so strong.
We can protect our children.

IV. *No you won't,* the young, composed woman taunts us
slowly, from the stage.
She is our teacher. She is teaching us our power.

Yes we will, We yell back.

No you won't.

Yes we will.

No you won't.

We are roaring, *YES WE WILL. YES WE WILL.*

Now she pauses *Say, Yes I will.*
Yes I will, I yell.
AGAIN, she bellows.
Yes I will, my eyes fill with tears. I am trembling.

YES I WILL. YES I WILL. YES I WILL.

I will.
I will protect my daughter.
How
will I protect my daughter?

Even if we dismantle the bombs, cement the power plants,
ban 2, 4, 5-T, men are still raping women.

Men raped women before they split the atom
before they concocted herbicides in their stainless steel laboratories.
They raped in war and they raped in what they called peace,
they raped in marriage,

they raped in groups, they raped old women, young women,
they raped when they were angry,
    they raped when they were scorned,
they raped when they got drunk, got high, got a weekend pass,
got on the Dean's list, got fired. They still do.

They rape women asleep, children asleep—
        fathers have easy access to children asleep.
They rape babies—
        doctors treat three month old babies for gonorrhea
        of the throat.

They rape women getting into their cars after late night shifts,
they rape old women washing up their breakfast dishes,
they call on the phone and threaten rape, they write songs like
your lips tell me no no, but there's yes yes in your eyes,
they design high heeled sandals so we can't run away,
they invent the pill—easy sex and we die from cancer when they're done.

They use knives and guns when subtler coercion is not enough,
sometimes they use the knives and guns anyway, afterward.

And how shall I protect her?
How shall we protect each other?

I can warn her not to talk to strangers
I can forbid her to go out at night
I can nag her to press her knees together
          and button her blouses to her neck,
but none of that will assure her safety
or even her survival.

I can enroll her in self-defense, judo, karate.
I can practice with her in our yard. We can grow
quick and deft, together.
And that will help, but it is not enough.
Three boys with razor blades, a man with a 45 . . .

We can castrate rapists. My mother suggested that.
She thinks simply, and I like the idea.
But the damage is already done, and the next time
they can use a broken bottle, it's not sex they want.
So what's enough? what's enough?

Only
to gather,
to gather as our foremothers gathered.
Wild plants, berries, nuts—they were gatherers
they gathered together, their food, their sustenance
reeds for weaving baskets, feathers, raven and flamingo
dyes, ochre and vermilion,
they gathered flat stones for pounding
scooped stones for grinding, they gathered rocks, they gathered
shells and the meat of the shells—conch, mussel, clam, they
gathered wood for fire, they gathered clay from the riverbank
they kneaded the clay, they pinched and pressed it with their fingers
they shaped bowls and jars, they baked the vessels

in the coals of the fire, they gathered water, they gathered rain
they gathered honey, they gathered the stories of their mothers
their grandmothers, they gathered under moonlight
they danced, the feel of cool packed dirt under feet
they sang praises, they cried prayers.
When attacked, they knew how to gather their fingers into a fist
they could jab with sharpened sticks, they could hurl rock.
They gathered their strength, they gathered together
they gathered the blessings of the goddess, their faith
in the turning of the earth, the seasons bleeding into each other
                leaves crumbled into earth, earth
                sprouting water-green leaves
they gathered leaves, chickweed, comfrey, plantain, nettles
they worked together, they fought together
they fed, they bathed, they suckled their young,
they gathered stars into constellations
and their reflections into shallow bowls of water,
they gathered an acknowledged, familiar harmony
one I have never known, one I long for
long to gather
with all you women.

V. Women, I want
to gather with you.
Our numbers are grand.
Our hands are capable, practised,
our minds know pattern, know
relationship, how the tree
pulls water up through root
through trunk, through branch, stem
into leaf, how the surface stomata release
water vapor into the air, the air cooled. We know
to honor trees. We know
the chrysalis, the grub, the earthworm.

We have handled baby poop and vomit
the incontinence of the old and sick.
We smell menses every month
from the time we are young girls.
We do not faint.
We do not titter
at mice.
We have handled horses, tractors
scalpels, saws.
We have handled money
and the lack of it
and we have survived

poverty, puerperal fever
forceps, scopolamine
footbinding, excision, infibulation
beatings, thorazine, diet pills
rape, witch burning, valium, chin lifts
female infanticide, child molestation
breast x-rays, suttee.

Some of us have died. Millions, millions
have been killed, murdered. We
mourn, we mourn
their courage, their innocence
their wisdom often lost to us.
We remember.
We are fierce
like a cornered animal.
Our fury spurts like geysers
like volcanoes, brilliant lava, molten gold
cascading in opulent plumes.

And every morning we gather eggs from the chickens
we milk the goat

or drive to the Safeway and push our cart
under fluorescent lights.
We feed our children.

We feed them blood from our womb
milk at our breast.
Our bodies create and nourish life.

We create. Alone
we are able to create.
Parthenogenesis. Two eggs unite. It happens.
It has always happened.
One women, alone, can create life.
Think what all of us could do

if we gather
gather like the ocean gathers for the wave
the cloud gathers for the storm
the uterus gathers for contraction
the pushing out, the birth.

We can gather.
We can save our earth.
We can labor like we labored
to birth our babies,
laboring past thirst, past the rising and the setting of the sun
past distraction, past demands
past the need to pee, to cry, or even to live
into the consuming pain
                                        pain
pain beyond possibility,
until there is nothing but the
inevitable gathering
gathering, gathering
and

the new is born,
relief spreading through us
like the wave after cresting
spreads over sand in a shush of foam, grace
our saving grace.

VI. *NO touch bee*
BITE my finger
my daughter explains to me
pulling back her hand from the wild radish blossoms
                    buzzing with furry bees.

My child
with your neck still creased in slight folds
the tiny white hairs of your back stemming up your spine
fanning out over shoulders like a fern,
you *may* live
you *may,* you *may,* oh I want to believe it is possible
that you may live
to handle bees, pick miner's lettuce
eat black olives in the sun,
            to gather,
                with me
                    with your daughters
                        with all the world's life-sweet women,
                            our stunning harvest.

Margaret Bacon
Nonviolence and Women: The Pioneers

Here is a wonderful story: The Rynder gang, Tammany toughs, were determined to break up the New York Women's Rights Convention of 1853. Other New Yorkers were snickering: the New York Herald *headline read "GRAND RALLY OF THE BLOOMERS." But the Rynder mob wasn't laughing. They had managed to break up the convention the night before and now were back to disrupt the gathering again. They jeered the speakers—Sojourner Truth, Lucy Stone, Ernestine Rose, Susan B. Anthony, Charles Burleigh, William Lloyd Garrison. Lucretia Mott, the self-possessed president of the convention and long-time radical Quaker activist, had tried to reassure those attending: "Any great change must expect opposition, because it shakes the very foundation of privilege." But that second night the violence escalated. The crowd panicked when the Rynder gang shoved the women. More gang members seemed to be waiting outside to beat up the leaders. The female speakers were afraid to leave. Lucretia immediately offered them her own escort and turned to the nearest bully saying, "This man will see me through." She slipped her hand under the man's arm. It was Captain Rynders himself! Stunned by this uncompromising expectation of courtesy, Rynder escorted Lucretia to safety, a gruff, blushing puppet on the string of this brave woman.*

This inspiring story is more fully told in Margaret Bacon's Valiant Friend: The Life of Lucretia Mott *(1980). In the following essay, Margaret shares some of her research on the foremothers who were prominent in making the first connections between feminism and nonviolence—Lucretia Mott, Abby Kelly, Susan B. Anthony, and Alice Paul. Indeed, we learn from this essay that, though our hearts sometimes despair at the task before us, we can take strength from the women who stood bravely before us, paving the way with their own courageous lives.*

In addition to Valiant Friend, *Margaret has authored five other books including* As The Way Opens: The Story of Quaker Women in America. *She is currently the Assistant Secretary for Information and Interpretation of the American Friends Service Committee. Her professional background includes journalism, public relations and social work and has taken her to Africa, Europe, Japan, the People's Republic of China, the U.S.S.R. and Greece. She and her husband Allen are members of the Religious Society of Friends and live in downtown Philadelphia. They have three children and three grandchildren.*

While the connections can be traced deep into human history, neither feminism nor nonviolence were expressed in specific social activism until the nineteenth century. With the organization of the New England Non-Resistance Society in the Fall of 1838 and the publication of a newspaper, *The Non-Resistant*, a movement to spread the ideas and to use the methods of nonviolence in the struggle for justice was begun. Less than ten years later, in July of 1848, the women's rights movement was launched with the "Seneca Falls Declaration of the Rights of Women."

The proximity of the birthdates of these two movements is no accident. Both grew out of the abolitionist struggle against slavery, and both were the product of a new group, the radical reformers, who believed that Christian principles must be translated into action and who saw the struggle for peace and for justice as one and the same. As Lydia Maria Child, a novelist and founding member of the Non-Resistance Society wrote:

"Abolition principles and nonresistance seem to me identical. . . the former is a mere unit of the latter. I never saw any truth more clearly insomuch that it seems strange to me that any comprehensive mind can embrace one and not the other."

Not all abolitionists agreed, however, and not all nonresisters understood and accepted the equal importance of the Woman Question. The one person who gave leadership to and embodied all three issues was Lucretia Mott, a small Quaker minister with a mighty spiritual stature.

When she died in 1880, the *New York Times* called Lucretia Mott "One of the greatest fighters of the world." She fought most of her long life for the slaves; for an end to racial discrimination; for the rights of women, Native Americans, workers; for freedom of thought and religion. To her the impulse to struggle for justice and to use the methods of "moral suasion" in that struggle were identical. When people suggested to her that she drop one cause to concentrate upon another she was perplexed. The Inner Light demanded that she oppose injustice wherever she encountered it and to oppose it always with the weapons of love.

Born Lucretia Coffin on the island of Nantucket, Lucretia came from a long line of strong, self-reliant women who drew upon the Quaker belief in the equality of the sexes and their position as the wives of seafarers responsible for the maintenance of shops and farms while their husbands were at sea for the formation of their characters. Lucretia grew up with a hot temper and a warm heart; early stories of the capture of slaves and their transportation to the Caribbean upset her and converted her to the antislavery position. Later, at boarding school in New York State, she learned that women teachers were paid less than half the salaries that men commanded and determined that she must do something also about the rights of women.

At eighteen Lucretia married a fellow teacher, James Mott, in Philadelphia, and here she spent the rest of her life. Although she was soon busy with a family of six children, she was independent and active, teaching school for some years after she was married, struggling against the growing conservatism in the Religious Society of Friends, and pushing the movement against the use of the products of slavery, an early form of boycott.

In 1833, when Lucretia was forty, William Lloyd Garrison came to Philadelphia to organize the American Antislavery Society which pledged to "use no carnal weapons for deliverance of those in bondage." The Society was made up of men only, as was the social custom of the day, but four days later Lucretia helped to organize the Philadelphia Female Antislavery Society. This group can be regarded today as the first active political organization of women, the launching pad for the women's rights movement and the marriage of nonviolence and feminism.

The women of the Antislavery Society circulated petitions, organized meetings, distributed literature and raised money. As they uncovered their own abilities, they began to question the rule that they could not speak before public meetings in which men were present or participate in all male organizations. Two women from South Carolina, Angelina and Sarah Grimke, having joined the Society, began to attract "mixed" audiences when they spoke against the slavery they had known in childhood. As a result, "The Woman Question" was hotly debated within clerical and antislavery circles.

The controversy came to a climax in May of 1838 when the First Annual Convention of Antislavery Women met in Philadelphia in newly dedicated Pennsylvania Hall. A mob formed around the building, angry that Black and white women were meeting together and angrier yet when it was decided to permit women to address a mixed male and female or "promiscuous" audience. On the night of May 17th the mob, with the tacit permission of the mayor and his police, burned the new structure to the ground. They then prepared to attack the home of the Motts, nearby, until a friend shouting, "On to the Motts," led them in the wrong direction.

Although Lucretia Mott had been raised as a Quaker pacifist

and was an advocate of the boycott, the events of the burning of Pennsylvania Hall began her lifelong practice of personal nonviolence. On the afternoon before the burning of the hall, she had shepherded the women to safety by asking them to walk with linked arms, one Black woman with one white woman, and to ignore provocations. On the night of the fire, she and James and their guests decided to await the arrival of the mob at their house as calmly as possible. The next day the women conducted their meeting in a nearby school room, pledged themselves to increase, not decrease, their practice of holding integrated gatherings and to struggle harder for equal rights for women within the antislavery societies.

When the women's convention met in Philadelphia the following year, Lucretia held a series of animated conferences with the mayor who wanted to provide police protection and who urged her to prevent Black and white women from walking together in the streets. Lucretia insisted that the women needed no such advice and were prepared to protect themselves. Some months later, travelling in Delaware with an elderly abolitionist, Daniel Neall, she offered herself to a tar and feather mob who had captured her companion. "Take me, since I am the chief offender," she insisted. "I ask no favor for my sex." Embarrassed by her persistence, the mob gave Neall only a token brush with the tar.

When the New England Non-Resistance Society was formed in the fall of 1838, Lucretia was unable to be present. Her good Boston friend, Maria Chapman, Lydia Maria Child, Anne Weston, and Abby Kelley of Worcester, Massachusetts, all members of the abolitionist crusade, were there instead. The next year, however, Lucretia played a leading role in the convention, arguing that nonresistance principles should be applied in the classroom and in raising children as well as in public life. This was regarded as too Utopian by some of the most ardent male nonresisters. Few, if any of them, had homes based on equality of responsibility as did the Motts, and consequently probably did not see the implications of nonresistance for the Victorian relationships between husband and wife, father and child.

Lucretia herself practiced both nonviolence and democracy in her home life. All the Motts, everyone, male or female, had his or her chore so that housework did not fall too heavily on any one member. Her marriage to James was a unique one of mutual support. She frequently urged newly-wed couples to follow her example. Her motto, often repeated at weddings, was "In the true marriage relationship, the independence of husband and wife is equal, their dependence mutual, and their obligations reciprocal."

The antislavery movement at this time was split over the issue of nonresistance as well as the Woman Question. Some conservative abolitionists, particularly clergymen, objected to the inclusion of these "divisive" issues in the antislavery crusade. There was a series of schisms climaxing in May of 1840, when Abby Kelley was placed on a business committee and half of the American Antislavery Society walked out to form a New Organization.

At the time of this meeting, Lucretia Mott was on the high seas on her way to London, England to represent the Pennsylvania Antislavery Society at the World Antislavery Convention. She and her followers had succeeded in obtaining equal rights in the Pennsylvania Society eighteen months earlier, and the New England Antislavery Society was also sending women. Having gotten rid of their conservative members through the schism, the old American Antislavery Society proceeded to name her their representative in absentia. When she reached London, therefore, she had dual sponsorship. She was nevertheless denied a seat; the British had not yet faced the Woman Question, and members of the New Organization from the United States were present to spread rumors about her as a heretic.

Lucretia fought vigorously against this exclusion and yet maintained such poise and good temper that she won many admirers. Among these was Anne Knight, a young British woman who later started a women's rights movement in that country, and Elizabeth Cady Stanton, present as the twenty-year-old bride of Henry Stanton, a New Organization delegate to the convention. Elizabeth Cady Stanton had believed in the strength and power of women all her life but she had never before seen her ideals acted out as they were by Lucretia Mott. She pledged herself then and there, she said later in her autobiographical notes, to do something about women's rights. On the last day of the convention the two took a walk and promised each other to hold a convention upon their return to the United States.

The convention was long in coming. Elizabeth Cady Stanton promptly became pregnant, and the next years were devoted to a string of baby boys and interesting social life on the outskirts of Boston. Lucretia meanwhile returned to do battle on a whole series of issues. She lectured vigorously against slavery, making a trip into the South, addressing Congressmen, and meeting with the President to express her feelings; and she became involved in an across-the-seas women to women exchange during the crisis between the United States and Great Britian over the Oregon territory, 54-40-Or Fight. She was also struggling within the Society of Friends for equal rights for women in the business of the church, and for a time she had to defend herself against efforts to have her disowned from the Society because of her radical views.

Finally, however, in July of 1848, while Lucretia was visiting her sister in upstate New York, she and Stanton met at a tea party and decided to have a convention that very next week. Hastily called, the Seneca Falls Convention was a success, winning advocates and critics as well. At the Convention, and for many years thereafter, Lucretia was recognized as the guiding spirit of women's rights, giving counsel and direction to the younger women. As the Woman Question became more and more controversial and angry mobs circled the national conventions, she was often called upon to chair the meetings in order to use her unique presence to keep order. She still had her sharp tongue, but she combined it with a warm spirit and was able to use wit and sarcasm delicately to put hecklers into place without offending them.

In her speeches at the women's conventions Lucretia frequently referred to the links between women's rights, nonresistance and peace. She often said it was actually human rights, not just women's rights, that they must try to achieve: "It has sometimes been said that if women were associated with men in their efforts, there would be not as much immorality as now exists in Congress, for instance, and other places. But we ought, I think, to claim no more for woman than for man; we ought to put woman on a par with man, not invest her with power, or call for her superiority over her brother. If we do, she is just as likely to become a tyrant as man is, as with Catherine the Second. It is always unsafe to invest man with power over his fellow being. 'Call no man master...' is a true doctrine. But be sure that there would be a better rule than now; the elements which belong to woman as such and to man as such, would be beautifully and harmoniously blended. It is to be hoped that there would be less war, injustice, and intolerance in the world than now."

During the turbulent 1850's she continued to practice nonviolence, helping with several slave rescues and making a daring trip into the South to preach against slavery. While many of her abolitionist colleagues were beginning to question nonresistance, and to support John Brown and his followers in their idea of encouraging an armed slave revolt, she remained faithful to the superiority of moral weapons. Following the tragic events at Harpers Ferry she wrote movingly of her belief in the power of nonresistance: "For it is not John Brown the soldier we praise, it is John Brown the moral hero; John Brown the noble confessor and patient martyr we honor, and whom we think it proper to honor in his day when men are carried away by the corrupt and proslavery clamour against him. Our weapons were drawn only from the armory of Truth; they were those of faith and love. They were those of moral indignation, strongly expressed against any wrong. Robert Purvis has said that I was 'The most belligerent Non-Resistant he ever saw.' I accept the character he gives me; and I glory in it. I have no idea because I am a Non-Resister of submitting tamely to injustice inflicted either on me or on the slave. I will oppose it with all the moral power with which I am endowed. I am no advocate of passivity. Quakerism as I understand it does not mean quietism. The early Friends were agitators, disturbers of the peace, and were more obnoxious in their day to charges which are now so freely made than we are."

During the Civil War she remained a pacifist, supporting conscientous objectors and arguing that the struggle should be pursued with moral force alone, while she lamented that the best and the bravest were dying on the battlefields. Following the war she devoted much of her energy to the cause of peace, serving as the spirited President of the Pennsylvania Peace Society for many years. At the same time she tried to make peace between warring branches of the women's rights movement while she continued to support women's admission to the professions and schools of higher education.

Far less well known, but at times more radical than Lucretia, was Abby Kelley who married a fellow radical, Stephen S. Foster. Abby attended the women's rights meetings, but made the abolition of slavery her first priority. In her marriage to Stephen, however, she practiced a complete sharing of household duties and a system where one partner took care of the farm and their only child, Alla, while the other travelled and spoke against slavery. She was not always well liked, but she was often admired as "The Woman of the Age." Both Stephen and Abby were devoted to nonresistance, and both practiced it dramatically. One weekend when they were arrested in Ohio for distributing antislavery literature on the Sabbath, Abby went limp and had to be carried by several sherriff's deputies to jail and later to the courthouse where she absolutely refused to cooperate until the Fosters' case was won by a young antislavery lawyer and two were set free.

Later, after the Civil War, when the drive for suffrage for women began in earnest, Abby and Stephen decided to refuse to pay taxes on their farm in Worcester since it was taxation without representation for Abby. Everyone was impressed that the Fosters, who loved their farm deeply, were willing to continually risk it for principle.

Civil disobedience, such as Abby committed, became a favorite technique in the long post Civil War battle for suffrage led by the Quaker feminist and pacifist, Susan B. Anthony. In 1872 Susan, with a group of sixteen women, voted illegally in an election in Rochester. Susan was convicted in a court of law for this action and fined $100. She refused to pay the fine and was never prosecuted for this refusal. Her courtroom statement was, "May it please Your Honor, I shall never pay a dollar of your unjust penalty...and I shall earnestly and persistently continue to urge all women to the practical recognition of the old revolutionary maxim, that 'Resistance to tyranny is obedience to God.' " Elsewhere other women conducted vigils and demonstrations at polling places. Four years later, in 1876, members of the National Women's Suffrage Association interrupted proceedings during the Centennial Celebration at Independence Hall in Philadelphia to present the startled delegates with a revised version of the Declaration of the Rights of Women.

The majority of the suffragists in the late nineteenth century were concerned with other reforms affecting women; temperance, protection for working women and children and elimination of military training from the schools. Although some Black women were involved in the movement, there was a tendency to move away from the earlier close alliance of Blacks and women and to make the women's movement a middle class white phenomenon. This became more pronounced as the drive for suffrage lingered on into the twentieth century and women began to narrow their focus to suffrage alone.

The growing conservatism of the suffrage movement was challenged at the time of World War I by Alice Paul, a Philadelphia Quaker who had participated in the British suffrage movement under the leadership of the Pankhurst women and came back to the United States to introduce more militant methods into the faltering campaign. She was opposed to the war, and, as the United States entered it, she organized pickets outside the White House, protesting a battle for democracy abroad while there was so little democracy at home. When the police began to arrest the picketers for "disturbing traffic," she taught them to refuse food in jail and to resist force feeding. The resulting news stories brought women flocking to Washington from all over the country and helped in the final passage of the Nineteenth Amendment.

Alice Paul recognized that suffrage was only one of a number of feminist issues, and decided to concentrate her attention next on the passage of an Equal Rights Amendment. She remembered that Lucretia Mott, who had been a lifetime hero of hers, had been the first president of the American Equal Rights Association at a time after the Civil War when it was thought possible to combine the interests of Blacks and women. She decided to name the ERA, as introduced into Congress in 1923, the Lucretia Mott Amendment.

Thus, ninety years after the Philadelphia Female Antislavery Society was formed, the central core of ideas—feminism, nonviolence, and social justice which Mott represented to her contemporaries—were present at the inauguration of a new phase of the struggle. Not all feminists in the nineteenth or the twentieth century have seen the correlations or shared the central vision, but all can attest that their challenge to male supremacy seems to challenge the whole system of society. Mott said it for her colleagues in 1853: "Any great change must expect opposition, because it strikes at the very foundation of privilege." Understood in its broadest sense, nonviolence can be a powerful tool in the feminist struggle for social change and justice.

Rosemarie Freeney-Harding
Ida B. Wells: "Free Speech" and Black Struggle

Ida B. Wells-Barnett (1862-1931) was best known among her contemporaries for her powerful anti-lynching lecturing, organizing and writing. As her commitment to justice for her people pressed her into the world of advocacy journalism she became the first Black woman in the United States to serve at once as editor, publisher and writer for a significant weekly newspaper—THE FREE SPEECH AND HEADLIGHT of Memphis, Tennessee. While all of her activities were informed by her concern for the rights and survival of Black people in the racist America of her time, she consistently demonstrated a deep sensitivity to the needs of the poor and exploited everywhere. Wells probably did not consider herself a pacifist (during at least one very dangerous period she reportedly carried a pistol for self-defense), but she spent a life time involved in what was essentially courageous, persistent, nonviolent struggle against the murderous violence of lynching in post Civil War America.

Born into Mississippi's slavery near the beginning of the war, Wells became a teacher while still in her teens, primarily as a means of supporting younger brothers and sisters who, with her, had been orphaned through the death of their parents in a cholera epidemic. Soon after her teaching career took her to Memphis in the early 1880s, she began contributing articles to various Black periodicals under the pen name of "Iola." Her career as an advocate of Black rights was stimulated by her own experience of bringing suit against the Chesapeake, Ohio and Southwestern Railroad in 1884 after she was violently forced off a train for refusing to move from a first class coach (for which she had a ticket) to the car reserved for smokers and Black people.

Ida was 30 years old and had already established herself as a brave, outspoken, and gifted journalist when Tom Moss, her close friend, was lynched in Memphis in 1892. The following essay is about this event and about Wells' subsequent life-long devotion to the anti-lynching campaign.

Wells was one of the first to point out that it simply was not true that lynching was justified in order to protect white women from Black rapists running rampant in the streets. Few of those lynched were even charged with rape. Indeed, many were children and women. In truth, Wells claimed, lynching was actually used to terrorize and intimidate the entire Black population and block their economic and political development. She also wrote about the more prevalent, even commonplace, rape of helpless Black women and girls which had begun during slavery and was continuing "without reproof from church, state or press."

Wells faced many challenges in her anti-lynching crusade both in England and in America, and she frequently disagreed publicly with less radical Black leaders (such as Booker T. Washington) who urged patience, compromise and public silence in the face of the brutal mob murders. She also exposed the racism of Frances Willard, a leading and esteemed white feminist, and tried unsuccessfully to persuade the Women's Christian Temperance Union to pass an anti-lynching resolution. ". . . that great Christian body which expressed itself in opposition to card playing, athletic sports and promiscuous dancing, protested against saloons, inveighed against tobacco, wholly ignored the seven millions of colored people whose plea was for a word of sympathy and support." Wells more gently challenged her friend Susan B. Anthony who had a single-minded conviction that everything would change once women got the vote. "Knowing women as I do," Wells said, "I don't believe that their exercise of the vote is going to change the political situation."

Wells' lectures inspired the renewed energy of the woman's club movement among Afro-Americans. When the Illinois legislature gave women the vote in local elections, Wells helped form the Alpha Suffrage Club for Black women. This group of activists canvassed house to house, urging women to register, and marched in Chicago demonstrations alongside white suffragists in favor of a federal suffrage amendment. Later, when Wells went to Washington to march in a suffrage demonstration, the officers of the National American Woman Suffrage Association forbade her to participate lest she antagonize southern white women, but Wells defied this racist order and joined the march with the Illinois delegation.

Rosemarie Freeney-Harding, a native of Chicago, has been an active participant in movements for peace, justice and new human community in America for nearly a quarter of a century. Her first visit to Ida B. Wells' native state of Mississippi took place in the early 1960s while Rosemarie was involved in the southern-based Black freedom struggle. Living now in Denver, Colorado, she is a research-practitioner in the arts of holistic health care and a student at the University of Denver's Graduate School of Social Work. With her husband, Vincent, she has raised two children, Rachel Elizabeth Sojourner and Jonathan DuBois.

"Free Speech" is a chapter in Rosemarie's M.A. thesis on Ida B. Wells for Goddard College's Graduate School. She received support for the research and writing through a grant from the Center for the American Woman and Politics at the Eagleton Institute of Rutgers University.

By the end of the 1880s it was clear that writing—especially advocacy journalism—was Ida Well's central vocation and public school teaching was simply her way of earning a respectable living. Her writing continued to focus on problems within the local regional southern community, but her reputation went beyond the city limits of Memphis and even the Mason-Dixon line. But Memphis was home, and in order to find means to express the growing interest she held for Black journalism, Miss Ida joined the local Black newspaper called the *Free Speech and Headlight* in the year 1890. From the outset, Ida's writings for the *Free Speech* were often sharply critical and created controversy. For instance, her criticism of her co-worker, Rev. Nightengale, who actually served as publisher (he was a minister of one of the leading Black Baptist churches and it was his church which housed the press from which the *Free Speech* came), for infidelity and suppression of her articles, finally resulted in his withdrawal from the paper.

Her writings in the local paper also began to reflect the dangerous disdain she held for the local board of education. She regularly criticized its treatment of Black schools, and then, in 1891, she implied in one editorial that there were white male members on the board who hired Black teachers for sexual favors that such teachers gave them, rather than for the ability these teachers possessed for teaching Black children.[1]

That was the beginning of the end. For it was one thing to write about Black ministers in a Black journal, or even to send articles outside the South criticizing brutal lynchings there, but it was another very threatening thing for a Black journalist to publicly criticize leading white men about their relations to Black women in the very community in which all parties resided. Because she was now clearly a threat, obviously the foremost public spokesperson for the Black community of Memphis, Ida B. Wells could no longer be ignored. Official notice of white attention came shortly after the critical editorial, and the outspoken journalist was told that her teaching contract would not be renewed.

The loss of her job was a release—a gift of freedom to give full time to her first love. Teaching was never the challenge that Ida needed, although she was confident that her work proved more than adequate. But even at that time, when her teacher's salary had been most inadequate to meet her responsibilities for her younger brothers and sisters and her need to buy her reading and writing materials, not to mention the paying of rent, Ida knew that if she remained in a white controlled structure, even with a higher salary, she would never be free to write the things that needed to be said.

For Ida Wells, nothing stood higher on the list of topics to be dealt with than lynching—the ruthless public murder of Black people. In the decades before the turn of the twentieth century, lynching, for all practical purposes, was a national pastime of torture, murder and destruction against the Black communities, especially in the South. This was usually done by young white males, although the crowd of lynchers (usually called "mobs" or "rioters" or "the lower element of the whites") might have women and children of all ages present to encourage the murder of the victims, who might also be men, women or children. Although primarily based in the southern portions of the United States, the sympathy and understanding of the lynching mania, indeed the subtle and sometimes not so subtle encouragement of the "justified passions of an outraged people" prevailed throughout the United States and its territories. Blacks were being hung from trees, riddled with bullets, mutilated with knives, burned in village squares and in isolated fields.

Except for a few brave editorials that raged from the Black press in the South and the North, national news coverage of anti-lynching protest was not consistently reaching nor influencing the public. There was no local or national legislation attempting to protect Black people and their property from the mobs. It was a common practice after lynching one or more Black citizens for the group of white lynchers, joined by an ever larger number of persons, to visit other Black sections of the county and burn, loot and murder people, until such passions had waned and until the reality of white supremacy went unquestioned.[2]

In the closing winter days of 1892, all these matters became forcibly personal to Ida. While traveling in the lower Mississippi Valley, Wells received word that lynching had reached the city limits of Memphis when three Black men were taken from jail, tortured and shot in the early morning hours on March 9. This time the victims were all known personally to Ida B. Wells, and one, Tom Moss, a letter carrier, was a close friend. Tom Moss' young daughter was Ida B. Wells' godchild. Moss and the other two men had owned a store, the People's Grocery, in a suburban area just outside the city limits, in a section called the "Curve." Before the three men had set up their clean and efficient establishment, a white grocer had had a monopoly on the trade of the largely Black population surrounding the "Curve."

When the three friends began their store and won customers away, the white merchant's hostile feelings were set in motion. One event led to another, with threats of destroying the People's Store coming from the white grocer. After the three grocers sought legal counsel as to their right to arm themselves against intrusion, they set up groups of Black men to guard their store in the evenings. One evening early in March a group of policemen in plain clothes and in the company of other white men broke into the store under the pretense of looking for a criminal. They found instead a barrage of shots from Black men, and three policemen were seriously wounded.

In the confusion and terror that followed the shooting nearly thirty-five Black men were arrested in the area. Houses in the Black section were searched for weapons, while the Black militia's guns were confiscated by official decree. For three days, the Black prisoners were held in jail and beaten without the right of legal counsel or other visitors. Any contact with relatives or friends was denied the men while they underwent all forms of punishment, leaving some permanently scarred and crippled.[3]

On the Tuesday following the shooting of the officers, the papers announced that the three white men were out of danger and the Black community rested with the knowledge and expectation that no further violence would take place. Instead, that same night, the three Black grocery store owners, Tom Moss, Calvin McDowell and Will Stewart, were taken from their cells in prison by " . . . the mob, in obedience to a plan known to every prominent white man in the city . . ." The three men were put on a "yard engine" in the railway yard that took them a short distance from the city. Here, they were beaten and tortured once again, but not without their resisting. Finally, they were killed.[4]

When the white newspaper reported the lynching the next day, a graphic description described the way in which the men fought. Ida B. Wells' friend, Tom Moss, was reported to have told the sea of white faces surrounding the three of them, "If you will kill us, turn our faces to the West."[5]

When Ida B. Wells received news of the lynching, she did not know the surrounding circumstances. However, she returned to the city and pieced together as much of the story as possible, including the detailed report of the lynching in the white owned paper the day following the murders. After accusing the white journal of having had a reporter on the death scene, she began a series of articles that carried the theme taken from the last words of Tom Moss, "If you will kill us, turn our faces to the West."

And so they turned, first by the hundreds and then by the thousands. Ida B. Wells took up the call with a fierce passion. The angry, distressed Black woman urged Memphis' Black community to migrate to the West, especially to Oklahoma where large numbers of Blacks had gone as early as 1875-1876. Her editorials in the *Free Speech and Headlight* blamed the white power structure for the murders and reminded her Black readers that they had every right to leave ". . . a community whose laws did not protect them."[6]

More than six thousand Black persons left Memphis within a space of two months. Whole blocks were left vacant. At least two church congregations departed en masse for the West, settling in both Kansas and California. Stores and shops were closed as their paying customers either stopped patronizing them or sent word to close their accounts. Black folk slowly began to walk to their jobs rather than ride the city trolleys. Soon there were so few riders that officials from the trolley lines were sent to the *Free Speech* offices to ask that the paper attempt to encourage Black people to ride the trolleys once again.[7]

Ida B. Wells listened as these emissaries claimed that the owners were northerners who had no feelings of hostility to the Black riders, and although service had been not the best for Blacks in the past, all such acts of insult and rudeness would be promptly settled if only the editors would promise to tell the riders to use the public conveyance again. When Ida B. Wells asked the men why they came to the offices of the *Free Speech,* they responded that revenue to keep the trolleys in operation came from her people. She then asked why they thought Black people were no longer riding the trolleys, and they answered that maybe Blacks were afraid of the electricity that moved the car along the tracks. Could it not be that exactly six weeks ago when they stopped riding the cars was the same time that the murder of the three Black grocers took place? When she raised the possibility that there might be a relation to the murders and the trolley boycott the white men went away with no hope that the *Free Speech* might end the boycott. Instead, Ida B. Wells continued to encourage the men and women to walk rather than ride.[8]

Many Blacks were leaving the city and quitting their places of work in order to join the swelling throng of migrants to the West. To combat the serious economic effects of the migration, a local white newspaper ran a series of articles on the horrible, fearful fate that awaited the new arrivals to the "wild" West. In response to these articles and the fears they engendered, Ida B. Wells decided to follow the migration. Using her press card she visited parts of Oklahoma to ascertain for herself the state of the resettlement of the thousands of migrants from Memphis, Tennessee. What she found was that there were many hardships. The ferry across the Mississippi from Memphis to the eastern shore of Arkansas could hardly carry the large number of fleeing Blacks. And the wagon trains on the other side of the river were loaded with families and friends, ready to brave the "wild" West. In this move away from the constant threat of death, the Black citizens of Memphis were reaching toward independence.

On May 21, 1892, Wells wrote another editorial. This time she reported lynchings in other parts of the South as more and more Black persons were being killed by mobs under the accusation of rape, usually without the benefit of facing their accusers, and always without trial by jury. She wrote:

> *Eight negroes lynched in one week. Since last issue of* Free Speech *one was lynched at Little Rock, Ark., where the citizens broke into the penitentiary and got their man; three near Anniston, Ala., and one in New Orleans, all on the same charge, the new alarm of assaulting white women—and three near Clarksville, Ga., for killing a white man. The same program of hanging—then shooting bullets into the lifeless bodies was carried out to the letter. Nobody in this section of the country believes the old threadbare lie that negro men rape white women. If Southern white men are not careful they will overreach themselves, and public sentiment will have reaction. A conclusion will then be reached which will be very damaging to the moral reputation of their women.*[9]

By this time, white business leaders were in conference almost daily about the Black "uprising" in Memphis. The exodus of the many thousand Black workers with the combination of brave and fearless words coming from the *Free Speech* raised additional concerns among the white power structure of the city. The main problem was how to stop the writing of Ida B. Wells in the *Free Speech.* It is not clear if these white leaders knew that she did the actual writing. As far as the white men were concerned, everyone connected with the paper was responsible for the writings. With Wells, there was J. L. Fleming, the business manager of the *Free Speech.* Another partner, Rev. Nightengale, was no longer associated with the paper when Ida B. Wells wrote her May 21 article.

So on the following Wednesday, after Ida B. Wells' article appeared on the streets of Memphis, the *Daily Commercial Appeal* wrote: "Those negroes who are attempting to make lynching of individuals of their race a means of arousing the worst passions of their kind, are playing with a dangerous sentiment. The negroes may as well understand that there is no mercy for the negro rapist and little patience with his defenders. A negro organ (the *Free Speech*) printed in this city a recent issue publishes *(sic)* the following atrocious paragraph:—." That "atrocious" paragraph was Ida B. Wells' statement on the reaction of the public to the reputation of white women. The *Commercial Appeal* editorial concluded with: "The fact that a black scoundrel is allowed to live and utter such loathsome and repulsive calumnies is a volume of evidence as to the wonderful patience of Southern whites. There are some things the Southern white man will not tolerate, and the obscene intimation of the foregoing has brought the writer to the very uttermost limit of public patience. We hope we have said enough.''[10]

The evening journal, *The Evening Scimitar,* another white paper, thought there was more to say to the Black writer. ''Patience under such circumstances is not a virtue. If the negroes themselves do not apply the remedy without delay, it will be the duty of those he has attacked, to tie the wretch who utters these calumnies to a stake at the intersection of Main and Madison streets (and) brand him in the forehead . . .'' The message was clear to the white leaders in the city: obviously, the *Free Speech* had to go.[11]

When all of these events were taking place, Ida B. Wells was in the North. The Friday before her article appeared, she had left the written copy to be printed and distributed in their weekly Tuesday edition and that afternoon or early evening had taken the train to Philadelphia to attend the A.M.E. Church conference. She had plans to travel on to New York, to meet with T. Thomas Fortune of the *New York Age,* and then return home after a few days. By the time she reached New York in the afternoon of May 25, 1892, word of the destruction of the *Free Speech* and the beating and humiliation of Rev. Nightengale had preceded her arrival. J. L. Fleming had already fled the city, after being warned by a white Republican that his life was in danger.[12]

By this time the white leaders of Memphis knew that the writer of the infamous editorial was none other than Ida B. Wells, a Black woman—not a man. The threats that emanated from white Memphis were just as fierce against her as they would have been for anyone else. She was warned never to return South and that if she did, she would be stripped and whipped to death. Even in the face of such danger, Ida considered returning to Memphis. Indeed a message from Black men there, promising to fight to the death to protect her, was both encouragement and deterrence. She knew that both the Black and white forces would keep their promises to her and the superior firepower and political power of the whites would lead to a terrible bloodletting. She decided she should not return to precipitate that further tragedy.

Nevertheless, if the white Memphis leaders thought that the Black crusader would for a moment halt her campaign against lynching, they were wrong. For Ida B. Wells continued to send anti-lynching press releases to the nation and the world from her new headquarters at the *New York Age.* Moreover, T. Thomas

Fortune, the publisher and editor of the *Age,* was instrumental in assisting Wells in setting up speaking engagements and putting her in touch with persons throughout the North who could give financial and moral support to her activities. In exchange for Ida B. Wells' list of subscribers to the *Free Speech,* Fortune offered her a position with his paper and encouraged her to continue writing on the horrors of lynching. Frederick Douglass came to the *New York Age* offices to see for himself this writer of such brave and critical attacks on a South that he was all too familiar with. They shared the growing fear of what the lynching mania was doing to their people.

Meanwhile, the support and encouragement that she got from women in Brooklyn and New York meant a great deal to Ida B. Wells, for it was her first experience of coming together with Black women around political and social issues. While still working with the *Age,* she went to their meetings and gave such a moving account of the current state of Black people in the South that the women determined to organize around the struggle for justice much more fully than ever before. Eventually, these contacts by Wells led to a new source of life for the women's club movement in the Black community.[13]

For instance, the gathering in Brooklyn of these sisters, who gave moral and financial support to Ida B. Wells, was inspiration and strength for her soul. To this young newspaper woman who only a few months ago was writing in Memphis about the need for Blacks to support one another in the migration West and in the boycotting within the area of Memphis, this reception and encouragement was a balm that both soothed and strengthened her for the yet unknown and difficult times ahead. And it was significant that such support came from that group of humans who were ordinarily assumed to be too weak, uninterested or, by "nature," unqualified to persist in demonstrating such solidarity and commitment about public issues.

There was no fireside at this gathering in Brooklyn, no sewing needles and small talk on the exploits of persons far and unrelated to the lives of these women. Instead, before them stood a woman who had defied the very foundations of racism by daring to challenge the myths of white supremacy and standing upon a platform, speaking with tears of the cost of such a challenge.

Actually, what was taking place in the life of Ida B. Wells was that for the first time she was coming into intimate contact with Black women who were in a tradition of social club work and she was also meeting Northern-based Black writers and spokespersons. From this beginning, she went to other parts of the north-east, speaking and describing the events that took place in Memphis and those that were taking place throughout the South within the Black communities.

For the next four decades she continued to carry out this dangerous vocation all over America and across the Atlantic, insisting that the world awaken to the conditions of her people, determined that the spotlight of truth would remain focused on the darkness of white America, hoping always that the light would eventually prevail.

Diana J. M. Davies/Insight

Peggy Terry, a tenant organizer for poor people who moved to Chicago from her native Appalachia, sits in her make-shift home at Resurrection City, Washington, D.C., 1968.

Jacquelyn Dowd Hall
Jessie Daniel Ames: Grass-Roots Anti-Lynching Campaign

Not until 40 years after Ida B. Wells began her campaign did white women take up the anti-lynching cause. For four decades Black women had led the anti-lynching campaigns without the visible or organized support of white women, though they repeatedly appealed to white women to join them. Ida B. Wells and Mary Church Terrell, the first president of the National Association of Colored Women, were both leaders in the anti-lynching movement, and Mary Talbert headed the Anti-Lynching Crusaders under the auspices of the National Association for the Advancement of Colored People.

The woman who spear-headed the white women's involvement in the campaign was suffragist Jessie Daniel Ames. She helped organize a grass-roots movement primarily made up of small-town church women. Eventually the women in the Anti-Lynching Association obtained over 40 thousand signatures to their pledge which stated in part, "(P)ublic opinion has accepted too easily the claim of lynchers and mobsters that they were acting solely in defense of womanhood. In light of facts we dare no longer to permit this claim to pass unchallenged, nor allow those bent upon personal revenge and savagery to commit acts of violence and lawlessness in the name of women."

The white women who began speaking out about lynching encountered threats and hostility from the white community but succeeded in adding their own courageous outrage to that of the Black women. They not only understood lynching to be a crime against the Black population, but eventually made the connection that they, as white women, were being used and manipulated as the possessions of white men. Thus, in this part of white women's history, we see a marvelous synthesis of realizations about the interconnected violence of racism and sexism in the patriarchy.

Jacquelyn Hall teaches history at the University of North Carolina and directs its Southern Oral History Program. She wrote Revolt Against Chivalry: Jessie Daniel Ames and the Women's Campaign Against Lynching *(N.Y.: Columbia University Press, 1979) which received the Lillian Smith and Francis B. Simkins Awards. Jacquelyn is now doing research on Southern working women.*

On May 3, 1930, a Sherman, Texas mob dragged George Hughes from a second floor cell and hanged him from a tree. Hughes was accused of raping his employer's wife. But the story told in the Black community, and whispered in the white, was both chilling and familiar: an altercation over wages between a Black laborer and a white farmer had erupted in mob murder. The complicity of a moderate governor, the burning of the courthouse, reprisals against the Black community—all brought the Sherman lynching unusual notoriety. But Hughes' death typified a long and deeply rooted tradition of extralegal racial violence.

Unlike other incidents in this bloody record, the Sherman lynching called forth a significant white response. In 1892, a Black Memphis woman, Ida B. Wells Barnett, had initiated a one-woman anti-lynching campaign; after 1910, the NAACP carried on the struggle. But the first sign of the impact of this Black-led movement on Southern whites came in 1930 when a Texas suffragist named Jessie Daniel Ames, moved by the Hughes lynching, launched a white women's campaign against lynching. Over the next 14 years, members of the Atlanta-based Association of Southern Women for the Prevention of Lynching sought to curb mob murder by disassociating the image of the Southern lady from its connotations of female vulnerability and retaliatory violence. They declared:

> *"Lynching is an indefensible crime. Women dare no longer allow themselves to be the cloak behind which those bent upon personal revenge and savagery commit acts of violence and lawlessness in the name of women. We repudiate this disgraceful claim for all time."*[1]

Unlike most suffrage leaders, Jessie Daniel Ames brought the skills and consciousness acquired in the women's movement to bear on the struggle for racial justice. The historic link between abolitionism and women's rights had been broken by the late nineteenth century, when an organized women's movement emerged in the former slave states. Ames herself had registered no dissent against co-workers who argued that woman suffrage would help ensure social control by the white middle class. But as the Ku Klux Klan rose to power in the 1920s, she saw her efforts to mobilize enfranchised women behind progressive reforms undercut by racism and by her constituency's refusal to recognize the plight of those doubly oppressed by sex and race. As she shifted from women's rights to the interracial movement, she sought to connect women's opposition to violence with their strivings toward autonomy and social efficacy. In this sense, she led a revolt against chivalry which was part of a long process of both sexual and racial emancipation.

Two interlocking networks of organized women converged in the creation of the Anti-Lynching Association. From evangelical women's missionary societies, Ames drew the movement's language and assumptions. From such secular organizations as the League of Women Voters and the Joint Legislative Council, she acquired the campaign's pragmatic, issue-oriented style. Active, policy-making membership consisted at any one time of no more than 300 women. But the Association's claim to represent the viewpoint of the educated, middle-class white women of the South depended on the 109 women's groups which endorsed the anti-lynching campaign and on the 44,000 individuals who signed anti-lynching pledges.

Ames' commitment to grass-roots organizing, forged in the suffrage movement, found expression in the Association's central strategy: By "working through Baptist and Methodist missionary societies, organizations which go into the smallest communities when no other organizations will be found there," she hoped to reach the "wives and daughters of the men who lynched."[2] Once won to the cause, rural church women could, in their role as moral guardians of the home and the community, act as a restraining force on male violence.

The social analysis of the Anti-Lynching Association began with its perception of the link between racial violence and attitudes toward women. Lynching was encouraged by the conviction that only such extreme sanctions stood between white women and the sexual agression of Black men. This "Southern rape complex," the Association argued, had no basis in fact.[3] On the contrary, white women were being used to obscure the economic greed and sexual transgressions of white men. Rape and rumors of rape served as the folk pornography of the Bible Belt. As stories spread, the victim was described in minute and progressively embellished detail: a public fantasy which implied a group participation in the rape of the woman almost as cathartic as the lynching of the alleged attacker. Indeed, the fear of rape, like the fear of lynching, functioned to keep a subordinate group in a state of anxiety and fear; both were ritual enactments of everyday power relationships.

Beginning with a rejection of this spurious protection, Association leaders developed an increasingly sophisticated analysis of racial violence. At the annual meeting of 1934, the Association adopted a resolution which Jessie Daniel Ames regarded as a landmark in Association thought:

> *"We declare as our deliberate conclusion that the crime of lynching is a logical result in every community that pursues the policy of humiliation and degradation of a part of its*

> *citizenship because of accident of birth; that exploits and intimidates the weaker element . . . for economic gain; that refuses equal educational opportunity to one portion of its children; that segregates arbitrarily a whole race. . . . and finally that denies a voice in the control of government to any fit and proper citizen because of race."*

The women, Ames proudly reported, traced lynching directly to its roots in white supremacy.[4]

Although the Association maintained its single-issue focus on lynching, its participants also confronted the explosive issue of interracial sex. They glimpsed the ways in which guilt over miscegenation, fear of sexual inadequacy, and economic tensions were translated into covert hostility toward white women, sexual exploitation of Black women, and murderous rage against Black men. Their response was to demand a single standard of morality: only when white men ceased to believe that "white women are their property and so are Negro women," would the racial war in the South over access to women come to an end.[5] Only then would lynching cease and social reconstruction begin.

By World War II, the anti-lynching movement had succeeded in focusing the attention of an outraged world on the most spectacular form of racial oppression. The Black migration to the North, the emergence of an indigenous Southern liberalism, the interracial organizing drives of the CIO all contributed to the decline of extralegal violence. This successful struggle against terrorism made possible the emergence of the post-World War II Civil Rights Movement in the South. Only with the diffusion of massive repression, of overwhelming force, could the next phase of the Black freedom movement begin: the direct-action assault on segregation in the Deep South.

On February 21, 1972, Jessie Daniel Ames died in a hospital in Austin, Texas. The civil rights movement had long since bypassed the limits of her generation's vision of interracial cooperation and orderly legal processes. Ames had not become part of the folklore of Southern struggle. But, with the rebirth of feminism from the crucible of the Civil Rights Movement, her career has come to be seen in a more favorable light. On February 12, 1972, as Ames lay dying, Congresswoman Bella Abzug of New York addressed a Southern Women's Political Caucus in Nashville. Exhorting her audience to use the political power of organized women to affect the issues of the day, she could find no closer analogy for such a movement than the Association of Southern Women for the Prevention of Lynching. Jessie Daniel Ames would have wanted no better tribute.

Karla Jay
The Amazon Was a Pacifist

Natalie Clifford Barney, "The Amazon," "The Lily," was one of the first women to live openly as a lesbian. She was an American heiress born on Halloween in 1876 and is most often remembered for the Paris salon she began in 1909 which was frequented by many celebrated writers and artists. She wrote over 20 volumes of essays as well as plays, poems, a novel and some autobiographical works. Probably her most important contribution was her Academie des Femmes (1927), an academy of women, formed in response to the Academie Francaise which did not admit women until very recently.

Barney was also famous as a lover. Her most important relationships were with Renée Vivien and Romaine Brooks. (She lived with Brooks for over 50 years.) In this essay, Karla Jay uncovers a seldom acknowledged period of Barney's life during which she was the central figure of a Paris anti-war group during W.W. I.

Karla became interested in Barney and her circle in the early 1970s when she read the book Sex Variant Women in Literature *by Dr. Jeannette H. Foster. When Karla was hired by Arno Press to read the works of Barney, Vivien and Brooks, she began to see patterns in their writings. She then embarked on a dissertation tentatively entitled, "The Disciples of the Tenth Muse," which she is still writing.*

Karla, a pacifist for many years, co-edited (with Allen Young) Out of the Closets: Voices of Gay Liberation, After You're Out, *and* Lavender Culture *(all in paperback from Jove). She also co-authored* The Gay Report *(Summit Books) with Young.*

Some historians would have us believe that every American and British woman in France during World War I drove a jeep or ambulance to help the war effort. Gertrude Stein, for example, learned to drive a jeep to aid the wounded. Pat Bond, portraying Gertrude Stein in the play *Gerty Gerty Stein Is Back, Back, Back,* relates a tale of how Stein learned to drive the jeep forward but never figured out how to get it into reverse (a story that seems to contradict Stein's self-professed genius, but which seems to support the male notion that women could support the war only in auxiliary positions—Stein would have been hazardous on the front lines).[1] Some rare film footage of Stein shows her still in a jeep cheering up the troops during World War II. Another stirring account of women assisting men in action can be found in Radclyffe Hall's *The Well of Loneliness,* in which various women, including the heroine Stephen Gordon, drive ambulances in and around Paris to assist the war effort and to prove that lesbians can be "patriotic" [sic] and noble.[2]

Some historians of that period have chosen to ignore the fact that another group of American and British women (and some men too) who were also living in Paris during World War I were not driving jeeps or ambulances. In fact, they actively opposed the war, despite the fact that it was such a popular cause in France and despite the fact that, like Stein and her lover Alice B. Toklas, they chose to remain in France for the duration of the war.

This anti-war group centered around American writer Natalie Clifford Barney (1876-1972), who, despite her fierce nickname, "the Amazon," was a dedicated lover of peace. She had moved to Paris at the turn of the century and, in October 1909, had opened a salon at 20 rue Jacob that attracted the best-known literary and artistic figures of her era, including André Gide, Paul Valéry, Paul Claudel, Jean Cocteau, Gabriele d'Annunzio, Anatole France, August Rodin, Rabindranath Tagore, James Joyce, Raine-Maria Rilke, Isadora Duncan, and Max Jacob among others.

Behind Barney's house was a Doric temple dating from the 1800s, which was called the Temple of Friendship. Barney used the temple as a site of plays and festivities, but when the war broke out, she held anti-war meetings on its steps.

These meetings seem to have been inspired by French writer Marie Lénéru, author of *Témoin, le Livre de la France* (1915), whom Barney admired greatly and who wrote, "The day will finally come when our duty will no longer be to accept [war] and be quiet, but to judge and to revolt. . ."[3] The rallies at the Temple of Friendship were attended by several members of Barney's salon, including writers Aurel, Rachilde, and Séverine, and American painter Romaine Brooks, who was Barney's lover for over fifty years. It should be noted that several central members of Barney's salon, such as Elisabeth de Gramont (the Duchess of Clermont-Tonnere) and Lucie Delarue-Mardrus, supported the war effort and drove ambulances. Barney ridiculed them as "ambulance flies" and prided herself on being totally useless to the war effort.[4]

Barney's active opposition to the war was unusual in that she did not consider herself to be—nor was she, in truth—a political person in any traditional sense of the word. She preferred to engage others in battles of wit or in romantic embraces rather than to engage in dreary political combat. She was in some sense a "feminist" and had great visions of the social transformation of women, which would be effected by and for an elite cadre of poets.[5]

Barney was a great lover of life (and other women), and nothing can be more antithetical to a true "bon vivant" than war. "Those who *love* war," Barney once wrote, "lack the love of an appropriate sport—the art of living."[6]

Thus when World War I erupted, she declared herself to be a pacifist. What is especially significant about her pacifism, as well as that of several of her close friends and contemporaries, is that she went beyond condemning and demonstrating against war merely because it was wicked or bloody: She brought her feminist perspective into her analysis of war.

Barney linked men and masculinity directly to the war. She said that men gave birth to war as naturally—and sometimes as choicelessly— as women gave birth to children.[7] Since Barney viewed men as being of a different "race" from the one women belonged to, and since she tended to view the world as divided into diametric oppositions, she saw men as belonging to—and choosing to belong to—a race that engendered, nurtured, and abetted war and other forms of destruction.

In her mind, war was clearly linked to the stupidities of nationalism. Unlike Stein, Toklas, Hemingway, Fitzgerald, and countless other American expatriots in Paris in the early years of the twentieth century who always considered themselves Americans no matter how long they remained abroad, Barney, Brooks, and another group of Americans (including poet Renée Vivien, who died in 1909) abandoned loyalty to their fathers' country, wrote in French for a French audience, and considered themselves either French or beyond the limitations of nationalism. Barney and Brooks, for instance, never considered returning to the United States during either war but neither did they consider it their duty to defend France.[8] "What one calls a country," wrote Barney, "is land insatiable for blood."[9] Even though there were supposedly "good reasons" for war, all wars were fought, according to Barney, for totally selfish ends. "God and the right cause are ever taken into some such compromise."[10]

Barney's sister, Laura Dreyfus-Barney, went even further and made an insightful connection between the behavior of individual men and that of their nations. Long a peace advocate, Dreyfus-Barney told the Los Angeles City Club in 1925 (when she was the French representative of the Peace and Arbitration Department of the International Women's Council) that "we must make the youth of the world realize that the moral code of the individual must be applied to the relations between nations. Theft, attack, rapine, all the crimes for which the laws of a nation penalize the individual, must be handled in an identical manner by a court or arbitration world court, league of nations or what you will.

"Once we have made the youth of the world realize this fundamental premise, we shall have taken the first tremendous step to end war and all its miseries."[11]

Exactly fifty years later, feminists in New York, including Andrea Dworkin, Barbara Deming, Leah Fritz, and myself, would try to make the same kinds of connections for a proposed issue of *Win*, a magazine which advocates "Peace & Freedom Thru Nonviolent Action." We argued that the way individual women are treated—rape, battery, assault, incest—was a paradigm for male aggression in the world at large and that a feminist perspective was essential for the continuation of the peace movement and for the evolution of a peaceful existence on this planet. The ideas we proposed were rejected by *Win* as was the issue we had hoped to publish.

While we probably realized that we were not the first women to think about the connections between masculinity and war, we were largely unaware that women so long ago and so far away had made the very same connections and had also tried to analyze war in a feminist context.

Today, there is a widespread feminist movement in which such ideas are welcomed and nourished, but in Barney's time support was not forthcoming, even from some of Barney's closest friends and associates. Barney, who never really felt that significant political change was possible for women, tried instead to reify poetic realities, to establish a new golden age of Sappho where ideas of beauty and truth would reign untroubled by the political realities and economic necessities of the world of men. But without the right kind of encouragement from other feminists who were also pacifists, Barney and Brooks became increasingly rightist and elitist, and they gradually abandoned their pacifist convictions; indeed, they finally wound up supporting the Fascists in Italy where they spent a portion of World War II. In fact, Barney was said to have encouraged Ezra Pound to make his pro-Fascist broadcasts.

Barney's transformation from a rally-organizing pacifist to a pro-Fascist is difficult to explain completely within the scope of such a short article, but there are several important lessons to be learned from her story. First, it is important in and of itself to know that feminist analyses of war existed before World War I and that the books of Barney, Vivien, Lénéru and others still exist (although some of them are almost impossible to find). Second, when pacifism among women or in any other group receives little support, then it is more likely to disappear. While this fact seems so obvious, there are far too few support networks for feminist pacifists even today. Finally, even though a brilliant woman like Natalie Clifford Barney was lost to the cause of pacifism, her words and actions have not been forgotten, as this article attests. While feminist pacifists may have lost and continue to lose many like Barney over and over, others happily take their places. Eventually we may overcome the resistance of some men (and some women too) to a feminist analysis of war. Eventually, we may win the peace.

Dorothy Marder

Women Strike for Peace brings women from the U.S. and Japan to the White House, 1975.

Susan Kling
Fannie Lou Hamer: Baptism by Fire

When Fannie Lou Hamer began to push the limits of her courage in Mississippi, she had no spotlight, no long-simmering theory, no money and only a little contact with the organized civil rights movement of the 1960s. She was, quite simply, a poor Black sharecropper who was profoundly moved to action by the voter registration drive in the South and the magic word "Freedom!" Her commitment to voter registration for Blacks led her quickly into conflict with the white power structure. The following essay is about her courageous baptism by fire, but this is just the beginning of the story of Fannie Lou Hamer. Once she got started working for freedom and justice she never stopped. She went on to join with others in challenging the constitutionality of the all-white Democratic Party of Mississippi and, after an unbelievable battle, eventually won seats for her integrated delegation at the 1968 Democratic Party Convention in Chicago.

Later in her life she saw the realization of a dream—the opening of The Freedom Farm Co-operative which, she announced in 1970, fed 1,500 people, Blacks and whites, from 40 acres. She helped open a garment factory to provide jobs for the people of her community and then a Day Care Center for the children of low-income and working parents. She spoke out against the war in Viet Nam. She was among 200 women who met in Washington D.C. to mobilize the National Women's Political Caucus and in 1972 was named "The First Lady of Civil Rights" by the League of Black Women. "I work for the liberation of all people," Fannie Lou said in Gerda Lerner's Black Women in White America, *"because when I am liberating myself, I am liberating other people. The freedom of the white woman is shackled in chains to mine, and she realizes for the first time that she is not free until I am free."*

Susan Kling is a long-time civil rights activist, writer and poet who lives in Chicago. She has written "slice of life" stories based on her experiences in Chicago for newspapers in England, Hungary, Poland Czechoslovakia and in 1981 won a prize for submitting one of the best articles to the Russian magazine Soviet Woman. *She has also written stories for confessions magazines and recently finished a full length novel about the Chicago of the 1930s which is going the rounds of publishers.*

Susan worked with Women for Racial and Economic Equality (WREE) toward their first National Convention in Chicago in 1977, and that year, when Fannie Lou Hamer died, Susan was asked to write a eulogy for the WREE-VIEW *(WREE's newspaper). This eventually inspired Susan to write a small book on Fannie Lou Hamer from which this chapter is taken.*

Then came the summer of '62, when the magic word "Freedom!" swept like a wild wind through the South. In late August, James Bevel of the Southern Christian Leadership Conference, came down to Ruleville, and together with James Forman of the Student Non-violent Co-ordinating Committee and other Black and white activists in the boiling civil rights movement, called a mass meeting at a church there.

Fannie Lou attended—and her life suddenly changed. "I had never heard the freedom songs before!" she said in wonder. And of the people she listened to: "They really wanted to change the world I knew—they wanted Blacks to register to vote!" They wanted Blacks to be able to have some small say about their destiny!

Fannie Lou felt that she was called, that this was the chance she had waited for, it seemed, all of her life. She and seventeen others in the church signed up to go to Sunflower County Courthouse in Indianola the next Friday. Without any vote or special arrangement, Fannie Lou became the leader of the group. On the following Friday, August 31, she and the seventeen other Blacks, fearful but determined, boarded a bus owned by a friendly Black man, and rode to Indianola.

Police and other whites began to mill around the bus when it stopped. But the eighteen, with Fannie Lou in front, marched bravely into the courthouse. There they were promptly told to go outside, and come in two at a time.

Fannie Lou was asked twenty-one questions, including one that asked her to copy and interpret a part of the constitution of Mississippi. "I could copy it," she said later, "but I sure couldn't interpret it—because up to that time, I hadn't even known Mississippi *had* a constitution." She failed the registration test, as did all the others. But she made up her mind that she would come back, no matter how many times, until she did pass.

In the late afternoon, after all the others with her had gone through the same frustrating, threatening day, with rifle-carrying whites strolling in and out of the courthouse past them, they boarded the bus and started for home. They had gone only a few miles when they were stopped by a policeman and ordered to return to Indianola. There the driver was fined $100 for driving a bus "with the wrong color."

Fannie Lou's real troubles began with that first effort to register to vote. But it was also the beginning of a new level of struggle against racism, which lasted for the rest of her life.

Here is her story of what happened that day she tried to register, as taken from a hearing before a Select Panel on Mississippi and Civil Rights, held at the National Theater, Washington D.C., on Monday, June 8th, 1964, and reprinted in the Congressional Record of June 16th, 1964:

". . . I will begin from the first beginning, August 31, in 1962. I travelled twenty-six miles to the county courthouse to try to register to become a first class citizen. I was fired the 31st of August in 1962 from a plantation where I had worked as a timekeeper and a sharecropper for eighteen years. My husband had worked there thirty years.

"I was met by my children when I returned from the courthouse, and my girl (her eldest daughter) and my husband's cousin told me that this man my husband worked for was raising a lot of Cain. I went on in the house, and it wasn't long before my husband came and said this plantation owner said I would have to leave if I didn't go down and withdraw.

". . . (The plantation owner) said, 'Fannie Lou, you have been to the courthouse to try to register,' and he said, 'We are not ready for this in Mississippi.' I said, 'I didn't register for you, I tried to register for myself.' He said, 'We are not going to have this in Mississippi, and you will have to withdraw. I am looking for your answer yea or nay.'

"I just looked. He said, 'I will give you until tomorrow morning.'

"So I just left the same night."

She told the Panel her husband was not allowed to leave the plantation until after the harvest time, but in spite of this restriction, he took his wife to the home of a friend in Ruleville. She said in addition, that the plantation owner had warned Pap that if he decided to go with Fannie Lou their furniture would be confiscated, and Pap would lose his job. Thus, because of the need for the family to have housing and some means of her husband earning a livelihood, Fannie Lou was forced to separate from her family.

Her report to the Panel continued, "On the 10th of September, they fired into the home of Mr. and Mrs. Robert Cuker sixteen times, for me. That same night, two girls were shot at Mr. Herman Sissel's; also, they shot into Mr. Joe Maglon's house. I was fired that day, and haven't had a job since . . ."

Her husband was fired anyway and the furniture confiscated

by the plantation owner who took their car as well, saying they owed him $300 on it.

Fannie Lou became a virtual fugitive, staying here and there with friends or distant relatives. At last the family found a bare house into which they moved. But even here, they were not left in peace. Cars full of white men armed with rifles would ride up and back in front of the house, shouting obscenities and threatening to shoot.

If any of the family left the house, for whatever reason, cars followed, with white men leaning out of the windows, shouting, cursing and threatening.

But these reprisals, as well as abusive letters that she kept receiving, only stiffened her resolve and made her even more determined to keep on, in the path on which she had set her feet. And her family, to their everlasting credit, stood solidly with her.

At last, word of what was happening to her reached the ears of the Student Non-violent Co-ordinating Committee (SNCC). Robert Moses, a leader in the Mississippi grass-roots civil rights movement, came down to Ruleville and invited Fannie Lou to attend a SNCC conference at Fisk University in Nashville, Tennessee, in the fall of 1962. That conference instilled in her an even more total commitment, and she went to work for SNCC "even when they didn't have any money." This work provided her with a kind of security, for after that she never felt alone in the ideals she had laid out for herself.

She not only worked for SNCC as a Field Secretary, but was tireless in half a dozen other avenues as well. She circulated a petition to get food and clothing from the government for needy families. She helped in getting welfare programs started, she got clothes from people who didn't need them to people who did, and she cooked for the many volunteer workers who came continually to help. In addition to all of this work, she was employed for a time at a Ruleville cotton gin, until she was fired. She had to leave her house again.

When she returned to the Sunflower County Courthouse on December 4th to take the registration test a second time, she said of that time, "There was nothing they could do to me. They couldn't fire me, because I didn't have a job. They couldn't put me out of my house, because I didn't have one. There was nothing they could take from me any longer." She told them, "You'll see me every thirty days, until I pass." And on January 10th, 1963, she passed—and became one of the first of Sunflower County's 30,000 Blacks to register to vote.

But on June 3, 1963, she paid heavily for that right and for the work she was doing to get other Blacks to register.

"I had gone to a voter education workshop in Charleston, South Carolina," she told the Congressional Panel. "We left Mississippi June 3, 1963. We finished the workshop June 8th. We left on the 8th by Continental Trailways Bus, returning back to Mississippi.

"We arrived in Winona, Mississippi between 10:30 and 11 a.m., June 9th. Four of our group got off the bus to get food in the bus terminal. Two got off to use the washroom. I was still on the bus. I saw the six people rush out, and I got off to see what was happening.

"Miss Ann Ponder told me the chief of police and a state highway patrolman had ordered them out. I said, 'Well this is Mississippi for you.' I went and got back on the bus.

"I looked out of the window and they were putting the Negroes in a car. I was holding Miss Ponder's iron. I got off to ask her what to do with it. My friends shouted, 'Get back on the bus!'

"A white officer said to me, 'You are under arrest. Get in the car.' As I went to get in, he kicked me. In the car, they would ask me questions. When I started to answer, they would curse and tell me to hush, and call me awful names.

"They carried me to the (Montgomery) County jail. Later I heard Miss Ponder's voice and the sound of licks. She was screaming awfully.

"Then three white men came to my room. A state highway policeman (he had the marking on his sleeve) asked me where I was from. I said, 'Ruleville.' He said, 'We're goin' to check that.' They left out. They came back and he said, 'You're damn right!'

"They said they were going to make me wish I was dead. They had me lay down on my face, and they ordered two Negro prisoners to beat me with a blackjack. That was unbearable. It was leather, loaded with something.

"The first prisoner beat me until he was exhausted. Then the second Negro began to beat. I have a limp. I had polio when I was about six years old. I was holding my hands behind me to protect my weak side. I began to work (move) my feet. The state highway patrolman ordered the other Negro to sit on my feet.

"My dress pulled up and I tried to smooth it down. One of the policemen walked over and raised my dress as high as he could. They beat me until my body was hard, 'til I couldn't bend my fingers or get up when they told me to. That's how I got this blood clot in my left eye—the sight's nearly gone, now. And my kidney was injured from the blows they gave me in the back."

She was left in the cell, bleeding and battered, listening to the screams of Ann Ponder, who was being beaten in another cell, and hearing the white men talk of "plotting to kill us, maybe to throw our bodies in the Big Black River, where nobody would ever find us."

At last, word of the beatings and detention at Winona reached the ears of Dr. Martin Luther King, Jr., who sent members of his staff to the jail, with the demand that she and the others be released at once. Andrew Young and James Bevel came to the jail, helped carry her out, half conscious, and took her to a doctor in Greenwood, Mississippi, where the blood was washed off her, and her wounds stitched and bandaged. Then they took her to Atlanta to some friends of the civil rights movement, where she remained for a month, convalescing. During this month, she refused to allow her husband to come to see how terrible she looked, until some of the scars were less livid and the swelling had gone down.

While she had been in the Winona jail, she told friends, "Medger Evers was killed, and they offered to let us go one night, but I knew it was just so they could kill us, and say we was trying to escape. I told 'em they'd have to kill me in my cell."[1]

The effects of the beatings plagued her the rest of her life, until sometimes she would say caustically, "I'm sick and tired of being sick and tired!"

This brutal experience only served to make her more determined than ever to continue to get Blacks to register. As soon as she was able, even limping and almost nauseated with pain, she was out in the cotton fields at sun up, lining up prospective voters, and telling how almighty powerful it would be to be able to vote. Evenings she spent going around to the many little churches in the countryside, talking about voter registration, and singing in that powerful voice that moved all who heard her, the freedom songs she had learned. But her base was always Ruleville, where she had been born and raised.

Neither did the constant hate letters and abusive telephone calls she received deter her from her work, and she refused to move away. "I ain't goin' no place," she insisted. "I have a right to stay here. With all that my parents and grandparents gave to Mississippi, I have a right to stay here and fight for what they didn't get." And after her experience in the Winona jail, she added, "I don't want equal rights no more. I don't want to be equal to men that beat us. I want human rights!"[2]

Cynthia Washington
We Started From Opposite Ends of the Spectrum

"The oppression of women knows no ethnic nor racial boundaries, true, but that does not mean it is identical within those boundaries. Nor do the reservoirs of our ancient power know these boundaries, either. To deal with one without even alluding to the other is to distort our commonality as well as our difference." (from "An Open Letter to Mary Daly" by Audre Lorde)

Cynthia Washington addresses this theme from the vantage point of her experience as a Black woman in the 1960s Civil Rights Movement. Of her white sisters she says, "We definitely started from opposite ends of the spectrum." This letter was written several years ago, and many things have changed since the 1960s, but the complex tangle of sexism and racism is still an issue for feminists and advocates of nonviolence in the 1980s.

Currently Cynthia is the Director of Publications at the Coalition for a New Foreign and Military Policy in Washington D.C. She writes, "My activism these days is limited to cranking out the many educational materials the Coalition produces for organizing around disarmament, human rights, budget priorities and self-determination for southern Africa. Add to this raising a 15-year-old son, taking care of a house, the veggie garden to save money, and some freezing and canning here and there, and the time is all gone. And doing all this alone doesn't get easier as I get older."

Cynthia believes that all women, no matter which end of the spectrum we start from, could agree on some things we would all want to work for and that it is imperative that we spend time developing this common vision. As we give voice to our many experiences of oppression and listen to and learn to trust these varied expressions, we will recognize our common humanity, our common need.

During the fall of 1964, I had a conversation with Casey Hayden about the role of women in SNCC. She complained that all the women got to do was type, that their role was limited to office work no matter where they were. What she said didn't make any particular sense to me because, at the time, I had my own project in Bolivar County, Miss. A number of other Black women also directed their own projects. What Casey and other white women seemed to want was an opportunity to prove they could do something other than office work. I assumed that if they could do something else, they'd probably be doing that.

I remember driving back to Mississippi in my truck, thinking how crazy they were. I couldn't understand what they wanted. As far as I could see, being a project director wasn't much fun. I didn't realize then that having my own project made a lot of difference in how I was perceived and treated. And I did not see what I was doing as exceptional. The community women I worked with on projects were respected and admired for their strength and endurance. They worked hard in the cotton fields or white folks' houses, raised and supported their children, yet still found the time and energy to be involved in struggle for their people. They were typical rather than unusual.

Certain differences result from the way in which Black women grow up. We have been raised to function independently. The notion of retiring to housewifery someday is not even a reasonable fantasy. Therefore whether you want to or not, it is necessary to learn to do all of the things required to survive. It seemed to many of us, on the other hand, that white women were demanding a chance to be independent while we needed help and assistance which was not always forthcoming. We definitely started from opposite ends of the spectrum. . . .

I remember discussions with various women about our treatment as one of the boys and its impact on us as women. We did the same work as men—organizing around voter registration and community issues in rural areas—usually with men. But when we finally got back to some town where we could relax and go out, the men went out with other women. Our skills and abilities were recognized and respected, but that seemed to place us in some category other than female. Some years later, I was told by a male SNCC worker that some of the project women had made him feel superfluous. I wish he had told me that at the time because the differences in the way women were treated certainly did add to the tension between Black and white women.

At a district meeting in Mississippi, I heard Stokely's comment that the only position of women in SNCC was prone—with the exception of women who either dressed or looked like men. I was standing next to Muriel Tillinghast, another project director, and we were not pleased. But our relative autonomy as project directors seemed to deny or override his statement. We were proof that what he said wasn't true—or so we thought. In fact, I'm certain that our single-minded focus on the issues of racial discrimination and the Black struggle for equality blinded us to other issues. . . .

In the late 1960s, some Black women were "producing children for the Black nation," while others began to see themselves as oppressed by Black men. For many, Black women were the most oppressed group in American society, the victims of racism, chauvinism and class discrimination. Chauvinism was often seen as the result of forces acting upon all Black people, and struggle between Black men and women as an effective way to keep us from working together for our common liberation. On the other hand, my son by this time was three years old; I was divorced, and the thought that anyone would want to have a child to support by themselves seemed like a mean joke. If women were becoming pregnant to counter the charge that they took "manhood" away, then the position of Black women, even in movement circles, seemed to have deteriorated. To me, it was not a matter of whether male/female oppression existed but one of priorities. I thought it more important to deal with the folks and the system which oppressed both Black women and Black men. . . .

The white people I talked with often assumed the basic necessities. That gave them the luxury of debating ideology and many things I felt would not change the position of Black women. Abortion, which white women were fighting for, did not seem an important issue for Black women. Women who already had children might need abortion in the future, but in the present they needed a means to support children other than welfare, a system of child care, decent homes and medical attention, opportunities for meaningful employment and continuing education. Again, we found ourselves in different circumstances with no program or tactic to begin building sisterhood.

Over the last two years, I find myself becoming more involved with women in Washington, discussing the impact of race, class, and culture on us all and concrete ways women can help each other survive. I also find that the same Black women I knew and respected during the 1960s are in the process of re-forming a network. Most of us have now spent the greater part of our adult lives as single women involved in movement activities. We have been married, divorced, some have children; we have gone from town to town, job to job, talking to each other. The problems of womanhood have had an increasing impact on us, and the directions of our own, of my own, involvement in the women's movement are still unfolding.

Sara Evans
Women's Consciousness and the Southern Black Movement

This is the story, from a white woman's perspective, of how the experiences of Black and white women in the nonviolent Civil Rights Movement of the early '60s led to the eruption of feminism later in that decade. Citing the repeated history of women involved in both the abolition and civil rights movements, Sara Evans writes, "Working for racial justice, they developed both political skills and a belief in human rights which could justify their own claim to equality." This is a story full of promise and pain. It is about women—both Black and white, Northerners and Southerners—who struggled to work toward the fullest expression of justice in a violently racist and sexist climate. It is a story full of lessons to be learned and questions still needing to be asked.

Sara has been active in the civil rights, anti-war and women's movements in the South for many years. This article originally appeared in Southern Exposure *in 1977. Sara also wrote a book which deals at greater length with these issues,* Personal Politics: The Roots of Women's Liberation in the Civil-Rights Movement and the New Left *(Knopf). Sara is now an associate professor of history at the University of Minnesota where she teaches women's history.*

Twice in the history of the United States the struggle for racial equality has been midwife to a feminist movement. In the abolition movement of the 1830s and 1840s and again in the civil-rights revolt of the 1960s, women experiencing the contradictory expectations and stresses of changing roles began to move from individual discontents to a social movement in their own behalf. Working for racial justice, they developed both political skills and a belief in human rights which could justify their own claim to equality.

Moreover, in each case, the racial and sexual tensions embedded in Southern culture projected a handful of white Southern women into the forefront of those who connected one cause with the other. In the 1830s, Sarah and Angelina Grimke, devout Quakers and daughters of a Charleston slave-owning family, spoke out sharply against the moral evils of slavery and racial prejudice. "The female slaves," they said, "are our countrywomen—*they are our sisters;* and to us as women, they have a right to look for sympathy with their sorrows, and effort and prayer for their rescue. . . . Women ought to feel a peculiar sympathy in the colored men's wrong, for like him, she has been accused of mental inferiority, and denied the privileges of a liberal education."[1]

When the revolt of Southern Blacks began in 1960, it touched a chord of moral idealism and brought a significant group of white Southern women into a movement which would both change their lives and transform a region. Following the first wave of sit-ins in 1960, the Southern Christian Leadership Conference (SCLC), at the insistence of its assistant director, Ella Baker, called a conference at Shaw University in Raleigh, N.C., on Easter weekend. There Black youth founded their own organization, the Student Nonviolent Coordinating Committee (SNCC) to provide a support network for direct action. SNCC set the style and tone of grass-roots organizing in the rural South and led the movement into the Black belt. The spirit of adventure and commitment which animated the organization added new vitality to a deeply rooted struggle for racial equality.

In addition to this crucial role within the Black movement, SNCC also created the social space within which women began to develop a new sense of their own potential. A critical vanguard of young women accumulated the tools for movement building: a language to describe oppression and justify revolt, experience in the strategy and tactics of organizing, and a beginning sense of themselves collectively as objects of discrimination.

Nevertheless, it was precisely the clash between the heightened sense of self-worth which the movement offered to its participants and the replication of traditional sex roles within it that gave birth to a new feminism. Treated as housewives, sex objects, nurturers, and political auxiliaries, and finally threatened with banishment from the movement, young white Southern women responded with the first articulation of the modern challenge to the sexual status quo.

The Decision

The first critical experience for most white women was simply the choice to become involved. In contrast to portions of the Northern student movement, Southern women did not join the civil rights struggle thoughtlessly or simply as an extension of a boyfriend's involvement. Such a decision often required a break with home and childhood friends that might never heal. It meant painful isolation and a confrontation with the possibility of violence and death. Such risks were not taken lightly. They constituted forceful acts of self-assertion.

Participation in civil rights meant beginning to see the South through the eyes of the poorest Blacks, and frequently it shattered supportive ties with family and friends. Such new perceptions awakened white participants to the stark brutality of racism and the depth of their own racial attitudes. One young woman had just arrived in Albany, Georgia, when she was arrested along with the other whites in the local SNCC voter registration project. By the time she left jail after nine days of fasting, the movement was central to her life. Her father suffered a nervous breakdown. But while she was willing to compromise on where she would work, she staunchly refused to consider leaving the movement. That, it seemed to her, "would be like living death."

For other women, such tensions were compounded by the fact that parents and friends lived in the same community. Judith Brown joined the staff of CORE and was sent to work in her home town. She wrote later of the anxieties she felt: "For that year I had to make a choice between the white community in which I had grown up and the black community, about which I knew very little."[2]

Anguished parents used every weapon they could muster to stop their children. "We'll cut off your money," "You don't love us," they threatened. The women who refused to acquiesce often responded with loving determination. On June 27, 1964, a young volunteer headed for Mississippi wrote:

Dear Mom and Dad:

This letter is hard to write because I would like so much to communicate how I feel and I don't know if I can. It is very hard to answer to your attitude that if I loved you I wouldn't do this . . . I can only hope you have the sensitivity to understand that I can both love you very much and desire to go to Mississippi. . . . There comes a time when you have to do things which your parents do not agree with.[3]

Even activist parents, who themselves had taken serious risks for causes they believed in, were troubled. Whether they kept their fears to themselves or openly opposed their children's participation, the messages from parents, both overt and subliminal, were mixed: "We believe in what you're doing—but don't do it." Their concern could only heighten their daughters' ambivalences.

The pain of such a choice, however, was eased by the sense of purpose with which the movement was imbued. The founding statement of SNCC rang with Biblical cadences:

> "*. . . the philosophical or religious ideal of nonviolence (is) the foundation of our purpose, the presupposition of our faith, and the manner of our action. Nonviolence as it grows from Judaic-Christian tradition seeks a social order of justice permeated by love. . . .*
>
> "*Through nonviolence, courage displaces fear; love transforms hate. Acceptance dissipates prejudice; hope ends despair. Peace dominates war; faith reconciles doubt. Mutual regard cancels enmity. Justice for all overcomes injustice. The redemptive community supersedes systems of gross immorality.*"[4]

The goals of the movement—described as the "redemptive community," or more often, the "beloved community"—constituted both a vision of the future obtained through nonviolent action and a conception of the nature of the movement itself.

Within SNCC the intensely personal nature of social action and the commitment to equality resulted in a kind of anarchic democracy and a general questioning of all the socially accepted rules. When SNCC moved into voter registration projects in the Deep South, this commitment led to a deep respect for the very poorest Blacks. "Let the people decide" was about as close to an ideology as SNCC ever came. Though civil-rights workers were frustrated by the depth of fear and passivity beaten into generations of rural Black people, the movement was also nourished by the beauty and courage of people who dared to face the loss of their livelihoods and possibly their lives.

New Realities

The movement's vision translated into daily realities of hard work and responsibility which admitted few sexual limitations. Young white women's sense of purpose was reinforced by the knowledge that the work they did and the responsibilities they assumed were central to the movement. In the beginning, Black and white alike agreed that whites should work primarily in the white community. They had an appropriate role in urban direct-action movements where the goal was integration, but their principal job was generating support for civil rights within the white population. The handful of white women involved in the early '60s either worked in the SNCC office—gathering news, writing pamphlets, facilitating communications—or organized campus support through such agencies as the YWCA.[5]

In direct-action demonstrations, many women discovered untapped reservoirs of courage. Cathy Cade attended Spelman College as an exchange student in the spring of 1962. She had been there only two days when she joined Howard Zinn in a sit-in in the Black section of the Georgia Legislature. Never before had she so much as joined a picket line. Years later she testified: "To this day I am amazed. I just did it." Though she understood the risks involved, she does not remember being afraid. Rather she was exhilarated, for with one stroke she undid much of the fear of Blacks that she had developed as a high school student in Tennessee.[6]

Others, like Mimi Feingold, jumped eagerly at the chance to join the freedom rides but then found the experience more harrowing than they had expected. Her group had a bomb scare in Montgomery and knew that the last freedom bus in Alabama had been blown up. They never left the bus from Atlanta to Jackson, Mississippi. The arrest in Jackson was anti-climactic. Then there was a month in jail where she could hear women screaming as they were subjected to humiliating vaginal "searches."[7]

When SNCC moved into voter registration projects in the Deep South, the experiences of white women acquired a new dimension. The years of enduring the brutality of intransigent racism finally convinced SNCC to invite several hundred white students into Mississippi for the 1964 "freedom summer." For the first time, large numbers of white women would be allowed into "the field," to work in the rural South.

They had previously been excluded because white women in rural communities were highly visible; their presence, violating both racial and sexual taboos, often provoked repression. According to Mary King, "the start of violence in a community was often tied to the point at which white women appeared to be in the Civil Rights Movement."[8] However, the presence of whites also brought the attention of the national media, and, in the face of the apparent impotence of the federal law enforcement apparatus, the media became the chief weapon of the movement against violence and brutality. Thus, with considerable ambivalence, SNCC began to include whites—both men and women—in certain voter registration projects.

The freedom summer brought hundreds of Northern white women into the Southern movement. They taught in freedom schools, ran libraries, canvassed for voter registration, and endured constant harassment from the local whites. Many reached well beyond their previously assumed limits.

Some women virtually ran the projects they were in. And they learned to live with an intensity of fear that they had never known before. By October, 1964, there had been 15 murders, 4 woundings, 37 churches bombed or burned, and over 1,000 arrests in Mississippi. Every project set up elaborate security precautions—regular communication by two-way radio, rules against going out at night or walking downtown in interracial groups. One woman summed up the experience of hundreds when she explained, "I learned a lot of respect for myself for having gone through all that."[9]

New Role Models

As white women tested themselves in the movement, they were constantly inspired by the examples of Black women who shattered cultural images of appropriate "female" behavior. "For the first time," according to one white Southerner, "I had role models I could respect."[10]

Within the movement many of the legendary figures were Black women around whom circulated stories of exemplary courage and audacity. Rarely did women expect or receive any special protection in demonstrations or jails. Frequently, direct-action teams were equally divided between women and men, on the theory that the presence of women in sit-in demonstrations might lessen the violent reaction. In 1960, slender Diane Nash had been transformed overnight from a Fisk University beauty queen to a principal leader of the direct-action movement in Nashville, Tennessee. Within SNCC she argued strenuously for direct action—sit-ins and demonstrations—over voter registration and community organization. By 1962, when she was twenty-two years old and four months pregnant, she confronted a Mississippi judge with her refusal to cooperate with the court system by appealing her two-year sentence or posting bond:

> *"We in the nonviolent movement have been talking about jail without bail for about two years or more. The time has come for us to mean what we say and stop posting bond. . . . This will be a Black baby born in Mississippi, and thus wherever he is born he will be born in prison. I believe that if I go to jail now it may help hasten that day when my child and all children will be free—not only on the day of their birth but for all their lives."*[11]

Several years later, Annie Pearl Avery awed six hundred demonstrators in Montgomery, Alabama, as a white policeman who had beaten several protesters approached her with his club raised. She reached up, grabbed his club and said, "Now what you going to do, motherfucker?''[12] Stunned, the policeman stood transfixed while Avery slipped back into the crowd.

Perhaps even more important than the daring of younger activists was the towering strength of older Black women. There is no doubt that women were key to organizing the Black community. In 1962, SNCC staff member Charles Sherrod wrote the office that in every southwest Georgia county ''there is always a 'mama.' She is usually a militant woman in the community, outspoken, understanding, and willing to catch hell, having already caught her share.''

Stories of such women abound. For providing housing, food, and active support to SNCC workers, their homes were fired upon and bombed. Fannie Lou Hamer, the Sunflower County sharecropper who forfeited her livelihood to emerge as one of the most courageous and eloquent leaders of the Mississippi Freedom Democratic Party, was only the most famous. ''Mama Dolly'' in Lee County, Georgia, was a seventy-year-old, grey-haired lady ''who can pick more cotton, slop more pigs, plow more ground, chop more wood, and do a hundred more things better than the best farmer in the area.'' For many white volunteers, they were also ''mamas'' in the sense of being mother-figures, new models of the meaning of womanhood.[13]

The Undertow of Oppression

Yet new models bumped up against old ones: self-assertion generated anxiety; new expectations existed alongside traditional ones; ideas about freedom and equality bent under assumptions about women as mere houseworkers and sexual objects. These contradictory forces finally generated a feminist response from those who could not deny the reality of their new-found strength.

Black and white women took on important administrative roles in the Atlanta SNCC office, but they also performed virtually all typing and clerical work. Very few women assumed the public roles of national leadership. In 1964, Black women held a half-serious, half-joking sit-in to protest these conditions. By 1965, the situation had changed enough that a quarrel over who would take notes at staff meetings was settled by buying a tape recorder.[14]

In the field, there was a tendency to assume that housework around the freedom house would be performed by women. As early as 1963, Joni Rabinowitz, a white volunteer in the southwest Georgia Project, submitted a stinging series of reports on the ''woman's role.''

> *"Monday, 15 April: . . . The attitude around here toward keeping the house neat (as well as the general attitude toward the inferiority and 'proper place' of women) is disgusting and also terribly depressing. I never saw a cooperative enterprize (sic) that was less cooperative."*[15]

There were also ambiguities in the position of women who had been in the movement for many years and were perceived by others as important leaders. While women increasingly became a central force in SNCC between 1960 and 1965, white women were always in a somewhat anomalous position.[16] New recruits saw Casey Hayden and Mary King as very powerful.[17] Hayden had been an activist since the late '50s. Mary King, daughter of a Southern Methodist minister, had visited SNCC on a trip sponsored by the Y at Ohio Wesleyan University in 1962 and soon returned to work full-time. They and others who had joined the young movement when it included only a handful of whites knew the inner circles of SNCC through years of shared work and risk. They had an easy familiarity with the top leadership which bespoke considerable influence. Yet Hayden and King could virtually run a freedom registration program and at the same time remain outside the basic political decision-making process.[18]

Mary King described herself and Hayden as being in "positions of relative powerlessness." They were powerful because they worked very hard. According to King, "If you were a hard worker and you were good, at least before 1965 . . . you could definitely have an influence on policy."[19]

The key phrase is "at least before 1965," for by 1965 the positions of white women in SNCC, especially Southern women whose goals had been shaped by the vision of the "beloved community," was in steep decline. Ultimately, a growing spirit of Black nationalism, fed by the tensions of large numbers of whites, especially women, entering the movement, forced these women out of SNCC and precipitated the articulation of a new feminism.

Racial/Sexual Tensions

White women's presence inevitably heightened the sexual tension which runs as a constant current through racist culture. Southern women understood that in the struggle against racial discrimination they were at war with their culture. They reacted to the label "Southern lady" as though it were an obscene epithet, for they had emerged from a society that used the symbol of "Southern white womanhood" to justify an insidious pattern of racial discrimination and brutal repression. They had, of necessity, to forge a new sense of self, a new definition of femininity apart from the one they had inherited. Gradually they came to understand the struggle against racism as "a key to pulling down all the . . . fascist notions and mythologies and institutions in the South," including "notions about white women and repression."[20]

Thus, for Southern women this tension was a key to their incipient feminism, but it also became a disruptive force within the civil-rights movement itself. The entrance of white women in large numbers into the movement could hardly have been anything but explosive. Interracial sex was the most potent social taboo in the South. And the struggle against racism brought together young, naive, sometimes insensitive, rebellious, and idealistic white women with young, angry Black men, some of whom had hardly been allowed to speak to white women before. They sat-in together. If they really believed in equality, why shouldn't they sleep together?

In many such relationships there was much warmth and caring. Several marriages resulted. On the other hand, there remained a dehumanizing quality in many relationships. According to one woman, it "had a lot to do with the fact that people thought they might die." Sexual relationships did not become a serious problem, however, until interracial sex became a widespread phenomenon in local communities in the summer of 1964. Accounts of what happened vary according to the perspectives of the observer.

Some paint a picture of hordes of "loose" white women coming to the South and spreading corruption wherever they went. One male Black leader recounted that "where I was project director we put white women out of the project within the first three weeks because they tried to screw themselves across the city." He agreed that Black neighborhood youth tended to be sexually aggressive. "I mean you are trained to be aggressive in this country, but you are also not expected to get a positive response."[21]

Others saw the initiative coming almost entirely from males. According to historian Staughton Lynd, director of the Freedom Schools, "Every Black SNCC worker with perhaps a few exceptions counted it a notch on his gun to have slept with a white woman—as many as possible. And I think that was just very traumatic for the women who encountered that, who hadn't thought that was what going South was about." A white woman who worked in Virginia for several years explained, "It's much harder to say 'No' to the advances of a Black guy because of the strong possibility of that being taken as racist."[22]

Clearly the boundary between sexual freedom and sexual exploitation was a thin one. Many women consciously avoided all romantic involvements in intuitive recognition of that fact. Yet the presence of hundreds of young whites from middle- and upper-middle-income families in a movement primarily of poor, rural Blacks exacerbated latent racial and sexual tensions beyond the breaking point. The first angry response came not from the surrounding white community (which continually assumed sexual excesses far beyond the reality) but from young Black women in the movement.

A Black woman pointed out that white women would "do all the shit work and do it in a feminine kind of way while [Black women] . . . were out in the streets battling with the cops. So it did something to what [our] femininity was about. We became amazons, less than and more than women at the same time."

Soon after the 1964 summer project, Black women in SNCC sharply confronted male leadership. They charged that they could not develop relationships with the Black men because the men did not have to be responsible to them as long as they could turn to involvement with white women.

Black women's anger and demands constituted one part of an intricate maze of tensions and struggles that were in the process of transforming the civil-rights movement. Within the rising spirit of Black nationalism, the anger of Black women toward white women was only one element.

It is in this context that Ruby Doris Smith Robinson, one of the most powerful Black women in SNCC, is said to have written a paper on the position of women in SNCC. Ruby Doris Smith Robinson was a strong woman. As a teenager she had joined the early Atlanta demonstrations during her sophomore year at Spelman College. That year, as a participant in the Rock Hill, South Carolina, sit-in she helped initiate the "jail—no bail" policy in SNCC. A month in the Rock Hill jail bound her to the movement with a zeal born of common suffering, deepened commitment, and shared vision. Soon she was a battle-scarred veteran, respected by everyone and feared by many; she ran the SNCC office with unassailable authority.

As an early leader of the Black nationalist faction, Robinson hated white women for years because white women represented a cultural ideal of beauty and "femininity" which by inference defined Black women as ugly and unwomanly. But she was also aware that women had from time to time to assert their rights as women. In 1964, she participated in and perhaps led the sit-in in the SNCC office protesting the relegation of women to typing and clerical work. Thus, when an anonymous paper entitled "The Position of Women in SNCC" circulated at the tension-filled Waveland Conference in the fall of 1964, most of the speculation about its authorship centered on Robinson. She died of cancer in 1968, and we may never know her own assessment of her feelings and intentions in 1964.[23] It appears that she did not go to any great lengths to refute the rumors. We do know, however, that tales of her memo generated feminist echoes in the minds of many. And Stokely Carmichael's response that "the only position for women in SNCC is prone" stirred up even more discontent. The persisting myth among white feminists that Robinson wrote and presented this first overt attack on sexism in the movement remains a testimony to the powerful image of Black women and of Robinson in particular. It has become a staple in accounts of the revival of feminism. In fact, however, the anonymous author was a Southern white woman, Casey Hayden.

For Southern white women who had devoted several years of their lives to the vision of a beloved community, the rejection of nonviolence and movement toward a more ideological, centralized, and Black nationalist movement was bitterly disillusioning. Mary King recalled, "It was very sad to see something that was so creative and so dynamic and so strong [disintegrating]. . . . I was terribly disappointed for a long time. . . . I was most affected by the way that Black women turned against me. That hurt more than the guys. But it had been there, you know. You could see it coming."[24]

Rebirth of Feminism

In the fall of 1965, Mary King and Casey Hayden spent several days of long discussions in the mountains of Virginia. Both of them were on their way out of the movement, though they were not fully conscious of that fact. Finally they decided to write a "kind of memo" addressed to " a number of other women in the peace and freedom movements."[25] In it they argued that women, like Blacks, "seem to be caught in a common-law caste system that operates, sometimes subtly, forcing them to work around or outside hierarchical structures of power which may exclude them. Women seem to be placed in the same position of assumed subordination in personal situations too. It is a caste system which, at its worst, uses and exploits women."

Hayden and King set the precedent of contrasting the movement's egalitarian ideas with the replication of sex roles within it.

They noted the ways in which women's position in society determined women's roles in the movement—like cleaning houses, doing secretarial work, and refraining from active or public leadership. At the same time, they observed, "having learned from the movement to think radically about the personal worth and abilities of people whose role in society had gone unchallenged before, a lot of women in the movement have begun trying to apply those lessons to their own relations with men. Each of us probably has her own story of the various results."

They spoke of the pain of trying to put aside "deeply learned fears, needs, and self-perceptions . . . and . . . to replace them with concepts of people and freedom learned from the movement and organizing." In this process many people in the movement had questioned basic institutions, such as marriage and child-rearing. Indeed, such issues had been discussed over and over again, but seriously only among women. The usual male response was laughter, and women were left feeling silly. Hayden and King lamented the "lack of community for discussion: Nobody is writing, or organizing, or talking publicly about women, in any way that reflects the problems that various women in the movement came across." Yet despite their feelings of invisibility, their words also demonstrated the ability to take the considerable risks involved in sharp criticisms. Through the movement they had developed too much self-confidence and self-respect to accept passively subordinate roles.

The memo was addressed principally to Black women—long time friends and comrades-in-nonviolent-arms—in the hope that, "perhaps we can start to talk with each other more openly than in the past and create a community of support for each other so we can deal with ourselves and others with integrity and can therefore keep working." In some ways, it was a parting attempt to halt the metamorphosis in the civil-rights movement from nonviolence to nationalism, from beloved community to Black power. It expressed Hayden and King's pain and isolation as white women in the movement. The Black women who received it were on a different historic trajectory. They would fight some of the same battles as women, but in a different context and in their own way.

This "kind of memo" represented a flowering of women's consciousness that articulated contradictions felt most acutely by middle-class white women. While Black women had been gaining strength and power within the movement, white women's position—at the nexus of sexual and racial conflicts—had become increasingly precarious. Their feminist response, then, was precipitated by loss in the immediate situation, but it was a sense of loss against the even deeper background of new strength and self-worth which the movement had allowed them to develop. Like their foremothers in the nineteenth century, they confronted this dilemma with the tools which the movement had given them: a language to name and describe oppression; a deep belief in freedom, equality and community soon to be translated into "sisterhood"; a willingness to question and challenge any social institution which failed to meet human needs; and the ability to organize.

It is not surprising that the issues were defined and confronted first by Southern women whose consciousness developed in a context which inextricably and paradoxically linked the fate of women and Black people. These spiritual daughters of Sarah and Angelina Grimke kept their expectations low in November, 1965. "Objectively," Hayden and King wrote, "the chances seem nil that we could start a movement based on anything as distant to general American thought as a sex-caste system." But change was in the air and youth was on the march.

In the North there were hundreds of women who had shared in the Southern experience for a week, a month, a year, and thousands more who participated vicariously or worked to extend the struggle for freedom and equality into Northern communities. These women were ready to hear what their Southern sisters had to say. The debate within Students for a Democratic Society (SDS) which started in response to Hayden and King's ideas led, two years later, to the founding of the women's liberation movement.

Thus, the fullest expression of conscious feminism within the civil-rights movement ricocheted off the fury of Black power and landed with explosive force in the Northern, white new left. One month after Hayden and King mailed out their memo, women who had read it staged an angry walkout of a national SDS conference in Champaign-Urbana, Illinois. The only man to defend their action was a Black man from SNCC.

Barbara Reynolds
Sailing Into Test Waters

In 1958 the Phoenix, carrying Barbara Reynolds and her husband, children and three crewmembers from Hiroshima, sailed into nuclear test waters in the Pacific Ocean and became peace movement history. Later, while living in Japan, the Reynold's marriage broke up and their divorce brought headlines and judgments. One Japanese newspaper concluded, "While she was traveling the world to make peace, the toast was burning in the kitchen."

This is Barbara's story. It is a story which documents her struggle for self realization within the confines of patriarchal expectations. It is a story of a woman who, in the course of her life, took for granted the roles of good daughter, helpful wife, loving mother but who felt compelled to push the boundaries of those roles to encompass a commitment to her own "peace pilgrimages" as an outgrowth of her faith. Finally, because Barbara had no access to a supportive system such as a feminist network might offer today, it is a story of self blame and loneliness. Indeed, she seems to concur with the observation made in the Japanese newspaper, concluding her story with, "Someone has to 'stay in the kitchen.' "

That Barbara rejects what she knows of feminist analysis makes her article an exception in this anthology by feminists, but her story does not represent an exception in women's experience. Indeed, it exemplifies the feminist accusation of sexism in the peace movement and the pain wrought by that oppression, and it effectively illuminates the struggles, choices and conclusions made by many women of Barbara's generation. It is movement history, a story younger feminists need to hear, a story which belongs in our "remembering rooms."

In a letter to me, Barbara wrote:

"Your request was a challenge and my struggles to respond honestly have been a blessing. I have had to come to grips with who I am: a woman who was born during World War I, whose father and mother loved each other and believed that marriage was for keeps, and who brought up their only child in the assurance that it is an exciting privilege to be a woman—but one that carries responsibilities: responsibilities for nurturance and servanthood and sacrifice, whether in a marriage relationship or in a life of singleness. That these responsibilities are for both sexes I have never questioned. Certainly it was so in my home.

"I am a product of that childhood. I am also a product of my marriage experience, of my divorce, and since 1964, of my commitment to Jesus Christ. And, because I am a woman who has longed for

approval and hated confrontation—and because "feminist" stereotypes stand for something other than what I have come to believe and "activist" stereotypes me—I was afraid to write of these things for fear of alienating many whom I love and admire as caring people, concerned about our world.

"But 'peace' is not brought about by keeping silent about deeply held beliefs. And perhaps the thoughts of one who has lived for 66 years and learned much, both from the living and from the looking back, will add something to the necessary dialogue. For I am *a woman and I am concerned about the direction in which we are headed, about the violence and injustice and unlove in the world. And I do believe that the answer to our problems will not be found if those who care withdraw from the pain. In tender and honest struggle there is growth, and only in victory shared lies wholeness."*

After some tender and honest dialogue about the ideas expressed in this essay, Barbara requested the addition of this statement: "I cannot concur with Pam McAllister's analysis that 'because Barbara had no access to a supportive system such as a feminist network might offer today, it is a story of self-blame and loneliness.' I suspect that any support group might have encouraged me in my own frantic activities without helping us all to see the interrelatedness of what we were trying to do. This might have hastened the dissolution of our family while doing nothing to increase our effectiveness. The overall plan, after all, was God's."

I believe in the nuclear family, one father and one mother and one lifetime commitment. I believe in the extended family—extended by close and responsible relationships with any grandparents, uncles, aunts and cousins that are available, and by the inclusion, in an ever-growing circle, of others whom God sends who are in need of loving support. Although I was an only child, my family was agglutinative in this way. A grandfather was "adopted" because I had none. Close friends of my parents became "aunts" and "uncles" to me. My grandmothers were an integral part of my growing up and my mother cared for each of them in their final years. I feel stronger and more able to give love because of this caring start.

My mother knew about sacrifice. She had been a kindergarten teacher and a teacher of kindergarten teachers, but she gave it up willingly to take care of me. She did not, however, give up being a person. Convinced of the importance of good playthings in the development of a child, she established a testing bureau in our home, published articles and pamphlets, and awarded a "best Toys" seal of approval which became widely recognized and much sought after by manufacturers of playthings. In all of her writings, she advocated dolls and homemaking toys for boys as well as girls and encouraged parents to buy sturdy, functional wagons, trucks, tools and the like for both sons and daughters. It would never have occurred to me to ask anyone to open a jar, pound a nail, or change a fuse—until I discovered in my teens that helplessness was one way of getting attention from boys and, later, my husband.

My father, who was drowned in a boating accident when I was fifteen, was a sensitive human being, not afraid to be tender or to weep during a showing of *All Quiet on the Western Front*, a circumstance that caused me acute embarrassment at the age of 14 but for which I am now profoundly grateful. To me, he was the measure of a man.

I married early, before the loss of my father had been fully accepted and resolved. For many years, I was happy to let my husband fill the father role of arbitrary decision making, a role which allowed me periodically to submit, rebel, or in devious ways, to circumvent. I doubt now if my husband enjoyed the role. I am sure he wanted a partner and helpmate rather than a child bride. But marriage relationships were not examined in those days. No one had ever heard of marriage enrichment groups, and I was given no assertiveness training. For us, it was either confrontation—which I sought to avoid at all costs because my husband could roar louder and inevitably walked out if I cried—or suppressed resentment which sooner or later built to an explosion.

My prolonged adolescence did not end until 1954, although my participation in decision-making had begun with a really tough one two years earlier.

At that time, we were living in Japan where my husband was studying the effects of radiation on the growth of children in Hiroshima. Having found an excellent shipbuilder, he was about to fulfill a lifelong dream of building a yacht on which to sail around the world. The decision I had to make involved both our family savings and our lives, not only in the sense of physical risk but in our ongoing relationship. Was I willing to let my husband design a 35-footer in which he would sail away alone while I stayed at home with our three children? Or would I insist that we put all of our resources into a yacht large enough to accommodate our entire family plus a couple of additional yachtsman to supplement our inexperience? Even with the memory of my father's death by drowning (or, perhaps, because of it) I chose to throw in our lot with my husband. At least our memories, for good or bad, would be shared.

On May 5, 1954, "Phoenix" ("Bird of Peace," according to Oriental mythology) was duly christened and launched. The next four years were the dreams of a lifetime fulfilled: for my husband, the experience and personal satisfaction of a circumnavigation accomplished; for me, the joy of a loving and increasingly close family relationship and a growing sense of personal worth. Paradoxically, this came about through accepting a role I had never particularly enjoyed. I became the ship's cook, responsible for laying in all culinary supplies and creating, from a repetitious inventory of rice, dried beans, canned fruits and vegetables, corned beef, tuna, and soups a varied menu of three hearty meals daily, plus *oyatsu* (an afternoon snack), for six ravenous shipmates. And all this on a two-burner stove.

For the first time I felt challenged, competent—and appreciated. There was never any doubt that my contribution was essential to the well-being of our group and I felt in every way equal to those who handled sails, calculated our position, stayed awake through stormy nights, or made the final decisions. That I might also have shared in some of the long-range planning or wielded a scraper or paintbrush during our periodic drydockings did not occur to me then, nor did my husband ever suggest it. I am sorry he did not for I realize now that he too was trapped in a role which forced him to carry alone a very heavy burden of responsibility. It was not until circumstances forced me to take a more active role in standing a watch and sharing time of anxiety that I realized I had missed out on much of the real satisfactions of the voyage. By then, it was too late.

My other, and highly enjoyable task, was to oversee our daughter's studies as she kept a daily journal and worked her way from fifth grade through junior high school. Our fifteen-year-old (whose older brother had elected to go on to college rather than sail with us), combined the roles of navigator and cabin boy. Short-circuiting his adolescence, he quickly became his father's right hand as well as an entertaining companion to his sister. With mutual respect, affection, and trust, the four members of our family were working as a team.

Because we sailed with three fellow crewmembers from Hiroshima, this was also a time for discovering some of the tensions and difficulties that arise between people whose language and culture are different—and for learning a great deal about Hiroshima and the continuing suffering of the *hibakusha,* those who had been exposed to the radiation of the atomic bomb.

By the time we returned to Hawaii (where we had stopped for four months on our outward voyage), two of the Japanese had left us and the third had become like one of the family. We had all experienced that "consciousness raising" which only life itself can give. We were ready to be shoved onto the stage as "peace activists."

It was at that point that Phoenix—Bird of Peace, risen from the ashes of Hiroshima—met the Golden Rule, sailed from California by four Quakers for the purpose of protesting the U.S. nuclear weapons tests in the South Pacific.

"Crackpots!" was our first reaction. What could four men on a tiny boat do to change government policies? But we were concerned about the dangers from radiation and soon realized that the presence of Golden Rule was stimulating a discussion of the issues.

For me, it stimulated much more. In court, where we went to a hearing on an injunction forbidding Golden Rule to sail—an injunction which was upheld—I heard George Willoughby's quiet statement: "When the laws of men are in violation of the laws of God, I must obey God. You can send me to jail but you cannot imprison my conscience!" I felt a deep affirmation.

For the first time, I knew that God *was* and that He was in charge. I knew, too, what it was to be God-fearing. For Phoenix to pick up the protest voyage after the crew of Golden Rule had been sentenced to sixty days in jail was not an action I felt we could evade. Rather, it was a decision for which our whole lives had prepared us. To have said, "No, I have other plans for my life!" would have taken more courage than I possessed.

I shared my conviction with my family. After some discussion (and perhaps for different reasons) we found ourselves in agreement. As for our Japanese companion, there was no hesitation. "I am from Hiroshima!" he said. And so, with no knowledge of the peace movement nor any background in nonviolent action, we sailed. Three weeks later, inside the forbidden nuclear testing area 2300 miles from Hawaii, we were stopped. My husband, my daughter and I were flown back to Honolulu, leaving our son and Japanese companion in the Marshall Islands with the ship. My husband was put under arrest. Almost overnight we found ourselves "peace activists," "leaders" in the anti-nuclear movement.

I became an "activist" out of a deeply felt inner compulsion, as instinctively as a dog responds to his master's voice. But now we found ourselves having to react to government pressures upon us while responding to the expectations of those who began to send money for our trial in the confidence that we were somehow representing them.

Because my husband was not allowed to return to Kwajalein for our ship and it would have posed considerable danger for the two men who had been left in charge to sail back alone, I was flown back to the Marshall Islands to prepare meals, stand watch, and give moral support on the return trip. For 60 grueling days, while my husband went through his trial alone and was convicted, I had to adjust to the loneliness and uncertainty of being without the "skipper" on whom I had come to depend.

That 60 days was a significant period in both of our lives, one that we never had time nor opportunity to examine. Events caught up with us. My husband had become the spokesman for the Phoenix protest—and his reasons were not always the same as mine. He spoke of "freedom of the seas" and the extent to which science was being twisted for political ends, while I, as a woman, felt the need to emphasize the immorality of endangering life and the health of the world's children, including those yet to be born.

During the next two years, while my husband's conviction as a felon was under appeal, we were seemingly as close as ever. But the seeds of disunity had been sown. My tentative motions toward God had ceased. Without being aware of my feelings, I resented the publicity that focused on my husband and did not recognize that, like my role as cook on board Phoenix, my function as secretary to send out fund appeals, prepare reports of progress, and write letters of thanks to contributors was equally as important as my husband's speaking tours and interviews with the media. Although I faithfully went through the motions, I was no longer a part of the team.

Eventually, my husband's case was won in the Court of Appeals, and we returned to Hiroshima. There, our entire family was overwhelmingly welcomed as a "family devoted to peace." Far from being able to put our action behind us and start recovering the memories, the joys, and the closeness of our four-year-voyage, we found that expectations upon us were even more demanding. In our efforts to meet the needs of everybody, we became even more fragmented. Our son entered college in Tokyo and became the idol of the student activists, our daughter studied Japanese and tried to keep up with the flood of fan mail from young people all over Japan, and my husband and I entered into frenetic activity in line with our own special "leadings"; he, to establish an Institute of Peace Science and I, to rush around the world with *hibakusha* on "peace pilgrimages." What had once, for a brief time, been a shared awareness of Light, was gone. Instead, we snatched up our own flickering candles and dashed off in all directions.

There was no one to prepare meals or make decisions or give encouragement or even to listen to anyone else. Our family had lost focus and splintered into just so many self-important individuals, each trying to save the world by his or her own efforts. When the final break came and my husband and I were divorced, our house built on sand collapsed "and great was the fall thereof." As one Japanese friend observed, "When the moon goes into eclipse, all the world sees." But a feature article in a Japanese newspaper sagely observed, "While she was traveling the world to make peace, the toast was burning in the kitchen."

Only in the aftermath of the "great fall" did I again seek God, whom I had begun to know six years before. I do not believe that His intention was to "keep me in the kitchen," but I do know that, in the course of our voyage, we had been given a glimpse of what a stable family can be if its members respect, appreciate, and cherish one another while sharing faithfully in all necessary tasks. I am sure that such a family, knowing themselves to be part of a higher plan and seeking together for God's guidance in the fulfillment of that plan, can *be* a center from which peace and justice will radiate and that the children, male or female, who grow up in such a family, will be nonviolent, less competitive, and more caring people. Without the old-fashioned virtues of nurturance, sacrifice, and commitment—which only God makes joyously possible—it seems doubtful that such families can survive. Someone has to "stay in the kitchen."

Caroline Wildflower
How Feminism Changed the Peace Movement

This article could have been titled, "But Can She Type?" Like the previous essay, Caroline's story documents the dilemma of women active in the peace movement who have too often found their energy, commitment and skills trivialized or ignored there. But this is also a story of how feminists have chipped away at the rigid, sexist expectations and limitations and begun to change the face of the peace movement.

Caroline writes, "Once, in a workshop, the participants were asked to define the words 'feminism' and 'nonviolence.' Many women came up with similar definitions for these two words. I think this was no accident: feminism and nonviolence go hand in hand."

"My essay is about what it was like for me as a woman, trying to break into organizing work in the peace movement, about the process two groups went through in becoming feminist-oriented, and about what feminist-oriented actions and groups look like."

Caroline has participated in the peace movement for over 20 years and has been an enthusiastic part of the women's movement since the late '60s. For the past five years she has been part of the Catholic Worker and active in the anti-Trident submarine campaign. She lives at Peter Maurin House of Hospitality with her husband, two children and another community member and works in the preschool and daycare which she helped found. She continues to be an active member of the Society of Friends.

I have been working against nuclear war since 1960 when I joined 1000 Quakers ringing the Pentagon in a 2-day Vigil for Peace. The following spring I joined the San Francisco to Moscow Walk for unilateral disarmament for three days and then participated in a vigil at a nerve gas factory in Indiana. Tangible results from these and allied actions were the nuclear test-ban treaty, the eventual closing down of Fort Detrick as a manufacturer of germ warfare, and the dismantling of some of the germ warfare weapons.

But the organizers of these actions had a lot to learn in the area of feminism. When I offered to do something more to help out at the nerve gas vigil, the man in charge put me to work typing addresses on envelopes. Most of the anti-war activities at that time were organized by individual men who worked alone. They did not like the idea of shared leadership and could be pretty bull-headed when it came to relationships with their own family members or friends. In other words, they were sexist. In spite of these drawbacks, I was really excited by my brief contacts with the peace movement in those years. I saw the potential power of nonviolence. It seemed to be a way for Quakers today to witness to the truth as the early Quakers did. So I dreamed of dedicating myself to the peace movement full time.

In 1969, I decided to work full time in the peace movement. My husband (we are no longer married) and I applied for a number of jobs. I had more experience in the peace movement, he had more education. My high expectations of serving the peace movement quickly turned to mud. We worked with a personnel director at American Friends Service Committee who sent Jim's name in for a number of prospective jobs, all of which I was qualified for and interested in. Each time, I had to write and ask her why she hadn't sent my name in. When we went to an interview at the American Friends Service Committee, they told us frankly that women usually started as secretaries and maybe moved up to other positions, while men could start out in jobs like peace intern or draft counselor. This was particularly distressing as I had experienced women being accepted as equal members of AFSC projects. At Fellowship House, the Black man interviewing us directed all his questions to Jim and then offered to hire us both. When I called him on it, he told me I should do as he did and learn to live with that kind of thing and not get too upset. I was afraid to get too angry for fear of not getting jobs, and I began to wonder what was wrong with me.

Finally, I was hired as office manager at A Quaker Action Group, a group which I admired for emulating early Quakers because several of its members had sailed a boat to North and South Vietnam during the Vietnam war with medical supplies for people on both sides of the conflict. Jim was hired as the head of the Draft Information Center though I had more knowledge in the area of draft counseling and was very interested in draft counseling. What was clearly happening in my case was that I was not being considered for a lot of positions simply because I was a woman. I was lucky to be supported and respected by Jim in my feeling that this was unjust. I was also lucky the Women's Movement came along right at that time to help me put power behind my anger at this injustice, and to change things for women coming after us.

1969 saw the beginnings of the modern women's movement. Women at A Quaker Action Group began raising questions about how the work was organized. We talked about the "shitwork" (the work no one liked to do) and who was doing it (the women). Why had we copied big business's way of doing things? Why did we have a male boss who hand-wrote letters for the female office manager (me) to type? Why did a woman have to start out in the peace movement as a secretary and then *maybe* move into organizing work, while men could start out in charge of things? I began refusing to type letters for my boss, and somehow they got typed. When we began to propose changes at meetings there were several vocal men who had been in the peace movement for years and made it clear that things were not going to change. At one meeting, as I was proposing a more collective structure, I was interrupted before I could even finish my sentence and told there was no way that would happen.

I came to believe A Quaker Action Group (AGAG) would not change and got myself a job as a youth worker at Friends Peace Committee, because that seemed to be the path to becoming an organizer in the peace movement. While there, I became a trainer for nonviolent action and a very competent organizer in the peace movement, although it took me a long time to believe it. I was still working in an hierarchical structure with a boss, a "front desk" who told the boss repeatedly that she did not like to be referred to as "the front desk," and organizers. The staff meetings were terrible—constant criticisms and putdowns. There was an attitude that there was something wrong with taking a day off, with taking care of oneself. During this time, I saw a lot of people (including me) burn out and leave the peace movement both because of the macho work ethic and because of the constant criticism and putdowns. People also left out of despair, because they did not see anything changing.

I feel a number of mistakes were made because of the office structure. During the time when people became aware of the U.S.invasion in Cambodia in May 1970 and began to strike and act in many ways, it was business as usual in our office. My boss insisted that I continue work on organizing a summer program for youth. I did that and also answered the call to give speeches and do nonviolence training, so I probably worked 90 hours that week. But my gut reaction was that we should have suspended our regular work to do nonviolence training with people who wanted to act and didn't know how. We had calls from people offering their services, and we didn't know what to ask them to do. We simply weren't ready to take advantage of a situation where many people wanted to move into nonviolent action. The summer program attracted maybe six people.

That summer I participated in the AQAG anti-chemical and biological warfare (CBW) campaign, a campaign I had helped to design. It had a sense of wholeness and of people being moved by God, in the Quaker tradition, to take these actions. I had to participate during my weekends and vacation times and missed all the exciting civil disobedience days. Again, I felt that because of my commitment to the peace movement, I would have been very valuable as a full time worker in that campaign, but the structure of our office did not allow for that. I probably had some influence on the people who attended the summer program, but my heart was with the CBW campaign.

What was lacking for me and for other activists was a sense of wholeness and some way for us to sense what was happening in the peace movement and how we could best be helpful and to then change our direction as workers. Qualities like gut reactions, women's intuition, heart, Quaker sense of being moved by God should all be a part of nonviolence, but the strong influence of a few men had erased these qualities in most cases. One of the things that had made both the sailing of the boat to North and South Vietnam and the CBW campaign "whole" actions was that the people involved felt moved to take these actions and listened to the call.

In the fall of 1970, women in the peace movement in Philadelphia started two consciousness-raising groups for pacifist women. We began to talk, as women, about what was happening to us. We began to share what we admired about each other and what was hard about being a woman. We took some actions as groups of women and began to joy in our coming together as women. It was a time for me to stop thinking of myself as a girl and identify strongly and proudly as a woman. It was good to have a place to talk where men were not present.

Each time we tried to take a stumbling step to change things in the peace movement, we endured terrible putdowns. We had men in the (draft) Resistance movement laughing at us and claiming the "work" needed to go on, that women's liberation was a non-issue. But over a couple of years things changed dramatically. A number of us were living in communal households where the work was supposed to be shared among everyone, but women were doing the major portions of housework in spite of the fact that women and men were putting equally long hours in the peace movement. There were a couple of strikes and threats of strikes in our living situations. With an actual strike at a house full of people in the Resistance movement, men were put on notice that women were indeed serious about this "women's liberation stuff." After that, we were taken more seriously other places, and some of the questions we were raising started to sink in although they took several years to bear fruit.

Through my study and thinking during that period, I became even more dedicated to a nonviolent way of life which included action and civil disobedience. But I couldn't stay within the structure of Friends Peace Committee, so I left in the fall of 1970, still seeking a place in the peace movement right for me.

During the following year, AQAG was transformed into Philadelphia's Life Center and Movement for a New Society. The new structure was thought about and put together with position papers and long meetings of fifty to seventy people during that year. The very person who had interrupted me to say that AQAG would not change was instrumental in proposing a model where people would live and work in a neighborhood. Anyone who wanted to be a member could be a member, and people would do the work in collectives. Indeed, all the work AQAG did is now carried on by collectives where everyone has an equal voice and decisions are made by consensus. The people doing the work make the decisions, so they don't have the situation of someone telling them to work on a summer program when they think something else is more important. It is not a perfect model—some work doesn't get done, and it's hard to figure out how to pay people and who should get paid. But there are built-in ways to change the structure, and it is constantly being refined. I believe the model is much closer to our vision of how to work in the new society. The Life Center and Movement for a New Society have also incorporated feminism as an important part of their analysis and way of doing things.

Friends Peace Committee took longer to change, though I no longer lived in the area when it began to change, and so don't know all the details. Basically, it took that particular boss leaving, and a group of people convincing the hiring committee of Quakers that they could do a good job as a collective. By 1974, staff people were taking collective leadership responsibility and rotating the job of answering the phone among themselves. They spent time in staff meetings appreciating themselves and each other and shared exciting things that were happening in their jobs. So there was a complete change that made it possible for people to stay longer without burning out, to enjoy their jobs more, and to make decisions about what to work on.

What is important about these changes is that they are permanent. Feminism is now a part of everything we do in the peace movement. We are living the new society now instead of waiting until after the revolution.

During the People's Blockade in 1972 (an action intended to block a ship loaded with bombs), we were able to experiment with new models of doing things. For a number of days we waited for the ship to leave the dock. Four of us were committed to civil disobedience, two women and two men. There were two canoes available. It was presumed that the two men were both better at handling canoes, but we had all gotten to the point of being sensitive to sexist expectations. We questioned whether the two women wanted to be stuck in the fronts of the canoes with men in the backs controlling the direction of the canoes. We women had also gotten the chance to practice being in the back, because we had demanded it earlier in the summer. This was important, because it takes practice to handle a canoe in the middle of the ocean. We had already been caught in a storm and had one canoe overturned, so we knew how dangerous the ocean could be. We talked it out and agreed to have a women's canoe and a men's canoe, with the men taking the wooden canoe which was more difficult to maneuver. Finally the ship began to steam away from the dock. People on shore who had telephoned the company and been told the departure time, quickly sent out a canoe which darted in front of the ship and slowed it down. We were waiting at a sandbar two miles out and thought we saw the ship getting up steam, but it became foggy and we were unsure. In a story which can now be told, a person came out from the coast guard and told us the ship was leaving. We paddled into the channel. The men's canoe was the next to block the ship. The coast guard kept putting grapeline hooks on the canoe and the men kept taking them off until they were finally taken aboard the coast guard cutter. Meanwhile, the women's canoe had outmaneuvered a coast guard boat to get directly in the channel. When we too were taken aboard the coast guard boat, Christiana and I looked at each other and nodded. We jumped into the water—something we had previously discussed, but not come to any decision on. The coast guard folks had to jump in and "rescue" us. All in all, according to a copy of the coast guard log supplied by our friend, we delayed the ship about 30 minutes. The action would have felt very different to me if there had been a man in the back of each canoe, "controlling things" and I don't think it would have come off with unspoken agreements and everything working like clockwork. It showed what we women have known all along—that we are just as good at "controlling things" and making decisions as are men and that "woman's intuition" can be very helpful in making quick decisions.

In 1975, I moved into a Catholic Worker house in Seattle. Our house provides temporary hospitality for homeless families. We pray together several times a week and attend a weekly neighborhood mass.

With this move I also got involved in the Pacific Life Community, which was conducting a nonviolent campaign against the Trident Submarine. My life finally seemed whole, the lacking elements had been added. I had found a place where I could dedicate my life.

There was a spiritual nature to the anti-Trident campaign. The Pacific Life Community was not religious, and yet there was a group sense of what we needed to do that I can only describe as being spiritual. We were a group of approximately 50 people living in Seattle, U.S.A., and Vancouver and Victoria, Canada, who made the anti-Trident campaign a top priority. Our statement of purpose came out of a two-day group effort and read:

> *Pacific Life Community seeks the truth of a nonviolent way of life. We recognize the Unity of all life. We affirm the wholeness of each individual and resist the fear and deceit that separate us from our own inner reality. We honor our relationships to members of living and working communities and resist any exploitation of the bonds between us. We recognize a special connection with all other people of the Pacific and join them in work for a nuclear free zone. We uphold our true identity as world citizens and commit our lives to resisting the militarism, poverty and oppression that threaten our future as a human family.*

This summed up my belief in nonviolence and our dedication, not only to stopping Trident, but to allying ourselves with the peoples of the Pacific and identifying all people as human.

We made decisions by consensus, and each person's ideas were considered important—women's and men's. We put together a slide show and a pamphlet, which both went through a group process. We carried the Trident Monster in Vancouver, Peace Arch Park (the border), Seattle, The Trident Base, and Bay Area, and Washington D.C. The Monster consisted of two ropes, 550 feet long (the length of a Trident submarine), held 10 feet in the air by bamboo poles, and 408 black plastic streamers attached to the ropes (each Trident will carry 408 nuclear warheads). We worked up to doing civil disobedience actions every couple of weeks. People tried to act as a community and to continue to decide things as a community during civil disobedience actions.

Feminism was an important issue to us. We tried to work out any problems with sexism as we went along. In general, people in Canada were not as aware of feminism as those in the U.S., so there was quite a bit of discussion of this issue in the beginning. At a strategy weekend leading up to the first big civil disobedience action, feminism was talked about as an integral part of the strategy and a man was challenged on his use of the word "men" for "people." By the time of the action, people felt fairly good about each other and able to act together. Over the years, we had our growing pains and personality clashes, but I cannot identify them as being particularly over sexism or feminism.

We developed some fine female speakers and writers, sometimes quite accidentally. For example, we co-sponsored a program featuring Phil Berrigan and discovered that all the other speakers were men, so we thought we had better have a woman. I was one of the few available at that particular time, and I rather reluctantly agreed to give the speech. Two weeks before the program I sat down to write my talk and the words just flowed out. I gave a good speech on why I, as a pregnant woman, had gone to jail to prevent nuclear war. Later, my talk was published in *Fellowship*.

The anti-Trident campaign continues now mostly out of Ground Zero Center for Nonviolent Action, a piece of land which shares a fence-line with the Trident Base. Ground Zero is also dedicated to feminism, to a spiritual basis for the campaign, and to group process. It now has collective leadership by the active people.

Our feminism permeates all aspects of life and MAKES A DIFFERENCE FOR EVERYONE. Though we still need to pay attention to feminism and keep raising issues that seem important to feminism, life is better for both the women and the men involved in the places where I used to work. Now that we have made these big changes, women are not constantly hurt and put down and devalued in the peace movement. We have successfully created a situation where we live the revolution now, where women and men are respected for their talents and potential, where women and men are living up to their potential.

Marion Bromley
Feminism and Nonviolent Revolution

Continuing our hard look at sexism in the peace movement, Marion takes us back to the early 1940's and (by focusing on the development of two groups—Peacemakers and CORE) documents women activists' metamorphosis from muffled second fiddles in the male domain to awakened sisters transforming the landscape of the peace movement.

Of course the struggle continues for Marion as it does for us all. She writes, "I went to New York in 1943 to work at the national FOR (Fellowship of Reconciliation) office. I was secretary to A.J. Muste, but since becoming a feminist I have stopped identifying myself as 'secretary to' or 'wife of.' I was at the originating conference of Peacemakers in Chicago in 1948, and Ernest and I were married the same year. Nonviolent activity against war and other kinds of oppression has been a major part of my life. I'm a member of Community Friends in Cincinnati.

"I've had a recent demonstration that it's not easy to break out of the role of being Ernest's helper in all the activities we've worked on. Just last Saturday the local Cincinnati Post *carried a feature story about the anniversary of the integration of Coney Island Amusement Park (in Cincinnati). Our part of the story is introduced by, 'Ernest Bromley remembers driving up to the auto gate of Coney in 1952, in a car carrying a black person. Bromley had the car window down but... a standoff ensued; they sat for 20 minutes. His wife, meanwhile, was sitting in the county jail in the first of what would be nine days in custody for her part in the demonstration.' It just misrepresents the truth of the matter to imply that Ernest was 'doing it' and I was a sidecar helping him. People who were involved know that and the young reporter who wrote the story wasn't around at the time, but it seems to be no different from ten years ago."*

The struggle continues, but in this essay, originally written as a speech for a 1976 conference, Marion encourages women to look to our foremothers for inspiration and courage and reclaim our rich heritage as leaders toward a peaceful, egalitarian society.

I have been anti-war from high school days and, since 1941, a pacifist with recognition that I was in conflict not only with nationalism but also with racism and other injustices. I have been committed to nonviolent direct action as the method for bringing my personal life and my social attitudes into harmony with Gandhian nonviolence since 1944. I have been a feminist pacifist only since about 1970.

Those of us committed to nonviolent direct action in the 1940's termed ourselves "radical pacifist." We based this term on the meaning of radical as: "Arising from or going to a root or source; fundamental; basic."[1] We considered the root of war and racism to be violence, and we experimented with various ways of trying to oppose that violence and to convince others of that basic philosophy. Nonviolence, as any student of Gandhi knows, is far from being a submissive or passive attitude about oppression and violence. It is, instead, an attitude of resistance to oppression, commitment to the struggle for freedom, both for oneself and for all others.

It is with some surprise that I now realize that all these years I and most others had overlooked the soil in which that root of violence grew—patriarchal attitudes, patriarchal institutions and patriarchal control. I must henceforth describe myself and express myself as a "radical-feminist-pacifist." The goal remains the same—in a word, freedom. That is, I want not to oppress any other and I will not accept oppression *by* any other—individual or group.

Origin of Peacemakers

In the late 1930's I was working as a secretary in a large manufacturing firm and spent a considerable amount of my free time in an anti-war organization, the Akron Council for Peace Action. Through that connection I learned of the Fellowship of Reconciliation, a religious pacifist group which broadened my concept of pacifism to one of accepting the essential equality of all human beings. This concept later attracted me to the Society of Friends, for that is a central belief of Quakers.

After Pearl Harbor and the U.S. entry into World War II on both continents, I could no longer tolerate my privileged position of earning a good secretarial salary, having a good time in several attractive circles of friends while men were being drafted and people were enduring the horrors of savage concentration camps, displacement, sending or receiving the results of the best death equipment afforded by the technology of the time. In 1943 I left home and job and began working for the Fellowship of Reconciliation in New York for a subsistence wage.

At the end of World War II, the U.S. used atomic weapons on a defenseless civilian population in Japan, not to complete the defeat of that nation, for Japan was by then helpless, but to warn the rest of the world, particularly the Soviet Union, that this weapon, which had been developed secretly in the United States, was not only ready for use, but that it would be used to maintain U.S. dominance. (What a *macho* thing to do!)

Many of those who had resisted World War II recognized that the Atomic Era brought to humankind greater peril than ever before. They began to think that what was required was commitment to a way of life that expressed nonviolence in all areas. The Peacemaker movement had its beginning in 1948, when a group met in Chicago to discuss these ideas. From the beginning, Peacemakers sought not merely the elimination of war, but the elimination of violence, coercion, exploitation and injustice. They advocated and practiced total rejection of conscription, refusal to pay taxes for war, and the creation of communities of work and sharing. The Peacemaker movement has remained small, but it has been influential. It has changed people's lives in a surprising number of cases.

The Congress of Racial Equality (CORE)

Another movement which I want to sketch briefly, developed from American pacifism during the early 1940's. CORE, the Congress of Racial Equality, began in Chicago during the spring of 1942.[2] I look upon the civil rights movement and the Black freedom movement as inspiration to those who yearn and hope and work for a women's movement that will not only free us individually, but will also vastly change the society in which we live. Part of that inspiration lies in the knowledge that CORE started from such small beginnings, and indeed in most of that organization's history there were very few people really working at CORE's objectives. A nucleus of six pacifists started CORE, two of whom were staff members of the Fellowship of Reconciliation. The F.O.R. at that time was beginning to move beyond opposition to war to experimenting with nonviolent direct action for social justice in the United States. Among the "peace teams" or "cells" into which F.O.R. members were organized, there was one established at the University of Chicago in October 1941, which was deeply interested in applying Gandhian principles to racial problems. From that race relations cell of about a dozen members emerged the first

CORE group, the Chicago Committee of Racial Equality.

They believed that discrimination must be challenged directly, without violence or hatred, yet without compromise. They worked against restrictive covenants in the University area, tackled the White City Roller Rink, and then developed the technique of "sitting in" at restaurants which refused to seat or serve the Black members of the action teams. This was precisely the method used 18 years later when four students from North Carolina A&T College sat-in at a Woolworth lunch counter in downtown Greensboro, igniting a major protest movement throughout the South.

CORE activists dreamed of a mass, nationwide, interracial movement of non-cooperation with segregation and discrimination. The first wider project they were able to launch was called the Journey of Reconciliation, in 1947. It was sponsored jointly by the Fellowship of Reconciliation and CORE, and was limited to the upper South—a two-week bus trip by 16 men, eight Black and eight white, designed to test compliance with a recent Supreme Court decision against segregation in interstate travel. That case involved the arrest and conviction of Irene Morgan for refusing to vacate a front seat on a bus traveling from Virginia to Maryland. In June 1945, the Court ruled that it was unconstitutional for the Virginia legislature to require segregation on interstate motor carriers.

As an aside, isn't it interesting to note how many of the landmark decisions in the civil rights struggle involved women? Irene Morgan, Rosa Parks, Linda Brown, Vivian Malone. Of course Black men were no doubt subject to harsher treatment when they "crossed the color line" in those barbaric rituals of racist America, but when we discuss the traits commonly thought of as more characteristic of one sex than the other, let us not allow courage to be catalogued as "male."

The Journey of Reconciliation aroused very little national attention, but it functioned as a dramatic high point and source of inspiration to CORE for years to come, and 14 years later it served as the model for the famous Freedom Ride of 1961, which demonstrated for the whole nation to see, the brutal suppression by all agencies of the society of even those rights supposedly guaranteed by specific legal decisions.

Along with the NAACP and CORE, two other organizations provided the backbone for the "Black Revolt" of the 1960's: Southern Christian Leadership Conference (SCLC), which grew out of the Montgomery bus boycott of 1955-56, and the Student Nonviolent Coordinating Committee (SNCC), which was the product of the southern college student sit-ins of 1960. Both SCLC and SNCC adopted the strategy of nonviolent direct action, which had been pioneered by CORE.

Some of the idealistic young leaders of the Black freedom movement, although involved most of the time in the pressure-packed momentum of one campaign after another, would sometimes speak of their larger objective. They would make clear that their goal was not merely an equal share with whites in jobs, income, housing, their "piece of the pie." They were critical of American society, no matter how big a share one might attain. They wanted a more equalitarian society in which people related to each other with warmth, and caring, and sharing.

CORE Reverses Policies

In CORE it seemed that the larger and more prominent the organization became, during its roller coaster history of ups and downs, the more males became the "leaders" and the women in most cases faded into the background. From the beginning, cornerstones of CORE policy were nonviolent action and interracial participation. Early CORE members were very serious about both these principles and for a period of 20 years or so there was a high degree of consensus among CORE members about the value of using interracial nonviolent direct action as the way to best achieve the goal of an integrated society based on racial justice. By the spring of 1964 the consensus over tactics and strategy had disintegrated. The struggle over gaining access for all to public accommodations in the north and upper south was all but completed by the tactics CORE had pioneered. When the focus shifted to helping ghetto dwellers organize themselves to achieve the improvements they saw as most necessary to them, there was an obvious conflict with the ideal of integration. Some chapters were controlled by nationalists. Basic changes occurred in removing whites from leadership positions, and relinquishing any remaining adherence to nonviolence. By 1966 "Black power" had arrived and national CORE officially excluded whites from active membership in the summer of 1968. It is interesting to note now that the new leaders of national CORE, when nonviolence was abandoned as either principle or tactic, also spoke in stridently sexist terms.

Waking Up

Turning again to personal experience of awareness of sexism, it seems that some women had the door blow open as with a rushing wind, once the door opened a crack. Others had the experience of the door opening slowly and gradually, squeaking on its hinges. The latter was my type of awakening. It began when I had access to literature of the S.D.S. women (Students for a Democratic Society) in the early 1960's. What they wrote about the male monopoly on power in S.D.S. was very familiar in the pacifist movement I knew. What I began to learn about more personal, day-to-day arrangements was revealing. But it was movement sexual politics that bothered me more. And here I and others, men and some women in Peacemakers, were hung up on dogma. This hangup lasted for years!

Peacemakers are committed to reaching agreement on movement matters by consensus. This means very personal, open and frank discussion and, as in the Society of Friends, action is not taken on group matters until there is unanimity. Of course Peacemakers want integration. When the Black freedom movement began to adopt separatist politics and even CORE, which had from the beginning been an interracial movement, began to move toward a Black nationalist position, Peacemakers felt this a denial of nonviolent principles. Similarly, when Peacemaker women began to suggest separate meetings for women, there was strong opposition to this procedure. Women who endured discussions of the "woman question" in a mixed group with Peacemaker men realized with a fresh clarity some of the frustrations Blacks had endured in a CORE chapter or an "Interracial Fellowship" dominated by whites. But the practice of women meeting with women and the recognition for the first time that "sisterhood is real," "sisterhood is powerful," swept aside the dogmas for most Peacemaker women, and they began to respond to the reality of experience instead of banging their heads against the wall of dogma.

The need and the determination of women to meet together has proved to be like the tide of "Black power." Separatist or not, no one could stop it.

Maleness

It is understandable that Peacemakers were slow to or unable to recognize their sexism. For pacifist men are probably, as a group, less chauvinist than most of the society. Peacemaker men do not exhibit the most flagrant characteristics of male-dominant behavior. They are not "success" oriented, they believe themselves to regard all humans as equals, and they have consciously and at some cost opted out of much of militarist, racist, punitive American society. Peacemaker women are likely to be more independent and self-reliant than most American women, since they, too, have adopted a lifestyle more in accord with nonviolence. In a word, both men and women may be more nearly androgynous than the average.

Unfortunately, however, the aggressive and dominating tendencies of the "masculine" personality cause even the less chauvinist males to assume that unconscious certainty of their innate superiority to females. On a one-to-one relationship, that may be the aspect of sexism which is the most maddening to deal with. This is particularly true in a group such as Peacemakers where men are sure they are not sexist. As any religionist knows, it is nearly impossible for the "already saved" to have any concern for their own salvation.

Consider the following: Pacifists have frequently denied that draft resisters, refusers and conscientious objectors are "feminine." Doesn't this denial indicate an acceptance of the correlation of "feminine" with "lack of courage?" "Courage" has generally been accepted by both pacifists and militarists as being a male characteristic. There seems to have been no recognition, by the pacifists themselves, that choosing to protect life rather than killing those pointed to as the enemy is a more female attitude than a male one. Eleanor Emmons Maccoby and Carol Nagy Jacklin have reported, after a three-year study of sex differences in motivation, social behavior, and intellectual ability of children, that they found many of the beliefs commonly held about psychological differences between males and females to be myths. Their findings on aggression are clear, however. They state their conclusion as:

> *Difference One: Males are more aggressive than females. A sex difference in aggression has been observed in all cultures in which aggressive behavior has been observed. Boys are more aggressive physically and verbally. They engage in mock fighting and aggressive fantasies as well as direct forms of aggression more frequently than girls. The sex difference manifests itself as soon as social play begins, at age two or two and a half. From an early age, the primary victims of male aggression are other males, not females.*[3]

In discussing sex differences in animals and in earliest human society, Evelyn Reed states:

> *A careful study of animal life and behavior shows that it is not the female animal but the male animal that suffers from a biological liability. This stems from the violent characteristics of male sexuality in nature, propelling males to strive for "dominance" over other males and limiting their ability to cooperate with one another. Females, on the other hand, far from being handicapped by their maternal functions, acquired from them the very traits conducive to advancing from animality to human life and cooperative labor. Insofar as the sexes were unequally endowed by nature, the biological advantages for humanizing the species were on the side of the females, not the males.*[4]

It is dismally clear now that the liveliest and most adventurous Peacemaker projects were previously carried out by all-male teams. Women have taken a more nearly equal part in recent Peacemaker activities, but discussions generally, and particularly of the "woman question" in the mixed group, with the "antler-clanking" performance of some men, are no longer tolerable to many Peacemaker women. They find in women's discussions a treasured quality of sharing, of consideration, of caring and, more important, a lack of "dueling," of using the group to demonstrate one's ability to debate, to overcome an "opponent."

Again the similarity of the women's struggle with the Black freedom movement comes to mind. Here is a fragment from James Baldwin's dialogue with Margaret Mead which applies:

> *(Baldwin): And now what's happened is that, for this moment in our history, anyway, black people no longer care what white people think. I no longer care, to tell you the truth, whether white people can hear me or not. It doesn't make any difference at all. If they can hear me, so much the better; if they can't so much the worse. For them.*[5]

Some Peacemaker women now feel like that about the opinions of Peacemaker men on "the woman question."

In the wider peace movement of the 1960's, where there was more organizational power to be divided among groups and strong leaders, the experience of women was more devastating than in Peacemakers. Shelley Douglass writes,

> *We were welcomed into the movement in lower-echelon positions, as somebody's woman, girl, old lady, wife, as sex ob-*

jects, as workhorses. Women were expected to make coffee and provide refreshments while men planned strategy and did resistance actions.

Another statement by Douglass sets the bells ringing for many women.

Women kept the homefires burning while men organized, acted and went to jail. Women bore and raised children and created the homes to which the men returned. Women did leaflets in the thousands, typed letters, licked stamps, marched in demonstrations. We rarely spoke at demonstrations; our actions did not make us celebrities like the men. When women went to jail, they lacked strong community support. They had no knowledge, by and large, of their historic role in the peace movement.[6]

The Recent Past

To obtain a realistic possibility that women can turn the society around by exposing and then removing the power of patriarchal institutions, attitudes and individuals, we must be aware of the pitfalls of imitating those male-dominant characteristics that have brought us to the present perilous state. We can keep a radical, total vision of androgynous society, a peaceful egalitarian society, before us while we work at specific projects to bring those changes to pass. Accepting the assistance of feminist males, we can make it happen—we can bring down the patriarchy.

One requirement is to discover our past. One of the real gains women have made since becoming conscious of our condition of servitude is that discovery, and I hope women who have the skill and scholarship will continue sharing that information with all of us. Quaker women are beginning to look to their 18th century foremothers for inspiration and courage. We can all look with pride on the contributions of American women to peace, protection of the young, organizing for improved conditions all the way across the social scene. Our job will be to expose for all to see, the contrast of that contribution with the role of the patriarchs who are most venerated in school texts, for leading others to battle, for gaining political power so they might rule others for the benefit of their own class or political group. School children and adults who read history will probably continue to be regaled with stories of patriarchal leaders; we will insist that they also learn about such women as these:

Mary Dyer, a Quaker woman whose heroism played a significant part in establishing religious freedom in America. Quakers were banished when they continued to hold meetings for worship in their homes in the Massachusetts Colony, where the Puritan law forbade any other religious practice. Returning after having been banished under pain of death and given an earlier reprieve, Mary Dyer was hanged on Boston Common in 1659. The British Crown then ordered the colony to stop their religious persecution, and the practice ceased.

Susan B. Anthony, another Quaker, born in 1820, was a teacher, and active in the New York State Teachers' Association, making many demands for higher wages and for recognition of the rights of women. In 1847 she joined the Daughters of Temperance and in 1852 organized the first open women's temperance organization, of which *Elizabeth Cady Stanton* was president. She identified herself with the suffragist movement, and abolition of slavery. Arrested and tried for voting at the presidential election of 1872, she refused to pay the $100 fine. She said to the judge: "Resistance to tyranny is obedience to God, and I shall never pay a penny of this unjust claim."

Elizabeth Blackwell, born in England in 1821, came to Cincinnati in 1838. By teaching she earned enough for her medical education. In 1853 with her sister, she established in New York City the New York Infirmary for Women and Children. In 1869 Dr. Blackwell settled in London where she practiced for many years and founded the National Health Society and worked in a number of social reforms.

Emma Goldman holds an honored place in so many categories of the struggle for freedom. Her life-long commitment to personal integrity and love of the people is brilliantly depicted in her autobiography, *Living My Life*, which is a text of great value for all of us.

Jane Addams, best known for founding Hull House in Chicago, the first settlement house, was an active participant in opposition to World War I. In 1915 she took part in the Women's Congress at the Hague to counteract growing tensions between countries; out of this came the Woman's Party and the Women's International League for Peace and Freedom. Jane Addams became its first president, *Emily Greene Balch* its first international secretary. Jane Addams' name was on the call for the first meeting of the National Association for the Advancement of Colored People (NAACP).

Sojourner Truth played a significant role in the struggle

against segregation after the Civil War. Streetcar conductors sometimes refused to stop for Black passengers, even after a law was passed in 1865 making such practice illegal. Sojourner Truth used nonviolent resistance to force the issue. When a streetcar stopped for white passengers she boarded the car and dared the conductor to throw her off. The man who accepted her challenge and ejected the eighty-year-old woman was successfully sued and lost his job.[7]

Women workers played a unique role in the 1912 Lawrence, Massachusetts, textile mills strike. The strike began spontaneously the first payday after Massachusetts passed a law reducing the maximum work hours for women and children. Mill owners used the law to justify lowering wages in an industry already marked by poor pay and working conditions. When Polish women opened their pay envelopes they began shouting, "Short pay!" and calling for a strike, which eventually involved 23,000 workers from 25 different ethnic groups. Tactics included mass picketing and huge solidarity parades, in which women carried signs reading, "We Want Bread and Roses Too!"[8]

Jeannette Rankin was one of 50 U.S. Representatives to vote against entry into World War I in 1917. Having been returned to Congress by Montana, she became the only member to vote against entry into both world wars when she again voted "No" in 1941. She worked for child welfare, for justice in labor, against social injustice and racial prejudice. She had a special interest in the development of public lands, including public parks. After World War II she went to India because of her interest in nonviolence, and became a Gandhian. She took part in opposing the war in Vietnam, in 1968 appearing in a wheelchair with the Jeannette Rankin Brigade of Women's Strike for Peace in a public demonstration in Washington.[9]

War Resisters League was founded in 1923 by three women, *Jesse Wallace Hughan, Tracy Mygatt* and *Frances Witherspoon.* Their purpose was to support conscientious objectors whose pacifism was secular or political, rather than religious. The WRL is one of the major anti-war organizations on the American scene.

Dorothy Day, founder of the Catholic Worker movement in 1933 with Peter Maurin, was the leading spirit of that pacifist, anarchist lay Catholic movement, unique for its identification with the poor. Through its widely-circulated monthly, *The Catholic Worker,* and its communities of work and sharing, in rural areas and city slums, the Catholic Worker movement has attracted thousands of Catholic and non-Catholic youth and has been a strong influence in the emergence of the Catholic left and anti-war movement.

Women Against Daddy Warbucks conducted a unique action against the draft and continuing war in Vietnam in 1969. This small group of women messed up draft files of 13 Uptown Manhattan draft doards, bringing the files' remains to Rockefeller Center in a public demonstration of their civil disobedience action.

Among women who took strong nonviolent action against the war and imperialism in the past few decades, and spent time in federal prisons because of their civil disobedience, are: Ruth Reynolds, who was imprisoned in Puerto Rico in 1950 for her association with the movement for Puerto Rican independence; Marj Swann, who climbed the fence in an open action of protest at the Omaha missile base in 1958; Rose Robinson, who was sentenced in 1960, in Chicago, for contempt in connection with her action of refusing taxes for war. These three women had also been active in CORE. More recently, Sali McAllister, Charlene Pope, Cathy Melville, Connie Grubbs McNamara, Marjorie Melville, Pat Pottinger Morrisson, Phyllis Burke, Jane Meyerding, DeCourcy Squire, Suzanne Williams, Joan Nicholson, Margaret Katroscik, Jo Anne Mulart, Pat Grumbles and Joan Kennedy did time in federal prison for such actions as draft board raids. Martha Tranquilli had a year's sentence in 1960 for refusing to permit war taxes to be withheld from her pay when she had worked as a nurse in Mississippi.

Conclusion

The history of the "male way" of countering violence with greater violence points directly to the grave. The nonviolent "female way" of life-giving, nurturing, protecting the young and cooperative labor has pointed to life, all through human existence.

Nonviolence as an organized, conscious movement has had a very brief and small-scale history, but those experiments have demonstrated the potential of nonviolent means for achieving the ends of peace, justice and freedom.

It is said that the most highly-developed brain has used a very small portion of its potential. To stir the human brain to design ways of meeting the human situation requires vast energy. We have all seen evidence of the stirrings of energy in the women's movement. May this energy supply vastly increase, so we may create the means whereby male aggression will be controlled and women's potential nonviolent power be enhanced, leading to more androgynous, creative individuals.

Diana J. M. Davies/Insight

In Harlem, 1965, a woman joins a demonstration in support of civil rights actions in Selma, Alabama. CORE, Congress of Racial Equality, was instrumental in popularizing nonviolent techniques.

Margaret Bishop
Feminist Spirituality & Nonviolence

Why are feminists leery of nonviolence? Margaret offers a few suggestions from her own experience: One reason is that, while pacifists want our help in anti-war organizing, they often reject our analysis that war is inherent in the patriarchal structure. Sometimes the male-led peace movement relies on manipulation of people rather than on empowerment. Moreover, because our models have been either warriors or victims, we fall for a common misconception—we fear we must be nice or silent when we're not planning a violent confrontation. "When we- . . . begin to identify ourselves as pacifists, we too often become more concerned that we not hurt or perhaps alienate anybody than that we fulfill the demands of living."

Still, for all our feminist reluctance, we usually do turn to nonviolent tactics—building alternative institutions, boycotting, starting C-R groups, demonstrating. And while this is largely because nonviolence is effective and practical, Margaret believes we turn to it in part because it is consistent with the process suggested by feminist spirituality. "We hold to the faith that, as we have found positive ways to change and grow, others can change as we have changed. . . This is a direct challenge to violence which always posits an unchanging enemy. . ."

Margaret teaches in an alternative elementary school in Detroit. She has been active in various feminist groups including a self-help health collective and a feminist bookstore. She writes poetry, flies kites and begins all sorts of projects like learning to play concertina and painting stars on her bedroom ceiling.

> *Feminism is an exploration, one that has just begun. Women have been taught that, for us, the earth is flat, and that if we venture out, we will fall off the edge. Some of us have ventured out nevertheless, and so far we have not fallen off. It is my faith, my feminist faith, that we will not."*
>
> *Andrea Dworkin*

Five years ago, in 1976, when we in the Hershelf Wimmin's Bookstore collective were planning workshops to hold at the store, I piped up with the perfect idea: we could invite some feminists in Ann Arbor, who had been trained in the Movement for a New Society, to hold a day-long training session in nonviolence. My friends stared back at me so coldly that I had that old, prickly feeling of having read from the wrong script. I was shocked by their reaction. Because we shared a common lifestyle, work style and analysis of world problems, I had assumed that we also shared the vision of nonviolent social change which was fundamental to my choice of political work. What puzzled me most was that many of these women were involved in feminist spiritual exploration like tarot, energy circles and various meditative healing practices. How could it be that these women's peacemaking with the soul did not lead them to a vision of nonviolence?

The climate has changed somewhat with the advent of the Women Take Back the Night marches which have been organized as nonviolent demonstrations. But although many more women are now getting nonviolence training and accepting the discipline of a nonviolent march, feminist commitment to nonviolence is still tentative, even while our protest against violence is growing.

Feminists have good reasons for mistrusting the current nonviolent movements. We have all attended large, expensive demonstrations which were ineffective because they were isolated from ongoing local campaigns. Such actions offered no sense of a realistic or daring strategy which would go beyond our day's adventure. This was how I felt about the May 27, 1978 demonstration at the special session on disarmament at the United Nations. I know many people worked hard on building this first demonstration of the Mobilization for Survival. I believe that in other areas of the country this action was made more clear. As a Detroiter, however, I was unsure about what we were doing. Were we expecting the United Nations to force worldwide disarmament? If so, what was to happen when the UN would inevitably fail to be conclusive in its recommendations or active in the implementation? I never learned, and so I spent the day in New York with a vague sense that I was "speaking out" against nuclear war.

Sometimes these marches have actually fit into a long-range strategy, but one that involves manipulation rather than empowerment of large numbers of people. This is the male left at its worst, and we have seen it repeatedly in the anti-war movement both during times of fighting and now, again, in the anti-draft movement. Groups like the Young Socialist Alliance form (or join) organizations which are mobilized around a single issue such as ending the war or preventing a new draft. The plan is that once a crowd is gathered, socialists will then speak in order to show the people the truth about socialist analysis. This often alienates the constituency. It also hamstrings the whole power of protest because the lack of shared vision between the organizers and the participants undermines any possibility for trust that would make forceful campaigns, including civil disobedience, possible.[1]

We women have learned how enervating it is to squander our trust on people who will not return the commitment that they ask of us.[2] And, while pacifists ask us to work against war and the draft, they often refuse our analysis of war and violence as being inherent to all patriarchal societies. They prefer to explain massive violence as part of a cosmic struggle between good and evil or as a product of the relentless machinations of capitalism. As a result, they neither see their own patriarchal behaviors at meetings and at home as relevant, nor do they understand the importance of women demanding control of our own bodies under all circumstances.

This is changing. The War Resisters League now has a feminist task force and has sponsored at least one conference on "Feminism and Militarism—a Conference for Women." Movement for a New Society (MNS) has responded bravely to feminist criticism of the left by integrating the theory and lifestyle of its members, decentralizing its organization, and taking seriously the methods by which decisions get made. However, this response is still not enough. The primary issues for MNS seem to be nuclear power, the draft and military spending. Other forms of violence, like forced sterilization or exporting of anti-woman drugs like Depoprovera to Third World countries, have that secondary place which is all too familiar.

These problems, which make it easy for feminists to turn their backs on nonviolent organizations, as well as lack of media information on nonviolent struggles and victories, mean that many feminists are not well informed on nonviolent struggles, victories and possibilities. For instance, how many of us know exactly what has happened in the fields of Fresno to make the UFW (United Farm Workers) a force to be reckoned with, or what happened at the various Seabrook demonstrations? We don't know what has been effective, nor where the mistakes were made.

Moreover, we have to face our fear of confrontations. Our

models, the products of a patriarchal society, have been either warriors or victims. This means that when we are not planning a violent confrontation, we have a strong pull to be either nice or silent. We need to learn that understanding our adversaries' lives and struggles is not the same as either giving up on ourselves or making things easy for them.

This fear of confrontation leads us sometimes to a rather blind rejection of our culture. We need to trust our ability to sort through arguments, test them against our lives, reject those things which attack us, enjoy those parts of our culture which *have* nourished us and *have* allowed us to survive. Blanket statements like "We must not accept, even for a moment, male notions of what nonviolence is"[3] weaken our belief in our ability to sort things out and therefore to confront those with whom we differ. Certainly we should not accept male vision of nonviolence, but neither should we dismiss it all. We should trust our desire to learn and our ability to detect shit when we see it. In my life my mistakes have not come so much from confusion, but from an inability to act on what I knew was true.

Despite all of these shortcomings with our present models and understanding of nonviolence, we still turn to nonviolent tactics such as education (as in consciousness-raising groups), boycotts (as in the anti-Nestle organizing), the formation of alternative institutions, and massive demonstrations like the Take Back the Night marches. Consciously or not, we know that embracing violence is the same as accepting defeat.

To begin with, any armed revolt must include a massive propaganda campaign which dehumanizes the opponent. Such campaigns are most successful when the opponent is vague and unknown. The "ruling class" is a remote and faceless group to the mass of peasants whose labor supports it, while people of other racial and/or cultural backgrounds are easily turned into subhumans as is done in military bootcamp. However, feminist vision goes beyond mere class changes because it recognizes that sexual oppression exists regardless of monetary gain or loss. Economic or class analysis cannot adequately explain rape or incest. Our lives are so embroiled with those we would fight against; can we really expect large numbers of women to objectify and dehumanize their fathers, brothers, husbands, and sons? Even if we could imagine such a possibility, we must face the racism of such a position. If we define men as a gender class which oppresses us and then decide to fight against that class, then we must realize that we would be asking Black women to participate in the destruction of Black men. Black women, however, are sick of the destruction of their people.

Second, we know that since "you can't kill all the unbelievers,"[4] a violent means of gaining changes would eventually force us to become part of a violent status quo. Not only would this be unacceptable to feminists, it would also be wildly impractical. When people are being attacked, they harden in their present state: Personal change is out of the question. Given the assumptions of much of the world, any violent solution would necessarily claim women as victims.

All of this has been borne out in our world's history—a history which has included many violent revolutions, none of which put women first even in countries like Cuba, Israel and China where women have fought in significant numbers.

Beyond all these practical questions, however, are spiritual imperatives for nonviolent action. Our politics must be rooted in a deep consciousness of the meaning of our lives if we're going to find the commitment to nonviolent discipline that any sustained campaign for social justice must include. I believe that no matter what course of action we take, these spiritual imperatives call out for our attention. We simply can't exist as human beings and not have to reckon with these concepts in some way.

It's important to say here that, while I'm committed to nonviolence, it is not my primary commitment. My primary commitment is to learning the truth about this earth and universe and working toward a human reconciliation with this truth. My commitment is to life, joy, creativity, love—in other words all those things which make us aware of energy and our essential harmony with the things outside ourselves.

Although my particular vision of "the truth" is largely an individual matter with a whole set of individual images which contain it, I do believe that it's this search for truth that must be our first item of business. When we turn from our compelling visions and begin to identify ourselves as pacifists, we too often become more concerned that we not hurt or perhaps alienate anybody than that we fulfill the demands of living.

It's quite possible that a biophilic[5] society based on truth will need to face a tremendous amount of hurt before it can truthfully celebrate the joy which is life.

But if we don't turn to theories of nonviolence for our primary inspiration, where do we turn? I believe that, first and foremost, we must turn inward. We must do what we did when we first tentatively started calling ourselves feminists; we must trust ourselves.

This means developing every part of ourselves—our strong bodies, our rationality, our music, our dreams and hunches. Naomi Goldenberg in *Changing of the Gods*[6] makes some good arguments for basing a feminist spirituality on our dreams. I find this exciting and personally very affirming because I have lived best when I have taken the time to explore my dreams and find expression for them.

It's this dipping into the nonverbal, but fertile, part of ourselves and bringing forth something which is complex and often frightening to acknowledge, which is, I believe, what Adrienne Rich is talking about when she speaks about "naming the unnamable."[7]

If we love ourselves, then we also love the changes that we must, as living beings, go through, as well as the changes that make life around us possible: changing seasons, changing vision, and the changing states of one's own body. We hold to the faith that as we have found positive ways to change and grow, others can change as we have changed. We hold to this in the face of the hopelessness that surrounds us because we know that there was a time when others looked at us and imagined that we, too, were lost souls. This is a direct challenge to violence which always posits an unchanging enemy and, in its most extreme form, embraces as a solution the most unchanging state of all—death.

learned from the Quakers—that truth does not come to us from books or any authority, but from careful exploration of ourselves, tempered by a love that embraces our world. This exploration involves not only our intellect, but all those less verbal aspects of our consciousness as well. I believe that those of us who have embraced feminist thinking have already begun to use this process. We must continue in this, and begin to bring deep reflection, "cosmic spinning," into our lives not only as a reaction to crisis, but daily. As we deepen our commitment to ourselves and the world, we will build a spirituality which will speak to us so deeply and seriously that we will never compromise with violence again. We will be moved to speak actively against the pervasive and deadly cultural passivity that surrounds us and isolates us from each other.

Kathy Bickmore

Feminism and Peace: The Issues We Work On

In this essay, Kathy, a lesbian feminist who teaches nonviolent skills in Cleveland, Ohio, outlines some ways in which feminists and peace activists can bridge the gap between their movements and challenges each to recognize the necessity of embracing a broader perspective on basic issues. "This piece was written while exploring differences between what 'movement' groups say *they're for and what they actually work for." Kathy became involved in radical feminism and peace and justice activism during her student days at Oberlin College (graduated, 1979).*

Patriarchy is violent both in its public manifestations—militarism, economic imperialism, capital punishment, and hierarchy-bureaucracy, and in its private manifestations—domestic violence, rape, job discrimination, and pornography. For some reason the mainstream peace movement has all but totally ignored "private," close to home violence in favor of combatting more "public" and remote wrongs. Surely we can guess the results of this separation. It is said that Susan B. Anthony encountered far more resistance among Quakers for sheltering a woman being battered by her husband than for housing escaped slaves.

Focusing only upon public, more remote, violence allows peace movement members to avoid taking personal responsibility for violence. So we find, for example, the irony of so-called liberal or radical anti-draft activists consuming a huge share of Third World products such as coffee, aluminum and oil, while cheap access to these products is "protected" militarily by the U.S.; men working to "save the people" of Viet Nam or an El Salvador while supporting the pornography industry and beating their wives or lovers; or "banning the bomb" while harassing the secretary.

Rape and the economic colonization of women, especially women of color, have traditionally been considered consequences of war, but rape and economic colonization of women (the average working woman earns 59% of what the average working man earns) are increasing here at home. It seems that the so-called "peace" movement can accept violence until it's men getting hurt.

There's another problem. If people seeking peace do not take responsibility for combating violence immediately around us, we do not learn about violence on a personal level, and so we do not discover the root causes and cures for it.

Feminist women, whatever our class background, cannot and must not side with the ruling classes. Oppression of young people or old people, people of color, or of anyone affects all women. While we must see the difference between the violence of the oppressed and that of the oppressor, we must not satisfy ourselves with using violence. To recognize that violence is an integral part of patriarchy is to know that women can and must develop alternatives to violence, and continue to be nurturers, healers, listeners, educators.

Feminists are challenged to deal with these peace issues:

- Funding for human needs will be available when and if national priorities are changed and the funding now wasted on military is spent for life-supporting goods and services. Local peace conversion efforts need feminist leadership and support.
- Our children will continue to grow up violent and be victims of violence until forces of militarist/macho socialization are eliminated. This means combating militarism in school texts and teaching methods, military recruitment in schools, and the lack of funding for education. And there will be an economic "draft" into the military until full, useful employment for all is available.
- Women can take the lead in "peace education," teaching the skills which will enable people to choose viable nonviolent solutions in their own lives.
- Women must continue their unrelenting resistance to the nuclear annihilation which is now believed by many to be "likely."

The peace movement is challenged to work for peace by dealing with these issues:

- Hierarchy, male-identification, and power-tripping within the movement must be stopped. This might, for example, entail putting some of the effort which now goes into centralized rallies and media events into locally initiated education, outreach, and action projects.

•The people in the peace movement can provide child care and be sensitive to the special needs of women and poor people in determining time and place of meetings.
•The movement should actively support liberation struggles within the U.S., including those of lesbians and gays, women, and people of color. Don't expect help from a group or community you will not support.
•The peace movement must speak out and act against violence against women: rape, incest, battering, sexual harassment, and the pornography which encourages it.
•Peace activists can develop and provide feminist nonviolent training.

There are many similarities between feminism and pacifism, and both movements need each other desperately. Both the feminist movement and the peace movement can enhance radical change by taking a hard look at the issues we take up and the methods we use. The leadership of feminist women is essential to making peace. And making peace is essential to human survival.

Dorothy Marder

Women Strike for Peace contingent of the 5th Avenue Peace Parade Spring March Against the War, April, 1972. WSP began in November, 1961 as a one day strike by "housewives and mothers" against the nuclear arms race.

Eleanora Patterson
Suffering

What begins as an effort to come to terms with an apparent contradiction between the suffering which the nonviolence movement traditionally embraces and feminists' resistance to suffering leads this writer to examine the occasions of suffering in her own life. This inquiry generates a range of questions about the distinctions to be made between suffering from a sense of worthlessness or from our wholeness, between misery and suffering, and between involuntary and voluntary suffering.

Eleanora lives in Vermont with her husband, daughter and four other housemates whose ages range from eight months to fifty years. She devotes some of her time to bookkeeping and to dreams and she is currently re-publishing a book for children. From her attic room she writes, "I look out to a garden, trees and a hillside and hear woodland, field and road sounds. I like May Sarton's image of what is most hopeful amidst the horrors in the world, that tough shoots of human imagination can break through the asphalt. I dream of tapping fully into powerful inner energies so that alone and together we can push through the asphalt of cynicism and brutality."

When I began to write this essay about suffering, I thought of misery as a synonym for suffering. I soon sensed, however, that this was misleading. Exploring suffering was not to be so easy or uninteresting. The dictionary, for one, pointed me elsewhere; suffering was defined as a way of experiencing rather than a kind of experiencing; as a verb rather than a noun. It was defined as putting up with and enduring in a situation. As I explored my own memories and shared them with others, I was led in a similar direction. Feelings of misery did not correspond with the impact of external events, but with personal conditions such as powerlessness and isolation. Situations in which people endured difficulties were not necessarily even times of misery; some, to the contrary, were moments of exhilaration.

As long as I had associated suffering with misery, I thought my talk would be to weigh the pros of the personal and political changes wrought by particular suffering against the cons of the misery of that suffering. The kinds of questions I thought I'd be dealing with included: how much misery can we ask ourselves and each other to go through, for what, and how sure do we have to be of the results?

My experience with the feminist and nonviolent movements had given me a sense that these movements and their underlying beliefs would give somewhat contradictory answers to such questions. My initial perception was that the nonviolence movement, in the footsteps of Gandhi, would speak to the necessity of considerable misery-suffering. Suffering would be advocated as necessary to achieve lasting structures based on shared power and mutual respect; creating such structures would entail considerable struggle and disappointment. Faith in the value of one's actions would be needed to get through harsh times before the hoped-for changes could show the tactics of resistance and suffering to be effective.

It was not clear whether the feminist movement would answer my questions with a unified voice. However, I felt there would certainly be many voices saying, "Enough of misery-suffering; women have been told for years to go through that at their own expense and for others' benefit." A very persuasive article I read in the early 1970's was "The Compassion Trap."[1] It spoke to women's role as the servicer and nurturer both of individuals and of society as part of misalignment in human relationships. As a result of this misalignment, men take little caretaking responsibility for others individually or on a social scale. To create a more balanced and compassionate society, women were advised, in this article, to step back from compassionate roles and push men to take them on. By this I understood that self-sacrifice on others' behalf was linked with misery-suffering, and I heard some feminists doubt that such suffering was a way to create a more respectful society. This, then, was the contradiction between nonviolence and feminism I thought I was tackling when I began to think about suffering.

I soon realized there was more to this than fascination with a mere conceptual wrangle. Suffering was a touchstone to deeply powerful experiences. Suffering took me to my childhood where the theme of illness wove in and out. I saw my sister's pain and fear wheezing in her labored, asthmatic breathing; I sensed it in the hush of gloom that hung over our household in the quarantine for her diptheria. In my own bouts with poison ivy, the misery of a body opened with yellow pus drew grimaces of repulsion from those about me. There were silences surrounding our illnesses. The sick were handed over to doctors even as the fear lay inside in welts, as questions went unformed and information was not given. There were crude healing methods; ether gases that numbed feelings while tongs removed the problem organ or while scissors cut the too-tense muscle. We woke up alone and nauseous in the dark.

I also experienced misery-suffering in feeling helpless to change another's pain. I watched my sister be taken to a doctor when she was very afraid. I saw a favorite caretaker fired when she was targeted as the diptheria carrier. I did not protest. I heard grim stories of war, of murdering, of living skeletons being tormented, of jungle fighting, of a huge bomb that killed a city. I did not know how to change any of this; thinking of it terrified me. I wondered if there were any way I could be protected from such tormentors and such tormenting, and if I could protect others as well.

I am not sure I would have moved beyond my desire to protect myself and others from misery-suffering if it had not been for the Civil Rights movement. Slowly the sit-ins, the marches and the protests penetrated into my life. First I became aware of the movement in conversations where hysterical and defensive formulations were made about what 'they' deserved. Then came TV images of barricades in front of schools, of marches and stirring songs. There was also the news of children killed in church. I started a job and found myself amidst people who had been at the march, had sung the songs and heard the speeches that had been a TV spectacle to me just the day before. Soon I began marching, singing, talking, and lobbying myself. What drew me was not the misery and righteousness of the cause; it was a power and sense of being that I had never experienced before. I felt an exhilarating sense of connection with others in standing up for more hopeful and respectful ways of living together. People made themselves vulnerable and took risks, while conveying an inner strength and compassion. During my involvement in the Civil Rights movement, I felt alive as I rarely have. This persisted even as I struggled with personal disappointments and was confused by growing dissension within the movement.

A few years later I was stopped by a man I did not know as I walked in Harlem. I had papers under my arm, and he mistook me for a welfare worker. He introduced himself as Dan and proceeded to barrage me with graphic descriptions of the injustices he, his friends and neighbors suffered daily: filth, medical services that don't respond, police brutality. He had been an ace pilot in Vietnam. This was his bitter reward. I acknowledged his list and the injustice. I tried to tell him that I had some feeling for his pain in part because of my experience in being mistreated as a woman. I did not want to compare or equate our miseries; I wanted to tell him I shared the experience of being disrespected. In his parting comment, he warned me I might be attacked as an enemy if I walked in Harlem; if so, I should tell my attackers he was my friend. They would stop.

Many feminists have spoken of making the leap from working for others' causes to working for their own as a breakthrough. These stories often have an edge of bitterness. In others' causes, many women felt devalued by the work they were allotted or the relationships they were expected to have. They experienced fighting for others' well-being as linked with not being fully respected themselves. I was much less aware of such a contradiction since my involvement boosted me to dare many things I'd never dreamed of doing before. Either way, the fight for self-respect became the spark that moved many women.

How do such recollections speak to my exploration of suffering? They have pointed me to some important distinctions. The first distinction has to do with our self-image and suffering; do we suffer out of a belief in our worthlessness or do we suffer out of a belief in our wholeness? This is a key to the quality of feelings we have as we endure (suffer) hardship. It is separate from the degree of brutality in the situation or even the intention to hurt on the part of those who oppose us. Dan protested and reached out in a brutal situation because he felt he deserved better; he did not accept that he and his neighbors were worthless and deserved horrible living conditions. As a child I accepted my misery with poison ivy passively, because I assumed I deserved it; in looking so gross, I felt I did not deserve more compassionate treatment. Dan and I had different images of the quality of treatment we deserved. They effected how we experienced our hardships. My belief that I did not deserve more empathetic help during my illness furthered my self-pity and diminished me. I imagine that Dan's speaking out against the atrocities in his situation furthered his self-respect and enlarged him even as he suffered them.

The second distinction I want to make is between voluntary and involuntary suffering. Involuntary suffering describes inevitable suffering; experiencing things we do not like and may wish were very different that happen no matter what we do. Some we may be able to change in time, usually with the help of others, but for the present we must accept their existence. Examples of things we suffer involuntarily are blizzards, traffic jams, separations and death, racism and the threat of nuclear war. No matter what we think or feel about these, we must suffer their existence. Even so, we do have important choices in facing these situations.

Voluntary suffering describes situations we actively place ourselves in knowing that it is likely our action will create stress for us given the way things usually happen and people usually behave. Examples are winter camping and deep-sea diving. More political ones include voicing controversial beliefs, interrupting degrading jokes, and participating in sit-ins and civil disobedience.

The elements of voluntary/involuntary suffering and worhthlessness/self-respect can interact in various ways. We can choose to suffer based on images of worthlessness or of dignity. An example of the first is a woman who returns to a relationship in which she is emotionally or physically assaulted because she believes that is all she deserves. An example of a choice that risks suffering based in self-respect is a woman who risks her job because she refuses to accomodate the sexual servicing expected of her. We can also suffer inevitable events and experience ourselves as worthless or as empowered in so doing. We can suffer nuclear power and its poisons and believe people are not worth a better environment, or we can suffer it and speak and act against it because we believe in treating ourselves and our planet respectfully.

Sometimes we risk suffering whether or not we act. When we let a degrading joke pass uninterrupted, we suffer degradation. When we interrupt it, we voluntarily risk suffering attack or insult, though the suffering is then based on an act of respect. So whether or not to suffer is not the issue. *How* to suffer and what choices we have are issues. What we can learn from suffering hardship and what that learning offers our personal and political transformation are issues.

Many of us have been wounded by sources of hardship, especially those based in denigrating imagery of ourselves. It can seem naive to suggest that such wounding can be a vital resource in our transformation, yet I believe it is so. Such a belief in no way validates the degrading reality, but does face that reality and uses it. The metaphor of the "wounded healer" exists in some ministerial and healing traditions. It refers to the belief that to be a healer to others, one must have experienced the wounding; in such wounding, additionally, lies the source of greatest strength.

The process of healing our wounds can be complex and painful. Very often it can mean reopening the wound and removing infection and dirt. Old pain recurs. Also there are often differing opinions about what caused the wound and what the best treatment is. The issues rarely greet us as crystal clear images that project a ready path to guide us.

As a woman, much of my wounding is rooted in experiences with sexuality, menstruation and child-bearing. I will explore some of my experiences in these areas to illuminate facets of facing and healing our wounds.

I remember being with a few other girls in my 6th grade class. We were at one girl's house, huddled in her bedroom with the shades pulled. We passed around the instructions to a tampon box, giggled and shrieked as we read from them. Words like "insert" and "vagina" brought the strongest howls. When we were at school, we would bump into each other and pull at whatever covered the other's buttocks in hopes of catching her with a telltale belt; telling the tale of her changeover. When I was older, I asked my mother why she hadn't told me the tale with different words. Why had she used "curse" rather than "menses"? Why had she not shared the wonder of this bloody bedding rather than highlighting a dreadful smell that must be hidden?

I later realized that the misery in the situation was not from the menstruation itself but from the negative imagery it conveyed to me about being a woman. The foreboding word "curse" threatened punishments; the teasing and secrecy created isolation and guilt. I felt most isolated and apart from those who shared my experience. When I first glimpsed the possibility of experiencing menstruation proudly and as a source of power, I began to sense a kinship with other women and a desire to resist and replace the culture's negative imagery with imagery that affirmed our bodies. I remember my sensing this alternative as a time of great exhilaration and energy.

I was stunned when it first occurred to me that giving birth might be a positive experience: that I might define my birth-giving and cope with the strong forces of labor. When I became pregnant many years later, I prepared myself diligently. I read, exercised and worked for new associations with painful sensations. I learned what I could about what to expect and how I might respond. In giving birth, I experienced little misery despite the considerable pressure and some intense pain.

When I spoke about childbirth as a positive experience, however, I was surprised that some women turned aside and even seemed to resent my "good news." It was then I faced the dilemma that suffering hardship can be a time of bonding or a time of feeling isolated; as with other powerful experiences, it is rarely neutral. Many women had painful and unpleasant childbirth experiences or thought they might. Many heard the advocacy of painless childbirth as an invalidation of their experience. Pain suffering, unfortunately, became a mirror of either worth or worthlessness and thus a divisive force.

I have also experienced the suffering of hardships as a divisive force in social change movements. Competition over the severity of experiences with a particular oppression has divided people and energized distrust. To find our common ground beyond the specific pains of our wounding and healing is vital. To do so, it is important to neither demean nor exalt the pain, nor to expect it to be the same in amount or form for each of us. The issue is not who is best because they have the greatest or least pain or hardship. The issue is how to create experiences out of hardship that empower and honor us and how to get the help needed to do so. so.

Another challenge to our ability to bond in suffering has to do with how we name the sources of our wounding and the remedies for healing them. Uncertainty as to cause and remedy can be harder to tolerate than the hardship itself. If we believe in the usefulness and appropriateness of our efforts, we make them without the anguish of doubting, though we may have to use great energy.

A tension sometimes arises within a woman and between women in the feminist movement as to whether heterosexual relationships inherently degrade women. In the urgency of desiring agreement on such a highly charged and critical issue, it is not surprising that women have at times treated each other disrespectfully. So that we do not undermine the grounding of mutual respect that transformation depends on, however, it matters deeply how we define our own oppression and how we resolve differences in our beliefs. I have recently heard wonderful stories of groups of women facing important differences through swirls of fear and anger, sometimes in pouring rain or in jail. They came to understandings. What was emphasized to me in the stories was not the content of the pulling together nor the rare event of unanimity: what was emphasized was the respect and listening that led somewhere not believed possible at first. There were still differences afterwards, but a grounding of respect was reached and became available to stand upon while the struggle continued. Such collective struggling is needed if we are to tease apart and reweave the elements for truly respectful ways of being and behaving.

Another crucial dynamic in the transformation from disrespect to respect is what I call the "no-yes" dynamic. This involves both saying "no" to the degrading image and intimidation that enforces degrading practices and saying "yes" to a hopeful image and respectful practices. The value of the "no" is in its call to our self-respect; it draws a bottom line against what we will allow. When powered by rage, it can provide a critical momentum to our change actions and inner work. To sustain and direct our transformation, however, we need a vision of what we are moving towards and how we want our life to be. Inspiration provides more sustaining energy than anger; it also directs us toward the beauty in others and opens us to a larger network of shared energy which can support us. Women who blocked a door to the Pentagon with a beautifully spun web symbolizing life's web were saying both "no" and "yes." Martin Luther King's "I Have a Dream" speech was a wonderful example of combining resistance with an animating vision. Gandhi spoke of having a "constructive program" and used the spinning wheel as his model and image for such constructive activity in addition to acts of civil disobedience.

In order to suffer hardships in ways that express and further mutual respect, most of us need to consciously prepare ourselves by undoing conditioning and imagery which is based on demeaning assumptions. When willpower and imagery are at odds, imagery holds sway. It takes more than "willing" a new sense of self. Preparation means rooting out demeaning images and steeping our words, thoughts and acts in respectful images of ourselves. Preparation means learning ways to shield ourselves from attacks and role playing ways of coping with blows or drawing on others' help. Preparation involves sharing in many ways: sharing stories, pain, resources, needs, risks, and differences. It means creating support structures such as affinity groups to facilitate bonding and sharing tasks. Preparation takes place in consciousness-raising groups or speak-outs where the sharing of painful experiences helps to break through the isolation of self-blame. Preparation means finding inner sources of power and nourishing and drawing on them. It means seeing our actions in relation to our vision.

What are helpful preparations in one situation, however, may not be so in another. Thus, speak-outs may not always be appropriate forms for purging self-blame; affinity groups may not always be the best way to generate support.

The power of acting to create a vision based on mutual respect is striking. When a person or a group actively chooses to confront a demeaning situation with a more respectful one, much thoughtful energy prepares the experience. People often describe such times as exhilarating. Many speak of feeling new strength and a deepening of bonds. Some of that strength is felt in realizing that one can cope with a difficult situation such as going to jail. Some of that strength is felt when old forms of intimidation no longer work; the authorities' orders no longer automatically command compliance. Some of the bonding occurs under stress when people listen to each other and allow differences, no longer having the usual pressures and separations that allow us to pass by untouched. But it is more than stress that forges bonding. Bonding is caused by acting respectfully on our own behalf; it is rooted in inspiration and hope.

In ending, I want to acknowledge some of my many teachers. One has been the prospect of death: personal death and Earth-death. I have been struggling to face both. Personal death is inevitable and not demeaning; Earth-death is not inevitable and is demeaning. I have learned I can face these stressful realities and still be hopeful, still feel respectful and still feel connected with others. In fact, as I learn to share from my vulnerability as well as from my vision, I feel more respect for and connection with others. My hope is no longer based, however, in the certainty of getting the results I dearly cherish; my hope is based in appreciating the present more fully, in sharing more openly with others, and in daring to further respectful images and practices.

Gandhi has impressed me in many ways. Because of his experimental curiosity, he acted and observed the results of his actions very carefully. I learn from him that we don't need to guarantee we will get the results we deeply cherish if we are encouraging ourselves and others to take risks on our/their own behalf; we do need to dare open ourselves to trying out forms to achieve what we cherish.

And finally, another source I draw upon when I wonder whether to act on behalf of mutual respect is the phrase "what else is there to be doing?" I have an image of Holly Near standing tall and speaking this phrase in a warm, exultant voice. She shared this as a response to her question, "why struggle against such formidable odds?" Unfortunately, bland utopianism still creeps subtly into my dreams so that images and memories of the exhilaration of daring to act respectfully are invaluable. Because of them I welcome tension as essential to happiness.

As I stop writing, I wander back over stories, conversations, and insights of people whose words and actions create the nonviolence and feminist movements. I smile in appreciation of the wisdom and willingness to struggle I have come upon in my explorations. I appreciate, too, those who took time to share their stories and perspectives with me directly. And I appreciate the challenge that writing this has given me to form and inform myself.

Dorothy Marder

Women's Pentagon Action (WPA), Nov., 1980 . . . a gesture of friendship as women doing civil disobedience wait to be arrested.

Judy Costello
Beyond Gandhi: An American Feminist's Approach to Nonviolence

Gandhi. Little wonder we still tremble in his wake.

In 1931 he arrived for tea at Buckingham Palace in a loincloth, and he observed every Monday as a day of silence (even when he appeared as a central figure at the ceremonial opening of the crucial Round Table Conference which had convened in London to consider the case for the independence of India.) And, even during a day of negotiations, press conferences and speeches, he met his daily quota of spinning two hundred yards of yarn. Indeed, he often spun as he addressed public meetings. What little cloth he wore was literally homespun (khadi), a symbolic gesture of great importance to Indian nationalists.

By all accounts, he was a seeker of Truth, a revolutionary, an unconventional character.

He brought us a gift, a finely tuned vision of Satyagraha, and demonstrated that nonviolence could be not only a viable political strategy but a way of life. But his vision was limited by his own world, his gender, and his time in history. What are we, late 20th century western-world feminists, to make of his gift? Do we swallow it whole or build on it to make it our own? What parts of his vision leave us out or impede the work of our lives?

This essay, like the one which follows it, is one woman's attempt to come to terms with her understanding of Gandhi's life, her interpretation of his teachings. She challenges what she sees to be the contradictions between his words and his actions. She calls him on his apparent inconsistencies. And she concludes that, while men should learn more of Gandhi's teachings, women should unlearn some of them.

Judy is a lesbian feminist who started doing political work as a Catholic Worker in 1975. She's been involved in Movement for a New Society since 1977, first in a collective in Omaha doing anti-militarism work, then in organizing national and regional MNS gatherings. She has been involved in the writing, editing and layout of leaflets about a wide variety of issues and has published small Catholic Worker and feminist publications. She is hoping to help start a women's print shop in Minneapolis within the next year.

An excerpt from my journal while I was living at a Catholic Worker House of Hospitality (June '75): "Eddie came in at lunch time and he was sober. He said he'd play a game of checkers with me after eating. But while he was in line for seconds, someone made a smart remark to him, and he stormed out. At suppertime I was in charge of the door. We've started to lock the door before supper and let people in one at a time in order to screen out those who are drunk. They've caused too much violence in the house. If they stick around we feed them outside. Well, tonight Eddie came back—drunk. Somehow he got inside but I stopped him and said he would have to leave because he was drunk. Eddie is a big man. People on the street are afraid of him, especially when he's drunk. He told me he was sober as he stumbled into the garbage cans. I asked him to leave again. He argued with me. I felt the whole room full of people watching me. If I allowed Eddie to take advantage of me in this instance, others would try. I asked if he would leave if I got him a sandwich, but when I turned to get it, he sat down and started an argument. He began threatening to beat up the other fellow. I tried every approach I could think of to get him to leave—joking, being very firm and expressing my anger, talking to him as a friend. I'm not sure what worked—maybe the accumulated harassment, but he finally left. He came back later to apologize."

I'm remembering this incident from my days as a Catholic Worker, as I sit down to write about wimyn and nonviolence. I remember too that when one of the male Workers was faced with a similar situation he settled the problem quickly by threatening to beat up the person.

Probably neither my approach nor his would meet Gandhi's guidelines of nonviolence, but mine meets my criteria for feminist nonviolence: recognizing my right to define who enters my space, feeling my anger and seeing it as an indication that something in my environment is wrong and needs to be changed, remaining firm in my will. I would now add being willing and ready to defend myself against attack, if need be, as consistent with my feminist understanding of nonviolence. How is all this different from Gandhian nonviolence?

Gandhi's program of nonviolence included "satyagraha"—the adherence to truth; "ahimsa"—action based on the refusal to do harm, involving the love and respect for the personhood of the enemy; "non-cooperation"—action based on the belief that all power is kept intact through cooperation and can be broken by the refusal of people to be subjected any longer; and "civil disobedience"—the breaking of a perceived "unjust" law and the willingness to go to jail for this belief. Gandhi confronted injustice with these political strategies and moral principles based on his religious understanding and found them to be powerful and effective.

My feminism has drawn me to Gandhi's philosophy of nonviolence. In answering the question, "What kind of change in society do wimyn want?," I believe most would say that we do not need a mere reversal of power with wimyn on the top. Male power has needed underlings—some who can be seen as less valuable than the holders of power, who therefore can be exploited, abused or killed if they get in the way. Men have relied on violence and have called it "law and order." But their violence, in the various disguises of justice, has not brought peace. There has been no "war to end all war." Wimyn, who are the child-bearers and nurturers of society, would have to shut down large parts of themselves to be able to take on this kind of power that demands they shoot down other wimyn's daughters and sons.

Gandhi noted that "we found the general work of mankind is being carried on from day to day by the masses of people acting in a harmony as if by instinct. If they were instinctively violent, the world would end in no time."[1] What Gandhi neglected to note here is that wimyn are the ones who carry that instinct to build harmony and who see all the world's people as connected. Wimyn are the ones who have picked up the pieces and kept things going, neglecting our own needs for nurturing and respect.

I believe that at this time, men and wimyn need to approach nonviolence differently. Gandhi would have us "hate the sin, but love the sinner," which is advice wimyn know all too well. But this advice to us has been twisted so that we feel more responsible for loving the sinner than we do for loving ourselves. Wimyn frequently make excuses for their abusers — "Maybe I shouldn't be mad, after all he didn't really mean it." Until we take care of our own needs, and until more men cultivate an instinct to nurture, our world will continue to move closer and closer to disaster. Men could stand to learn more of Gandhi's "ahimsa"—"For we are all tarred with the same brush, and are children of one and the same Creator, and as such the divine powers within us are infinite. To slight a single human being is to slight those divine powers, and thus to harm not only that being but with him the whole world."[2]

Wimyn need to unlearn the ways this kind of advice has been used to keep us responsible for the world, giving men the freedom to plunge into business and war without thought for morality. The anger of wimyn about this situation is a shock to men who expect to find us passively or fearfully accepting it. It is the first stage of our resistance and the very thing needed to make abusive men stop and think about what they are doing. Wimyn's anger, whether or not it is clearly directed at the sin as Gandhi would have it, is a significant step in interrupting an old pattern. Our resistance to the pattern of dominance and submission is a radical step in ending the cycle of violence in this society.

Gandhi espoused suffering and self-sacrifice as the essence of nonviolence. For wimyn, self-love is what is called for. Most of us know all about self-sacrifice and do not find it powerful. People who are in the category of aware "oppressors" are the ones who need to learn about self-sacrifice. We wimyn and other oppressed groups need to learn to love and value ourselves. We too have a right to be nurtured and no one has the right to abuse us—mentally, sexually, physically or emotionally. Oppressed people who know their own strength can choose when they want to be self-sacrificing or nurturing.

My current prescription for myself in gaining a clearer understanding of nonviolence is to take self-defense classes. I want the option of being able to use force so that the times when I don't use it are all more powerful. Learning in a practice session to look a would-be attacker in the face without smiling, feeling my anger and my right to my body and space, and then learning to think and breathe enough to respond, is something I don't think can be learned any other way. Knowing that I have an option to fight makes me feel more confident about trying other methods. For my men friends I prescribe that they learn how to nurture each other by forming support groups. Learning about sexism means learning to see the violence that is committed against half of the human race.

I respect Gandhi's philosophy and believe he has much to teach Americans—especially men. Some of his personal actions, however, are not consistent with my understanding of nonviolence. Wimyn see the personal as political. When we look at nonviolence theory we also look at the personal lives of those who preach it. Although Gandhi once said, "Of all the evils of men . . . none is as degrading as his abuse of the . . . female sex,"[3] he wasn't consistent with this belief in his personal life.

Looking at Gandhi I see that he did not renounce his male privilege. He traveled without his family whenever he felt like it, leaving his children to the care of his wife. He sometimes ignored his family's need for security, for attention and for physical affection. He took advantage of his authority as head of the household and as decision-maker. For example, after 23 years of marriage to

Kasturbai, Gandhi announced to her that he was becoming celibate. He said, "I took the vow of celibacy in 1906. I had not shared my thoughts with my wife until then." Of his lack of communication with his wife about decisions which affected both of them, he said, "It is likely that many of my decisions have not had her approval even today. We never discuss them, I see no good in discussing them. For she was educated neither by her parents, nor by me . . . But she is blessed with one great quality to a very considerable degree, a quality which most Hindu wives possess in some measure. And it is this; willingly or unwillingly . . . she has considered herself blessed in following my footsteps and has never stood in the way of my endeavour to lead a life of restraint."[4] Wimyn, generally, are more sensitive to the need for balance between body and mind, personal and political. If Gandhi had heeded more of the truth Kasturbai had to offer, he might have learned that our bodies are gifts, not hindrances.

William Shirer, in his book *Gandhi: A Memoir,* points out, "There were the contradictions in the man which often baffled one, and sometimes they were disturbing to all who revered him, as when in the last years of life, when he was in his late seventies, he took pretty young women to bed with him."[5] Gandhi, along with men of every culture, occasionally saw wimyn as objects for his needs. In this case, he explained his practice of lying down with naked wimyn, as a way to keep warm and a way to test his vow of celibacy. Gandhi said, "My meaning of brahmacharya (the vow of celibacy) is this: 'One . . . who by constant attendance upon God, has become . . . capable of lying naked with naked women, however beautiful they may be, without being in any manner whatsoever sexually excited.' "[6] Gandhi describes it as his "darkest hour" when "(I) suddenly felt I wanted to see a woman."[7]

Gandhi didn't repudiate the pattern of dominant and submissive roles set up for men and wimyn, although this power structure is a basic model for violence. Other leftist men who are followers of Gandhian nonviolence are similarly blind to the struggles of wimyn. But wimyn are raped daily, wimyn are battered, wimyn fear going out at night. Wimyn are portrayed in the media as victims and as objects for men's pleasure. And men play the role of terrorist and saviour to wimyn. They abuse their wives and then beat up other men who make passes at "their" wimyn. Leftist men who don't renounce the violence that comes with their male privilege aren't our allies until they figure out their error.

I believe in non-cooperation and civil disobedience, but in practice I have seen men use these tools as weapons—seeing who can suffer the most, counting up jail records, feeding on the glory of being able to suffer more. They know that a womyn behind the scenes is answering the mail or taking care of children or making sure there is something for him to come home to. Wimyn aren't as ready to go to jail because they often have families to care for and other people who need them. Even in the midst of the worst political strife wimyn carry on—feeding the children, caring for the elderly, healing the sick.

Though Gandhi frequently was sexist in his failure to consider the humanity of the wimyn around him, he also glimpsed their importance in revolutionary movements. Wimyn participated fully in his civil disobedience campaigns and of this he said, "They are as brave as men. You have no idea how what they did and suffered increased my faith in our people. The awakening of our women has helped mightily to awaken India. We cannot achieve freedom without them."[8] He also said in an article for *Young India,* "If by strength is meant moral power, then woman is immeasurably man's superior . . . If nonviolence is the law of our being, the future is with women."[9]

Gandhi is an important figure for those committed to nonviolence. But looking beyond him takes us into the lives of wimyn for a broader definition of nonviolence. We have powers we haven't even begun to tap . . . those powers that come from our own psyche, our spirit, our connectedness with others.

Lynne Shivers
An Open Letter to Gandhi

"Gandhi, every time I read your writings, you turn my head around." In this open letter, Lynne Shivers carefully re-examines Gandhi's views on women's issues in order that those of us in the feminist/nonviolence movement can have an accurate perception of Gandhi's ideas and not argue about rumors and myths. She writes, "I think Gandhi is a profound thinker in many areas. People who conclude easily he was unrealistic have not read him closely." While Lynne concedes that several of Gandhi's stands seem to be unacceptable to late 20th century U.S. feminists, by and large she is forced to conclude that Gandhi's record on women's issues was remarkable for his circumstances and that if we read him carefully, he still has a lot to teach us. Whether or not we agree with her conclusion, there is no doubt that we can learn much from the wealth of research and knowledge Lynne has to offer about Gandhi. Lynne uses the Indian system of dating when she cites her sources of information: day, month, year, and writes that the best source of information and quotations came from the book Women and Social Injustice, *by M.K. Gandhi, published by the Navajivan Press, India, 1947. This is, unfortunately, not widely available.*

Lynne has worked on the staff of the Hiroshima Friendship Center, London Friends Peace Committee and Friends Peace Committee in Philadelphia. She helped to train 4,000 marshals for the Mobilization against the War demonstration in Washington in 1969, a project she calls pivotal in her political education. In 1970 she made her first visit to Northern Ireland where she has visited many times since. She has also worked on Middle East issues, and in 1980 was one of 49 Americans who went to Iran at the invitation of the students holding the hostages. Writing has increasingly become a center of Lynne's energy and thinking.

Lynne writes, "Nonviolence training is important because it empowers us and forces us to consider means and ends and because it decentralizes power. Most important, however, it strengthens the movement for social change. Feminism remains as important as nonviolence in my thinking. It is my concern to work out any apparent contradictions since I think that one without the other will be unsuccessful. I insist on the double commitments to personal and political, means and ends, private and public, community and world, music and chores, and watching the tide come."

The Life Center/Movement for a New Society in Philadelphia has been Lynne's political home, "with visiting rights to other groups and activities."

Dear Mohandas Gandhi,

Since I joined the peace movement in 1966, I have read books and articles by and about you, and I have been tremendously inspired by your thinking. You have examined the intricate and complex strands of nonviolence theory and how the threads are related to each other. I am especially inspired and strengthened to see how you took the concept of nonviolent action and experimentally applied it on the mass social scale to achieve the independence of India. Of course, hundreds of groups and societies used the power of nonviolent action to create social changes before you. But I think one of your main contributions was that you were conscious about that process and shared your thinking with others.

Up to now, my learning from you has primarily dealt with applying nonviolence concepts to the political change process. But now I want to examine your thinking about women's rights. You do not have a good reputation among people in the U.S. social change movement. I think this is partly because there are problems to learning exactly what you thought. The first problem is the length of time that has passed from the 1920's and '30's when you did your most energetic thinking about these issues, to now. Some new perspectives have developed since then about women's rights. It is not fair, of course, to judge you from today's vantage point but then again, it is hard not to. In some ways, it is impossible to remove ourselves from the limits of our time.

The second problem is even more difficult, perhaps, since the American culture remains distant from the Indian culture; it is not possible to remove the differences even if we wanted to! Basic differences in values in the United States and India create very different ways of life and institutions.

The third problem is that you wrote so much! You did little systematic writing, apart from your *Autobiography* and the account of the time you worked in South Africa. You mainly wrote for weekly newspapers which served the independence movement. And like anyone else, your thinking changed over thirty years from the time, in 1915, when you returned to India for good. So there is a fair amount of sorting and sifting that we have to do to discover your thinking on women's issues.

Mohandas, just where did you stand on equality, political power, access to all jobs, birth control, and other issues that concern women today? After re-reading many of your essays, I think that you can be proud of your stand on a great many issues dealing with women's rights. You can still teach us some important lessons. Your stands against child marriage, enforced widowhood, the dowry system, sati (a wife's suicide at the husband's funeral), and wife beating, were all important. However there are a few issues that I find you ambivalent about. Your call for two separate campaigns for women, and your belief that women are capable of greater self-sacrifice than are men, are both troubling to me. More crucially perhaps, you never seemed to grasp women's perspective on birth control and rape. You had your own unique ideas about sexuality, spirituality and the nature of power which derived from the way these played out in your life.

Your Support of Women's Issues

In spite of the problems, it is exciting to read your writing. You were clear and passionate about many issues that are important to women! Throughout your life you were passionately opposed to child marriages, partly, no doubt, since you and your wife, Kasturbai, were forced to marry when you were both only 13 years old. Later on, you discouraged marriage before the age of 18. In addition, you were equally strongly opposed to enforced widowhood, the Indian tradition which held that once the husband died, the wife never remarried. (Fortunately this custom is less common today, especially in the cities.) You insisted, especially for people who married as children, that widows had the right to remarry, otherwise a women would not even have the option of marrying as an adult.

You also spoke against the custom of sati, that is the ancient tradition of a wife proving her selfless devotion to her husband by her self-immolation on his funeral pyre. You described it as "barbarous" and wrote that the practice "had its origin in superstitious ignorance and the blind egotism of man." (*Young India*, 21-5-31) Today, the custom of sati is, happily, prohibited, although it is reported occasionally in Indian newspapers.

Closely tied to this is your rejection of the dowry system that requires the bride's family to provide finances. The dowry system is part of the patriarchal thinking that a bride is the husband's possession, and I am glad you opposed it. In addition, you linked it with classism and the caste system. Of course the dowry system continues. Your opposition to the caste system, and especially to how harijan ("Untouchables") were treated seems intimately connected with your support of women's equality.

In a culture and time when men were more valued than women, you wrote, "I make no distinction between son and daughter. Such distinction is in my opinion invidious and wrong. The birth of a son or a daughter should be welcome alike." (*Harijan,*5-6-37) You wrote, "Remember your wife is not your property any more than you are hers." (*Harijan,* 13-4-40) In your weekly column, you made an issue of wife beating, when you contested a court ruling which recognized the legal right of a husband to beat his wife. *(Harijan, 3-10-36)*

Purdah, the custom of enforced segregation and seclusion of women, meant that women would sit behind a wall or veil at a public meeting, so that they would not be visible. Forms of the practice vary widely, and since it is a social custom, it dies slowly. In 1927, you wrote against the purdah, calling it a "barbarous custom" which had become "totally useless and was doing incalculable harm to the country." (*Young India,* 3-2-27)

Personally, I like the life-style issue you raised the same year, when you exhorted women not to wear jewelry, often part of the dowry. You wrote, "If you want to play your part in the world's affairs, you must refuse to deck yourselves for pleasing man....Refuse to be slaves of your own whims and fancies and the slaves of men." (*Young India,* 8-12-27) Some Indians remember the anecdote that one time you were pleading with women not to wear jewelry, and women from the audience spontaneously came up and took off their jewels! And local princes joined them!

I also find it comforting that you insisted that men, as much as women, be responsible for spinning. This had to do with your encouragement to all Indians to produce khadi, home-spun cloth, in order to cut the Indian economic dependence on British imported cloth. As early as 1925, you wrote, "It is contrary to say that any vocation is exclusively reserved for one sex only." You surely were way ahead of not only your culture but also your time!

You proposed an action that I wish Western Christian churches today would take up, if they are serious about supporting the women's movement. In 1936, you noted religious texts which put women down. For example: "Women should follow the word of their husbands. This is their highest duty." (*Yajnavalkya,* 1-18) Your response was this: "It is sad to think that the Smritis contain texts which can command no respect from men. The question arises as to what to do with the Smritis texts that are repugnant to the moral sense. There should, therefore, be some authoritative body that would revise all that passes under the name of scriptures, expurgate all the texts that have no moral value or are contrary to the fundamentals of religion and morality, and present such an edition." *(Harijan,* 28-11-36*)* If only our churches would be that brave!

Where You Were Ambivalent About Women's Issues

There are two areas where it seems your thinking was ambivalent, and I would like to discuss them with you. A number of women in the Indian independence movement seemed impatient to be more involved at the time of the 1930 Salt March. You did not encourage or discourage women from taking part, and many thousands did. What is a little troubling to me is that you called upon women to take up two campaigns that would be theirs exclusively; men would not take part in them. Those issues were the boycott of foreign cloth and the challenge of drunkenness in Indian culture. You wrote that in 1921, the picketing of foreign cloth shops and liquor stores by men had ended in violence. You went on:

> *If a real impression is to be created, picketing must be resumed. If it remains peaceful to the end, it will be the quickest way of educating the people concerned. Prohibition of intoxicating liquors and drugs and boycott of foreign cloth have ultimately to be by law. But the law will not come till pressure below is felt in no uncertain manner. Drink and drugs sap the moral well-being of those who are given to the habit. Foreign cloth undermines the economic foundations of the nation and throws millions out of employment. The distress in each case is felt in the home and therefore by the women...Let the women of India take up these two activities, specialize in them; they would contribute more than men to national freedom.*

I feel uneasy about your decision here. On one hand, these issues *seem* to be less important aspects of the main struggle for political independence, (the Salt March was one of many events in that struggle). The campaigns you called for did encourage women to be less involved in that mainstream. Another part of my uneasiness rests with the hint of sex role stereotyping. Did you ask women to address the issues of cloth and alcoholism because they are typically associated with women's roles and housewifely duties?

On the other hand you were offering women organizing jobs that were in their self-interest; anyone who has lived around alcoholics knows alcoholism is an important issue. You always insisted that Indian independence rested on two things: the Indian people's willingness to take on responsibilities as well as British withdrawal. And, both cloth and liquor were economic issues. It was important to the strengthening Indian economy to keep that income in the country rather than see it disappear into the British treasury.

There are numerous advantages, too, to having separate women's actions, as any who have participated in them know. What a sense of exuberance and power the participants experience! This must have been true for Indian women fifty years ago as well. And, of course, these actions gave an opportunity to organize women across class and caste lines, clearly important. We forget that you were creating a mass movement, larger than the U.S. anti-war movement during the Vietnam War. I realize now that it was important to identify issues that women of all stations and situations could immediately relate to.

You did not forbid women to participate in the other campaigns, and, indeed, many of those who led them were women. You insisted earlier that men as well as women spin and weave khadi as the constructive program, that is, the positive side to saying no to British cloth. In 1921, the All India Congress Committee sponsored a special demonstration, climaxing a campaign, several months long, of boycotting British cloth. People ceremoniously set fire to costly saris and other expensive dresses made with foreign cloth. I wish I could have been there!

The second ambivalence has to do with your insistence that women are capable of greater self-sacrifice than men are. In 1930, you wrote:

> *In this non-violent warfare their (i.e., women's) contribution should be much greater than men's. To call women the weaker sex is libel; it is man's injustice to woman. If by strength is meant brute strength, then indeed is woman less brute than man. If by strength is meant moral power, then woman is immeasurably man's superior. Has she not greater intuition, is she not more self-sacrificing, has she not greater powers of endurance, has she not greater courage? Without her man could not be. If nonviolence is the law of our being, the future is with woman.*
>
> *(Young India, 10-4-30)*

Two years later, you wrote, in response to the question how women in Europe might help in fighting militarism:

> *If only women will forget that they belong to the weaker sex. I have no doubt you can do infinitely more than men against war....I do not know if I have the courage to give the message...that you asked for. If I am to do so without incurring their wrath, I would direct their steps to the women of India who rose in one mass last year, and I really believe that, if Europe will drink in the lesson of nonviolence, it will do so through its women. Woman, I hold, is the personification of self-sacrifice, but unfortunately today she does not realize what a tremendous advantage she has over man. As Tolstoy used to say they are laboring under the hypnotic influence of man. If they would realize the strength of nonviolence, they would not consent to be called the weaker sex.*
>
> (*Young India,* 14-1-32)

In 1938, you wrote this:

> . . . *woman is more fitted than man to make explorations and take bolder action in ahimsa* [non-injury]. *For the courage of self-sacrifice woman is any day superior to man, as I believe man is to woman for the courage of the brute.*

This is where a lot of confusion sets in since to you self-sacrifice is an important component in nonviolent resistance. To many women, however, self-sacrifice means giving in to other people's priorities and not being able to act on one's own values, thus, never being a full person. Here is where nonviolence and feminism seem to be contradictory; yet, I believe on closer analysis, they are not.

You defined nonviolence as having three components: (1) Ahimsa, or non-injury. You meant deliberately intending not to injure the opponent, either physically or emotionally; (2) Adherence to Truth. By this you meant being open to new information, admitting when the opponent is right, and being willing to compromise on lesser issues; and (3) Willingness to take on unearned suffering in order to interfere in the spiral of violence, either as direct physical brutality or institutional structural violence on others. Joan Bondurant, a writer, and scholar of your political philosophy, has properly identified this last component as the most difficult for Westerners to understand, especially when we as women feel that we have been victims of so much violence, both direct and indirect.

I am clear, Mohandas, that you would never counsel women to give up their values and priorities for the sake of other people. I am sure you would call this timidity and fear; you would insist that women not cooperate with that sort of compromise. Indeed, you once wrote, "The first principle of non-violent action is that of non-cooperation with everything humiliating." I am equally clear that you would insist that nonviolence occasionally requires that we break through the spiral of violence by momentarily accepting to be the target of violence, rather than impose it upon others. Examples of such sacrifices might be dealing with tax resistance (which I have always thought women should take on in greater numbers, since men bear the suffering of draft resistance), jail (people who have served time know this is a real sacrifice), or the various other pressures and hurts that movement work can mean (alienation from society, loneliness, poverty, and harassment, to name a few).

To women, the term "self-sacrifice" too easily sounds as though it means passivity. To you, Mohandas, I think "self-sacrifice" meant having a compassionate heart. You thought that women instinctively understand this third component of nonviolence so much more than men do.

You wrote that women have five qualities superior to men: greater moral power, greater intuition, more aptitude for self-sacrifice, greater power of endurance, and greater courage. This is the point when the discussion breaks up into an infinite number of views. My response is, "You may well be right!" But how else can we answer, since our response is based on our own experience? There are two parts to the issue of sacrifice, I think. The first (which might be asked by feminists) asks, "Am I free to make a sacrifice of my own choice, or am I forced to make a sacrifice that men decide for me?" I insist that women be free to make their own choice, of course. The second part of the issue of sacrifice (which might be raised by a nonviolent activist) is that some groups in the feminist movement do not accept the concept of sacrifice in the struggle for social change. These issues around sacrifice need to be seen as important, and they need to be disscussed openly and widely.

Where You Do Not Support Women's Issues

The two issues around which I think you never clearly understood women's perspectives are birth control and rape. In 1936, Margaret Sanger visited India, hoping to introduce birth control there, and she wanted to get your approval. Throughout your life, you remained opposed to all artificial means of birth control. Margaret Sanger did not persuade you otherwise. As I understand it, you thought that the only natural birth control method was abstinence. And you practiced what you preached, since you upheld "brahmacharya," deliberate denial of sexual activity ("observance of chastity in quest for God"), from 1899, when you were 30, for the rest of your life.

At this point, most Western women (as well as men!) throw up their hands in despair at ever being able to understand you. But then again, few people, women or men, Westerners or whatever, are able to follow you at this point. To you, spirituality and purity were important values, and you often wrote about them using language unique to you and strange to us. Some people criticize you for having made the vow of brahmacharya after Kasturbai had four sons, but I think that is unfair. It takes a little searching into your thinking and life to understand your brahmacharya position. You thought that sexual abstinence was deeply related to dominance and power over yourself and events. This is a deep theme in Indian legend and codes of conduct. One of these codes states, "Chastity is the highest law." According to one of your biographers, Robert Payne, you thought that chastity is power. Thus, we see that your position on birth control is not identical with what is classed as "right wing" in the U.S. now; you do not oppose birth control for "pro-life" reasons. At one point, you wrote that you did not blame women for lack of discipline regarding sexual activity: "I blame the men. Men have legislated against them. Man has regarded woman as his tool....I do not suppose that all husbands are brutes and if women only know how to resist them all will be well. I have been able to teach women who have come in contact with me how to resist their husbands. The real problem is that many do not want to resist them."

What many people do not know about you is that you had a particularly painful sexual experience which strongly molded your thinking about sexuality. You recounted in your *Autobiography* that you and Kasturbai were making love when your father died, and you were only 16 at the time. You felt anguished and guilty and wrote that if only you had used restraint, you would have held your father when he died. It must have felt as though you were willfully disobeying Indian tradition by not showing the proper respect that a son should pay his father—especially when he was dying. It is clear to me and others that your guilt from this experience shaped your thinking about sexual activity, not only for yourself, but as general rules of conduct for humanity. I think the proper question to raise is not whether it is logical to develop general principles based on painful experiences (though that is a valid question). I am more interested in whether or not your thinking is valid.

You had three reasons for opposing birth control: you believed that sex should be only a means for procreation; you opposed all forms of artificiality; and you believed that sexual activity and spiritual power are related. I agree with some of your thinking. If the world were more rational about physical touching and the expression of tenderness, I believe sexual intimacy would (and should) be limited only to procreation. But since we have a long way to go in this regard, I think it is unlikely that people will limit sexual activity in this way. Your argument around artificial control seems hopelessly archaic. But, numerous artificial birth control methods which use physical devices or chemicals have been declared dangerous with long-term use. Thus, your thinking may be more sensible than at first glance. I am not saying that only natural birth control methods are acceptable: I am only saying that there is some truth in what you wrote. I think we still need to search for artificial birth control means which are completely safe. I do not think, however, that there is much real evidence to support your third argument that chastity preserves power. Catholic orders and religious sects have claimed this through the centuries, I know. Abstinence may have the effect of redirecting spiritual power for some people. But I think that the issue is based on unique, individual experiences and that it is not possible to develop a general principle.

I would see you as a closer ally of the women's movement if you had recognized how women's lives are often controlled and narrowed when children are born because society places the responsibility for raising children with the mother. As a Western woman, I am aware that I may not completely understand how my Third World sisters see children and motherhood. But I am aware that your refusal to accept artificial birth control seems to be related to the value of large families in Third World countries today.

If your writings about birth control are difficult to understand, your comments about rape are even more complex. In 1942 you wrote:

> *The main thing is for women to know how to be fearless. However beastly the man, he will bow in shame before the flame of her dazzling purity. There are examples of women who have thus defended themselves. I therefore recommend women to cultivate this courage. They will become wholly fearless if they can and cease to tremble as they do today at the mere thought of assaults. But such faith or courage can-*

not be acquired in a day. When a woman is assaulted, her primary duty is self-protection. She is at liberty to employ every method or means that comes to her mind in order to defend her honour. God has given her nails and teeth. She must use them with all her strength and, if need be, die in the effort. *(Harijan, 1-3-42)*

In 1938 you wrote:

But if they i.e., women find that their very chastity is in danger of being violated, they must develop courage enough to die rather than yield to the brute in man. It has been suggested that a girl who is gagged or bound so as to make her powerless even for struggling cannot die as easily as I seem to think. I venture to assert that a girl who has the will to resist can burst all the bonds that may have been used to render her powerless. The resolute will gives her the strength to die. But this heroism is possible only for those who have trained themselves for it. *(Harijan, 31-12-38)*

A few years later, your secretary, Pyarelal, wrote that:

His [i.e., Gandhi's] *advice to them* [women] *to commit suicide* [referring to the above quotation] *rather than allow themselves to be dishonoured has been much misunderstood. They could use a dagger for self-defense if they wished to. But a dagger was of no use against overwhelming odds. He had advised them to take poison and end their lives rather than submit to dishonour. Their very preparedness should make them brave. No one could dishonour a woman who was fearless of death. They had two ways of self-defense—to kill and be killed or to die without killing. He could teach them the latter, not the former. Above all he wanted them to be fearless. There was no sin like cowardice!"* *(Harijan, 3-11-46)*

Finally, in 1947, you were asked what a woman should do if attacked. This, in part, was your answer:

If there are women who when assailed cannot resist themselves without arms, they do not need to be advised to carry arms. They will do so. There is something wrong in this constant enquiry as to whether or not to bear arms or not. People have to learn to naturally be independent. If they will remember the central teaching, namely, that the real effective resistance lies in nonviolence, they will model their conduct accordingly. And that is what the world has been doing although unthinkingly. Since it is not the highest courage, namely, courage born of nonviolence, it arms itself even unto the atom bomb. Those who do not see in it

> *the futility of violence will naturally arm themselves to the best of their ability.*
>
> *A woman would most certainly take her own life rather than surrender. In other words, surrender has no room in my plan of life.* *(Harijan, 9-2-41)*

No wonder people have misunderstood your thinking around rape prevention! You applied to the discussion the same themes that were always important to you: nonviolence and fearlessness. And people understand these concepts just as poorly here as anywhere else you applied them.

You never meant nonviolence to mean passivity. (The only people who do are those who define nonviolence as non-resistance, and they are a very small minority, usually not active in the U.S. social change movement.) You always understood nonviolence to be militant and active, and this applied to rape prevention, especially when adding fearlessness to the discussion. I thoroughly agree that a militant nonviolent approach to rape assaults, combined with combating the paralyzing dynamic of fear, goes a long way to empowering women.

It probably comes as a surprise to modern readers that you wrote that a woman can use any method of defense.

However, people begin to call you crazy when you write about an assailant bowing "in shame" before the flame of her dazzling purity. I roll my eyes in amazement at your apparent naivete here! Yes, it is true that women have successfully escaped injury or death by skillful and clever nonviolent resistance to assaults. And, to the uninitiated, these stories are hard to believe. But your use of the phrase "bow in shame" makes me think you connected rape with the purity-of-women issue, which was discussed earlier in this letter.

Some people really give up on you when you talk about a woman taking her own life rather than surrendering. I am sure that honor and dying meant different things to you than to most people. But I do not agree that it is better to be dead than raped. I am sure that most women concur with me. I think, again, you are hung up on seeing women as virtue and, as you yourself wrote, "the embodiment of self-sacrifice." It is confusing to us also, to see you write about woman as self-sacrifice and women's resistance to rape. The terms seem to contradict.

I need to remind myself as well as my sisters that just because we disagree with you on this basic point does not mean we should dismiss you entirely. Plenty of people think clearly in one area and not so well in another. But we do not need to write you off because you do not have the answers on everything. That smacks too much of hero worship.

In summary, there were some women's issues that you whole-heartedly supported. You opposed child marriages, enforced widowhood, the custom of sati, and the dowry system. You always spoke on behalf of the harijan, the Untouchables. You opposed purdah. You encouraged women not to wear jewelry; you insisted that men, as well as women, be responsible for spinning. Yet, there were two areas where I found you ambivalent: you encouraged women to take up two special campaigns, and you thought that women are capable of greater self-sacrifice than men are. Where you seem not to support women's issues are on birth control and rape.

There were a lot of issues I wanted to take up with you, and we have covered most of them. In closing, a few thoughts come to mind. So what if you took a certain position on an issue? We should not expect you to be the final determiner of what is correct in the area of nonviolence. In fact, you often insisted to your followers in India not to make you out to be a saint.

Throughout this essay, I have mainly used your writings to understand where you stood on women's issues. Another valid way of examining your point of view is to look at your relationships with women. You have a poor reputation about how you treated your wife, Kasturbai, but I think most of us have very little information about that. Sishila Nayyar, an M.D. who treated you, wrote a brief biography of Kasturbai. She wrote that there was a profound and close love between you and your wife. Another biographer, Payne, recounts that at one time you were about to do another stint in jail, and that you said to Kasturbai, "You may come with me if you cannot bear to be without me." The truth was, you could not bear to be without her. After being married for 62 years, you went into a deep decline when Kasturbai died in 1944. You wrote later on that you had hoped to die before her.

Mohandas, I did not know you well at all until I learned how you related on a personal basis with Madelaine Slade, better known as Mirabehn. She was the daughter of a British navy admiral, and she came to work in the India independence movement in 1927. She published your letters to her, written over twenty years. One letter is worth quoting here since it shows you as a loving and vulnerable person, writing to someone you cared for:

> *I want you to be a perfect woman. I want you to shed all angularities. All unnecessary reserve must go. Without be-*

ing a burden on people with whom we come in contact, we must get the things we need from them. We must feel at one with all. And I have discovered that we never give without receiving consciously or unconsciously. There is a reserve that I want us all to have. But that reserve must be a fruit of self-denial, not sensitiveness. Yours is due to sensitiveness. This must go. Do throw off the nervousness. This is how I would grow if I were you. But you must grow along your own lines. You will, therefore, reject all I have said in this, that does not appeal to your heart or your head. You must retain your individuality at all cost. Resist me if you must. For, I may judge you wrongly in spite of all my love for you. I do not want you to impute infallibility to me.

With love, Yours,

Bapu

(You closed with the term of endearment used by your close friends, the term you used with all the movement leaders, roughly meaning "Papa.") Another letter written in 1940 shows similar tenderness and caring:

I was wondering why I had not heard from you for so long. Anything beyond a week will be too long for me. Though your descriptive letters are welcome (they are your speciality), a post card when you have time would be enough.

Do I take it that you have left Oel for good? I don't mind if you have. I want you to feel free and make yourself happy. Your description of your new place is attractive, but I do not know that I shall ever reach there. There is no prospect of my going to Simla. Though Sevagram is a furnace just now, I feel like not moving at all. The work before me takes up all my time.

Love,

Bapu

Gandhi, every time I read your writings, you turn my head around! I want to write you off as a crazy old man who did not understand women's issues at all. Yet, when I take the time to study your essays carefully, I conclude that I need to do more thinking about the issues. If we look carefully enough, you still have some things to teach us.

Love,

Lynne

Lisa Leghorn
The Economic Roots of the Violent Male Culture

In this essay, Lisa presents the argument that men's common culture around the globe is economically rooted in the separate male and female work spheres of the patriarchal family. The word "family," incidentally, is from the Roman "famulus" meaning a household of servants. The separation which results from men's activity being outside the home confuses little boys who seek male role identification and isolates adult men from involvement in birthing and nurturing. Only the institutionalizing of female values will bring about the new society and undo the harm done by centuries of patriarchal blundering currently exemplified by the Reagan administration's budget.

Lisa has been active in the feminist movement since 1968, writing, lecturing, teaching and community organizing. Very active in the movement to end violence against women, she helped start Transition House, a shelter for battered women in Massachusetts, and co-founded Aegis: A Magazine on Ending Violence Against Women. *She has co-authored a number of publications, the most extensive being* Woman's Worth: Sexual Economics and the World of Women, *which she wrote with Katherine Parker (Boston: Routledge & Kegan Paul, 1981).*

Violence, in this country and around the world, has historically been used to sustain economic exploitation. By redefining economics from a feminist perspective, we can clarify the economic roots of the domination ethic in the violent male culture, illustrating the links between sexism, militarism, racism, economic exploitation and over-development.

In looking at the economics of women's lives from women's perspectives, we must include a wide variety of interactions and duties not considered by most economists to have economic value or purpose, yet which sustain every economic system the world over. Women's economic sphere consists largely of unpaid work, from housework and childcare to subsistence agriculture and fishing. It also includes much of what economists call "informal" work, from market trading and prostitution to domestic work in other people's homes. This "informal" work of women, disguised as "housewifery" in most economic and census reports, comprises 4/5 of the world's unpaid work hours. When combined with women's underpaid work the world over, we find that women perform 2/3 of the world's work hours, yet only receive 10% of the world's income and own less than 1% of the world's property.[1] An extremely conservative estimate of the annual value of women's unpaid work in the U.S.A. alone, in 1970, was $650 billion. To understand the enormity of the value, internationally, of women's unpaid and underpaid work and how completely it subsidizes the world's economy, is to begin to understand the necessity, to the male order, of maintaining women's continuing performance of this work by whatever means necessary.

As one extreme along the continuum of dominating and terrorizing behavior, violence against women functions as a means of social control, assuring women's servility. The issue of reproductive rights is imbued with violence in the struggle over who will control the means of reproduction. As a result of the falling birth rate, women's right to abortion is currently being threatened. At the same time, racist and classist population planners implement policies for the sterilization of women of color without their informed consent as a means of determining who will have children. 20% of married Black and Chicana women under the age of 45, 14% of Native American women and 35% of Puerto Rican women have been sterilized.

Other forms of violence used to circumscribe women's behavior are rape and battery. All women are terrorized by the threat of rape (1/3 of American women will be raped in their lifetimes), and make life choices—including where and with whom to live, work and socialize—based on the fear of rape and sexual harassment. Every 18 seconds in this country a woman is beaten by her husband or lover on whom she is probably economically dependent. Men beat and rape their female "property" because they live with the acceptability and the assumption of the use of violence in their environment; and they have grown up with a deep-rooted sense of entitlement, combined with insecurity and a lack of nonviolent conflict resolution skills. These latter effects of male socialization are economically rooted in the male-dominated family and help to explain much of the masculine behavior and values we find the world over. (When speaking here of male or masculine, female or feminine values, traits and behavior, I'm referring to the social ideals and traditional behavioral norms for men and women, and of necessity making broad generalizations. That individual exceptions exist, and that we are capable of transcending these norms is crucial to the change process ahead.)

In almost all cultures, men's economic activity lies outside the home, and men are relatively uninvolved with childcare. With masculine role models outside the home, boys must *learn* to be men, learn an abstract set of rights and duties. Thus a profound insecurity about their sexual identity and a preoccupation with proving their manhood is, ironically, fostered in the patriarchal family which has been structured around women's unpaid work. In many cultures, the socially approved masculine role is also imbued with aggression and the need to be in control. This forges an implicit link between manhood, strength and violence, with power thought to be acquired through the humiliation and degradation of others. In addition, most men are rarely encouraged to develop nonviolent conflict resolution skills such as communication, diplomacy, the ability to bargain, compromise, find common values and empathize. Finally, most men grow up with a belief in their entitlement to the free services of women—mothers, sisters, daughters, girl friends and wives who are constantly performing small acts out of love, duty or fear.

Thus we have a group of people who are profoundly insecure, with poorly developed nonviolent conflict resolution skills and a deep-rooted sense of entitlement, who feel a need to prove themselves through aggression, achievement and competition. These people, who are the least equipped to deal with absolute power, are then put in positions of absolute power, from the heads of families to the heads of nations. And we ask ourselves why we live in a world which spends more money *in one day* on arms than what it would cost to feed, clothe and house at a minimally adequate level, every person in the world for one year.

We are living in a violent male culture which is worldwide and economically based. It requires and justifies systematic dehumanization and has created a climate of violence, whereby violence against women, from genital mutilation to marital rape and abuse, and violence against humanity, from agent orange and the neutron bomb to starvation and poverty, has become the social norm. The model learned in the home, the inequalities of wealth and leisure time produced by women, have also translated outside the home, to the poor producing for the wealthy, people of color in this country and around the world creating the wealth of the white minority.

Our problem, the world over, is not simply that men are in power, but that the world is run along a masculine value system. Most patriarchal economic systems—capitalist and socialist—have based their development on a growth model, with a notion of efficiency that values profit and surplus over social and environmental considerations and with decision-making and a division of labor which are stratified with structural inequalities.

An extreme example of the masculine culture is the right-wing movement of the late '70s and '80s, given voice and platform by the election of Reagan. The Reagan mandate (27% of the 51% who voted) originated out of an accurately perceived economic self-interest of the wealthy minority and, in the case of the majority, a fervent desire to believe in the viability of the male culture and the economic promise of Reagan's Hollywood-style fantasy. The nationalistic fervor of the male culture was fanned by the threat of the loss of its unlimited, exploitative access to the resources of other countries and of the earth itself, and by a resurgence of extreme racism and sexism. The economic crisis (intrinsic to capitalism's diminishing markets and the hidden, inflationary cost of militarism) became a justification for supply-side economics, selling the fantasy that if the rich get richer, the rest of us will have jobs and not get poorer. The bedrock of patriarchy—the family (household of servants)—became targeted for "defense" as the right-wing moved on the fear and hysteria generated by the gains of feminism.

With Reagan's administration came the implicit sanction of the right-wing, including right-wing terrorism and violence against women, people of color and gay people, and an awakened spirit of militarism. The Reagan administration initiated policies aimed at eradicating every gain we have made in the labor, feminist, gay, environmental, peace and Civil Rights movements. The patriarchal Golden Rule of economics (he who has the gold makes the rules) and the priorities of the male culture are most visible in the Reagan budget allocations, where the subsidies of the rich equal the budget deficits: \$1½ trillion on defense by 1985 for a *peacetime* economy is 2 to 3 times what it would cost to pay women for their unpaid work for one year; \$2.2 billion cut from the food stamp program equalling the \$2 billion allowed for businessmen's tax deductions on meals and entertainment; AFDC (93% of whose recipients are women and children)[2] cut by \$1 billion, while the nuclear power industry is subsidized at \$1 billion a year[3]; and of the 3 million people receiving the minimum monthly social security benefits of \$122 that Reagan wants to eliminate, 86% are women.[4]

The Alternative

Cross-culturally, the more female value-based the culture, the higher the status of women (including greater economic independence and reproductive freedom), the less violence against women and cultural violence, and the more men, without the distant aura of authority, are active in domestic life and childcare. In the more egalitarian cultures, as Anthropologist Michelle Zimbalist Rosaldo has pointed out, men are even symbolically and/or actively involved in birthing. The closer men are to the creation of life and the caring of others, the more it transforms their cultural experience and world-view.

Most women are socialized into behavior and develop skills useful for their economic role as servicers. Not only do women not face the same identity crisis (as Wilma Scott Heide says, women don't need to prove their manhood), but they develop an identity grounded in serving others. While on the one hand this perpetuates their performing free and underpaid labor, it also offers the qualities of empathy and sensitivity, the skills in administration, cooperation and arbitration, and an alternative world-view which, if used on a policy level in the world around them, would provide exactly what's needed to redirect the world from its destructive path.

The institutionalizing of female values necessitates a process of social change integrating the means and the ends which isn't based in violence against people, because any coercion, in itself, is a form of violence. This commitment to nonviolence in the truest sense, on the part of women and men alike, has successfully informed much social change organizing, from India's independence movement, to the Civil Rights movement in this country, to the multiple gains of the feminist movement here and around the world. Non-compliance, based on the recognition that it is women's work that keeps everything going, has been used both by individual women picketing their own homes and refusing to return until their families signed contracts renegotiating the division of labor, and by the women of Iceland in 1974 who stopped doing both paid and unpaid work, 90% of them gathering in public meetings to draw up lists of demands.

As believers in a new society, we have visualized alternatives and are manifesting them. The feminist movement has visualized new ways of working, of resolving conflicts, of organizing groups and new institutions to allow the best in us—our creativity—to flourish. Out of our higher selves we must continue to speak—with respect, compassion and a belief in human possibility—to the higher selves of others. We, individually and collectively, have the power to create whatever changes are necessary and that we believe in.

Karen Malpede
A Talk for the Conference on Feminism & Militarism

"All has to be admitted in our hearts," writes Karen. "Whatever we cannot tolerate inside us will rise outside in demon shape to plague us. . . " In this paper, originally written for and read at the April, 1981 War Resister's League Conference on Feminism and Militarism, playwright Karen Malpede presents a kaleidoscope of images from rituals, stories, myths, dreams—mirrors which help or hinder our inward search for the truths we crave. Carefully, candidly, Karen opens some windows to her own life—sharing a dream which frightened and enlightened her, her ambivalence toward an angry stepson, her empathy for a young neighbor unable to live with what he'd seen in Vietnam, her insights from reading Greek plays.

Karen is a playwright and theater historian. She is cofounder, with Burl Hash, of New Cycle Theater, a pacifist-feminist theater in Brooklyn, NY, which has produced her plays, "The End of War," "A Lament for Three Women," "Making Peace: A Fantasy," and "A Monster Has Stolen the Sun: Part One." Her books include People's Theater in America, Three Works by the Open Theater, *and the forthcoming* Women in Theater: Compassion and Hope *which she edited.*

I must confess to you my terror of speaking at a political gathering, even a gathering of strong, warm women, for I am not primarily a political organizer or a political theorist. I am a playwright, a theater historian, a mother and a stepmother. It is in these four capacities that I wish to speak with you today. I was asked here specifically to address myself to the linked issues of anarchism, pacifism and feminism. While these are ideas to which I am passionately attached and they represent a life-style to which I passionately aspire, the joint tasks of playwriting and mothering singularly ill-equip one to make definitive statements about anything. Thus I have no "anarchist, pacifist, feminist line;" I can offer no "anarchist, pacifist, feminist manifesto." Instead I want to speak with you about violence, and about possible effective nonviolent responses to it. This is a subject of endless fascination to me; it is the major question in my plays. It seems to me to be the major challenge of my life, and, perhaps, of all our lives. It is also a subject about which I know nothing absolute, hence I can offer only stories, tales, dreams.

Two weeks or so before this conference I was rereading Barbara Deming's book *We Cannot Live Without Our Lives* in order to reaquaint myself with one of our most brilliant pacifist-feminist thinkers. In the book, Barbara relates a dream dreamt by a friend of hers. In her dream, Barbara's friend was living with her ex-husband. He had just killed a young girl and he asked Barbara's friend to help him cover up this crime. The murdered young woman in the dream was, of course, the dreamer's Self, and the dream was, of course, about women's loss of life, of Self, of creative potential in traditional heterosexual alliances under patriarchy.

I read this part of Barbara's book just before I went to sleep. I then dreamt that I killed a young woman. I was at a campfire on the beach when a woman came up to me and said she didn't like my plays. The reason, she explained, was that in my plays I was afraid to face my own rage. After listening to her complaint, I calmly picked up a log and beat her to death. Immediately, I became frantic to cover up the murder. I began to look for an alibi, or for someone else on whom to pin the crime. Soon, though, I became aware that no one seemed to care that a woman had been murdered. I began to feel comfortable. I had done a terrible thing, but no one seemed to notice, no one cared. And just as I relaxed, a horrible thought struck me. Despite the fact that no one cared, I would, I realized, have to spend the rest of my life in jail. Not in an actual jail of bars and concrete, though that would be most unwelcome, but in a psychic jail built of my own remembrance of the crime I had committed, reinforced by the memory of the lies I had told about it, guarded by my fear of discovery of myself by myself. My every moment, I realized, would be constricted, and certainly my creative power would be lost, for the artist must above all be available to herself, and honest with herself. It was from the nightmare of this psychic jail I awoke, shaken and alone in the middle of the night.

The woman I killed was, of course, a part of myself whose energy I feared. That no one else cared that the woman was dead or that I had killed her is, I think, about the terrible truth of our lives under patriarchy, where no one does care about women's deepest selves. No one cares whether or not we live out our full potential—in fact, it's better if we don't, for the truths we would have then to tell are most unwanted, are, in fact, unspeakable within society as it currently exists.

It's interesting, isn't it, that when I was accused of not facing my own anger and rage, my immediate response was to kill. And what I killed was my own creative voice, the Fury who plagues us with her insistence that we follow where we need to go to arrive at our own truths.

There is a way of looking at killing as coming not so much from the wish to make the Other dead, as from the felt need to take the power of the Other inside oneself, to be energized, enlivened, one might even say eroticized by it. This was the nature of much animal sacrifice in so-called primitive cultures where people lived closer to the truths of the unconscious than we do now. The sacrifice was made, the blood spilled, so that the "god-like" power of the beast might pass, by way of its eaten flesh, into the body of the ones who had killed it for that purpose.

I should say "goddess-like" power, of course, for the original sacrifice, upon which recorded history proceeds, is the sacrifice of women's power as creatrix, seer, world-weaver and world-spinner, magical bringer of life and, therefore, of death. The original murder is not of brother by brother, as the Old Testament would have us believe, but of the Mother by her sons, and, by the ineffectiveness of their resistance, by her daughters, too. And the great redemptive act is not the sacrifice upon the cross of the son by the father as the New Testament tells us, for this event prefigures the exact apocalypse we must avoid. The great redemptive act is the defense of the Mother by her children, the reinstatement into the world of the feminine principle of warm nurture, welcome generation and also contact with the irrational, instinctual, untameable mysteries of the unconscious mind—those forces which, when ignored within us, become the so-called evil against which all holy or patriotic wars are waged. But how, I wonder, are we to accomplish such a feat as this?

I remember very well the first time I saw my step-son, now aged 12. He was a slim, slight, blond and cute 8 year-old, with narrow, untrusting eyes, an angry thrust-out chin. I looked at him, and I seemed to see two children standing there, one superimposed upon the other like a double exposure on a photographic plate. I saw Chris as he presented himself to the world, a hostile child who would not speak of anything but car and bicycle wrecks, would not make any sounds but sounds of crashes, collisions, and machine gun fire, or what sounded to me like an almost preverbal whine, demanding cokes and hamburgers, skate boards and water toys. At the same time I could see the child Chris was meant to be—for periodically this child would show himself to us—a delicate, tender, inquisitive little boy with a gay laugh, eager for love.

A year or so ago we were riding in the car when Chris announced to us he was so tough he could not feel anything. "Go ahead," he said, "hit me, punch me, put my head through the windshield; I don't feel. I can't feel anything." My first impulse, as it is too often with this child, was anger. I wanted to scream at him, to shake him into feeling. Instead I took my hand and gently stroked his cheek and arm. "Of course you feel," I said to him. "You feel this, don't you? . . .and this?" He looked at me in stunned and frightened silence, then giggled and wriggled away from my caress.

My first response to this child is often anger because I perceive such a need for love whenever I look at him—and such a need to push love far away—I feel if I were to give myself wholly to the task of parenting, his need would devour me. I would become that ancient sacrificial animal. Chris would take my life into himself and be enlivened by my energy, but there would be nothing left of me. But, more and more, as his father establishes the nurturant relationship his son missed in infancy, Chris dares to show his real self. His intelligence quickens, his sense of humor reappears, at times he seems almost carefree, almost gay. He becomes gentle with his cats, beautifully gentle with the baby half-sister who approaches him instinctively with trust.

When I first met Chris's father, Burl, I had sworn off men forever. I would never again be personally abused by male anger, male hurt. My own father was a violent man who died of stomach cancer when I was 18 and he was only 44—died of the same rage turned inward he used to shower out upon the world. My relationship with him, though not actually incestuous, had all the emotional components of a father-daughter love affair. When he died I felt that I had failed; I had not learned well enough how to comfort him.

I gave up my adolescent fiction then. Ten years would pass before I would attempt to tell a tale again. At 28, I wrote *A Lament for Three Women,* a play about three women who were losing three men—a father, a husband, and a son—from terminal cancer. In the play, the women make the decision to disconnect the men's life support systems and to let them die. Before they do this, however, the women have had to turn toward each other for support. In the play, cancer is a metaphor for patriarchy; cancer is a disease of patriarchy, after all: The life support systems the women disconnect from the men's bodies are meant to stand for the life energies a mother, wife and daughter so often give to others at the sacrifice of their own self-realization. In the play the women turn to one another, touch and embrace each other, to put into our minds an image of a woman's community that extends across the generations, across economic and cultural barriers and which has become a refuge for us, a place where we can grow into ourselves at last.

I have written four plays since that first one; I have yet to write a story of a reciprocal, vital, caring relationship between a woman and a man—though I feel I am living one and perhaps this will be the tale I tell next. In my most recently produced play, *A Monster Has Stolen the Sun*, there is a scene in which a man, put into a deep trance by a midwife, enacts the birth of his own child. The actor did this brilliantly, I thought, miming the growth of his belly, his labor pains, then with great effort pulling the child out from between his legs, biting the umbilical cord and speaking the same awesome feelings, put into verse, I spoke to my own baby daughter when she first appeared to me. Then this man, a king, fantasizes that the world is mocking him for what he's done. He smashes his imagined child on a rock, beats his own chest, screams that he is who he's always been, "a man whose mute and shuttered loins hold fast against unknown, unwanted things." He falls in tears upon the ground.

In the working class neighborhood where we live many men are veterans of Viet Nam. We once had a neighbor, Karl, who had been a Green Beret. He had been among the forces sent into Cambodia who were not expected to come out alive, and, in fact, most of his buddies perished there. Toward the end of his tour of duty, he had been sent to massacre a village. A six or seven year-old girl-child, whose family had all been killed, reached her hands out to him, touched him and begged him for her life. What fleshly sensation did he feel as he looked into her eyes and spared her? What quickening of heart and mind and soul made him put down his gun? "I cannot feel," Chris said to me. But this child touched a killer and he let her live.

After that, Karl shot only to miss but he had to endure the accusations of his fellow soldiers who began to call him coward. Returning home a "misfit," no longer able to glorify war or his part in it, he began drinking heavily and roaming the block, offering protection from imagined hoodlums to Burl, myself and others whom he liked. He lived at home with his parents. He had no job and, it seemed, was frightened of and impotent with women. The day our daughter was born, Karl knocked and kicked at the door until we opened it. We weren't ready to have company, Burl told him. Karl said he would not leave until he had seen the new-born child. Burl brought the infant to him in his arms and Karl stood over her and wept. "You can make new life," he said to Burl, "and all I've ever done is kill." A month or two later he was dead, of drinking and despair. Having renounced the role of murderer, he knew no choice but to become his own last victim.

In *Gyn/Ecology*, Mary Daly cites a book called *A Sexual Study of Men in Power* which documents that powerful men who act sadistically in their jobs are often extreme sexual masochists. These men are called "the slaves" by the prostitutes they hire to beat them, urinate and defecate on their bodies. Daly concludes: "the 'men in power' are the playwrights who create and identify with the roles of both the victimizers and the victims." The sado-masochistic dynamic takes place inside a single psyche which then projects this torture scheme outward to the world. Male torturers, as Mary Daly says, "vicariously enjoy" their victim's sufferings. If they were simply not allowed to be the victors any longer, powerful men would be unable to imagine another role save that of victim. As victims, they feel that they themselves would be subject to the actual torture their tortured minds project. This is one reason pacifism is so feared by men in power, one reason all discussions of pacifist options are rigorously censored in the press, media, film and theaters reflecting the world view of these men. The men in power have confused their fantasy of the passivity of the victim with what would be a vibrant self-affirming pacifist response to injustice—and they are afraid.

In Daly's chapter on the witchburnings, she convincingly proves that the women who were tortured and burned as witches were strong, visionary healers, women who lived outside marriage, church or state. As pacifists, feminists, anarchists and lesbians, these women posed a threat to men in power. It was not so much that they threatened to overturn the rule of these men as that they, themselves, paid that rule no heed. They lived another way and were closely in touch with mysteries far beyond the sado-masochistic mind-set of the men in power. Through their involvement with healing arts, hallucinatory plants and herbs, communal rituals, and ancient verbal lore, these women were vibrantly, sensually awake; they dreamed prophetic dreams, practiced regular ascents to regions far beyond the bounds of the rational mind. They knew, as a modern day healer friend of mine just said to me, that the universe is beautiful—knew this because they, themselves, had flown beyond the confines of a shattered sado-masochistic consciousness and had seen a great and kindly cosmic plan. Their very lack of fear struck fear into the hearts of men who hated them. And in towns in France and Italy they walked into the sea, singing a joyous hymn, rather than be destroyed on torture wrack and pyre.

Beginning in pre-Homeric times, but lasting through the golden age, a kind of sacrifice called holocaust was practiced by the Greeks. Nothing of this sacrifice was consumed by those who offered it, no feast was shared by man and god for there was no communion between the two. Everything of the sacrificial beast, be it animal or human, was turned to ash, all of its burnt flesh was meant to placate angry ghosts, malevolent spirits of the dead.

We are controlled still by rites of holocaust; this is clear. We need only cite the horrors of modern times as proof: witchburnings, Nazi murder of the Jews, the fire bombing of Dresden, the atomic bombings of Nagasaki and Hiroshima, the napalm bombings of the Vietnamese and defoliation of their countryside, the radiation poisoning at Three Mile Island, and who knows where else.

Along with holocaust, the Greeks also practiced rites which involved the beating and slaying of men and women called pharmakoi, or scapegoats. The pharmakoi were fed special, purifying food, then beaten as they marched around the town, then taken to its outskirts and slain. This sequence of purification, beating and murder was supposed to expel any evil forces which plagued the rest of the people. The scapegoat rites were often practiced in the springtime when the very promise of the stirring earth awakened fears of latent impurities. The pharmakoi, themselves, were often chosen from among people already condemned to die for one crime or another. Supposedly, they would take the malevolent force of those who had condemned them into themselves. By dying, the pharmakoi would purify the ones who had sentenced them to death. Such spectacles of expulsion of evil are still very much in evidence; we have only to cite the frequent persecutions of lesbians, Blacks, Jews, homosexual men, children, political dissidents.

Unfortunately, rites like the slaying of the pharmakoi intended to expel evil, or the offering of a holocaust aimed at placating an angry ghost, have similar, perfectly predictable, horrible results; they create guilt in the minds of those who practice them. And what is "guilt" after all but the persistent will of the silenced part of being to manifest itself again. Speaking of the effects of such sacrifices upon their practitioners, classical scholar Jane Ellen Harrison explains: "Man expects the dead man will behave as he would behave were he yet living—pursue him for vengeance; the ghost is an actual, almost physical reality. It needed a Euripides to see that this ghost was purely a subjective horror, a disordered conscience." She then cites a sentence from Euripides' play *Orestes* in which Menelaos asks the mad Orestes: "What doest thou suffer? What disease undoes thee!" And Orestes answers: "Conscience, for I am conscious of fell deeds."[2]

What crime had left Orestes conscience-struck? He had murdered his mother, Clytemnestra, because she killed his father, Agamemnon. There are many salient features to this myth which developed, as myths do, to explain the psychological-social changes already occurring in a people. Let's read the myth as if it were a dream, for myths are communal dreams. Agamemnon, you remember, sacrificed Clytemnestra's and his own daughter, Iphigenia, in order to raise winds propitious for his coming battle. We might agree Clytemnestra felt good cause to kill him in return. Upon his triumphant return from battle, she murdered him while he was luxuriating in a bath. Agamemnon was murdered while submerged in water, at a moment, that is, when he had reentered a womb-like state. Clytemnestra threw a net around him. He was ensnared by woman's power. The message is clear; having once dishonored his female self to feed his own warrior impulse, man cannot then return safely to the Mother. He can no longer make himself vulnerable to female energies inside or outside himself or, he fantasizes, these same energies will rise against him in revenge.

Agamemnon's son, Orestes, becomes the hero who manages to be acquitted for the actual crime of matricide. The decisive vote in favor of Orestes is cast by Athena; she was born from the head of Zeus and is proof, therefore, that the mother is not needed to produce the child. Athena says:

> "No mother ever gave me birth;
> I am unreservedly for male in everything. . ."[3]

The Orestia marks the moment of transition from matriarchal to patriarchal order. Matricide is no longer counted as a crime of blood, since, as Apollos tells us, "The mother is not parent of her so-called child, but only nurse of the new sown seed. The man who puts it there is parent."[4] And so, under patriarchy, neither son nor daughter owes allegiance any longer to their mothers.[5]

Something else happens in the final play of *The Orestia* which is of interest to us. The Furies, who have been haunting Orestes, spooking him in punishment for his deed, are domesticated by

Athena, rendered kindly guardians of female pregnancy (not of fertility in a broader sense which must include the creative Self). Then Athena leads them to shrines beneath the earth.

In Aeschylus' version of the myth, the Furies represent Clytemnestra's raging ghost. By the time Euripides wrote, he knew they were Oreste's own conscience.

In either case, for patriarchy to exist the Furies had to be tamed and quieted. That Athena leads them to shrines beneath the earth is evidence that their pacification did not wholly work. It was to the spirits of the underworld that the Greeks offered their holocausts and pharmakoi. The underworld spirits were always treated fearfully, since they were felt to be vengeful ghosts of those who had been wrongly killed. They were, I think, the ghosts of the female principle.

The Furies are rendered superficially harmless by Aeschylus, as they had to be for patriarchy to take hold, but they haunt us and control us still. Western civilization has been desperately attempting to placate the rage of these murdered women through its repeated holocausts. For what we have once killed, we need to kill and kill again, in order to make certain it is truly dead. And the great mystery of life is that nothing can be really killed. All has to be admitted to our hearts. Whatever we cannot tolerate inside us will rise outside in demon shape to plague us, taunting us to strike it down. Nuclear weapons have been developed to silence once and for all the murdered Mother and her Furies, for they have resisted each and every holocaust to date.

I do not mean to trap us into gender. Though I have called the initial murder that of the Mother, I believe it is actually the murder of our intuitive selves, our openly erotic selves, our prophetic, seer-like selves; the murder of our ability to dwell trustingly, with healthy awe of the unknown inside our own living flesh, alive on the living earth.

"Why do you like to be involved in muggings?" I asked my step-son Chris. "It makes a good story," he answered, even though, because he's small, he is usually in the victim role. Chris has no concept of a good story that does not include violence or the threat of violence. He is captive of the culture in which he lives. He will have no other stories unless we begin to dream for him and with him, and for and with ourselves, all the alternatives to violent murder and the ensuing violence of revenge. I mean quite literally that we need new rites, new myths, new tales of our beginnings, new stories that speak of new options open to us. The task before us is a task of the imagination, for whatever we are able to imagine we will also be able to become.

Cynthia Adcock
Fear of "Other": The Common Root of Sexism and Militarism

Cynthia Adcock, recently a staff person for the Women's Pentagon Action network, struggles in this essay to formulate a theory to explain the "why" of sexism—why have men sought such devastating power over women? Cynthia confesses that she wants a "no-blame" theory with neither women nor men being the scapegoats for the evils of the world. She presents a theory similar to that found in Dorothy Dinnerstein's The Mermaid and The Minotaur, *and, like the child who saw the Emperor and not his new clothes, asks us to look honestly at the role of motherhood—a role which has almost exclusively given women the power to either give or to withhold love and nurturance in the lives of small children. This role, a division of labor that was originally forced on women by natural circumstances and economic convenience, has, Cynthia says, perpetuated the cycle of domination and submission and has been the root cause of the hatred of women. Elsewhere Cynthia has written, "The exclusive role of females in child-rearing is, I think, quite a sufficient explanation for sexism—for hatred of the female, for economic exploitation and oppression, and for the massive violence we call militarism."*

This essay presents a controversial point of view and, despite Cynthia's denial, can seem to be a psychoanalytical feminist expression of the old line, "You can always blame your mother." This will most likely generate debate, as it has among those of us involved in assembling this anthology. It is included here for the sake of dialogue. Cynthia's essay raises many questions and contains a fragment of truth, but only a fragment.

Cynthia has taught "Women and Revolution" at the University of Pennsylvania and at the Free Women's School of Philadelphia, and has led workshops on women's sexuality, spirituality, and peace. She received her doctorate in history from Bryn Mawr, has worked as a freelance writer and editor, and has participated in a variety of women's and peace organizing activities. She now works for the Peace and Justice project of the University of Pennsylvania Christian Association. She gardens and plays guitar, is married and is the mother of two daughters.

This piece is unedited at the author's request.

We are out to glorify war!
The only health-giver of the world!
Militarism! Patriotism!
. . . Ideas that kill!
Contempt for women!

Filippo Marinetti

These words of an early 20th century poet make a chilling connection between sexism and militarism. It is no accident that the greatest threat to all human life, militarism, is also the most virulent expression of woman-hating and contempt for the feminine. Both sexism and militarism, I believe, grow from a common root. They feed on fear and hatred of the "Other," be it a female or the male foreigner, the tribal enemy. It is this fear and hatred that I wish to explore.

Militarism is primarily a male phenomenon, and the ultimate power of patriarchy is the organized, legitimized violence of the nation-state. For millennia, part of women's role has been to decry male aggression. We often see ourselves as posing a better way—a more loving, nurturing way of life than the masculine mode poses. Sometimes love and hatred seem polarized along sex lines.

I have been deeply saddened by this apparent polarity, and have felt an urgent necessity to re-examine it. I have hoped that somehow I could find the historical roots of the problem, so that we could see how to move beyond it.

In my re-examination, what first struck me is that women, too, exhibit fear and hatred of the Other—in particular of males who pile weapon upon weapon, or who rape and abuse women. Our fear and hate often seem quite realistic. As a sex, we have repeatedly been oppressed, dominated, and violated. Masculine violence has individually or collectively killed millions of women, and now endangers all life on this planet. Yet—once I recognized *our* fear and hatred—I had to ask whether those same emotions in men might also be rooted in reality.

In asking that question, I am trying to move beyond blame to an examination of the real causes of sexism and militarism. Understanding these, we may be able to change them in a way that simple blame and shame will never accomplish. The feminist psychologist Dorothy Dinnerstein was once asked what women want. She replied that we want an end to being blamed and scapegoated for the evils of the world. Indeed we do. In all fairness, I think it is important to extend the same perspective to men—if only so that our perception is not clouded by hasty judgments.

Seeking a common root of sexism and militarism means digging into the soil of primordial human culture. Current social science suggests that sexism is the oldest form of inequality or class division. Often the suggestion is made that human culture is inseparable from an antagonism between the sexes and from male domination over women. For instance, anthropologist Claude Levi-Strauss identifies the origin of human culture in the exchange of women by men.

The real discussion centers on how and why men achieved power over women. Various approaches are used. First is an explanation based on the biological fact that men have higher testosterone levels than women. This makes males in general more assertive. Added to this is the fact of their slightly greater average strength in shoulder and arm muscles, permitting men to coerce women physically.

Another explanation of male domination cites the greater vulnerability and dependence of women because of pregnancy, birth, and lactation. These factors are also cited as causes for the primitive division of labor in which women worked in the village or camp, while men became hunters and developed the weapons which eventually could be used to dominate women.

Other theories of male supremacy focus on economic factors. In hunting, gathering and agricultural tribes, women often provided over half of the group's food. When male hunters began to breed animals for domestic purposes, women became economically dependent on men for this new, substantial source of wealth. Economic dependency made women subject to male domination.

All of these explanations seem valid, up to a point. They do not, however, explain the "why" of sexism. No approach suggests why so many men, in so many cultures, over so many centuries, have *wanted* to dominate women. Our culture simply assumes that the wish to dominate is natural, and that it waits only for the opportunity and the means. We have no evidence for such an assumption.

In my own experience, the desire to dominate others usually stems from the experience of *having been* dominated. For example, there is evidence that a significant percentage of rapists were themselves sexually abused as children. I have therefore asked myself whether men might wish to dominate women because they were themselves subject to an earlier inequality that we have thus far ignored, an inequality that somehow predates sexism. If that inequality affected males with particular intensity, it might be the basic cause of their greater propensity for violence, their generally stronger need to dominate others.

That is the case, I think. The oldest inequality of all is that between parent and child. Human beings are born terribly helpless. Because of our larger cranial capacity, we are born very early, before we can feed ourselves or even cling securely to the warmth of a parent. Our dependence is vastly prolonged and it conflicts mightily with the desire of the infant for control over its environment—control over access to food, love, security, and freedom. Most of the factors present in the rise of sexism are thus also present in the inequality between adult and infant: physical strength versus weakness and vulnerability, economic power versus the dependency of infant need.

Mother as "Other"

It is difficult enough to be born. Once we were bathed in the warmth and rhythms of the mother's body, the chemicals of her feelings, and we were nurtured with her blood and spirit. Then we are forced out, born, separated, suddenly chilled and forced to use our muscles to fill our gasping lungs with air. We are our selves.

For each child, the creation of its own identity begins in crisis, with the loss of the mother as its world. The transition is difficult, but if we are lucky we find new delights, sweet milk and gentle touching, as we begin our separate lives. With luck, we are surrounded by love and security. Our experience of the first parent as "the Other" is grounded in a shared identity as lovers.

The problem of shared and separate identity is crucial to human culture, I think. It is a problem that lies at the root of sexism and militarism. There is a delicate tension between individuality and one-ness with the rest of humanity or with any other human beings. It is difficult for us to maintain the sense of being both fully, uniquely, our individual selves, and also a part of the whole. The balance between the two cannot survive an atmosphere of domination and submission. In the long run, it depends on relatively egalitarian power relationships that preserve the uniqueness of the individual while facilitating an harmonious community. My sense is that males have much greater difficulty in feeling a shared identity with other people. This is rooted in the original parent-child situation, I think.

The infant is terribly helpless and vulnerable compared to the parent (no matter how powerless the adult *feels* in the situation).

It is not an equal power relationship. Moreover, even the most devoted parent cannot always be available for food or love, cannot always bring release from pain, and cannot permit the infant total freedom. Our reasons, to the baby, are meaningless and arbitrary. That I, as a mother, was exhausted by feedings every two hours through the night, or that I was frustrated and lonely, meant nothing to my babies then. From the infant's point of view, the parent holds a terrible and arbitrary power. Until this generation, that power was almost exclusively female. This common condition was true across a huge range of cultures and across thousands of years.

The power, the immediate power over the infant, was female. We cannot help but live in fear, in dread, for any power on which we are so deeply dependent. In this fact, I think, lies the origin of sexism.

Torn from the mother by birth, needy for her milk and love, we feel a terrified ambivalence toward her. This painful alienation dances maliciously, invisibly, throughout the rest of our lives. The Mother becomes the primal Other in a way that cannot always be pleasing. *And it was not our fault as mothers.* Even the most loving and nurturing among us were *by that very fact* seen as the most powerful Other. The contradiction is inherent in the situation rather than the virtures and faults of individuals.

One of the human race's early responses to alienation from the mother was to create the notion of the Goddess. Woman was plastered against the sky as alien deity, the eternal, powerful Other, giver and taker of life, the symbol of all our beginnings and of life itself. When we observe the treatment of the Goddess in history, we can see that the patriarchy itself grows out of its own opposite. We can see that alienation from the powerful female Other was especially problematical for young men.

Unlike girl children, boys could not identify with the power of the female. They could not imagine growing up into her role. ("When I grow up, I'll be *your* Mommy," my daughter Iris often told me.) Instead, female deities were seen as especially dangerous for men, partly because of their attractive power. A male's love for a goddess could destroy him. The worship of Cybele, for example, reached orgiastic heights of male self-destruction. Young men would castrate themselves, throwing the bloody parts on the goddess' statue. The male priest became a eunuch. The power of the female was her biology, and this was forever denied to men, despite their yearning for her. The contradiction, the ambivalence, must have sometimes seemed unbearable. In the end, of course, the Goddess was de-throned, ousted by a masculine God. Her power went underground. Similarly, the matriarchal power set-up experienced by eons of children was overcome by the power we call patriarchy. Yet exclusive female power over child-rearing continued, underground as it were, in the privacy of the home. In contrast, men developed alternative forms of power in the world at large.

The inevitable alienation between powerful female parent and helpless infant thus continued through the centuries to weigh more heavily on men. To some degree, and quite naturally, the mother herself contributed to this dynamic. From the moment of birth, the boy-child was perceived by the mother as being essentially different from herself. She knew he would never follow in her footsteps, bearing and suckling children. She inevitably communicated this attitude to him. She saw him as "Other." It is only as we women move away from a biologically-determined identity that we can create a sense of shared identity with males. This new sense of *human* identity is at the core of feminism. But at least until the present, the mother-son dynamic made it especially difficult for males to develop a sense of shared identity with the first parent, and thus with all humanity. Lacking that sense, they tended to develop forms of power based on competition and aggression—economic and military power, used both to control females and to gain ascendancy over other males.

Yet another factor made males more prone to militarism. In mysterious ways, the mother comes to represent not only the source of life but also the beckoning doorway of death. She symbolizes the original perfection from which we were brutally separated by birth—a perfection both secure and totally unconscious and thus vaguely resembling death. Ernest Becker, in *The Denial of Death*, asserts that our ambivalence toward the mother results in ambivalence about both life and death. This is especially true for men, I think. Their inability to accept the power of the mother results in an "heroic" denial both of her and of death itself. That denial is accompanied by an unconscious fascination with death. It is as if by denying the life-and-death power of the mother, men themselves take on that same power in terrifyingly catastrophic ways that now endanger all life on earth.

The ambivalent primal relationship between parent and infant is so crucial because it occurs so early, when we have no words to objectify it, no way to distance ourselves to a safer plane. But this early difficulty is then compounded as we grow older, as we are "civilized" by adults. We then come to know ourselves as separate beings who must obey laws made by others or suffer the consequences. In most of human history, the original authority of the mother was reinforced throughout the formative years by *primarily female* teachers, nurses, nuns, housekeepers, babysitters, etc. The felt authority in a child's life was thus mostly female, unlike the more remote male authorities such as Daddy, Santa Claus, the policeman, the president, and the masculine God.

The special role of women in "civilizing" children inevitably produced anger and resentment toward women. This role was forced on us by the economics of our history, with terrible consequences. Because of this role, all human beings are prey to resentment of female authority. Daughters mistrust authority—power—in ourselves. Sons grow up to mistrust power in adult women. Thus we all become subconsciously and consciously fearful of letting adult women have power. That fear is at the root of sexism. It is a sex-linked fear, a sex-linked resentment and even hatred upon occasion.

Then, when women suffer the results of that sexism—when we are dominated by male power in the public world or in the patriarchal family—the vicious cycle of domination and submission is completed. We learn fear, resentment, and hatred of adult men, a sex-linked set of emotions altogether justified by our experiences as women in a patriarchal world. This in turn often led us to excessive use of power over the small children in our care, especially boys who reminded us of the men who dominate us.

The child who was blamed and shamed into "right" behavior (let alone the child who is beaten) then tends to perpetuate the cycle in the next generation. For male children, in search of alternative forms of power, the effect was often a grasping for destructive power, the power to kill. Resentment of the mother (earth) often twisted his creativity towards a technology that destroys life. A man's need often became greed, the desire to amass overwhelming wealth as his mother once controlled all the nourishment in his small world. Denied identification with the power over him, he often sought its opposite, power over females, over the earth, over all life, the power of making death everywhere. All of us, male and female, now suffer the consequences of the patriarchal economic and military systems that as a result have developed over the centuries, systems that now perpetuate themselves independently and that could destroy us all.

It is feminism, of course, that has challenged this entire division of labor and of power between males and females. From the beginning, we insisted that power be shared both in the home and in the public world. Instinctively, we argued that it is important for both sexes to share both the work and the power of childcare. We have asserted a shared human identity that transcends and undergirds our separate male and female selves, a shared identity that is our common hope for survival.

Yet through this revolutionary message there often runs an unfortunate, self-pitying sub-theme. We have generally portrayed ourselves as the victims of male domination, down-playing the arenas in which we have ourselves held power. We have thoroughly described and documented that half of the age-old saga of domination and oppression in which we are the victims. We have not yet fully recognized the effects of maternal power over children as a root cause of resentment, fear and hatred of females. Rarely do we admit that males have sometimes been our victims, as we have been theirs. The anti-war chant "Take the toys away from the boys" reveals how deeply we are still wedded to that ancient maternal power. After all, it was our only power. We have not yet gone beyond this position for a variety of reasons, I think.

First, we have desperately needed to reclaim for ourselves a loving and positive sense of shared identity with our own mothers, who were often clearly victims of the patriarchy. In addition, we have rightly feared our tendencies to understand and sympathize with men to the detriment of our own needs. We were also justifiably suspicious that—once again—we might blame ourselves for all the world's problems. There is also another factor involved. Our upbringing as females tended to place great emphasis on being "nice" girls, doing "good," acting "right," and avoiding anything that might be "bad." Our minds were conditioned by a manipulative blame-and-shame dynamic designed to keep us in our places. It is thus all too natural for us to resort to blaming and shaming others, rather than trying first to understand the problem and then solve it.

We need not remain stuck in the blame-and-shame mindset. As we ourselves refuse to be blamed for the world's ills, so also we can let go of the tendency to blame others. That tendency, as I experience it in myself, is a very nasty way to exercise power over other people, a manipulative and sneaky form of power, one that makes people feel bad rather than offering them concrete avenues of change and hope.

For me, a moment of horrible clarity came when I heard myself snarling in rage and contempt, "but people are *supposed* to be loving with each other." In my sneer, I heard echoes of the voice from my childhood, laying down the law that controlled my life, smothered my natural resistance, and manipulated me into being a "nice girl." I heard myself blaming and shaming another human, and I did not like that.

I hated hearing myself speak those sarcastic words, but at last I understood why men fear and resent the women they love. I had tried to turn that affection into a moral obligation, like the duty a child owes its mother. In my own feelings of desperation at the moment, I had tried to revive the old parental power of blame-and-shame. It didn't work too well, despite the fact that I was playing on the unconscious fear we all carry, that mother will abandon us if we do not "act right." I was reinforcing and using the cycle of domination and submission that begins with the infant's dependence on the "civilizing" parent. It is this cycle that must be ended.

The polarity of domination and submission lies at the heart of militarism as well as sexism. The military, for example, takes young men who are still unsure of their individual identities. It systematically undermines their sexuality, deriding them with words of feminine identification: "faggot," "girl," and "cunt." The military then offers men a masculine identification based on aggression and dominance.

Men are thus systematically taught to hate the "feminine" in themselves. What they hate in themselves (weakness) is defined as "feminine" by the military. This tactic works only because men wish that the "feminine" were weak. At a primal, unconscious level, what is female seems much too strong.

The military also *requires* men to be "feminine" as it defines the term. Men are required to be submissive to military orders. Yet every act of submission to authority instigates the desire to dominate someone else in turn. A double bind is imposed: men must be both submissive *and* dominating. To live in a double bind situation creates a terrible need to be aggressive, assertive, violent towards someone else. That someone becomes an "Other," a female or a male enemy. The cycle goes on and on, without an end.

It must be broken. The fear and hatred that drive it must somehow be short-circuited. And so I ask myself again, what does the feminist revolution have to offer? Che Guevara once said that every true revolutionary is motivated by love. I therefore ask myself, what is the concrete nature of that feminist love now?

Certainly it means a blossoming of love among women for each other and for the self, and for that which is "feminine" in our mythology—the earth, our mother, for example. Jill Johnston, the lesbian feminist, once wrote in the *Village Voice* that the feminist revolution would triumph through a healing of the split between the "mothers" and the "daughters." For her, those terms referred to heterosexual and lesbian women, and to the heterosexual and the lesbian within each woman. Nevertheless, the insight resonates on other levels as well.

It means to me, among other things, a healing between those who hold power and those who are powerless. Such healing can take place only when the contradiction itself is resolved—when the power is shared, when a shared identity is created to transcend the contradiction. The cycle of domination and submission continues *only* because it is a cycle of opposites split off from each other at the conscious level.

As feminism moves through a reconciliation of the mothers and the daughters, we learn a shared identity as women. We transcend the primal polarity between powerful mother and helpless child—a girl child in this case. That shared identity is powerful and is often felt as threatening to men. It need not be. The bridge we have built between mothers and daughters can become a means of understanding why males are so driven and so alienated. By recognizing our own conflicts with our mothers, we can make a leap of imagination to understand the greater alienation of males.

At one time or another, hatred of the female and fear of her power have afflicted us all in this human civilization. Hatred for life itself, the lust for destruction and violence, the cycle of domination and submission, are contradictions within this whole society. But there is a way out.

I find great hope in the fact that women today are liberating ourselves from our ancient roles and, in the process, are freeing our children to be themselves and to be free of sexism. We are short-circuiting the cycle of oppression and violence at its starting-point.

The gift of the feminist movement is that we are trying to dissolve the rigid separation of kinds of power. We are trying to share both parenting and power in the world at large, and we seek new forms of power that do not oppress others. That is why, for me, feminism is truly the most revolutionary movement in all human history.

There is, of course, an inevitable inequality of power between any parent and child. But when parenting is shared, both sexes can later identify with the giant—or giantess—in the nursery. Both can identify with that primal power, as well as with power in the world. Moreover, when parenting is shared, neither parent holds such exclusive power over the child. Neither parent is deprived of all power *except* over children. Abuse of power is less likely. Males will not have to "get back" at female power by dominating us when they become adults. Males will also carry the pre-verbal subconscious memory of a masculine power to nurture. They will learn that, as it were, at Daddy's knee.

We need not scapegoat either sex. As we try to free ourselves from old roles, we will also free our children. In that freedom there will be healing for all. The violence of patriarchy is, at root, a violence born of oppression, however unintentional. As we break the sex-linked alternating cycle of domination and submission, we will find new openings to peace. That is the crux of the link between feminism and nonviolence.

Dorothy Marder

Public Action Coalition on Toys (PACT) sponsors a demonstration at New York's annual Toy Fair for toy manufacturers and buyers, 1973.

Erika Duncan
The Lure of the Death Culture

We stand in the rubble of decay, bewildered by the rush toward destruction we see all around. We call ours a "sick society." In this essay, Erika Duncan asks us to take our own pulse, pause in our condemnation of the male warrior heroes and death-lovers long enough to look at our own complicity, face the ways in which we, women, have collaborated in the take over of the death culture. This is a bitter pill, but one which Erika suggests can provide us with the power to shut off the support systems and heal, heal. Erika uses, as her primary metaphor, a section from her novel, Those Giants: Let Them Rise, *about a dying giant and the deadliness of a woman's attempt to give her love to him—the destructiveness of the lure of a violent death culture which has been our human history.*

Erika's first novel, A Wreath of Pale White Roses, *was published in 1977. She is currently working on a novel about a blind child in a traveling pacifist theater company, exploring themes of change and healing both from a political and personal perspective. Her non-fiction appears frequently in* Book Forum *where she is a contributing editor. She is one of the founders of the* Feminist Book Review *and is a founder of the Woman's Salon, an alternative literary network to give audience support and serious critical attention to new works by women. Her New York City appartment where she lives with her three daughters is the home of the Salon with its monthly public readings and weekly fiction writing workshops. Her article on the Hungry Jewish Mother recently apeared in* The Lost Tradition: Mothers and Daughters In Literature *(Ungar) and will soon be reprinted in a new anthology on feminism and Judaism (Shocken).*

Last week one of our students announced that she might have to take a leave of absence from the Woman's Salon Fiction writing workshop. Her job as a probation officer was putting enormous pressure on her, pulling her away. She had just recently begun a project exploring "naming the Self" and dream and syncronicity, exploring woman's search for identity. Her writing was fresh and new, expanding rapidly. Her job, she explained, involved being the only woman working with big men who carried guns. They had pornographic pictures on their desks and mediated in cases of violence, often violence against women. It was stirring many feelings in her, she said. She could not concentrate upon her other work. Immediately we realized that the solution to her problem was not to drop out of the feminist fiction writing workshop, but rather to use it to explore her own attraction to the situation she was in, as well as the horror of it. As the sister of "powerful" brothers, what did it mean to her to be in this position among men? What had drawn her to it?

Too often in the feminist community, the focus upon what has caused the violence done to humankind comes from without, from a focus upon the ways of men, which puts women in a very mixed position as regards our own potential power. For as long as we ascribe our oppression to what we can't control, we also remain helpless to change it. It is far more frightening to look into ourselves to see how we have collaborated in allowing the death culture to take over, than to place the blame entirely outside ourselves. Yet ultimately it is perhaps also our only hope, for if there are forces within women, as well as within men, leading to violence and violation of our human potential, we as women can play a very big part in turning the course of events, by trying to probe and understand and act on what we are beginning to find out.

Just as in individual psychotherapy the internalization of "the problem" gives the patient the power to start to solve it, regardless of the stance of others in her personal orbit and her world, while the continued looking to the Other to mend the wounds once inflicted only brings paralysis and helplessness. So too, on a societal level, can women begin to undermine the destructive aspects of our culture, by understanding our role in its perpetration, regardless of whether men cooperate or resist. That does not mean that we ought to abandon our anger at the patriarchy, or that we ought to pretend that it would not be a far better world if men stopped oppressing us, nor does it mean that we should stop our struggle against what keeps us from being free. It only means that we must start to take more power into ourselves, and the responsibility for WHAT IS, not forgetting the causes, or our anger at the causes, but refusing all the while to let our anger at the outsider waylay our own powers to actively effect our world.

When the student began to tell her stories of her work in the probation office, it was difficult to not react with horror to the descriptions of the girlie pictures and the guns and to let the student begin to explore the reasons for her own attraction to the job and through the exploration grow beyond them. It was all that we could do to silence ourselves. Yet we did so, for such an exploration of what lures us to the violence of the death culture seemed crucial to our understanding and to change.

When I was asked to contribute to this anthology, almost without thinking about it, I sent in a few pages from my second novel, about a suicidal adolescent girl in love with a physiological giant who is convinced that he'll die young. She looks to him to fill her up, I explained in my covering letter.

The giant section of this book, *Those Giants: Let Them Rise*, begins as Melanie, the young protagonist, is haunting all the city book stores, looking for lore about death.

> *It was while she was stealing that she met the giant Gabriel, in the psychology section of the Eighth Street Book Store. She could still remember their first conversation.*
>
> *He told her all there was to know about himself quite fast, as if there was not time for gradual unravelling. Indeed there never had been time in Gabriel's exaggerated universe, for he was constantly outgrowing everything that came his way. Many people were standing in the mobbed book store that afternoon, but Gabriel towered above them all, a dark garbed scarecrow wearing last year's clothes. "My mother keeps on sewing them with tight cross stitches," he told her, "but nothing holds me in." No one knew how long he would keep growing. No one wanted to guess. "My mother can scarcely afford to keep me in shoes, which always have to be custom made," he said pointing to his new looking pointed leather boots.*
>
> *No one knew how long the giant Gabriel would live. Each new inch was robbing him of hopes of longevity, if statistical findings could be taken seriously. "There was a giant in Ireland once named Charlie Byrne," he said to her, "who died surrounded by quarreling anatomists. They all wanted his bones and they were very powerful. He tried to foil them by having his body shipped to sea. But they caught up with him and stole the coffin from the horsemen in the dead of night. His skeleton now hangs in the London Museum of Natural History." He had read every book on giants that there was.*
>
> *Often now Melanie would try to imagine how they must have looked together on that first day in the book store, she so very fat and awkward she could hardly steer between the shelves, and not at all flamboyant yet, and he so tall his*

head had almost struck the ceiling lights. He had stopped her from stealing and had given her a horrible lecture on being melodramatic without a reason. He had belittled the adolescent nature of her drive towards death. For even though he was her age, he felt he had a reason to explore such subjects. For he knew he would die young. All giants did.

Gabriel, like Melanie, was very pale, but there was a luminous glow about him, as if he was already in communion with his imminent passing. Maybe that was why Melanie could not recall the feeling of his hand in hers, the rhythm of his heart beating against her own. Gabriel had about him the air of a ghost, but one who bore the shadow souls of all his vanished tribe. He even seemed to share their nightmares.

Rarely having been hurt himself, he was terrified of the little superficial blemishes that never could be felt which suddenly grow gangrenous, for such had been the rather recent death of Robert Wadlow, scarcely older than Gabriel now was. He was careful never to walk without his custom fitted shoes, for even a splinter could be dangerous, he explained. He never went to the theater, for he feared the partly rotted floorboards in old fashioned auditoriums.

"Sometimes I shut my eyes and dream the dream of Charlie Byrne," he said, stroking her arm, "only it is my bones turning, turning in the famous scientist's enormous kettle, separating slowly from my flesh, becoming specimens." Then he told her how all the later giants had devised elaborate methods to protect their bodies after death. "Some had their coffins made of lead and lowered into beds of solid rock, or covered over with layers of brick and iron bars. Robert Wadlow, whom I think was buried in a piano case, had it encased in a full shell of reinforced concrete."

It was a most peculiar conversation for two seventeen-year-olds embarking upon their first romantic attachment. With a wonderful elation, Melanie followed him out of the book store. In her uncomely thick fur coat, being touched by him despite how she appeared, she felt she was the Beast in "Beauty and the Beast," the frog in "The Frog Prince." She felt like a rescued princess, only they were never ugly, never had a hidden noble soul. Gabriel looked so large that day, it seemed that he alone could save her.

Children believe very easily. They have a romantic nature which for all its sores had not completely disappeared. So they stood hand in hand, already making rapid plans.

Melanie had fascinated Gabriel because she was so fat and buried and so set on death. And he had fascinated her, with all his tales and abnormal obsessions. For there was something God-like in the way that he was constantly outgrowing his surroundings, in his helpless height that shut him out of ordinary life. His touch was too powerful, even when he meant to be gentle. And he had a hard time doing simple human things like opening locks or lighting matches. Whenever he entered other people's houses, he would have to be careful not to knock into crystal chandeliers and ceiling lights. Everything became fragile when he approached, became endangered. He was afraid to cross unknown bridges or sit down in strange chairs. Yet he was really quite weak, in a way. The bones in his lower legs were getting softer as he grew. There was almost no sensation left in his extremities and he was unusually susceptible to infections in these parts. Every night before he went to bed he would take off his shoes and check his boney long white feet for the bumps and bruises that he could not feel which threatened to destroy his body. Also, his voice was so soft and diffused that it often got lost in the air long before its meek vibrations could descend to normal ear level.

The giant Gabriel is a poet and painter, and Melanie looks to him for the beauty and largeness that she can't find in herself. But he is impotent, as are most giants. His heart is only normal sized and cannot pump the blood to his far off extremities. It can't last long. His hands are numb and cold. He cannot hug her properly and make her safe and warm. His feet are so numb they cannot feel injuries that may turn fatal. Therefore he is afraid to really walk on them. He's totally obsessed with images of death.

I was twenty-eight years old when I wrote these pages. I was married to a sculptor from a Scottish mining town. With him I traveled to Scotland and spent many wonderful hours listening to the wild wistful balladry of blood and violence, beauty and decay. We visited the old graveyards with their fieldstone angels missing noses and the crumbling castles of old legendary kings and queens. Back in this country, every free weekend we would take our three young daughters to old ruined churches with their golden angels outside in the wind and rain, their madonnas and martyted Christs left all alone in rubble and brick dust. Late at night from our window we'd watch the wondrous blaze of orange fires along the Hudson River where hoodlums had set the piers aflame. And later we would walk into the ruins of those piers, beneath the charred remains of roof and rafters, watching the magic brightness of the sky come through the open spaces in the darkness of the brown and grey. Rembrandt colors we would say to one another, El Greco, Kafka, Gorky. Whenever we had a free Sunday morning we would put the youngest children in their tandem stroller and take the oldest by the hand and walk to demolition sights to see the skeletal remains of houses that had once been lived in, rooms with pictures still hanging or hats on hooks, that once held people's hearts and lives. We would collect new images to put into our art.

Now, less than ten years later, I often ask myself what does it mean? What did it mean, my youthful equation of beauty and violence and images of death? What does it mean, not only for me personally, but for a whole culture which has based so much of its aesthetic on images of sorrow, pain and death? For indeed, this is the subject of so much great literature and art.

The other day I went to the Cloisters with the British poet David Gascoyne, originally a child prodigy among the surrealists (having published four books by the time he was twenty). He had been silent for more than twenty years, after writing a series of religious poems of prophesy based on the "handwriting on the walls" of the British Mass Observation Movement and the slow take over of Europe by the Nazis. He had stopped writing after letting forth his "cry" over British Radio from Civil War torn Spain. In his earliest surrealist poems, it had seemed to me, he used the unpredictable and ugly, the cruel, the excrement and putrification of Dali-like imagery with courageous lust to try to dare himself to become "man" enough to partake in the terrible world into which he was coming of age. But underneath the inventive surrealistic bravado, I could feel a mounting of the pain. Then the surrealist bravado disappeared, and only the pain, the prophecy of doom, remained, and then two decades and more of silence. I had gone to visit him on the Isle of Wight during the tail end of the silence, to interview him for *Book Forum*. Together we had watched the Verdi *'Macbeth'* broadcast on his color T.V., had seen the cruciform configuration of the singers silhouetted black against an orange fire background, watched the flashing white English translation letters "The Oppression is upon us" come upon the screen along with the wild other-worldly rising of the song. When I asked David Gascoyne why he no longer wrote, he answered quite simply that he had nothing else to say and felt that poetry should say something.

David Gascoyne had been brought up as a choir boy in

Salisbury amidst great beauty, and even his most lustful daring entries into the Ugly through his eary poetry did not inure him to the horrors of the world he had to face. Just recently he wrote another poem. It begins almost polemically about the brink of world disaster, almost coldly. Then suddenly he asks:

—If this is a poem, where are the images?
—What images suffice, Corpses and carrion,
Ubiquitous bloodshed, bigger, more beastly bombs,
Stockpiled atomic warheads, stanchless wounds,
Ruins and rubble, maniac messiahs and mobs.

—But poets make beauty out of ghastliness...
—You think I want to? Think truth beautiful?
—"A terrible beauty is born..." It is indeed.

In youth I did in spite of everything
Believe with Keats and Shelley such things as
That poets can "legislate" and prophesy;
Or like Stravinsky when he wrote "The Rite"
Become transmitting vessels for new sounds
From an inspiring, unknown world within.

I'm over sixty now...

I sat in the cloisters with David Gascoyne, silently, in an old stone antichamber which had no images, but only a high vaulted ceiling of the simplest archings of stone. It was very quiet. And I thought about how his poem continues from the cry "make beauty out of ghastliness... You think I want to?" to a "litany of lurid headline names," beautiful as any piece of music.

Vietnam, Angola, Thailand and Pakistan,
Chile, Cambodia, Iran, Afghanistan,
Derry's Bogside, Belfast and Crossmaglen;
Up in Strathclyde or down on Porton Down,
On Three Mile Island or Seveso, Italy:
Then there are Manson, Pol Pot, and Amin,...

For a few more lines he lets the litany of horror rise. Then suddenly he says

And yet I yearn to end by trying to evoke
A summer dawn I saw when I was not yet eight,
And having risen early watched for an hour or more
A transcendental transfiguration of auroral clouds,
Like a prophetic vision granted from on high.
I cannot see much now. The dawn is always new
As nature is, however much we blind ourselves and try
To poison the Earth-Mother...

We sat in silence in the vaulted room for a long time. What was it? a shelter? a void? a place of peace?

Then I left him to wander into a room with a Mary holding an infant Jesus made with the perfect adult proportions common for the sculpture of babies and children of the medieval period. The baby Jesus in Mary's arms was a perfect replica of a grown man, except for the expresison on his face which was so expectant and fresh and new, still so capable of everything, alive and pink-cheeked even through its tarnish of centuries of terrible, terrible things gone by.

Then I wandered into another room and saw the dead saints lying there, all marbleized in their crypts, with the wrinkles of their hands and faces and broken noses and fancy lace all the same texture of latticework stone, so exquisite and fine. How beautiful the sculptor had made their death, their stillness. And the crucified Christs in the room after that—they were such scary things, all black and skeletal and bone, their rib cages bare and big holes rent in their ankles and wrists where the wounds had been. They were what we did to the baby who had the head of the grown adult, who contained and expected it all. These terrible martyred Christs of dark black rib and agony and severed bone—were they the punishment for expectation, for trying to turn into an adult not dulled and stilled and killed? I went back to look at the wonderfully textured lying down saints, the exquisite perfection of their stillness. I was drawn to that room, over and over, as I wandered away, but I forced myself also to go back to the baby again, and look at its little upraised hand of painted wood, a few of the fingers broken off through time, but the ones that remained still reaching out, reaching forth.

What did it mean that I, at the age of twenty-eight, not yet a feminist, with three young babies of my own, was writing about a girl in love with a giant utterly obsessed with death, a giant born too large and short-lived for this world. My first book, *A Wreath of Pale While Roses*, written even earlier, was about four old people dying. It climaxed at the moment when sexuality completely merged with death. What did that mean?

"Alexy's body rose and fell over Laura's, slowly, so slowly, that the sound of his breathing roared in her ear like the crashing of the surf, and all was black beyond him. Laura had not imagined that her death would be like this, so like her life, only confused in time and place, less vivid, her sensations and her vision bone. She had imagined that there would be a feeling of fulfillment and finality, a supernatural embrace that would make her feel as warm as she had been within the waters of the womb, and would mould her into the shape that she wished to be, and not just this slow restless pounding as of unrelenting surf which did not reach her. Sometimes she had imagined that death would be a deeper vaster emptiness than any she had known, a knowledge of the infinite void which held her little human hopes, another birth into a larger disappointment... She had hoped in death to find the infinite pain which would completely kill her and the infinite emptiness by which she would recognize the end..."

What was it that I was trying so hard to end? I had not yet known women's love and women's warmth. Rereading this ending of my first book, later in retrospect, I thought of how when Olga Broumas accepted the Yale Younger Poet's Prize she told the audience that when pain is our primary and our most intense experience, it must inevitably become the material for our fantasies, for our poetry and our art. I felt a real sense of kinship in what she said. Then she read us her poem, "Beauty and the Beast," which begins:

For years I fantasized pain
driving, driving
me over each threshold
I thought I had, till finally
the joy in my flesh would break
loose with the terrible
strain...

Pain the link
to existence: pinch your own tissue, howl
yourself from sleep. But that night was too soon
after passion
had shocked the marrow alive in my hungry bones...
...and I leaned and touched, leaned
and touched you, mesmerized, woman, stunned

by the tangible
pleasure that gripped my ribs, every time
like a caged beast, bewildered
by this late, this essential heat.

As I became involved in the feminist movement and women's energies, the tone of my fiction gradually changed from one of despair to hope. And images of death and pain became vehicles for forward growth rather than ends in themselves. Because the giant, large and wondrous as he is, cannot live long, because he is impotent and cannot fill anybody up, Melanie must leave him and search for the inner largeness in herself she was afraid to see before. She must, through learning to love women, find the kind part of the mother she left and the peaceful person and the "mother" in herself. This became the "journey" of the final portion of my book, as well as the journey of my life.

The other day I heard Tille Olsen reading "Tell Me a Riddle" to a spell-bound audience. Every so often she would interrupt her story about the despairful, disappointed older people to talk about politics or hope. For her final interruption, as the woman of her story nears her death, she suddenly began to read a passage from the novel of her youth, *Yonandio*. It was the passage about the baby banging a jar cover with absolute seriousness. And she spoke of how she believed that we were all that baby once, with all of human potential and wonder, and all possibility in us, how she believed that we could all become that baby still. I will never forget that moment.

Yesterday, for no particular reason, I was reading the childhood memoirs of Albert Schweitzer. I came upon a passage about how he had to fight to restrain himself from desiring to whip his neighbor's aging horse to make it trot, how he had to force himself to see the effort and the sorrow in its flanks to relinquish his pleasure in watching it gallop so fast ahead. Then there was a short annecdote about how another boy insisted that they take their catapults into the trees to see if they could kill the birds. The trees were still wintery and bare, so the birds could be perfectly seen. And they were singing so beautifully. He didn't want to kill them. But he didn't know how to say no. Then suddenly the church bells started ringing, and adding their music to the bird song. They gave the boy the strength to brave his friends' contempt and shoo the birds away. From then on Schweitzer vowed never to hurt another creature, no matter how great the social pressure. And whenever the pressure would be upon him, he would hear the church bells and the bird songs, mixing up their echoing.

This article is dedicated to Tille Olsen's baby in us all, and to David Gascoyne's sunrise, to Olga Broumas in her fresh joy at finding woman's love and to my student trying to find her Truth, and to all people, women and men also, turning painfully from the age old lure of the death culture we have been dipped and dyed in, trying to clear away all the rubble of decay enough to hear the bells and singing birds, to grow into the giants we can really be, loving and affirming life.

Diana J. M. Davies/Insight

Dump Nixon/Anti-War Rally in New York City, 1970.

Bruce Kokopeli and George Lakey
More Power Than We Want: Masculine Sexuality and Violence

By now we might call this essay a "classic." Since it appeared in Win *(the magazine devoted to "peace and freedom thru nonviolence") in July, 1976, it has been reprinted in the U.S. and Europe 12 times. It has generated this wide circulation for the same reason that it is being included here as an exception, the only contribution by men—it is one of the few truly perceptive and articulate expressions of the interdependence of violence and the patriarchy's creation, masculinity, written from a male perspective. "More Power Than We Want" represents an awareness by some men (primarily coming from the gay rights movement) that feminists, gays and pacifists are fighting a common enemy—patriarchy. It is argued here that masculine sexuality, which the patriarchy has shaped to express the theme of domination, directly involves the oppression of women, competition among men and homophobia (fear of homosexuality), and locks men into justification of the military state. Bruce and George conclude, "...the struggle for a world without war must also be a struggle against patriarchy with its masculine character ideal and its oppression of women and gays," and they suggest we embrace androgyny as an alternative character ideal.*

Bruce, who writes songs and does construction work, was one of the founders of the Men's Resource Center in Seattle and is presently on the staff of the Fellowship of Reconciliation/Seattle. He is a member of Movement for a New Society and co-authored the 1979 MNS pamphlet Leadership for Change.

George was a founder of Movement for a New Society and currently lives in the Philadelphia Life Center. He is the author of Strategy for a Living Revolution *(W.H. Freeman, 1973) a new edition of which will be released by New Society Publishers (NSP) in 1982, and is co-author of* No Turning Back: Lesbian and Gay Liberation For the '80s *(NSP, 1982). George also teaches Social Change at the University of Pennsylvania.*

Patriarchy, the systematic domination of women by men through unequal opportunities, rewards, punishments, and the internalization of unequal expectations through sex role differentiation, is the institution which organizes these behaviors.

Patriarchy is men having more power, both personally and politically, than women of the same rank. This imbalance of power is the core of patriarchy, but definitely not the extent of it.

Sex inequality cannot alone be enforced through open violence or even blatant discriminatory agreements—patriarchy also needs its values accepted in the minds of people. If as many young *women* wanted to be physicians as men, and as many young men *wanted* to be nurses as women, the medical schools and the hospitals would be hard put to maintain the masculine domination of health care; open struggle and the naked exercise of power would be necessary. Little girls, therefore, are encouraged to think "nurse" and boys to think "doctor."

Patriarchy assigns a list of human characteristics according to gender: women should be nurturant, gentle, in touch with their feelings, etc.; men should be productive, competitive, super-rational, etc. Occupations are valued according to these gender-linked characteristics, so social work, teaching, housework, and nursing are of lower status than business executive, judge, or professional football player.

When men do enter "feminine" professions they disproportionately rise to the top and become chefs, principals of schools, directors of ballet, and teachers of social work. A man is somewhat excused from his sex role deviation if he at least dominates within the deviation. Domination, after all, is what patriarchy is all about.

Access to powerful positions by women (i.e., those positions formerly limited to men) is contingent on the women adopting some masculine characteristics, such as competitiveness. They feel pressure to give up qualities assigned to females (such as gentleness) because those qualities are considered inherently weak by patriarchal culture. The existence, therefore, of a woman like Indira Gandhi in the position of a dictator in no way undermines the basic sexist structure which allocates power to those with masculine characteristics.

Patriarchy also shapes men's sexuality so it expresses the theme of domination. Notice the masculine preoccupation with size. The size of a man's body has a lot to say about his clout or his vulnerability, as any junior high boy can tell you. Many of these schoolyard fights are settled by who is bigger than whom, and we experience in our adult lives the echoes of intimidation and deference produced by our habitual "sizing up" of the situation.

Penis size is part of the masculine preoccupation, this time directed toward women. Men want to have large penises because size = power, the ability to make a woman "really feel it." The imagery of violence is close to the surface here, since women generally find penis size irrelevant to sexual genital pleasure. "Fucking" is a highly ambiguous word, meaning both intercourse and exploitation/assault.

It is this confusion that we need to untangle and understand. Patriarchy tells men that their need for love and respect can only be met by being masculine, powerful, and ultimately violent. As men come to accept this, their sexuality begins to reflect it. Violence and sexuality combine to support masculinity as a character ideal. To love a woman is to have power over her and to treat her violently if need be. The Beatles' song "Happiness is a Warm Gun" is but one example of how sexuality gets confused with violence and power. We know one man who was discussing another man who seemed to be highly fertile—he had made several women pregnant. "That guy," he said, "doesn't shoot any blanks."

Rape is the end logic of masculine sexuality. Rape is not so much a sexual act as an act of violence expressed in a sexual way. The rapist's mind-set—that violence and sexuality *can* go together—is actually a product of patriarchal conditioning. Most of us men understand that mind-set, however abhorrent rape may be to us personally.

In war, rape is astonishingly prevalent even among men who "back home" would not do it. In the following description by a Marine sergeant who witnessed a gang rape in Vietnam, notice that nearly all of the nine-men squad participated:

They were supposed to go after what they called a Viet Cong whore. They went into her village and instead of capturing her, they raped her—every man raped her. As a matter of fact, one man said to me later that it was the first time he had ever made love to a woman with his boots on. The man who led the platoon, or the squad, was actually a private. The squad leader was a sergeant but he was a useless person and he let the private take over his squad. Later he said he took no part in the raid. It was against his morals. So instead of telling his squad not to do it, because they wouldn't listen to him anyway, the sergeant went into another side of the village and just sat and stared bleakly at the ground, feeling sorry for himself. But at any rate, they raped the girl, and then, the last man to make love to her, shot her in the head. (Vietnam Veterans Against the War, statement by Michael McClusker in *The Winter Soldier Investigation: An Inquiry into American War Crimes.)*

Psychologist James Prescott adds to this account:
What is it in the American psyche that permits the use of the word 'love' to describe rape? And where the act of love is completed with a bullet in the head! (Bulletin of the Atomic Scientists, November 1975, p. 17)

Masculinity Against Men: The Militarization of Everyday Life

Patriarchy benefits men by giving us a class of people (women) to dominate and exploit. Patriarchy also oppresses men, by setting us at odds with each other and shrinking our life space.

The pressure to win starts early and never stops. Working class gangs fight over turf; rich people's sons are pushed to compete on the sports field. British military officers, it is said, learned to win on the playing fields of Eton. Competition is conflict held within a framework of rules. When the stakes are really high the rules may not be obeyed; fighting breaks out.

We men mostly relate through competition, but we know what is waiting in the wings. John Wayne is not a culture hero by accident. Men compete with each other for status as masculine males. Because masculinity equals power, this means we are competing for power. The ultimate proof of power/masculinity is violence. A man may fail to "measure up" to macho stereotype in important ways, but if he can fight successfully with the person who challenges him on his deviance, he is still all right. The television policeman Baretta is strange in some ways: he is gentle with women and he cried when a man he loved was killed. However, he has what are probably the largest biceps in television and he proves weekly that he can beat up the toughs who [sic] come his way.

The close relationship between violence and masculinity does not need much demonstration. War used to be justified partly because it promoted "manly virtue" in a nation. Even today we are told that the Marines are looking for a "few good men." Those millions of people in the woods hunting deer, in the National Rifle Association, and cheering on the bloodiest hockey teams are overwhelmingly men.

The world situation is so much defined by patriarchy that what we see in the wars of today is competition between various patriarchal ruling classes and governments breaking into open conflict. Violence is the accepted masculine form of conflict resolution. Women at this time are not powerful enough in the world situation for us to see mass overt violence being waged on them. But the violence is in fact there; it is hidden through its legitimization by the state and by culture.

In everyday middle class life, open violence between men is of course rare. The defining characteristics of masculinity, however, are only a few steps removed from violence. Wealth, productivity, or rank in the firm or institution translate into power—the capacity (whether or not exercised) to dominate. The holders of power in even polite institutions seem to know that violence is at their fingertips, judging from reactions of college presidents to student protest in the 1960s. We know of one urbane *pacifist* man, the head of a theological seminary, who was barely talked out of calling the police to deal with the nonviolent student sit-in at "his" seminary!

Patriarchy teaches us at very deep levels that we can never be safe with other men (or perhaps with anyone), for the guard must be kept up lest our vulnerability be exposed and we be taken advantage of. At a recent Quaker conference in Philadelphia a discussion group considered the value of personal sharing and openness in the Quaker Meeting. In almost every case the women advocated more sharing and the men opposed it. Dividing by gender on that issue was predictable; men are conditioned by our life experience of masculinity to distrust settings where personal exposure will happen, especially if men are present. Most men find emotional intimacy possible only with women; many with only one woman; some men cannot be emotionally intimate with anyone.

Patriarchy creates a character ideal—we call it masculinity—and measures everyone against it. Many men fail the test as well as women, and even men who are passing the test today are carrying a heavy load of anxiety about tomorrow. Because masculinity is a form of domination, no one can really rest secure. The striving goes on forever unless you are actually willing to give up and find a more secure basis for identity.

Masculinity Against Gay Men: Patriarchy Fights a Rear Guard Action

Homophobia is the measure of masculinity. The degree to which a man is thought to have gay feelings is the degree of his unmanliness. Because patriarchy presents sexuality as men over women (part of the general dominance theme), men are conditioned to have only that in mind as a model of sexual expression. Sex with another man must mean being dominated, which is very scary. A non-patriarchal model of sexual expression as the mutuality of equals doesn't seem possible; the transfer of the heterosexual model to same-sex relations can at best be "queer;" at worst, "perverted."

In the recent book *Blue Collar Aristocrats,* by E.E. LeMasters, a working class tavern is described in which the topic of homosexuality sometimes comes up. Gayness is never defended. In fact, the worst thing you can call a man is homosexual. A man so attacked must either fight or leave the bar.

Notice the importance of violence in defending yourself against the charge of being a "pansy." Referring to your income, or academic degrees, or size of your car is no defense againt such a charge. Only fighting will re-establish respect as a masculine male. Because gay appears to mean powerless, one needs to go to the masculine source of power—violence—for adequate defense.

Last year, the Argentinian government decided to persecute gays on a systematic basis. The Ministry of Social Welfare offered the rationale for this policy in an article which also attacked lesbians, concluding that they should be put in jail or killed:

As children they played with dolls. As they grew up, violent sports horrified them. As was to be expected, with the passage of time and the custom of listening to foreign mulattos on the radio, they became conscientious objectors (El Caudillo, February 1975, excerpted in *Peace News,* July 11, 1975, p. 5).

The Danish government, by contrast with Argentina, has liberal policies on gay people. There is no government persecution and all government jobs are open to gays—except in the military and the diplomatic service! Two places where the nation-state is most keen to assert power are places where gays are excluded as a matter of policy.

We need not go abroad to see the connections between violence and homophobia. In the documentary film *Men's Lives* a high school boy is interviewed on what it is like to be a dancer. While the interview is conducted we see him working out, with a very demanding set of acrobatic exercises. The boy mentions that other boys think he must be gay. Why is that? the interviewer asks. Dancers are free and loose, he replies; they are not big like football players; and "you're not trying to kill anybody."

Different kinds of homosexual behavior bring out different amounts of hostility, curiously enough. That fact gives us further clues to violence and female oppression. In prisons, for example, men can be respected if they fuck other men, but not if they are themselves fucked. (We used the word "fucked" intentionally for its ambiguity.) Often prison rapes are done by men who identify as heterosexual; one hole substitutes for another in this scene, for sex is in either case an expression of domination for the masculine mystique.

But for a man to be entered sexually, or to use effeminate gestures and actions, is to invite attack in prison and hostility outside. Effeminate gay men are at the bottom of the totem pole because they are *most like women,* which is nothing less than treachery to the Masculine Cause. Even many gay men shudder at drag queens and vigilantly guard against certain mannerisms because they, too, have internalized the masculinist dread of effeminacy.

John Braxton's report of prison life as a draft resister is revealing on this score. The other inmates knew immediately that John was a conscientious objector because he did not act tough. They also assumed he was gay for the same reason. (If you are not masculine, you must be a pacifist and gay, for masculinity is a package which includes both violence and heterosexuality.)

A ticket of admission to Masculinity, then, is sex with women, and bisexuals can at least get that ticket even if they deviate through having gay feelings as well. This may be why bisexuality is not feared as much as exclusive gayness among men. Exclusively gay men let down the Masculine Cause in a very important way—they do not participate in the control of women through sexuality. Control through sexuality matters because it is flexible; it usually is mixed with love and dependency so that it becomes quite subtle.

Now we better understand why women are in general so much more supportive of gay men than non-gay men are. Part of it of course is that heterosexual men are often paralyzed by fear. Never very trusting, such men find gayness one more reason to keep up the defenses. But heterosexual women are drawn to active support for the struggles of gay men because there is a common enemy—patriarchy and its definition of sexuality as domination. Both heterosexual women and gay men have experienced firsthand the violence of sexism; we all have experienced its less open forms such as put-downs and discrimination and we all fear its open forms such as rape and assault.

Patriarchy, which links characteristics (gentleness, aggressiveness, etc.) to gender, shapes sexuality in such a way as to maintain male power. The Masculine Cause draws strength from homophobia and resorts habitually to violence in its battles on the field of sexual politics. It provides psychological support for the military state and is in turn stimulated by it.

Patriarchy and The Military State

The parallels between these two powerful institutions are striking. Both prefer more subtle means of domination but insist on violence as a last resort. Both institutions provide role models for socialization: the masculine man, the feminine woman; the patriotic citizen. Both are aided by other institutions in maintaining their legitimacy—religion, education, business, sport.

The sexual politics of the family provides the psychological model for the power politics of the state. The oft-deplored breakdown of the family may, from this point of view, have positive effects. Future Vietnams may be ruled out by the growing unmasculinity of soldiers and unfeminine impatience of women.

The business allies of the military are no doubt appalled. The patriarchal family gets constant bolstering from that camp: family services are traditionally the best funded of the private social work agencies; business promoted the Feminine Mystique quite consciously.

The interplay at the top levels of the state between violence and masculinity is becoming clearer. Political scientist Richard Barnet refers to the "hairy chest syndrome" among National Security Managers in government agencies.

The man who is ready to recommend using violence against foreigners, even where he is overruled, does not damage his reputation for prudence, soundness, or imagination, but the man who recommends putting an issue to the UN, seeking negotiations, or—horror of horrors—"doing nothing" quickly becomes known as "soft." To be "soft"—that is, unbelligerent, compassionate, willing to settle for less—or simply to be repelled by homicide, is to be "irresponsible." It means walking out of the club. (Men and Masculinity, by Joseph Pleck and Kack Sawyer, p. 136).

The Mayaguez incident, in which the US bombed Cambodia with no real effort at negotiations or other steps, was a clear example. In fact, it was so clear that Henry Kissinger felt impelled to deny that the US response was to "prove our manhood."

An Angolan leader tried to touch the masculinity nerve in an appeal for US help for the anti-Soviet FNLA. Holden Roberto told *Newsweek* (12/29/75):

> *Most of the world is sniggering up its sleeve at America's detente efforts and the way the Soviets pay lip service to it while consolidating their position. Maybe, like the cuckolded partner in a betrayed marriage, the United States will be the last to learn the truth.*

From all this it seems obvious to us that the struggle for a world without war must also be a struggle against patriarchy with its masculine character ideal and its oppression of women and gays. Pacifist men, by rejecting violence, have taken a healthy first step in dropping out of masculinity. Some have sought to compensate for that by being more rigorously "tough" in other ways and by participating in the oppression of women and gays. This must stop. Peacemakers need to see women and gays as the potential allies they are and develop a feminist perspective as they act for peace.

It seems equally obvious that feminists and gays must include, in our list of patriarchal enemies, the military state. The sexual politics of domination/submission is so reinforced by militarism that one cannot be eliminated without the other. Masculinity and violence are so intimately related that one cannot be defeated by itself.

Androgyny: New People For The New Society

If the masculine character ideal supports militarism, what can support peace? Femininity? No, for that character ideal also has been shaped by patriarchy and includes along with virtues such as gentleness and nurturance, a kind of dependency which breeds the passive-aggressive syndrome of curdled violence.

We are encouraged by the vision of androgyny, which acknowledges that the best characteristics now allocated to the two genders indeed belong to both: gentleness, intelligence, nurturance, courage, awareness of feelings, cooperativeness, rooting one's sense of identity in *being* as well as doing and not tying it to ownership of people or things, initiative, befriending persons rather than physical characteristics, sensuality with appreciation for the erotic dimension of everyday life.

Many of these characteristics are now allocated to the feminine role which has led some men to conclude that the essential liberating task is to become effeminate. We don't agree, since some desirable characteristics are now allocated to the masculine role (for example, initiative, intelligence). Further, some characteristics are not assigned to *either* gender in this culture: having an identity independent of ownership of people and things, for example. Women are expected to be as jealous as men and as absorbed in material accumulation or consumerism.

We urge people to continue the exploration of what a peaceful and sexually liberated society will be like and what kind of people will inhabit it. Let us allow our creativity to flow beyond the definitions patriarchy has given us.

Also needed are strategies for moving toward the androgynous vision which will show us how to change our organizations, campaigns, and lifestyles. All of us in this struggle have a lot to be proud of, and none of us needs to be guilt-tripped into changing. Let's all find the support we need to keep on growing. The future is ours if we only claim it.

Dorothy Marder

Native American women and children at "The War Is Over" celebration in New York's Central Park, May, 1975. An interesting historic note: it is said that in 1600 Iroquois women organized a successful "Lysistrata" action, refusing sex or childbearing until unregulated warfare ceased.

Betsy Wright
Sunpower/Moonpower/ Transformation

Betsy grew up in suburban New Jersey, and dropped out of college in 1977 to join the Movement for a New Society because she was excited about feminism, nonviolence, and moonpower.

What's moonpower? This is perhaps best answered by metaphor. Beneath the moon we dream, rigid distinctions melt and shapes are transformed, archetypal images bubble up to receptive imaginations, the tides ebb and flow. The sun, on the other hand, cuts the world into light and shadow. Beneath it we think our logical daytime thoughts, compete with each other, grow food and flowers, tell time, sweat in its forceful glare.

One is not better or worse than the other, but a predominance of one spells trouble. According to Betsy's analysis, our society is out of balance with excessive sunpower and because of this our response to change tends to be either rigid adherence to law and order or chaotic self-destruction.

Betsy builds a case for a Third Way, a response to change based on balanced sun/moonpower which will enable us to meet uncertainty creatively. She maintains that the re-development of moonpower "may be the most important historical task of our time," and that feminism and nonviolence are two vehicles with which to achieve this.

Betsy has lived in the Philadelphia Life Center since 1977 and has worked with the Keystone Alliance as a newsletter editor, grassroots organizer, fund-raiser and planner of demonstrations against nuclear power. She is the bookkeeper for the Central Committee for Conscientious Objectors.

God bless the grass that grows through the crack
They roll the cement over it and try to keep it back
The concrete gets tired of what it has to do
It breaks and it buckles and the grass grows through
And God bless the grass.

God bless the grass so gentle and low
But its roots they are deep and its will is to grow
And God bless the truth, the friend of the poor
And the wild grass growing at the poor man's door
And God bless the grass.

—*Malvina Reynolds*

Who could imagine something as small and soft as grass triumphing over something as hard and solid as concrete? Who could imagine a tree growing through an iron fence, when anyone knows that iron is stronger than wood?

The constant and obviously strong power of concrete is here being called sunpower; the elusive and organic power of the grass is here being called moonpower.

In a world where concrete and other oppressions seem to pave over everyone and everything, it is very important to learn the secrets of moonpower that the grass knows.

Sun/Moon

The sun's influence on our lives is obvious: it gives the warmth that lets our food grow and the light that lets us see, and its 24-hour cycle is our basic unit of time, the day.

The moon's influence is more subtle but just as real. It pulls the tides with its gravity and purifies our water with its ultraviolet rays; many plants and animals regulate their life cycles by the changes in the moon. It affects human beings, too, in ways we don't completely understand yet. Most mental hospitals routinely give their inmates extra sedatives at the full moon, and 82% of bleeding crises in hospital patients are reported to occur when the moon is full.[1] The moon's phases and women's menstrual cycles are of a similar length, and in some primitive cultures all women are said to menstruate together at the same phase of the moon.

By analogy we can use the sun and the moon as symbols for the two kinds of human power discussed in this article.

Sunpower: forcefulness, control, clear-cut boundaries and distinctions between things, logic and analytical thinking, orderliness, clarity, an emphasis on the individual and on the conscious mind, restraint, competition and ranking, being unyielding and unchanging.

The sunpower image of success is to overcome by superior logic, skill, or force.

Moonpower: receptivity, intuition, flexibility and fluidity, an emphasis on the collective and on the non-conscious and non-logical parts of our minds, acceptance of ambiguity and disorder, creative use of conflict, uncontrolled flows of energy, wisdom about and responsiveness to constant change, organic growth, the dissolving of individual or group ego boundaries, recognition of the unity of all life, and listening, resonating the rhythm of the other, being in harmony.

The moonpower image of success is to transform and to be transformed in the process.

Ideally, human personalities and societies should be a perfect balance of sunpower and moonpower. In fact, we live in a super-sunpowered society, and most of our problems come from this imbalance. The excessive sunpower mode of competition, hierarchy, rationality, and the separateness of each isolated individual can be seen everywhere in modern patriarchal society, from its philosophy to its economic systems to its sex roles.

As sunpower has come to predominate, with no moonpower to balance out its ethic of drawing distinctions and valuing force and control, a terrible process of objectification has happened. Over the centuries, women, animals and plants, the earth, people of color, non-land-owning people, the human body, and now, with modern psychology, even much of the human mind have come to be seen as Other, as objects to be studied, desired, used, and exploited. These Others have also been feared at times and seen as wild forces to be tamed and controlled.

This objectification is at the root of most of the problems of the modern world. Third World exploitation, environmental damage and resource depletion, the oppression of women, militarism, the profit system and the exploitation of working people's labor are all symptoms of the process of objectification.

The official solutions to these problems put forward by the over-sunpowered system are based in the concepts that change happens either through control or through progress. With the first, we can "put a lid on" out-of-control forces through regulation, stricter authorities, will power, etc. With the second, history is a straight line towards better times, and problems are leftover imperfections from our barbaric past that just need to be cleaned up, usually by more education or more sophisticated technology.

The conservative and liberal social philosophies prevalent today are combinations of different elements of these two concepts. Neither type of solution is effective and hopelessness is spreading like a disease throughout our society as people see these remedies fail.

The reason that sunpowered solutions are failing to solve the problems of excessive sunpower is that the concepts of how change happens (both on a social and a personal level) are wrong. Seeing the essential historical or personal drama as the alternating predominance of natural selfishness and barbarism and the controlling influence of civilization, and seeing historical change as smooth progression from one stage to the next, each better than the last, are both largely inaccurate.

To understand how change really happens requires some understanding of moonpower. Change, both social and personal, can happen in unexpected shifts of people's paradigm, or world-view, that seem impossible before they happen; the old way puts up resistance to change, and there is always struggle, polarization, and conflict both before and after the shift occurs. The change is often dormant, like a seed, for a time, and during much of the process nothing much seems to be happening. Both positive and negative change can be explained this way.

Moon wisdom is understanding this principle of change and interpreting events this way. To turn the tide of history for the better also involves people learning the moonpower skills of working with the principles of change and using them to create personal and social liberation.

This redevelopment of moonpower may be the most important historical task of our time.

A Third Way

Where will it come from, this vital re-creation of moonpower as a real power? What will it look like? Where are we historically in sunpower and moonpower terms?

The point of history we're living in now is one of chaos and the break-up of some old values and institutions. Thirty years ago in the US, the reign, for better of worse, of the nuclear family, Christian morality, and American technological superiority was almost unchallenged. But in recent decades there has been a great shattering of these secure traditions. Church attendance is down and divorce is up, to name some obvious signs of the shattering. Whereas in the '50's most people had their values and beliefs handed to them in a package which they seldom questioned, now many people have to decide what they believe from scratch.

It is obvious that there is a shift away from traditional American institutions, but what are we shifting *to*—something better or something worse? So far we have mostly shifted to uncertainty.

There are two responses to this uncertainty that people in touch with only sunpower can make.

The first is chaos and isolation—giving in to the lack of values and the lack of coherent connection to other people through stable institutions, and so acting in ways that seem self-centered but in fact are self-destructive. Crime, drugs, the arms race, and material ambition are examples of the chaos response. The survivalist movement, the people who are hoarding food and weapons and building shelters for an apocalyptic future thay see coming, are another example. The out-of-balance sunpower qualities of the isolation of the individual and the objectification of other people reach their peak in these trends.

The other over-sunpowered response to uncertainty is to cling to something and try to make a new security of it. Any dogma is more comforting than the torments of uncertainty. Security can be found in something new, for example the Moonies (followers of Sun Myung Moon), or in something old, e.g. the Jesus freaks or the Moral Majority. The key factors are a source of infallible truth such as a guru or a book, and a group to join that has a clear-cut distinction between "us" and "them." Millions of Americans, of all ages, of both left and right wing, have tried to build a new cocoon to replace the one that is splitting open.

There is a Third Way. The balanced sun/moonpower response to the shattering is to use the uncertainty creatively, to give birth to new values, new culture, and new, more just relations between people. Truth becomes neither relative ("you do your thing and I do mine") nor absolute. Instead, there is the view of truth articulated by Gandhi, in which there *is* an ultimate truth, but everyone has only a piece of it, and we shift to closer and closer approximations of it as we struggle with each other and learn from the experience. Raising conflict and struggling over injustice, and experimenting with all the possible ways of doing things better are two aspects of this response. These are done with joy and hope and excitement, because to a moonpower practitioner, the shattering of old values and institutions is a tremendous opportunity.

Another meaning of the Third Way: The sunpower-only world-view makes people choose between being a victim and being a victimizer. It is a comfortable choice for no one, but most people eventually settle into one or both roles. The pioneers of moonpower are those who are struggling to find a Third Way to act, neither being victimized nor victimizing others.

The physical expression of this Third Way, the moonpower way, can be found in the martial arts. With skill in Aikido or Judo or Jiu-Jitsu, one can fight bigger and stronger attackers and win. By using the opponents' weight and strength against them, the martial artist can effectively prevent herself from being hurt, yet inflicts no severe pain or damage on the opponents. No weapons are needed besides the resources of the human body, but the skills don't come naturally; it takes years of work to manifest the moonpower in our bodies. Like any moonpower interaction, this kind of fight can be initiated by one side alone, even if the opponent doesn't play by judo rules; any situation can be turned upside-down with moonpower, and we don't have to wait until the whole world is run that way.

Much that happens in radical social change groups and New Age spiritual groups and alternative communities has at least some element of experimenting with a Third Way, though there is no movement or ideology in this society which some people aren't clinging to as a security blanket. Two places where moonpower is being developed, where seekers of a Third Way are gathering, are feminism and nonviolent direct action.

The Key Role Of Women And Feminism

Men are conditioned to have sunpower qualities, and to the extent they don't have them, they are looked down on as weak, or even tormented.

Women are conditioned to have sunpower qualities only in moderation; we are despised for not having them but seen as strange or a threat if we display them too much. The personality traits expected of women are *not* moonpower, but are crippled, trivialized vestiges of moon qualities. Women are supposed to be nice, sociable, willing to serve others, pliable, and "motherly"—qualities that are the opposite of sunpower qualities and help moderate and humanize the viciousness of the imbalance. But they are weak and trivial compared with true moonpower, and they pose no fundamental threat to the reign of sunpower.

Resistance and fighting back by all the groups of people who have been objectified and exploited is an important challenge to sunpower dominance. The message of Third World liberation movements and labor organizing is also, "We will not be your Other anymore."

But because of the different conditioning of men and women,

women are an oppressed group that is key to the moonpower renaissance. The sun/moon imbalance can be shaken up and unlocked by women re-claiming sunpower as our birthright *and* rejecting the trivialized moon qualities we've learned. We must dare to experiment and search for the real thing. Women are closer than men, despite the trivialization, to the vestiges of moonpower (e.g. "women's intuition") and less indoctrinated in sunpower. To the extent that the feminist movement says, "We're not just joining the game, we're changing the rules," it is a movement of moonpower rebirth.

With our lives shaken up by the shattering of old institutions, women are experimenting with restructured lives—trying single parenthood, lesbian relationships, career/parenthood combinations, and all-women's communities. With so many options, women are in a position to insist that men change, to insist that they stop being oppressive, give up privilege, and drop the hard sunpowered armor that the system requires them to wear.

Feminists have all along emphasized developing new ways of doing things that change the quality of experiences and the relationships between people. Since the early 1970's when Jo Freeman wrote the article "The Tyranny of Structurelessness," pointing out that unstructured groups naturally develop domination and informal hierarchy, the creation of equalitarian meeting process and organizational structure has been a central project of feminists. The Women's Pentagon Action in November 1980, was an attempt at a different kind of demonstration, with active participation by everyone instead of a passive crowd and speeches from a stage. The slogan of Assertiveness Training, "Not passive and not aggressive, but assertive," reflects this awareness of the need for a Third Way.

The richness of recent feminism has been in feminist culture and spirituality, and the moon search is apparent there. In "And the Water Comes Again," a song by Holly Near and Meg Christian, there is a vision of the moonpower that women have to win our goals. Between verses that describe the worst of women's oppression is the chorus: "Can we be like drops of water/falling on the stone/splashing, breaking, dispersing in air/weaker than the stone by far/but be aware that as time goes by/the rock will wear away."

The best vision yet of a balanced sun/moon society is the one described by Marge Piercy in *Woman On the Edge of Time,* where conflict is accepted as normal and as what keeps the society growing; where families and other institutions are stable and nurturing but fluid and varied in form; and where intuition and psychic powers *and* analytical thinking are developed in everyone.

The revival of feminist spirituality from the traces of ancient goddess and pagan religions is another part of the moon search. Rituals celebrated at certain phases of the moon, including Rosh Hodesh, the new moon ceremony being revived by Jewish feminists, and full moon rituals, attempt to bring back the sense of time as cyclical, not linear, and an awareness of cycles in our lives. The book *The Spiral of Dance* by Starhawk (Harper and Row, 1979) contains an eloquent section on "The World View of Witchcraft" which relates closely to moonpower. It says that the goal of feminist spirituality is transformation, a never-ending process of change toward individual and social liberation, set in motion by experiences of dissolving the boundaries of the individual and of oneness with the human race and with nature. The nature of the universe is understood here to be basically good, with no Satan or force of evil (no "Other"). This does not lead to complacency or passiveness, because our energy and caring is part of the natural order, and it makes sense to use it to fight injustice and bring out the best in all situations.

Pitfalls For Feminists

There are some trends in the feminist movement that I see as subverting its incredible potential as a transformative movement re-birth.

De-valuing sunpower: Even though our society as a whole is over-sunpowered, many situations and many people, including most women, are lacking kinds of sunpower necessary for becoming whole and healthy. Putting down analytical thinking and toughness, or women who display them, is making the mistake of seeing sunpower as bad instead of seeing the imbalance as bad.

Restoring moonpower to our society is a huge task. To pull it off, individual women need self-discipline, ambition, and clear thinking; feminist movements need strong leadership and tight organization; and women as a group need enough economic and political clout and enough control of our lives and our bodies to have some room to maneuver. So even to restore moonpower, more sunpower is needed. Remember that moonlight is sunlight reflected, with new power added, but some of the old power too.

The struggles to get "equality" for women have sunpower goals that are important. The struggles of individual women to love ourselves—to get our needs met and to have more time for ourselves—are sunpowered in the sense of making a sharp distinction between self and other and asserting the individual; and they are vital.

Clinging to the imbalance of sunpower: The classic sunpower pitfalls which have been criticized often elsewhere are seen in the examplès of the female corporate climbers who just want a share of male privilege and of some old-style lesbians who play masculine roles. Instead of these, I'd like to point out two newer trends in radical feminism that I see as falling into excessive sunpower and violating the spirit of moonpower.

One is the theme that, "The patriarchy is the force of death and we are the force of life." Reducing social change into a struggle between good and evil and saying that oneself and one's movement belong entirely on the good side is simplistic and similar to the objectification that has hurt women so much. Under moonlight, distinctions blur and there are shades of gray on all sides. Social forces are seen *in motion,* not fixed. It is also not consistent with organic imagery to speak of death as something negative; death is a part of th cycle of life. With an analysis like that, one would expect feminists either to withdraw from struggle and just create a lovely, isolated, life-affirming counter-culture, or to hammer away at the power structure as if it were a monolith. Of course the institution of patriarchy has been terribly cruel and destructive, but it is not a monolith, and understanding its internal dynamics will help enable its opponents to topple its institutions and replace them with something better.

The other way feminists have clung to sunpower is by promoting an analysis which labels men as the problem and which further advocates separatism as a solution. (Separate space for women as a *means* to the creation of feminist culture and the healing of women hurt by sexism is fully consistent with moonpower.) Again, this is the same old objectification come back to haunt us—men are not like us, they are Other. It is a central principle of moonpower politics to give the oppressors a way to shift positions and then to make it extremely uncomfortable for them not to change. To say men are inherently oppressive gives them an easy excuse for not changing. Moonpower is inclusive, boundary-dissolving. No distinctions are rigid, and ultimately everything is very closely linked together.

Attachment to trivialized moon qualities: Another major pitfall for feminists has been the tendency to cling to or idealize trivialized moonpower, women's conditioned ways of operating.

Many women have learned subordinate behaviors—smiling, speaking softly, not asking for things directly. Women have also been limited mostly to the private spheres of life—to home, relationships, service jobs and indoor jobs with limited contact with the world. Our experience has taught us some valuable lessons and skills that we can be proud of. But the limitations have also left us with some weaknesses that need to be identified and struggled against.

One such weakness is conflict-avoidance. Women often play the pacifier role, and it is difficult for us to counteract that old role enough to raise and wage conflict well. Thinking that social change or personal growth should happen smoothly, without struggle, is a great temptation to many women.

"An all-women's space is so wonderful and comfortable." Of course it's comfortable, with no one to rock the boat by challenging our self-imposed limitations! People in touch with moonpower tend to be somewhat wild, bold, and disrespectful of established conventions; they often make people very uncomfortable.

Politically, the main manifestation of moonpower is nonviolent direct action. Even though the modern feminist movement was started by women active in the black civil rights movement—a movement which demonstrated the most skillful use of nonviolent direct action in our history—this method has been under-used by feminists. One reason for this is probably our attachment to conflict-avoidance and our restriction to the private spheres of life that were so thoroughly ground into us. The Take Back the Night marches in many cities in 1979-80, in which women demonstrated against the violence against women by marching on dangerous streets at night, were powerful direct actions and might be the beginning of a healthy trend.

Nonviolent Direct Action

Who could imagine it possible that the board of directors of JP Stevens would turn around and threaten to quit if the workers weren't allowed to unionize?

Who could imagine the Shah of Iran fleeing his country, when he owned millions of dollars' worth of the most sophisticated weaponry and his people owned no weapons at all?

Who could imagine the banks who stood to profit from the Seabrook nuclear plant pulling their money out of it?

Who could have imagined blacks and whites allowed at the same lunch counters when the white men in power in the South were passionate segregationists?

The most entrenched corporate and governmental powers, too hard-hearted to be reached by persuasion or negotiation and too big to be toppled by any amount of sunpowered force, can be changed by the power of nonviolent direct action. Described as political jiu-jitsu, it is the political power of the "powerless," and, although it involves long and difficult struggle, it works.

The method involves:

1) the coming together of a number of people who want to end the same injustice into a collective entity tight enough that they can act in *unity;*

2) *public actions* which put a spotlight on the issue and raise people's awareness of it. These actions should be dramatic enough that they create controversy and force people to take sides on the issue, and so human and in tune with mainstream morals that the people doing the action are seen as "the good guys" and the opponents are exposed as unjust. The result of this will be a polarization in which more and more of the public, and sometimes of the power structure, will side with the direct actioners; and will feel uncomfortable siding with the oppressor.[2]
oppressor.[2]

3) the campaign *continuing no matter how much repression* comes down on it, and never responding with violence in return. The oppressor then feels forced to escalate the repression to the point of wasting its resources and looking bad, and ultimately is demoralized;

and sometimes 4) organized, mass *noncooperation* with the oppressor, by identifying how the system needs the oppressed to cooperate in order to keep functioning and then withdrawing that cooperation, either symbolically or in full force, through boycotts, sit-ins, blockades, strikes, mass breaking of oppressive laws, etc.

Success results either from people in the power structure making the desired changes (because a changed political climate resulted from the polarization), or from the actual crippling of the opponent through noncooperation, or from a combination of the two. The first type of success may be invisible, and often it feels like "all our direct action didn't do a thing," when in fact it effected major changes. (The moon seems to do nothing, too).

To think of how little sunpower is necessary in this method, how little physical force, money, legal or social status, and expert knowlege its practitioners must have, and then to read the history of nonviolent direct action and see its staggering success rate, is to get a glimpse of the vast potential of moonpower.

Nonviolent direct action often involves doing things that appear weak in sunpower terms, yet it is those very moonpower qualities of being flexible and unified, of not retaliating and yet persisting, that are the method's strengths. The oppressor tries to push down this force rising up against it, only to find that it can't be pushed because it won't push back; it is slippery, as fluid as water, and as elusive and ever changing as the moon.

The history of nonviolent direct action is too long to go into here, but all seekers of a Third Way should study it. People have been practicing nonviolent direct action for centuries in a spontaneous way, just as an untrained person fighting off an attacker might use some judo moves without knowing it. Examples include resistance to the Nazis in the Scandinavian countries, and the battles for unions and the 8-hour day in the US labor movement. After 40 years of state referenda and other unsuccessful work within the system, the vote for US women was finally won by a 10-year campaign of marches, civil disobedience, and fasts in jail. Most national revolutions, including those in the US and China, were won in part by the methods of nonviolence.

The systematic theory and practice of nonviolent direct action was developed first by Gandhi and was continued by the black movement for desegregation and voting rights in the 1960's. This conscious evolution, as opposed to spontaneous practice, is crucial for the future use of moonpowered politics in turning th oppressive power structure over.

Conclusion

It's hard to see the similarity between doing a ritual celebrating the phases of the moon, flipping someone over in Aikido class, starting a women's group, and sitting around with a bunch of organizers (often including some very sexist, elitist, or otherwise difficult people) planning the next stage of a campaign to change some injustice. But the only way to learn moonpower skills is to practice, in these and other ways. In particular, the best way I know to learn these skills is to get involved in a nonviolent direct action campaign about a single issue and stay with it long enough to see the dance of the moon in its dynamics.

I wrote a paper on sunpower and moonpower exactly four years before writing this article, when the concepts first occurred to me. Since then I have worked for three years in a campaign against a nuclear power plant; I've also spent a lot of time in moon-cycle rituals, studied group dynamics in all kinds of groups, read social change history, got to know the feminist movement, and worked with the Movement for a New Society. I've been trying to learn about moonpower from all my life experiences.

These are some of the lessons we can learn from a moonpower process:

** The ability to listen and take in new information and constantly adjust our actions in response to it; the ability to notice and learn from the effects of our actions even if there is no direct feedback. This ability is the root of skills like "street smarts," awareness of and responsiveness to what's going on in city streets, and of good strategizing.

** A feel for how ideas emerge from a group or crystallize in a person; acceptance that things take time.

**Knowledge that there are no absolutes in tactics; ability to tailor actions to the circumstances. Skepticism toward people who argue that one certain tactic is always right.

** Understanding of the back and forth between when to let our voices blend in and when to speak out as individuals; being capable of both.

** Lack of rigidity and ego pride; knowledge that the appearance of strength and weakness is not important, but the situation being transformed is important.

** Tolerance of imperfect and ambiguous situations; not insisting that every truth be said by every person at every time.

** Ability to balance long-range ideal vision and realistic assessment of what's possible, and to hold on to both.

** Recognition of all people as our potential allies, while understanding what their limitations are and being willing to challenge them.

A very important lesson to be learned is that we are not stuck in the place we've been. The old, over-sunpowered order offers its own solutions which lead nowhere. But there is a Third Way, a way to come at any situation from a new angle, powerfully, ready to turn it upside-down. This moonpowered way can be learned, and in feminism and nonviolent direct action we have two vehicles to learn it and to start the creative and joyful struggle towards liberation. The connection between feminism and nonviolence is not that both are so nice and humane compared to patriarchy and violence. It is that both are so potent, with the same kind of power, that they have the potential to turn the violent, patriarchal system over and give birth to something healthier in its place.

Paula Rayman
Utopian Visions: Reflections On Feminist and Nonviolent Thought

In this essay, Paula examines the "utopian mentality" which is evident behind the thinking of both feminists and pacifists and looks at how this is reflected in their speculations on individuality, primary relationships and new forms of community. She writes, "This article is a beginning exploration of the utopian visions reflected in feminist and nonviolent thought, where these visions intersect and diverge, and the significance and difficulties of utopian thought in our times. This is a large and ambitious subject which can only be tentatively begun in the space allotted. And just as this effort is built upon the work of others, it is hoped a bit of a new path will emerge for future travel."

Paula teaches sociology at Brandeis University. She co-edited Nonviolent Action and Social Change *(Irvington Press) and wrote* The Kibbutz Community and Nation Building *(Princeton University Press). She is currently a member of Bay State Conversion Project and conducts research on job loss in military-defense industries. Paula invites people to write to her on issues relating to her article at Brandeis University, Waltham, Massachusetts 02154.*

La guerre revolutionnaire est le tombeau de la revolution. . ."
(The revolutionary war is the death of the revolution. . .)

Simone Weil

"Nothing short of a total revolution in all present modes of acting and thinking among all mankind, will be productive of the great change so loudly called for by women's miserable state. . ."

from the "Women's Page" in Owenite newspaper, The Pioneer

Historically, feminism and nonviolence, in both their theoretical and activist modes, have shared the need for envisioning an alternative to the existing society. Rejecting the inequalities, oppression and violence of previous and present societies, they have employed a utopian mentality as an inherent part of their metaphor. A utopian mentality is meant here to convey a state of mind or a way of acting that is incongruent with the dominant reality and "tends to shatter, either partially or wholly, the order of things prevailing at the time."[1] Assuming a utopian mentality combats a feeling of impotency in regard to the current situation. It also reveals an assertion of choice—that new possibilities can be chosen and acted upon—and a rejection of a static view of existence. Moreover, and this is a critical point for feminist and nonviolent thought, a utopian mentality necessitates an awareness of the prevailing social conditions and conditions under which a new social form can be born.

This utopian mentality is evident in the thinking of modern nonviolent activists such as Gandhi, Dorothy Day, Martin Luther King, Jr. and feminists such as Simone de Beauvoir, Emma Goldman and Barbara Deming. The recognition of the necessity for an alternative vision among these individuals and, more generally, within the nonviolent and feminist movements, does not however imply a consensus of what the new society should look like or how it should be created. Divergence exists within and between each movement though there are important areas of agreement.

The remainder of this article examines three areas of concern central in utopian speculations—individuality, primary (intimate) relationships and new forms of community—in order to outline salient points of consensus and disagreement. A final note will raise questions concerning the relationship between utopian mentality and social change dynamics.

Individuality

The discussion of individuality as it appears in the utopian outlook of both nonviolent and feminist thinkers has important implications for the possibilities of equality. Equality has been viewed as a supreme virtue of most utopian societies. It was a focal point in King's "I Have a Dream" speech, in Gandhi's vision of an independent India, in Ursula Le Guin's feminist-utopian novels and in Charlotte Perkins Gilman's writing.

In a review of utopianism, a tension appears between the idea that freedom must allow for individual differences and the belief that happiness within a given society is based on uniformity of experience. Another question arises when "equality" is thought to connote sameness which would greatly impair individual freedom and uniqueness. There has been a varied response to these conflicts within the feminist movement, revealing struggles concerning political ideology, class and racial distinctions and sexual preferences. Kate Millett, for instance, argues that matriarchy may not imply a social order of one sex dominating the other such as patriarchy does but rather, "Given the simpler scale of life and the fact that female-centered fertility religion might be offset by male physical strength, pre-patriarchy might have been fairly egalitarian."[2] Matriarchy here refers to an egalitarian order based upon individual differences. Marge Piercy, in her utopian work *Woman on the Edge of Time*, presents another picture:[3]

> *He had breasts. Not large ones. Small breasts, like a flat chested woman temporarily swollen with milk...he began to nurse.*

In this book, the ideal is a society which is classless and androgynous and where equality is founded on the variety of individual expressions of creativity. While renouncing biological determinism, Piercy also rejects the superiority of lesbian separateness and reaches for an androgynous solution. In her utopia, people are alike in striving to have their separate abilities fulfilled, but she does not assume that all people would be fulfilled in the same way.

In recent years, feminist visions of utopia sparked intense debate, often centering on the wisdom of separatist or marxist ideologies. Socialist-feminists, while dismissing Eleanor Marx's demand, "we will organize not as women but as proletarians...for us there is nothing but the working-class movement," remain convinced of the necessity of reconciling class issues with sexual politics.[4] Susan Griffin's provocative prose-poetry, *Women and Nature*, has added a voice to the separatist stance that women are in more harmony with the natural environment and have a more pacific character than men have. Some separatists are now positing the position that the only true women are lesbians since they are not bound by the social structures dominated by men. Other feminists argue that lesbian culture is a product of certain class and historic conditions and thus is not an island unto itself.

The debates within the feminist movement extend to questions of the relationship between the personal and political and the way in which change should be procured. A major premise of the women's movement is that the "personal is political." This was posited as a response to the political left of the 1960s which had termed concern with issues of marriage, reproduction and domestic work as bourgeois individualism of only private concern. Moreover, this slogan focused feminist thinking on the means and ends issue for liberation struggles.

It is on the issue of means and ends that nonviolent thinking expands upon its view of the dignity of the individual and the utopian ideal of universal equality. For Gandhi, "If the individual ceases to count, what is left of society?...No society can possibly be built on a denial of individual freedom."[5] In the nonviolent society Gandhi envisioned, the sanctity of individual life was to be preserved through the practice of satyagraha or "truth-force." The nonviolent doctrine of satyagraha advanced the idea that all life was an experiment in seeking truth and that no one person could ever grasp the final or absolute truth. Thus, when social conflict occurs, the testing of truth can only be performed through ahimsa—action based on the refusal to do harm.

In order to build a nonviolent society, coherence must be maintained between the means of social change and the ends: "the means are the ends in process and the ideal in the making."[6] Barbara Deming gives this explanation:

> *The advocate of nonviolence believes—and finds an irresistible logic in believing—that the only way to bring such a future into full being is to begin right now as best we can—though this will be at first imperfectly, since we are caught still in the habits of the past—begin nevertheless to act out that respect for one another, right now.*[7]

Martin Buber, in *Paths in Utopia,* criticizes Marxist separation of means and ends and the Marxists' tradition of centralization that permits no individual initiative, that suggests 'a means of compulsion' can miraculously change into 'an end of freedom.' The obliteration of the individual by state bureaucracy, according to Simone Weil in her 1933 essay, "Reflections on War," weakens all human values and spreads the march of facism. Weil goes on in her work to stress that truth is destroyed by violence.

In their speeches against the caste system, racial oppression and economic injustice, Gandhi, Martin Luther King, Jr., and Ceasar Chavez have all stressed universal equality and renounced the assumption of superiority of any person over any other. Although they each denied the power of their charisma—

Gandhi said, "Let no one say he is a follower of Gandhi. It is enough that I should be my own follower,"[8]—they embodied singular, not collective, positions of authority. Their form of leadership contradicts the feminist/nonviolent advocacy of non-hierarchical modes of organization.

Questions pertaining to the role of the individual in a new society therefore remain unresolved for feminists and adherents of nonviolence. It would appear that while some feminists suggest that a truly feminist process for change would only take a nonviolent form, this view is not universally held in the feminist movement. Positions concerning relationship to the State and to the structure of leadership remain unclear for both movements. And nonviolent male activists, in separating the personal from the political, have often demeaned the role of women and not taken the liberation of women seriously.

Intimate Relationships

What does an intimate relationship based on feminism and/or nonviolence mean? This is clearly an area of speculation, as neither movement has evolved a definitive reply. However, certain guidelines seem predominant in each movement's utopian construct.

Buber's formulations in *I and Thou* appear to echo in the works of pacifists Weil and Gandhi, and of feminists Le Guin and de Beauvoir among others. It is only through a genuine encounter with another that an individual becomes the self. Through loving, the process by which the separateness of an I-It relationship is overcome, a relationship of full reciprocity is established. An individual's dignity is reflected in the dignity of the other.

Generally nonviolent literature posits either an acceptance of heterosexuality or an endorsement of celibacy (generally to aid self-purification and renunciation of worldly delights). Feminist writers, on the other hand, have stated that sexual oppression in all its forms—economic, social, psychological, and physical—disallows genuine encounters between men and women. In *The Second Sex,* de Beauvoir analyzes the repercussions of a patriarchal system where the male is understood to be the authentic being and the female is "the Other." While de Beauvoir has generally believed that the liberation of women and male-female relations would emerge as a result of a socialist revolution, radical feminists now speak of a "feminist revolution" and a "post-androgynous society."[9]

Ursula Le Guin, in *The Left Hand of Darkness*, creates a

picture of post-androgynous society where I-Thou relations abound:

> *The entire pattern of socio-sexual interaction is nonexistent here. The Gethenians do not see one another as men or women. . . They are not neuters. They are potentials; during each sexual cycle they may develop in either direction for the duration of that cycle. . . There is no division of humanity into strong and weak halves. . . One is respected and judged only as a human being.*

In addition, the feminist descriptions of utopia, such as Le Guin's, challenge traditional gender-linked terms as being barriers to I-Thou types of relationships. For instance Marge Piercy uses the pronoun "per" to substitute for "his or her" and "he or she." Others (including the contemporary USA commune Twin Oaks) have used the term "co," and the term "herstory" has been substituted for "history."

Neither language reorientation nor an androgynous ideal have been a part of traditional nonviolent writings on intimate relationships, but recently, a number of nonviolent activists, including Barbara Deming, George Lakey and Leah Fritz, have attempted to bring feminist consciousness and language into the nonviolent movement. They argue that the feminist call for an end of relationships based on dominance and submission is inherently part of an ethos of nonviolence. Advocates of nonviolence, in their view, must oppose not only war between nations but the violence of daily life, the common episodes of wife beating, rape, prostitution, forced sterilization, and assault. Virginia Woolf wrote on this theme in *Three Guineas*, 1938:[10]

> *They [feminists] were fighting the same enemy that you are fighting and for the same reasons. They were fighting the tyranny of the patriarchal state as you were fighting the tyranny of the Fascist State. . .And abroad the monster has come more openly to the surface. . .He has widened his scope. He is interfering now with your liberty; he is dictating how you shall live. . . You are feeling in your own persons what your mothers felt when they were shut up because they were women. Now you are being shut out, you are being shut up because you are Jews, because you are democrats, because of race, because of religion. . .*

For her and the nonviolent-feminists, sexual oppression and political repression are cut from the same cloth.

New Forms of Community and Social Change

Martin Luther King, Jr. thoughtfully commented in 1960 that the choices confronting the world were no longer between nonviolence and violence but between "nonviolence and nonexistence." The choice seems even more stark as we move into the 1980's. This is a world where the language of first strike capability, integrated battlefields, nuclear proliferation and radiation kill-ratios abound. Virginia Woolf and Gandhi and Simone Weil and Martin Buber were among those watching the clouds gather.

In response to the darkening horizon, both the feminist and nonviolent movements have recognized the great importance of community-building, or creating new networks on local, regional and transnational levels. Concepts of self-help, decentralization, grass-roots organizing, volunteerism and mutual aid are common to the utopian mentalities of each movement. Rejecting the modern individualizing process which produces atomization and new modes of alienation, feminists and advocates of nonviolence have spoken of the necessity of associating individual integrity and liberty with first, I-Thou types of relationships and then with larger scale co-operative institutions.

There have been strong connections to socialism among left-feminists and much of the nonviolent movement. The socialist communities they conceive and work towards build on the ideas of the 19th century utopian socialists who called for a reorganized sexual and family existence alongside of an economic revolution.[11]

The parallels in the following remarks reveal a common vision of community design that would inhibit competition, encourage cooperation, limit isolation, and promote empowerment of all individuals.

> *Women must transform the sexual division of domestic labor, the privatized economic basis of domestic work, and the spatial separation of homes and workplaces in the built environment if they are to be equal members of society.*[12]
>
> *—Dolores Hayden*

> *Perhaps, as men take on new roles which encourage human values, nonviolence will seem more realistic to them too. Those who care for children and who understand their value as derived from caring will be less willing to kill.*[13]
>
> *—Mary Roodkovsky*

With the establishment of a world-wide network of Communities of Mutual Association, all institutional and ideological impediments to sexual equality would disappear, including oppressive marriage laws, privatized households, and private ownership of wealth.[14]

—*Barbara Taylor*

Other forms of community are wished for by different sectors of the feminist and nonviolent movements, including visions of an Amazon-type of collectivity, communities based on capitalist premises or more egalitarian environments. And, as previously mentioned, how to effect such social change is an issue of debate, not consensus.

A Note of Caution

Though this essay applauds the existence of utopian vision there are some points of caution. First, as George Kateb eloquently discusses in *Utopia and Its Enemies*, utopian planners are often guilty of emotional imperialism—playing with arrangements of reality in whatever way pleases them. Secondly, utopian visions usually emphasize a predilection for order that undermines the range of human experience. Lastly, utopias rarely incorporate the necessity for continual radical change but rather try to "secure basic values permanently; and if there is to be change, it is change only, as it were, on the margins."[15] Despite these warnings, the need for individuals to maintain a utopian mentality is of paramount import so that we can continue to understand and shape history and so that "we are not passive spectators doomed to unresisting obedience but by our thoughts and actions can ourselves change. . . ."[16]

Alice Walker
Only Justice Can Stop A Curse

". . . it would be good, perhaps, to put an end to the species in any case, rather than let white men continue to subjugate it . . ." Echoing an ancient curse for revenge, Alice Walker lifts her voice in rage and bitterness against white men who have brought us all to the edge of nuclear annihilation. She explains that this hope for revenge, though it would catch in its cruel net those who hope it, is at the heart of people of color's resistance to the anti-nuclear movement. "Let the earth marinate in poisons. Let the bombs cover the ground like rain. For nothing short of total destruction will ever teach [white men] anything."

And yet, though she doesn't forsake this rage, this bitterness, Alice cannot truly hope that this curse be fulfilled but rather that her courage not fail her love and that justice be done. Her words become a prayer of passionate yearning and enraged impatience for justice, and of the love which, finally, is what sustains us in the struggle to survive.

This speech was delivered at a San Francisco anti-nuclear rally in March,1982. Alice, an activist, poet and writer, has published five books of fiction including Meridian, *her second novel, which is generally considered the best novel of the civil rights movement. The following tribute is a quote from an article by Gloria Steinem in the June, 1982 issue of* Ms. Magazine *which featured Alice.*

> *"She's certainly not the only writer who sees personal cruelty and social injustice clearly," explained a woman who has grown old in the struggle for civil rights in general and Black women's dignity in particular. "But she's the only writer I know who sees it all: what happens to Black people here, to women everywhere; the outrages against history and the earth; everything. Yet she has taught me that cruelty turns back on itself—which gives me faith to keep on fighting. She also takes people who seem completely irredeemable, and then writes about their redemption. That gives me faith in change—and allows me to change, too. When I read something by Alice, I'm never quite the same person when I finish as I was when I began."*

Those who know Alice's work will know this tribute rings true. Her poems, essays, short stories and novels do indeed have the power to change lives.

"To the Man God: O Great One, I have been sorely tried by my enemies and have been blasphemed and lied against. My good thoughts and my honest actions have been turned to bad actions and dishonest ideas. My home has been disrespected, my children have been cursed and ill-treated. My dear ones have been backbitten and their virtue questioned. O Man God, I beg that this that I ask for my enemies shall come to pass:

That the South wind shall scorch their bodies and make them wither and shall not be tempered to them. That the North wind shall freeze their blood and numb their muscles and that it shall not be tempered to them. That the West wind shall blow away their life's breath and will not leave their hair grow, and that their fingernails shall fall off and their bones shall crumble. That the East wind shall make their minds grow dark, their sight shall fail and their seed dry up so that they shall not multiply.

I ask that their fathers and mothers from their furthest generation will not intercede for them before the great throne, and the wombs of their women shall not bear fruit except for strangers, and that they shall become extinct. I pray that the children who may come shall be weak of mind and paralyzed of limb and that they themselves shall curse them in their turn for ever turning the breath of life into their bodies. I pray that disease and death shall be forever with them and that their worldly goods shall not prosper, and that their crops shall not multiply and that their cows, their sheep, and their hogs and all their living beasts shall die of starvation and thirst. I pray that their house shall be unroofed and that the rain, the thunder and lightening shall find the innermost recesses of their home and that the foundation shall crumble and the floods tear it asunder. I pray that the sun shall not shed its rays on them in benevolence, but instead it shall beat down on them and burn them and destroy them. I pray that the moon shall not give them peace, but instead shall deride them and decry them and cause their minds to shrivel. I pray that their friends shall betray them and cause them loss of power, of gold and of silver, and that their enemies shall smite them until they beg for mercy which shall not be given them. I pray that their tongues shall forget how to speak in sweet words, and that it shall be paralyzed and that all about them will be desolation, pestilence and death. O Man God, I ask you for all these things because they have dragged me in the dust and destroyed my good name; broken my heart and caused me to curse the day that I was born. So be it"[1]

This is a curse-prayer that Zora Neale Hurston, novelist and anthropologist, collected in the 1920s. And by then it was already old. I have often marvelled at it. At the precision of its anger, the absoluteness of its bitterness. Its utter hatred of the enemies it condemns. It is a curse-prayer by a person who would readily, almost happily, commit suicide, if it meant her enemies would also die. Horribly.

I am sure it was a woman who first prayed this curse. And I see her—Black, Yellow, Brown or Red, *"aboriginal"* as the Ancients are called in South Africa and Australia and other lands invaded, expropriated and occupied by whites. And I think, with astonishment, that the curse-prayer of this colored woman—starved, enslaved, humiliated and carelessly trampled to death—over centuries, is coming to pass. Indeed, like ancient peoples of color the world over, who have tried to tell the white man of the destruction that would inevitably follow from the uranium mining plunder of their sacred lands, this woman—along with millions and billions of obliterated sisters, brothers, and children—seems to have put such enormous energy into her hope for revenge, that her curse seems close to bringing it about. And it is this hope for revenge, finally, I think, that is at the heart of People of Color's resistance to any anti-nuclear movement.

In any case, this has been my own problem.

When I have considered the enormity of the white man's crimes against humanity. Against women. Against every living person of color. Against the poor. Against my mother and my father. Against me. . . . When I consider that at this very moment he wishes to take away what little freedom I have died to achieve, through denial of my right to vote. . . . Has already taken away education, medicine, housing and food. . . . That William Shockley is saying at this moment that he will run for the Senate of my country to push his theory that Blacks are genetically inferior and should be sterilized. . . . When I consider that he is, they are, a real and present threat to my life and the life of my daughter, my people, I think—in perfect harmony with my sister of long ago: *Let the earth marinate in poisons. Let the bombs cover the ground like rain. For nothing short of total destruction will ever teach them anything.*

And it would be good, perhaps, to put an end to the species in any case, rather than let white men continue to subjugate it, and continue their lust to dominate, exploit and despoil not just our planet, but the rest of the universe, which is their clear and oft-stated intention, leaving their arrogance and litter not just on the moon, but on everything else they can reach.

If we have any true love for the stars, planets, the rest of Creation, we must do everything we can to keep white men away from them. They who have appointed themselves our representatives to the rest of the universe. They who have never met any new creature without exploiting, abusing or destroying it. They who say we poor and colored and female and elderly blight neighborhoods, while they blight worlds.

What they have done to the Old, they will do to the New.

Under the white man every star would become a South Africa, every planet a Vietnam.

Fatally irradiating ourselves may in fact be the only way to save others from what Earth has already become. And this is a consideration that I believe requires serious thought from every one of us.

However, just as the sun shines on the godly and the ungodly alike, so does nuclear radiation. And with this knowledge it becomes increasingly difficult to embrace the thought of extinction purely for the assumed satisfaction of—from the grave—achieving revenge. Or even of accepting our demise as a planet as a simple and just preventative medicine administered to the Universe. Life is better than death, I believe, if only because it is less boring, and because it has fresh peaches in it. In any case, Earth is my home—though for centuries white people have tried to convince me I have no right to exist, except in the dirtiest, darkest corners of the globe.

So let me tell you: I intend to protect my home. Praying—not a curse—only the hope that my courage will not fail my love. But if by some miracle, and all our struggle, the earth is spared, only justice to every living thing (and everything is alive) will save humankind.

And we are not saved yet.

Only justice can stop a curse.

Sally Miller Gearhart
The Future—If There Is One—Is Female

Given the perspective that nothing could be more extreme than the total destruction of our precious planet and all the life on it—a prospect which has crept into our psyches with little more than a shrug and a sigh—the proposal that the affairs of the world be placed in the hands of non-patriarchally aligned women really isn't as extreme as it might at first seem.

Most feminist activists accurately identify oppressive institutions and make demands for change or even call for revolution. We tend, however, to shy away from answering how *we actually could bring into being an environment so changed that rape, slavery and the specter of nuclear annihilation would become mere nightmares of the past. In what is probably the most radical and concrete strategy for earthly survival presented in this anthology, Sally Gearhart provides careful, step-by-step justification for her three-part proposal: I. Every culture must begin to affirm a female future. II. Species responsibility must be returned to women in every culture. III. The proportion of men must be reduced to and maintained at approximately 10% of the human race. "I believe we are at a great watershed in history," she writes here, "and that we hold in our hands a fragile thread, no more than that, that can lead us to our survival. I understand the rising up of women in this century to be the human race's response to the threat of its own self-annihilation and the destruction of the planet."*

Sally is careful not to say that men are innately destructive or women innately nurturing. Indeed, she says there is no way to prove such a claim. She asks us to look, instead, at the weight of history, its centuries of male rule accompanied by the growing power and likelihood of total earthly destruction. It is this history/tradition/pattern which must be broken, a pattern intimately tied to patriarchal control.

Though Sally's proposal is unique, others have suggested similar plans. According to the book The Grand Domestic Revolution: A History of Feminist Designs for American Homes, Neighborhoods and Cities *by Delores Hayden, (MIT Press, 1981), a feminist activist Lois Waisbrooker proposed a plan in 1893 similar in intent to the one Sally proposes here—almost one hundred years later! In Waisbrooker's novel,* A Sex Revolution, *men agree, reluctantly and under pressure, to change roles with women for fifty years as a social experiment. The women's concern in that book is to end all war.*

Barbara Stanford's anthology, On Being Female *(Pocket Books,*

1974), contains a reprint of a 1971 Chicago Daily News *item, "Let Women Rule the World, Asks Scientist." It quotes a Dr. Peter A. Corning of the U. of Colorado as saying, "In an age when the masculine virtues are becoming less adaptive for our survival, government by women might actually prove to be superior adaptation in evolutionary terms."*

New French Feminisms, *an anthology edited by Elaine Marks and Isabelle de Courtivron (U. of Mass. Press, 1980), includes segments from Francoise d'Eaubonne's essay, "Le feminisme ou la mort" (Feminism or death): "Thus a transfer of power is urgently needed,* then, *as soon as possible, a destruction of power. The transfer must be made from phallocratic man, responsible for this sexist civilization, into the hands of the awakened women." And elsewhere in that volume, "Therefore, with a society at last in the feminine gender meaning non-power (and not power-to-the-women), it would be proved that no other human group could have brought about the ecological revolution because none other was so directly concerned at all levels... And the planet in the feminine gender would become green again for all."*

There is something in d'Eaubonne's essay which seems to be missing in Sally's proposal as it currently stands, and that is the sense that this transfer of power would be a temporary measure, a step toward the ultimate hope that, as d'Eaubonne writes, "the male would once again become the expression of life and no longer the elaboration of death; and human beings would finally be treated first as persons, and not above all else as male or female." Sally, on the other hand, proposes that the proportion of men be reduced to and maintained at approximately 10% of the human race, though, she says, this must be done by increasing the birth of females and not by any loss *of lives. Still, it is the word "maintained" that disturbs even those of us otherwise intrigued by her proposal, for it seems unnecessary that this drastic measure become a part of a new order, but rather that it could conceivably accomplish its purpose in a couple generations—could break the chains of patriarchal tradition, erase from our collective memory the lies about male supremacy, interrupt the habit of female victimization and servitude, and, this done, could give us a chance to start over, refreshed, unburdened by the accumulation of past madness. Sally's essay, in all its intensity, is welcomed to this anthology in the spirit of dialogue (despite its unresolved complications) as we collectively struggle to come to terms with the death culture and our hope for salvation.*

Sally, a long time lesbian-feminist activist, is perhaps best known as the author of what has been called "the new underground classic" The Wanderground: Stories of the Hill Women *(Persephone Press, 1978, highly recommended—see the annotated bibliography at the end of this anthology) and co-author of* A Feminist Tarot *(Persephone Press, 1981). She is also chairperson of the Department of Speech and Communication at San Francisco State University, a member of a beauty shop quartet and is "a double Aries with Virgo rising." She is committed to criticism/self-criticism, anti-racist action and animal liberation.*

Sally writes, "I'm grateful for dialogues with a number of women and for the written words of others: Baba Copper, Jane Gurko, Sarah Hoagland, Pat Labine, Alice Molloy, Julia Penelope, Cynthia Secor and, over the last eight years, the members of the "Seminar in Patriarchal Rhetoric" at San Francisco State University. I'm also grateful to women like Mina Caulfield, Joanna Russ and Barbara Smith who continue to challenge and creatively criticize some of the ideas expressed in this paper."

In a remarkable science fiction work, *Rule Golden*, Damon Knight wipes violence from the face of the earth by having every agent feel in his/her own body any physical blow she/he delivers: kick a dog and feel the boot in your own rib; commit murder and die yourself. Similarly, stroking another in love results in the physical feeling of being lovingly stroked. Doris Lessing, in *Shikasta,* her recent venture into science fiction, lays the destruction of earth to a lack of the "substance of we-feeling." Both Knight and Lessing articulate for me the necessary connection between *empathy* and *nonviolence*; they remind me that *objectification* is the necessary, if not sufficient, component of any violent act. Thinking of myself as separate from another entity makes it possible for me to "do to" that entity things I would not "do to" myself. But if I see all things as myself, or empathize with all other things, then to hurt them is to do damage to me; I will move around this world with lots less pushiness and lots more care; I might adopt a more respectful nurturing attitude toward the world, wishing all things health and longevity.

But empaths don't live long if the Rule Golden is not in effect. Our world belongs to those who can objectify (or who are forced to objectify) and if I want to protect myself from them I learn to objectify and fight back in self-defense. I seem bound to choose between being violent and being victimized. Or I live a schizophrenic existence in which my values are at war with my actions because I must keep a constant shield of protectiveness (objectification) intact over my real self, over my empathy or my identification with others; the longer I keep up the shield the thicker it gets and the less empathic I am with those around me. So every second of protecting myself from violence makes me objectify more and ensures that I am more and more capable of doing violence myself. I am caught always in the violence-victim trap.

But most people, I'm convinced, do not want to rape the earth or exploit each other. While 53% of the U.S. public may expect nuclear war in its lifetime, nobody wants such an event. Violence has reached such monumental proportions that the ordinary citizen of the world feels impotent and increasingly cynical in the face of the immensity and complexity of the issue. A destructive technology is launched by the discoveries of "morally neutral" scientists; a proliferating consumerism urges 6% of the world to waste what 94% of the world starves in order to produce; clean air, clean water, arable land, wilderness, wildlife, forests and lakes—all are becoming "endangered species," as are "safety," "security," "freedom" and "equality." As one scholar has expressed it, our global society is a train on a downhill grade accelerating at an increasingly rapid pace. There is no engineer. And we are laying the track in front of us as we go. We may not be able to stay ahead of ourselves, much less stop the train.

There are three assumptions that I believe have led to the violence-victim trap. The first two assumptions underlie the science and the technology that have sprung from men: 1) *If it is possible then it must be done* and 2) *anything done in the service of mankind is praiseworthy, even necessary*. Human knowledge as we know it these last ten thousand years has been the bringing into reality of that-which-is-possible, including nuclear research, genetic engineering, computerized living; and it has been an exercise in human chauvinism testified to by the death of millions of laboratory animals, dessicated continents and polluted oceans.

While the first two assumptions underlie *knowledge* the third assumption underlies *power* as men have used it over the millennia: 3) *might makes right,* actually the crudest and most honest expression of the other two assumptions and a kind of justification for them. The stronger always has the greater possibility of subduing the weaker (if it's possible it must be done) and the stronger is of course the Crown of Creation who has dominion over all other things (he must be served, even to the destruction of the rest of the planet).

These three assumptions are responsible for the familiar and highly formalized duet between knowledge and power that we now identify as "western civilization." Put another way, malekind has seen the possible, he has consistently done the possible, he has justified his acts as manifestations of his human superiority, and he has made seem natural and right the use of force in human affairs. His assumptions have guaranteed us all of a strong and constantly proliferating civilization built upon objectification and violation. For me, the exercise of these assumptions on the part of male knowledge and male power is sufficient to indict the male of our species as the source of violence.

In this paper I want to say what I have carefully avoided saying for a long time: that if the world is to move away from the escalating violence that shapes all of our lives, then the affairs of the world, and of the human species specifically, must be placed in the hands of women.

I believe we are at a great watershed in history and that we hold in our hands a fragile thread, no more than that, that can lead us to our survival. I understand the rising up of women in this century to be the human race's response to the threat of its own self-annihilation and the destruction of the planet. In small ways, in big ways, it seems up to the world's women to take back their responsibilities as life-givers and sustainers.

Even after decades of feminist research we do not know for sure about the nature of female and male people—whether or not the male is "naturally" violent, the female "naturally" nurturant—and we are not likely, while sex roles still exist, to ascertain anything in this regard. This paper then, presupposes that the last ten thousand years of global patriarchy have given us a vivid and grim idea of what happens when men are in charge; it further assumes that as a species and as a global village we have nothing to lose and everything to gain by reversing the present power circumstances and returning to women the fundamental responsibility for human affairs.

But to say "return affairs to women" says too little, for the patriarchal system could continue quite well run by patriarchal women. We need the further understanding that the present system will not do, that even matriarchies—class societies that they were—will not do, and that not just any women will do. Enslaved by male-identification and years of practice within the system as we all still are to one degree or another, the assumption must be that the present system of monopoly capitalism and patriarchy must be replaced and that non-male-identified women must be the responsible ones. This calls for both action and education, for both a freeing of women from the strictures of patriarchal law and custom and an education of both women and men in the voluntary and vast changes that must take place. The call for action and education is not new to feminists, but the specific changes that I feel must happen may not be so familiar.

At least three further requirements supplement the strategies of environmentalists if we are to create and preserve a less violent world. I) *Every culture must begin to affirm a female future.* II) *Species responsibility must be returned to women in every culture.* III) *The proportion of men must be reduced to and maintained at approximately 10% of the human race.*

I.

What does a *"female future"* mean? First of all, it means the affirmation in all people of characteristics historically associated with the female, specifically: empathy, nurturance and cooperation. For the present, leave aside the question of whether these qualities accrue to women by nature or by acculturation. Let us just be sure that we do not make the common premature leap that insists upon calling these qualities "human" ones. To grant them to all human beings loses the point. Precisely the reason that they have taken a back seat to "male" qualities (objectification, violence, competitiveness) has to do with the fact that they are considered "soft," "weak," or "womanlike." When, in western culture, men are empathic or nurturing or cooperative, they are simultaneously branded as "feminine" or "like women" and they lose power accordingly. However loudly they're preached, from Christian pulpits or from the pages of *The Reader's Digest,* these are not the qualities or the values that govern western civilization. They are characteristics associated with the female of the human species. To act upon them is automatically to lose, to be less than a man. They are regularly set aside when the realities of life call for toughness, heroism, patriotism, *i.e.*, objectification, violence, competitiveness.

Some feminists object on strategic grounds to the labeling of these characteristics as "female" qualities. By touting women as less violent, less competitive, less objectifying than men we give support to the antifeminist notion, best articulated in the nineteenth century, that women are too pure for politics, that they are by nature different from men and thus must be limited to their domestic domain. But if by believing that women are by nature less violent we reinforce the sex roles that have held women down for so long, then perhaps it is time to dare to admit that some of the sex-role mythology is in fact true and to insist that the qualities attributed to women (specifically empathy, nurturance and cooperativeness) be affirmed as human qualities capable of cultivation by men even if denied them by nature. That kind of flipping of the coin can only be beneficial, *i.e.*, to insist that men become nurturing and empathic just as patriarchy has insisted for so long that women who enter its hierarchy become violent and competitive. In a system that has deforested, stripmined and dessicated the earth to the point where population far exceeds the carrying capacity of the land, where nuclear stockpiles are sufficient to destroy the earth forty or fifty times over, an affirmation of such "softer" qualities or such flipping of the coin seems long overdue.

Besides affirming female values, a female future requires that the whole concept of hierarchy be challenged. Male power figures (and female power figures) would have to descend from the high places and acknowledge the travesty that their empowerment has been. In other words, the vertical system itself, which provides the structure for the violence-victim trap would be replaced by horizontal patterns of relationship. If there were in such a revamped system any "supreme power," that power would be understood to be the tangible material earth herself and her biosphere, and any reverence for her would take the form of respect and deliberate care rather than fear and obedience. For that is the point, after all. The earth is ourselves; she is not "out there" giving orders or being worshipped. And the only divinity to be discerned about her has to do with our recognition of the energy we share with her and with others. The earth would not be conquered, tamed, raped in the service of greed; she would rather be related to and cared for in the service of all who live together with her.

Most important a female future means that femaleness itself, being female, would be understood everywhere to be positive, joyful: women would affirm themselves and other women; women would be affirmed by men and by children—much as males are affirmed in our present society. More important, the female would be acknowledged as primary, as the source of all life. The female encompasses the male, can exist without the male, can in a number of species, perhaps including the human one, reproduce without the male. The universal acknowledgement of these capacities is the *sine qua non* of a female-based society. The present unspoken acknowledgement of these female capabilities has been the motivation for patriarchy's desperate widespread and violent dedication to female slavery.

Let us be clear here. The primacy of the female does not mean that men would crawl away and expire. It is, or would be, when all the manufactured evidence to the contrary is swept away, simply a fact of existence that has no better or worse value put upon it. I realize how these words sound, how time after time in human history such words have been used in condescension or benevolent despotism to assert the superiority of one (usually ethnic) group above the other. I'm aware of the dangers of biological determinism and fear it in precisely the ways that each of us should. And yet, here on the level of human sexuality, I am at last forced to say that I believe the differences to be those of primacy and differentiation, *i.e.*, the most fundamental difference between members of the human race. Precisely because the difference is so fundamental, there is no analogy available to demonstrate how the acknowledgement of female primacy would be qualitatively different from a fascist demand that people of color acknowledge the primacy of caucasians; I fall back again on what ultimately seems to be the truth to me, that female primacy is the fact, the truth, as acknowledgeable by men as by women, while any higher valuing on the basis of race or ethnic background is simply—and obviously—absurd. Further, my belief is that the very nature of the female would preclude her use of the kind of hierarchical power displays that accompany the usual use of biology as a social weapon, both by whites who hold down people of color and by men who hold down women.

Since there is no existing comparison to a world in which femaleness is accorded its proper place in human affairs, the best we can do is to imagine a hypothetical society in which half the population lives twice as long as the other half, say a hundred years and fifty years. That difference between them, recognized at birth, is a fundamental and immutable one that shapes the self-image and social spirit of every person in the community. The portion of the population destined to live longer has an investment in a long-range view and in the overall good of the group. It does not seem far-fetched or unjust to me that the monitoring of the community's survival should fall to the longer-lived people. Nor does it seem incomprehensible to me that the shorter-lived group could acknowledge that reality of existence without hostility. The very fact of having double the number of years to live significantly alters the manner in which the longer-lived group looks at life and its relationship to the environment.

Women, who by their physical nature, bear a different relationship to children than do men and who, I believe, feel more connected and empathic with the environment than men have demonstrated that they do, see life and the role of the human species through experiences and sensitivities that men can possess only second-hand. Historically, they have not objectified quite as readily, and they have exhibited a more group-oriented and less violent attitude toward human beings and the world in which we live than men have done. I would expect then that, in view of this evidence, men are capable without defensiveness of acknowledging the female nature of the species and the male's role as subsidiary.

Perhaps I am wrong. Perhaps there is no way to avoid the hostility that men would harbor if they "had to" acknowledge the female as primary. Perhaps the best thing to do here is to admit, then, that the coin must be flipped, that the flipping *is* merely an exchange of power, and that women would have to hold men in check by myths, ideologies and education. In fact I don't believe that myths and ideologies would have to be constructed; the truth of female primacy, once it is reestablished, is sufficient unto itself and would make such constructions unneccessary. And the "exchange" seems more a *restoration* of the natural order of environmental processes. But if we must use such language at the outset, I'm ready to say—for the first time in my feminist life—that we should begin thinking of flipping the coin, of making the exchange of power, of building the ideology of female primacy and control. Simple justice suggests that if men have been in power for so many thousands of years and have botched so badly the job of human and environmental health, it is time to give the other alternative a chance.

The most formidable objection to the notion of female primacy points to the women who have gained power in the male system, those who turn out to be cruel, ruthless, or violent or who at least seem to espouse the very destructive values that women, according to this proposal, are supposed to transcend. (The woman governor of Washington campaigns for nuclear plants, the prime minister of England wants to move away from collective power, Phyllis Schlafly opposes abortion, and the woman mayor of my own city vetoes rent controls.) Would the female of the species, if given the chance, repeat the violence of the patriarchy? I argue no, for it seems to me that the system itself guarantees that anyone remaining within it will be affected by its corruption. If we would see how women really manage power and government, then let them demonstrate their abilities in a system that they themselves create out of their own values. There has never been an antipatriarchal woman in power since the beginning of male domination, but only women who are puppets of men behind the scenes, or women who are the pawns of male business interests.

To say that if women had the opportunity for such power they would use it as men have done, is to assume that men gained patriarchal control by mere luck or chance. The very fact that women were subdued might testify to their reluctance to use violence even in the face of gradually rising male control. Women are certainly capable of taking up arms, of protecting themselves and their offspring, of training themselves in war or politics just as men have done. But women do not, in my experience, *choose* to become violent, particularly on the large scale that men seem so to choose. To say that women would abuse the power as men have done is to refuse the risk of flipping the coin despite the message of history that women would use that power less violently.

One final objection: there is a contradiction inherent in the idea of bringing about a global "female future," for though some women in the United States and Europe may be articulating the need for such a goal, the majority of the world's women inhabit very different realities. How then, without the same kind of cultural invasion we have witnessed for centuries, can we expect that women of all cultures can respond to the hope of a female future? Who will "go in" to the appropriate African and Arab countries and "stop" the genital mutilation? What right does western culture, even the women of western culture, have to question *purdah, suttee,* female infanticide? Even the righteous rage and empathy we have for women does not justify the imposition of our standards on other cultures.

Several things occur to me in this regard. First of all, we sell short the women of other nations to assume that they are unaware of their status as women. With the intensification of economic realities, there are enough rumblings in countries other than European-based ones to suggest that women do know their power and do not need liberation by any outside force. Second of all, consciousness cannot be halted by border patrols, and even consumerism and advanced technology may turn out to be aids in our learning about the lives of most of the world's women, in their learning about the benefits and the strictures of the lives of westernized women. If it is true that women universally have some fundamental sensitivity to the land and air and water and energy with which they live, and if it is true that there is some connection between the critical point that the earth is now reaching in terms of resources and women's awareness of that, then the tide of women's rage may well rise up in response to those conditions. We may talk here in our English words of a female future, but it may well be the women of other nations who ultimately lead us in the most significant steps toward that future. Finally, nature seems to be giving us unmistakable signals that human beings must begin to think of ourselves not as nations or as employees with loyalties to this or that multinational corporation but as a single entity in relation to its environment. More than at any other time in history "loyalty" is going to have to be a term applied to the species as a whole—and again, perhaps "loyalty" is not the term at all: perhaps "empathy" is. Communication among "nations" of non-patriarchal women offers the natural, most effective, and most revolutionary avenue for global unity.

II

If we would have the world a less violent place *species responsibility must be returned to women in every culture,* that is to say, women must regain their say-so over the proper size and character of the human race. There is no way to achieve that without our traversing some very familiar ground. The whole of feminism in these last two centuries has been concerned with the liberation of women from their role as sexual servants of men; even to approach the place where women's own bodily freedom is a given, we have to raise all the economic and psychological questions of male domination. But once they have control of their own bodies, then women stand in exactly the critical position necessary for their reclaiming of the more essential responsibility, that of monitoring the reproduction of the species. Certainly the fear of that development must be a part of the male-identified forces that oppose women's reproductive rights even today. We are now negotiating at the bedrock level of societal values and with the fundamental precept of the entire women's movement.

To return species responsibility to women means in very practical terms that erotic and reproductive initiative must be restored to women all over the globe. The task is so familiar, we need only remind ourselves of the following specifics. Place entirely in the hands of every woman the decisions about whether or not intercourse will take place, where and with whom and how often it will take place and under what conditions and with what physiological result to her body. Make the decision entirely that of the woman as to how she will be impregnated and how often, if indeed she chooses to be so at all, and whether by heterosexual intercourse, artificial insemination or a form of ovular merging. Restore to each woman the inalienable right to say what shall become of any fertilized egg and to control absolutely the number of children she wishes to emerge from her body. Begin now to fight against and to dismantle the religious and financial interests that oppose women's bodily freedom. Introduce and uphold globally the disintegration of the very customs themselves that secure women's bodily enslavement. Grant without delay any woman's right to free abortion on her demand, her right to keep any child she wants, her right to safe birth control and to the freedom from forced sterilization, her right to love sexually other women. Guarantee her freedom from rape, from battering, from genital mutilation, from the sexual slavery that keeps the traffic in women a thriving global business. Explode the mythologies that reinforce women's weakness in contrast to the brute strength of individual men or institutionalized male power. Release women from the economic dependency upon men that requires them to say "yes" to a sex act, whether as wife or as prostitute. Make nonexistent any male's say-so in the process of human reproduction. Create and protect alternative structures of economic and psychological support for independent women—women not attached to men—who are child-bearers and child-raisers.

We may be closer than we think to the reality of women's freedom. The very fact that all over the globe in one form of protest or another women are awakening to their oppression suggests that an old Darwinian principle is emerging; the species must adapt or die. No other female has endured as has the human female the assault by males upon her individual person. No other female has endured such usurpation of her natural functions. No other female has been forced by her male counterpart to endanger not only her own species but the life of every other species on the globe. The female, arbiter of life, must take back the power wrested from her: her rightful power to control the size and the quality of life within the human species.

Other mammals do a better job of regulating their species than humans do. If the environment is not fouled (by humans) a number of species maintain themselves without growing beyond their ecological support base. If flocks of ducks can number the same every year whether two of its members die or ten, then the human animal, particularly with our highly touted "intelligence," should be capable of regulating itself. But the human female does not have the freedom of her own reproductive processes, much less control of the species, and the unfortunate result is that the earth suffers with the weight of an overproliferated—and very violent—species called "mankind." A worldwide reduction of human beings to approximately one-tenth of the present number and maintenance of it at that figure would move our species back to some proportionate and appropriate relationship with the environment.

The patriarchal myth is that it is women who cause overpopulation. The reality is that overpopulation is the direct result of male control of female bodies. Men have imposed on women their "right" to unlimited sexual intercourse. They have protected that "right" and that practice through the careful construction of whole societal institutions: marriage, incest, rape, compulsory heterosexuality, pornography, prostitution, the nuclear family, the church, the law, medicine, and psychiatry to name only the most overt offenders. Men even have us believing that they have a right to our bodies.

Return to women their erotic and reproductive rights and an automatic governor of population will be in effect. Women will bear the number of children they know can be sustained not just by their own social group but by the wide ecological system. They will not bear the children that some man wants only to perpetuate his name or the family possession of his property; they will not bear the children they presently convince themselves they must have because their only role is obedient wife and mother; women will not have the children *men* think are necessary to perpetuate the tribe or the religion or the specific culture. Instead they will bear the children that *they* want, that *they* can care for, and that *they* assess are needed by the specific group and the entire species.

When we consider the efforts of patriarchy to control population we are faced with epics of slavery, genocide and misogyny. For the colonized people of the world, the residents of cultures invaded by educational and later technological models of western civilization, "population control" has meant white men manipulating the reproductive life of less powerful cultures, sometimes encouraging the production of babies (when the labor market needs them, when they can be bought cheap and sold high) and other times conversely holding nondominant groups to a lower density either by forced or uninformative sterilization practices or by birth control propaganda aimed at the destruction of family structures, or by both. The violence done to female bodies when population control is in the hands of men is legendary by now—the pills, the I.U.D.'s, the tubal ligations, the hysterectomies—while vasectomies or male birth control pills go unpublicized or unresearched. The masculine code requires that men control other cultures and, above all, control women. Never are men called upon to reduce their potency, to take responsibility themselves for a sane human population, particularly when there's a pile of money to be made manipulating human life. It's primarily women who pay the price of men's manipulating.

Imperative then is that population reduction is never done "to" a group but that "we" reduce "our" population, culture by culture, without interference from colonizing influences, monied interests or the exigencies created by cultural invasions. Again, we have to trust the spirits of women in every nation, and the flow of information among us to avoid the mistakes of male history. In every culture it must be women in charge of the changes: woman-identified women, not women who are pawns of men, not women who out of their fear of losing their lives or those of their children, still hold to the securities of that dangerous patriarchal culture, but women utterly free of coercion, free of male influence and committed to the principle that the right of species regulation is their own, and not the prerogative of any man. I suggest that lesbians and other independent women are already moving in this direction.

The objection of men to female bodily freedom and control of the species may well be that they will lose their own rights in the process, the right to have a child, the right to the consequences of their own seed. While that of course is not entirely true, the real argument does stand: except at the will of a woman no man will be able to sire a child, and that constitutes a considerable abridgement of their present power. I have argued precisely the injustice of this and I've talked with men about those deep feelings of wanting a child of "their own." I contrast that desire on their part with the more communally oriented desires on the part of lesbian mothers, for instance, or "single mothers" to share the "possession" of the child, to move toward sets of three, four, five, and seven parents for any child. I contrast the individualized desire for my-child (to inherit my-property, my-name, my-physical-and-psychological-characteristics) with the tendency of lesbian and "single" mothers to form extended families and with the belief that I hold that women move naturally into more communal and cooperative settings than do men.

So in response to that painful outcry of men that they will no longer have the right to have "their" children, I ultimately admit that that is true. Men may have to content themselves with the love and nurturance of the community's children. But if we are taking from men a "right," then let us also remember that it is a right that they have viciously abused. The more fundamental right must go to the person who has more physical involvement at stake and that is the woman. To risk letting men retain any "right" over children is to risk having them take it all over again.

If we had a world in which women controlled their own bodies and the issue of their bodies, a world in which the most sacred conviction a man possessed was his belief in the necessity for the female's control of her own body, if we had a world in which the value of female freedom and responsibility were the foundation of the culture, then we would have a world vastly different from the violence and greed of the present one. Resistance to the notion of women's bodily freedom makes clear the necessity for a universal change in attitude to a female value system, a female-based future. The re-valuing of the female must occur concurrently with the lifting of the restrictions on her body, for neither can be successful without the support of the other. Essential attitudes for the solution of scores of world problems would flow, I believe, from the change in values and from the female freedom that accompanies that change.

III

But even if the female body were at last free, and a female future guaranteed, and even if the race began its more proportionate and gentle relationship to its environment, there is still no guarantee that the level of violence, competition, and alienation could be held in check. To secure a world of female values and female freedom we must, I believe, add one more element to the structure of the future: *the ratio of men to women must be radically reduced so that men approximate only ten percent of the total population*. This would have to be done, not by men's traditional methods of war or execution, but without loss of any present human life in the endeavor. Further, it would have to be done within cultures themselves, without outside intervention.

Though women will increasingly demand their rights all over the globe, still it is men who have the power at present and who can act. The likelihood is slim that women could gain the necessary power in time. Men would have to see and understand the necessity for a reduction in their own number. They themselves, the group that would be most affected, would have to take the initial responsibility and be the leaders in education and consciousness. Where men have served the male-bonded Masculine Code they would now see the race as a whole and move toward the affirmation of a female future and preservation of all of us.

To be sure, by reducing the proportion of males, humans would be in good emulation of other species, very few if any of whom have as high a male population as *homo sapiens* does. But more to the point, the reduction of men is necessary because men resort to violence more quickly and more intensely than do women, both among themselves and toward others—women, animals, the earth. Whether by nature or by nurture, competitive, violent and alienated acts the world over and as far back as recorded history goes seem consistently to be associated with the male of the species, whether in the form of war, rape, gladiatorial games, cock-fighting, or buffalo shooting. That evidence is hard to deny. And beyond history, current sociological studies (such as Paul Erlich's crowding experiments of the late sixties) suggest that individual men are more violent and competitive than women.

But the danger is not individual men, because they can resist the demands of the masculine role and certainly are capable of developing nurturance and empathy. The real danger is in the phenomenon of male-bonding, that commitment of groups of men to each other whether in an army, a gang, a service club, a lodge, a monastic order, a corporation, or a competitive sport. That tightly woven power structure actually defines patriarchal society; it can allow into its ranks at best only tokens from non-dominant groups—*i.e.*, in western culture, people of color and last of all women. A large portion of any male-bonded group's energy and spirit is expended in the exclusion of women and in the derogation of female values and qualities. Women must be the brunt of jokes; their experiences and emotions must be trivialized. Male-bonding's success depends upon that exclusion and that constant derogation. When such bonding escalates with the proportion of available males, the resultant power and power-trips are insurmountable. If men were reduced in number, the threat would not be so great and the placement of species responsibility with the female would be assured.

Some have asked, given the overwhelming association of men with violence, why the reduction to ten percent only? Why have any men at all? I take that question quite seriously. First, I have no desire (and I know few women who do) to do away with men as a group; I cannot bring myself fully to the conviction even in spite of their behavior that men are beyond redemption; the moment I indulge in that conclusion a very gentle and loving man, woman-identified or "sissy"-identified, appears to give the lie to my generalization. Second, sexual intercourse is the easiest means of reproduction and one that some women prefer; those women must have the freedom to choose it. Finally we need to maintain ten percent males for the simple reason that I may be wrong; we may discover that violence does not disappear with the reduction of males and that for the human species at least the present 47% ratio of males is more nearly appropriate.

We now come to a critical point: how is such a reduction in male population to take place? One option is of course male infanticide. It differs very little from the female infanticide that has apparently been carried out even into the twentieth century by some cultures. Such an alternative is clearly distasteful and would not constitute creative social change.

Cloning, a process that is itself the response of frightened scientists to the female capacity to give life, does not yield a mixed gene pool. But another genetic breakthrough may be an option: ovular merging, the mating of two eggs, seems not only possible now (after Pierre Soupart's 1979 successes with mice at Vanderbilt) but likely. Human females already volunteer for such experimentation. However difficult the technology that must accompany such merging, the possibility of its perfection is significant, for under such circumstances only female children are produced; if women are given the freedom of their bodies then they may well choose that alternative in great enough numbers to make a significant difference in the sex ratio of women to men. A 75% female to 25% male ratio could be achieved in one generation if one-half of a population reproduced heterosexually and one-half by ovular merging.

Such a prospect is attractive to women who feel that if they bear sons no amount of love and care and nonsexist training will save those sons from a culture where male violence is institutionalized and revered. These women are saying, "No more sons. We will not spend twenty years of our lives raising a potential rapist, a potential batterer, a potential Big Man."

It's significant that little or no money is allocated for research on ovular merging. The threat that it poses to the Code of Masculinity, to the male ego and to the male supremacist system is extraordinary, demonstrating in itself the work that is yet to be done in the education of men—and in the education of women who must still identify according to male standards in order to survive. Yet if we are to make the necessary changes then the financial support of research on ovular merging is only part of the picture. We must begin as well to change our attitudes toward women who defy the patriarchal limits on motherhood—

the single mothers, the lesbian mothers, the women raising children in groups of women—for these women are assuming species responsibility, are reproducing without the influence of men and with some awareness of what the needs are of the entire human race.

A growing number of women feel that still another method of securing a male reduction is possible: if reproductive initiative were returned to women and if female values were the values of the society in its everyday operation, then the natural ratio of females to males would be significantly higher. The present 47% male figure is engendered, they believe, by the high value placed upon males in the world-wide patriarchal system. Women presently survive by producing sons; in some places their lives literally depend upon that capacity. If childbearing women were relieved of that pressure and allowed to value females, even to *desire* daughters in far greater numbers than sons, they might well produce a far greater proportion of female children. Though women cannot presently "will" their children's sex, some believe that if women had the freedom of their bodies that control could be nearly foolproof. It remains to be seen if, with a different adult sexual ratio, such a different natural birth ratio would result.

Even though we can't know that a female future would save the world, we have nothing to lose from acting *as if* it would. Even though the restoration of her bodily rights to the female might not make the crucial difference, we have nothing to lose and everything to gain by acting *as if* it would. Even though we have not yet discovered the cause of alienation or violence, we have nothing to lose and everything to gain by approaching the problem *as if* it were caused by the overabundance of males within the human species.

When we speak of a female future and its attendant realities of the female's species responsibility and the reduction of men to 10% of the population, we are not talking about women imposing their morality or their values upon men. We are not talking about any violent act whatsoever. We are not talking about some arbitrary choice of innocent victim, or even, necessarily, the elevation of one group at the expense of another. When we talk of a female future we are talking of something that once existed and that has been deliberately and with full malice held down and controlled by means so violent that no nonaggressive entity could hope to resist. We are talking here about the power of women, felt by every woman at some time in her life, that tremendously rich and life-giving, life-affirming force that functions for both men and women, for the earth and her creatures as well as for the human species. When we talk about a female future we are talking about a force that has been denied, hidden, trivialized, ridiculed and suppressed. That's where the violence lies—in the minute-by-minute, day-by-day suppression of the very force that gives us all life. A female future means the challenge to and the obliteration of that violence.

But time is short. And the species may not be able to adapt fast enough. For that reason it's imperative that the rising up of the female future be not just the arising of women but an action on the part of men as well—a movement of men who not only cease to hold down women but who earnestly lend their tremendous male power to the hastening of the female future. We can count on it: it will be for us all the most crucial, the most profound act that women and men have ever undertaken together. It may well be the very last act that we ever undertake together. For it becomes clearer with every moment: EITHER THE FUTURE IS FEMALE OR THE FUTURE IS NOT.

Dorothy Marder

Stop raping, stop warring! WPA, 1980.

Part II

the passion to make and make again
where such unmaking reigns

—Adrienne Rich

Holly Near
Foolish Notion

Deep inside a city, a circle of women sit around a cluttered table sticking mailing labels on envelopes. Someone puts a Holly Near record on the stereo and soon the women are all singing along. "Oh, there's something about the women, something about the women in my life." One woman lets out a whoop and the others chuckle and sing some more as they put the labels on the envelopes.

Holly's music resonates with our pain and our rage and sometimes with our deepest anguish, as when she moans, "No, no don't melt into one." But her music then lifts us up, and inspires, indeed compels us to move, to carry on, to work even harder for social change and liberation from oppression. She sings about prison and militarism and nuclear energy and unemployment and women who have disappeared in Chile, but also about the joys of women loving women and people fighting fear and about people working together, of women fighting back.

Holly grew up in a Northern California farming community where her family supported her in both political awareness and development as an artist. In 1971, after working in the television and film industry, Holly was invited to join Jane Fonda and Donald Sutherland in the Free the Army *show which became known as an "alternative to the Bob Hope Show" for G.I.s overseas. In 1973 she formed Redwood Records (which she now co-owns with two other women) and recorded her first album* Hang In There. *Her award-winning fourth album,* Imagine My Surprise, *was made with an all-women team of musicians, technicians, graphic artists. The song Holly contributed to this anthology is from her fifth LP,* Fire In The Rain, *released in March, 1981, by Redwood Records. The future work of Redwood Records is coalition, international solidarity, and outreach into much larger mass audiences by using existing communication media such as radio, TV and film.*

Why do we kill people who are killing people
To show that killing people is wrong
What a foolish notion
That war is called devotion
When the greatest warriors are the ones that stand for peace

War toys are growing stronger
The problems stay the same
The young ones join the army
While general whats-his-name
Is feeling full of pride
That the army will provide
But does he ask himself

Why do we kill people who are killing people
To show that killing people is wrong
What a foolish notion
That war is called devotion
When the greatest warriors are the ones that stand for peace

Death row is growing longer
The problems stay the same
The poor ones get thrown in prison
While warden whats-his-name
Is feeling justified
But when will he be tried
For never asking

Why do we kill people who are killing people
To show that killing people is wrong
What a foolish notion
That war is called devotion
When the greatest warriors are the ones that stand for peace

Children are so tender
They will cross the earth if they think they are saving a friend
They get drawn in by patriotic lies
Right before our eyes
They leave our home
And then they find out once they're all alone
They're asking the age old question
Why?

Why do we kill people who are killing people
To show that killing people is wrong
What a foolish notion
That war is called devotion
When the greatest warriors are the ones that stand for peace

Diana J. M. Davies/Insight

Holly Near

Catherine Reid
Reweaving the Web of Life

From Vermont comes this moving account of women who picked up the thread of nonviolence and knotted it securely to feminism through the genius of guerrilla theatre. The Spinsters, an affinity group of women-identified-women, began spinning their symbolic web of many colors on March 30, 1980 in support of a week long occupation at the Vermont Yankee Nuclear Power Plant in the town of Vernon.

With this action the women began weaving a web to entangle the powers that threaten this vulnerable planet; mending the ragged edges of our misinformed, fragmented lives; spinning the delicate threads that will connect us to each other.

Catherine brings the clear vision of an artist, the sensitive ear of a poet and the heart of a true Spinster to the spinning of this tale. She writes, "I knew the story had to be written. It was hard to write when it was raw and uncertain in my thoughts. I sat under the sugar maple whose huge limbs seemed to embrace the small cabin in which I was living. From where I sat I could see three spiders on delicate threads, weaving webs for their sustenance and survival. I was reassured."

It was a year and three days after the accident at Three Mile Island. The Vermont Yankee Decommissioning Alliance (VYDA) occupiers were just waking up from their eventful night—punctuated by arrests, shift changes of plant employees and state police and strategy meetings and half-sleep on the pavement. Just as the next employee shift began, a group of women began weaving intricate and spontaneous designs between the trees of the entrance to the plant.

With thousands of yards of colored yarns, threads and strings, the Spinsters, an all-women affinity group, had begun at different trees, secured their ends, and started spinning and weaving before the police could respond.

We will meet, all of us women of every land,
we will meet in the center, make a circle;
we will weave a world web to entangle the powers
that bury our children.

We, as life-givers, will not support any life-threatening force. Nuclear madness imminently endangers our children, their future and the earth. On Monday, March 31, women will be reweaving the web of life into the site of the Vermont Yankee.

We will meet, all of us women of every land, we will meet in the center, make a circle; we will weave a world web to entangle the powers that bury our children.

We, as life-givers, will not support any life-threatening force. Nuclear madness imminently endangers our children, their future and the earth. On Monday, March 31, women will be reweaving the web of life into the site of Vermont Yankee.

So read the small leaflet distributed by the Spinsters. The woven patterns were symbolic of the interconnectedness of life, the delicate balance of our dependencies with all living things. They were a reminder of how abusive a nuclear power plant is in its indiscriminate destruction of these webs.

In contrast, the disregard for the future that seems to be an arrogance of men was symbolically represented in the gestures of the police officers: the ripping and cutting of the webs with hands and knives; their refusal to discuss the issues of nukes, waste disposals, freedom of speech, etc.

"Would you hold this end?" I asked the officer unravelling a big tangle, and I headed off to a tree to tie down the other end.

"Ohh, you dropped it!"

Slash! went the officer's knife down through several strands. "Just like a knife through butter," said Alex, "just like radiation through DNA."

"He will someday make the connection," said Cora, "his mother tied his shoes a thousand times, his clothes were woven-mended. Watch him wrap up the yards of yarn. He's had practice holding skeins while his mother wound balls."

"A spider's work is never done," someone else said. "Every morning she must remake her web where it has been torn."

The police continued cutting with their knives, then resorted to wrapping and wrapping the multicolored ends of pieces together. The Spinsters began knotting and reknotting the breaks in the threads, trying to make continuous the interconnections.

One officer looked real young and uncomfortable. "Such beautiful colors!" I said. "You can have this gold one; I'll take the lavender."

"Is it wire?" A man had stopped his car and shouted out his window at a trooper; he wouldn't go any farther until the string was snapped.

For an hour the dance continued. A Spinster would travel out to another anchor, tying together different colors and textures, repairing the breaks, finding new orbs to connect to. Other women joined the dance, from other affinity groups, this dance of creativity and life. Soon, however, the police had confiscated all the yarns, while refusing to arrest anyone.

Meanwhile, Julie had begun with spools of thread, tying, designing, covering the heavy metal fence surrounding the plant. The other Spinsters joined her, spools appearing from their pockets, to add more incongruity to this absurd fence, with its triple strand of barbed wire on top.

"Yes, I have a child, that's why I'm here," said Julie. But the officer was playing "flirt with the women," a common game when they don't want to take women seriously.

Another officer, responding angrily to a comment about protecting the earth, said he had relatives who were Abenaki Indians. "Then you must know of their decision-making ways!" said Cora. "Before making a decision that would affect their environment or themselves, they asked: 'what will this do to our children seven generations from now?'" He didn't answer.

We continued to discuss the implications of nukes with the long line of officers watching us. We showed them leaves from last year, the acres of veins clearly displayed in the beginnings of the decaying process. "These webs are everywhere. Playing blind to them doesn't mean we aren't destroying them," we said. No answer.

"Listen, we aren't allowed to debate with you. We aren't even supposed to be talking with you," an officer said.

Cora was furious. "Who gave you that order?" She approached the lead man, closely and pointedly, and told him, "I'm going to give you another order. You have the right to free speech and to speak to whomever you choose to speak to. This is America."

Again, the officers arrested no one.

The VYDA village was bustling—town meeting planned, soups simmering, workshops scheduled. The Spinsters who had planned their action to be a second wave to the VYDA occupation now had to decide what to do. If the first group wasn't going to be arrested from where they were established at the entry to the plant, how could the Spinsters be a second wave?

We could continue the action we had set for ourselves: creatively, spontaneously symbolic. An action independent from the VYDA occupation; blowing breezes into their sails, but not detracting from their impact.

We had chosen to work together as Spinsters because we were all women-identified. We resented the still-present sexism of working with men and knew the comfort and strength of working with women. We informed VYDA of our intent, but asked no consensual support from them.

Tuesday morning we were back. With dozens of balls of yarn, we wove between the trees and fence, creating one big tapestry. The weft was mostly supplied by cornstalks, tall dried goldenrod, pine and willow and birch branches, leaves and acorns and pinecones. The day was intensely blue, the sky hazy; faces sunburned, sleeping bags flapped, and dry, stiff bodies warmed through. When we had finished weaving we lay in the grass beneath our design, watching the light catch and scatter the the hairs of the yarns.

Soon, the police came. Again, with knives they cut and tore while Cora read aloud to them from Helen Caldicott's *Nuclear Madness*:

> *Whether natural or human-made, all radiation is dangerous. There is no "safe" amount of radioactive material or dose of radiation. Why? Because by virtue of the nature of the biological damage done by radiation, it takes only one radioactive atom, one cell, and one gene to initiate the cancer or mutation cycle. Any exposure at all, therefore, constitutes a serious gamble with the mechanisms of life.*

The men were silent, embarrassed, uncomfortable. Before they had quite finished cutting the web, they had had enough. "Come on, let's get out of here."

Wednesday we came again. We wove first between the trees of the entry to the site. The police looked at us familiarly, pulling out their knives, ready to repeat the steps of the dance they knew so well: cut, tear down, destroy. The kite string we used this time, however, merely stretched below the blades, until one man shouted in disgust, "It breaks. Use your hands."

We started in on the railings of the stairway to the Information Center (closed due to the occupation going on), and, while Cora read aloud, we spun. This time, however, five women from VYDA approached us, "We women would like to talk to you women. We want to tell you we don't support what you're doing. We weren't involved in the decision-making process and resent the litter you're leaving behind."

Ow. Wounded, hurt, sad. Undermined by women, sisters who don't yet understand.

Cora answered them articulately and eloquently. We weren't competing with their action. We knew they were the real heroes, spending the long nights and days. "And if you call this litter, what do you call that?" asked Alex, angrily pointing at the power station.

We had attended a VYDA meeting, had informed the spokespeople of our intentions, had invited other women to join us. Ours was an act of theatre, an art form made difficult for some to evaluate because to many it was still threatening.

But it was time for us to leave. Saddened, we drove away, but not before we saw VYDA-ers pouncing on the tiny remaining bits of string, reminders of life-symbols and sanity which were now being captured and thrown into plastic garbage bags.

We returned at the end of the week to fly the 16' wide, vivid orange kite that Mary and Alex had made. Its stark warning, "NUKES KILL," was clearly visible from the site. At the final meeting of all VYDA, Grace Paley jumped up, pointed at the kite, and said that these women had provided the only originality to the week, that their weavings were all too symbolic of the life we were all wanting to protect.

So who are the Spinsters? and why spin?

A woman whose occupation is to spin, to create, to remember the integrity (wholeness of being), is a Spinster. Weaving symbolizes our need to maintain the connections between all life and to avoid male-defined hierarchies and dominances.

We have reclaimed the word "spinster," refusing to succumb to the reversed definition found in contemporary language. The word has long functioned as a "powerful weapon of intimidation and deception" (says Mary Daly in *Gyn/Ecology*). The fear of being a spinster has driven women "into the 'respectable' alternative of marriage, forcing them to believe, against all evidence to the contrary that wedlock will be salvation from a fate worse than death, that it will inevitably mean fulfillment."

We acknowledge the integral work that women have long done: spinning, weaving, tying, knotting, repairing, mending. We endorse these attributes and let them give us creative strength in responding to the work that men have long done: ripping, tearing, destroying, killing.

Webs of life.

The webs are only just beginning to appear. In Groton, Connecticut, on April 26, 1980, Womyn Spinning for Life wove near the gate of Electric Boat where celebrants were entering to cheer the launching of the second nuclear-powered Trident submarine. Each Trident has 408 warheads, each with an explosive force five times that which destroyed Hiroshima.

These Womyn were reminding the celebrants that this is a threat to all life.

Several were arrested. After all their yarns had been confiscated, they began unraveling their clothes and sheets, and their webs appeared in the jails, the paddy wagons, the court house. The tiny, fragile designs were an ominous threat to the armed, white male authorities.

On November 17, 1980, spontaneous groups of women moved from the circle of women surrounding the Pentagon. Again, yarns and string and scarves appeared, and two of the entrances of this oppressive, police covered building were suddenly filled with color and motion.

In March, 1981, VYDA gathered at Vermont Yankee for a one day "Warning Strike." Some of the original Spinsters came, many other women joined them, and the dance for life was repeated.

And so it shall continue to be repeated. For as long as we feel life is being threatened, we will continue to talk about it and spin about it and point to those who are destroying life's webs.

Grace Paley
Cop Tales

Grace, a long-time political activist, is a beloved and familiar face to many at East Coast demonstrations. Acclaimed author of The Little Disturbances of Man *and* Enormous Changes at the Last Minute, *Grace has been a typist, housewife and writer and currently teaches at Sarah Lawrence College.*

This essay is a collage, a kaleidoscope tinted uniform-blue, made up of her random observations and overheard conversations of those men who consistently stand on the other side of the sawhorses. She shows us their moments of loveableness and their unrelenting armored distance.

At the Wall Street Action in October 1979, the police were on one side of the sawhorses. We were on the other. We were blocking Wall Street workers. The police were blocking us. One of them was very interested in solar housing. Our solar expert explained the science and economics of it all. Another cop from Long Island worried a lot about Shoreham. "Can't do anything about it," he said. "They'll build it. I hate it. I live there. What am I going to do?"

That could be a key to the police I thought. They have no hope. Cynical. They're mad at us because we have a little hope in the midst of our informed worries.

Then he said, looking at the Bread and Puppet Theater's stilt dancers, "Look at that, what's going on here? People running around in the street dancing. They're going every which way. It ain't organized." We started to tell him how important the dancers were. "No, no, that's okay" he said. "The antiwar demonstrations were like this at first, mixed up, but they got themselves together. You'll get yourself together too. In a couple years you'll know how to do it better."

Earlier, about 6 a.m., two cops wearing blue hardhats passed. One of them looked behind him. "Here come the horses," he said. "Let's get the hell out of here!" And they moved at top casual walking speed in the opposite direction.

Also at 6 a.m., but about fifteen years ago, we would walk up and down before the Whitehall Street Induction Center wearing signs that said "I Support Draft Refusal." It wouldn't take more than a couple of hours for the system to gather up its young victims, stuff them into wagons, and start them off on their terrible journey. At 9:30 on one of those mornings, about twenty women sat down all across the street to prevent the death wagons from moving. They sat for about thirty minutes. Then a plainclothesman approached an older gray-haired woman, "Missus, you don't want to get arrested." "I have to," she said. "My grandson's in Vietnam." Gently they removed her. Then with billy clubs, a dozen uniformed men moved up and down that line of young women, dragging them away, by their arms, their hair, beating them, I remember, (and Norma Becker remembers) mostly in the breast.

Last May at the rainy Armed Forces Day Parade, attended by officers, their wives, and Us, some of Us were arrested by a couple of Cops for Christ. At the desk, as they took our names, smiling, they gave us "Cops for Christ" leaflets. We gave "Disarm for Human Life" leaflets.

Another year, one of the first really large antidraft actions—also at the Induction Center at dawn. We were to surround the building. The famous people, or *Notables* as the Vietnamese used to say, sat down to bar the front entrance. That's where the TV cameras were. Our group of regulars went around to the back of the Center and sat down. Between us and the supply entrance stood a solid line of huge horses and their solemn police riders. We sat cross-legged, speaking softly as the day brightened. Sometimes someone would joke and someone else would immediately say, "Be serious." Off to one side, a captain watched us and the cavalry. Suddenly the horses reared, charged us as we sat, smashing us with their great bodies, scattering our supporting onlookers. People were knocked down, ran this way and that, but the horses were everywhere, rearing—until at a signal from the captain, which I saw, they stopped, settled down, and trotted away. That evening the papers and TV reported that a couple of thousand had demonstrated. Hundreds had been peacefully arrested.

At Wall Street too: A gentleman with a Wall Street attache case tried to get through our line. The police who were in the middle of a discussion about Arabian oil said, "Why not try down there, mister. You can get through down there." The gentleman said he wanted to get through right here and right now and began to knee through our line. The cop on the other side of the sawhorse said, "You heard us. Down there, mister. How about it?" The gentleman said, "Dammit, what are you here for?" He began to move away, calling back in fury, "What the hell are you cops here for anyway?" "Just role playing," the cop called in reply.

There were several cheerful police at the Trident demonstration last year. One officer cheerily called out to the Trident holiday visitors to be careful as they trod the heads of the demonstrators blocking the roadway. "They're doing what they believe in." He asked us to step back, but not more than six inches. He told a joke. He said he hated war, always had. Some young state troopers arrived—more help was needed. They were tall and grouchy. A Black youngster, about twelve, anxious to see what was going on, pushed against the line. One of the state troopers leaned forward and smacked the child hard on the side of the head. "Get back, you little bastard," he said. I reached out to get the attention of the cheery cop, who wore a piece of hierarchical gold on his jacket. "Officer," I said, "you ought to get that trooper out of here, he's dangerous." He looked at me, his face went icy cold, "Lady, be careful," he said. "I just saw you try to strike that officer."

Not too long ago, I saw Finnegan, the plainclothes Red Squad boss. I hadn't seen him in a long time. "Say, Finnegan," I said, "all these years you've been working at one thing and I've been working at the opposite, but look at us. Nothing's prevented either of us from getting gray." He almost answered, but a lot of speedy computations occurred in his brain, and he couldn't. It's the business of the armed forces and the armored face to maintain distance at all times.

Dorothy Marder

Grace Paley, center (left)

Meg Bowman
Letter to the IRS

While Benjamin Franklin was rallying Pennsylvanians to arm against the "Indians," John Woolman and Anthony Benezet were urging their radical Quaker friends to consider tax refusal. Tax resistance is an old technique of noncooperation, one which was used by Henry David Thoreau who did not want to support slavery or war with his actions or money, and one which is still used today. Barbara Deming, a war tax resister, justified this act of noncooperation in her essay "On Revolution and Equilibrium." "Words are not enough here. Gandhi's term for nonviolent action was 'satyagraha'—which can be translated as 'clinging to the truth.'...And one has to cling with one's entire weight... One doesn't just say, 'I don't believe in this war,' but refuses to put on a uniform. One doesn't just say, 'The use of napalm is atrocious,' but refuses to pay for it by refusing to pay one's taxes."

Meg, a 57-year-old life-long Quaker from Massachusetts, has been a war-tax resister since 1967. She offers here the text of a letter she wrote to the Internal Revenue Service in 1972 when she began resisting payment of all federal taxes. "The I.R.S. has never acknowledged this letter," she writes, "though they have occasionally snatched my cars."

Meg plans to enter the Peace Corps in the near future and is presently learning organic gardening with Juanita Nelson (also a contributor to this anthology.) Meg hopes to someday "live gently on the land."

February 7, 1972

To: The Internal Revenue Service, Washington, D.C.

From: Meg (Bowman)

Re: Payment of federal taxes

> "Do you carefully maintain our testimony against all preparations for war and against participation in war as inconsistent with the teachings of Christ?" Query, *Discipline* of Pacific Yearly Meeting, Religious Society of Friends (Quakers).

The above quotation is from the book that is intended to give guidance to members for daily living. The book repeatedly stresses peace and individual responsibility.

It is clear to me that I am not only responsible for my voluntary actions, but also for that which is purchased with my income. If my income is spent for something immoral or if I allow others to buy guns with money I have earned, this is as wrong and offending to "that of God in every man" as if I had used that gun, or planned that bomb strike.

When I worked a five-day week it seemed to me that one-fifth of my income went to taxes. This would be equivalent to working one full day each week for the U.S. government. It seemed I worked as follows:

> *Monday for food.* I felt responsible to buy wholesome, nourishing items that would provide health and energy, but not too much meat or other luxuries, the world supply of which is limited.
>
> *Tuesday for shelter.* We maintain a comfortable, simply furnished home where we may live in dignity and share with others.
>
> *Wednesday for clothing,* health needs and other essentials and for recreation, all carefully chosen.
>
> *Thursday for support of causes.* I select with care those organizations which seem to be acting in such a way that responsibility to God and my brother is well served.
>
> *Friday for death,* bombs, napalm, for My Lai and overkill. I am asked to support a government whose main business is war.

Though the above is oversimplified, the point is clear. I cannot work four days a week for life and joy and sharing, and one day for death. I cannot pay federal taxes. I believe this decision is protected by law as a First Amendment right of freedom of religion. If I am wrong it is still better to have erred on the side of peace and humanity.

Sincerely,
signed Meg Bowman

Juanita Nelson
Fragment from a Play in Progress

Set in a jail cell, this lively play within a play explores the significance of nonviolence, noncooperation, integrity and the power of the individual. Alice, a character in the play, has been arrested for tax resistance and, much to the bewilderment of her sister inmates, has continued her resistance in jail by refusing to walk or eat for her captors.

Juanita, born in Cleveland, Ohio in 1923 and active in CORE (Congress of Racial Equality) in the 40's and early 50's, based the play on her own jail experiences. "The longest sentence for me was a seventeen day stint in Elkton, Maryland in 1961 where I was arrested for trying to eat at a truck stop on Route 40. In those days people with skin my color were not served there. Other arrests have included one for tax resistance. (I haven't paid income tax since 1948.)"

Now living in Massachusetts, Juanita and her husband try to be self-provisioning and less dependent on "the system" by growing eighty percent of their own food.

Scene 2: ***Second Day***

The cell block gate is open. Guard and matron go out, gate clangs shut. Alice slips the tray of food back under the barred door. She paces off the dimensions of her world, measuring with her arms. Stands on bed and tries to reach ceiling. Touches everything: bedstand, bed, slop bucket, glass and pitcher of water, towel rack. Sits on bed, head in hands.

Door to cell block clangs open as inmates return from dinner, some sullen and silent, some joking. Gate clangs shut. Bertha, Rita and Mary stop at Alice's cell; Marion, Stella and Pearl, curious, stand around.

Bertha: Hey, aren't they ever gonna let you out to eat?
Alice: Oh, room service is ever so much better. *(Points to tray.)*
Bertha: *(groaning)* Aren't you hungry? You haven't eaten a bite since they brought you in yesterday.

Alice: I'm beginning to feel a little hungry. But as long as they keep me in jail I'm not going to feed myself.
Rita: You gotta not eat to be nonviolent? How come you don't just go out and shoot yourself?
Mary: Half the time I don't eat. The food's lousy.
Rita: The Ritz this is not.
Bertha: How long you not gonna eat?
Alice: As long as I'm locked up. As far as I'm concerned I've been kidnapped, and I'm not going to help anybody violate me like that. They have taken my body and as long as they have it they're responsible for it. *(Sounds belligerent and is; realizing this, tries to get into her classic nonviolent pose.)* It's not that I hate or dislike the matron or the judge or the guards or even the folks who run the wars I don't want to pay for. They're all people like me and in my better moments I love them. I try to love them. Love the evil doer, hate the evil. Detest the sin, understand the sinner. And feel sorry for all of us. *(Earnestly, almost too earnestly)* I really, truly don't dislike the people who put me here. But I do detest what they're doing and I'm going to resist that with all my strength. They may be doing what they think is right. Anyway, in a sense we're all the same, so I must love them: If I love myself, I must love them.
Mary: *(gently)* Relax, honey, you ain't in no church—we're in jail, remember?
Bertha: It's not a question of love in this game—it's power, baby, power.
Alice: You're absolutely right. *(With some animation)* Power and love. The power of love, instead of the love of power. Hey, how's that? I just thought that up!
Rita: Give me the power and you can have the love.
Alice: *(Almost completely into herself)* The courts and the jails have the power because we give it to them. Right? My only power, our only power at this point, is to take the power away by refusing to cooperate. But with compassion for our common humanity, with love. Do you see that?
Bertha: Hey, girls, what do you 'spose would happen if one of us acted like her?
Pearl: Shi-i-i-t. They'd put us under the jail, you better believe it.
Marion: Hey, let's have a trial and I'll be the judge. Man, you bring me a motherfucker like this one, I'd make her straighten up.
Rita: You mean cause she won't eat? That ain't hurting anybody but her. What's it to you, Judge?

Marion: It's not natural. Besides, the court has got to be respected. Or else your criminal elements take over.

(Lots of noise, comments about this)

Marion: Shut up. I'm the judge. You all be quiet while the court gets its shit together.

(Bedlam ceases and everyone arranges herself spontaneously for the proceedings. Bertha, who has decided to be the prisoner, goes to one side and sits on the floor with her arms folded. Pearl and Rita, the police officers, hover near her. Stella sits as if at a stenotype machine to record the trial. A chair is placed on a table and the rest help Marion mount the pedestal. Bailiff Mary stands at her side. Everyone's in the action, with Alice the lone spectator.)

Marion: *(bangs gavel, a rolled up* True Confessions, *while the Bailiff stamps her foot for sound effects)* This court will come to order. Hear ye, hear ye.

Bailiff Mary: Hear ye, hear ye.

Marion: Bring in the prisoner.

Bailiff Mary: Bring in the prisoner.

Marion: Hey, you're the bailiff, not a parrot. You're supposed to bring in the prisoner.

(Bailiff goes "out," returns immediately)

Bailiff Mary: The prisoner won't come, Your Honor.

Marion: What do you mean, the prisoner won't come? It's your business to get the prisoner before the bar of justice. Do your job or I'll have you arrested.

Bailiff Mary: But she won't walk, Your Honor.

Marion: Pour some cold water on her head.

Bailiff Mary: She's not drunk, Your Honor. I don't think she is. I can't smell anything. She says she's not going to cooperate with this court, Your Honor, because she's a nonviolent cooperator, a violent noncooperator. *(Calls back to the prisoner)* Hey, you explain it.

Bertha: Because I don't believe folks ought to be locked in cages like, like hyenas, that's how come. I'm not a baby and you are not my mamma. I am a grown woman and I am responsible for myself.

Marion: That's enough. Bring the prisoner in.

Bertha: I am not a prisoner.

Marion: What do you mean? Have we got the wrong...

Bertha: I don't feel like a prisoner.

Marion: Hey, you two are the police. Bring that whore, bring that woman before the bar of justice.

Police Officer Pearl: Bar, shit. I bet she'd walk if it was the 57th

Street Bar and you was the bartender. Hey, why don't you offer her a drink?

Marion: *(raps gavel)* The courtroom will be cleared if there's any more lip.

Pearl: But I'm the policeman.

Marion: So? You can be arrested, too. And you will be if you don't bring that woman in.

(Pearl and Rita try to pick Bertha up; they tug but get nowhere)

Bertha: Keep you hands offa me.

Rita: You supposed to be nonviolent. You're not supposed to offer any resistance...

Bertha: Excuse me. I'm new at this stuff. I gotta learn how to stick a knife in your guts, in my mind, and look like I'm giving you a lollipop. *(Assumes praying hands attitude, composes face into beatific expression)* How's that?

Pearl: Shi-i-i-t. That grin don't take off one pound.

(They tug at Bertha; she goes limp and they can't budge her)

Rita: Judge, Your Honor, we can't budge this bitch. She is naturally too heavy. It'll take a crane to move her. Shit, I'll never get a hernia carrying her around.

Marion:*(with a rap of the gavel)* Don't tell me your troubles. I want the prisoner before the bar. Or I'll charge you with gross neglect on five counts.

(Rita and Pearl roll Bertha in like a hoop)

Pearl: You may be nonviolent, but you're making me violent as hell. I'd like to bash your head in, and I would if I was the Judge.

Marion: The prisoner will stand before the bar of justice.

Bertha: I'm too dizzy to stand up.

Marion: The prisoner will have three minutes to get her balance back.

(Takes out imaginary watch)

Now stand up.

Bertha: Un-unh.

Marion: Are you defying this court?

Bertha: That's my intention. But with love, Judge, with love.

Marion: What's your name?

Bertha: Not going to tell you. *(Pause)* But it's on that sheet in front of you. Can't you read?

Marion: This court will not tolerate back talk. Of course I can read. What's your name?

(Only a great sigh from Bertha breaks the silence)

Marion: All right, name unknown. It really doesn't matter, you

know. We've got your fingerprints, footprints, Mobil credit card, Sears credit card, food stamp number. And your social security number.
Bertha: Ain't that a bitch.
Marion: *(raps gavel)* Stop calling me names. The bitch, I mean the bench must be respected. Somebody, read the charge against the prisoner.
Mary: Ber...the unknown prisoner did, on three separate, distinct and different occasions, extract money from the First National Bank under a false name.
Marion: The charge is forgery. Stealing. How do you plead?
Bertha: I am not pleading. I am protesting. With love. I really do love...
Marion: What are you protesting? You're getting a fair trial, at least I'm trying to give you a fair trial, but you refuse...
Bertha: I am protesting being brought into this court like a...like a common criminal.
Marion: Stealing is a crime. It is also common. Happens everyday. And right from this throne I put them in jail everyday. You think you ought to get different treatment?
Bertha: Depends. Like, you're stealing my freedom. What's the penalty for that?
Marion: I am going to hold you in contempt of court pretty soon. You're on trial, not me. I ask, you answer. Guilty or not guilty?
Bertha: I got only one answer, Judge. I love you. I mean, can't you respond to that?
Marion: I love you is not a plea; it's just another four letter word. You can slobber all over me as much as you please, but I am going to put your ass in jail if you don't stand up. And show the proper respect to this court.
Bertha: *(sotto voce to the others)* Oh, she's mad now. That shows I got her by the balls. Just play it cool and you throw them off base. They don't know what to do when you lay this love stuff on 'em. *(To Judge again)* I really do love you, Judge. You're up there and I'm down here. But we're sisters under the skin, right?
Marion: No. No, I am a judge, and you are a thief and don't you forget it.
Bertha: Oh, no. That ain't the difference. The difference is you got on a robe and I'm wearing a jailhouse dress.

(At this point everyone but the Judge becomes an empathetic prisoner again)
Mary: You tell her, Bertha.

Marion: I am giving you one more chance, prisoner. Stand up and give your name or I'll...
Pearl: Don't you do it, Bertha. Keep the knife in.
Rita: Twist it.
Marion: Order in the court or I'll have all of you arrested.
Chorus: We love you, we love you, we love you, we love you, we love you!
Marion: I sentence you to one hundred years in solitary. And don't tell me you won't eat. Makes me no difference. Next case.
Bertha: Hey, Judge, I tell you what, I'll give you my name if you'll tell me yours. I mean, what's in a name?
Pearl: No, no, don't do it. Don't let her scare you.
Rita: Don't tell that bitch a thing.
Bertha: *(to Judge)* To hell with you. *(Raises hands to conduct the chant)*
Chorus: We love you, we love you, we love you, we love...

(Matron enters)

Matron: What's going on here? I told you girls to leave this prisoner alone. I don't want anybody near this cell again. I try to be nice to you girls, but I got my orders. You wanna get me in trouble? No television tonight and you can all go to your rooms, right now. That's so you'll remember. Next time it'll be lock up for three days.

(For a moment everyone is frozen)

Alice: You don't have to do it, you know.

(They look at each other, at Alice, at the Matron. Dazed still from the playacting. But they come out of the trance and go slowly, as if sleepwalking, to the cells and close themselves in.)

Charlotte Marchant
Sweet Life

What was it like to be arrested at a sixties anti-war demonstration, believing that the revolution "was only a matter of months" and be put in prison for a sentence of 30 days? In this short story we see prison from this special perspective, a point of view probably familiar to many of the contributors as well as to many readers of this anthology. Charlotte writes, "My story is semi-autobiographical, which I've decided is just another way of saying 'I've changed the names to protect the innocent.' I spent a number of years being pretty arrogant about life, the world, and the changes I thought only I knew the correct way to make happen. Now, when someone asks me about politics and the revolution, I tell them that I have more questions than answers these days. My heart, though, continues to be with the people's struggles of the world, and 'power to the people' is still a slogan I embrace."

This story may raise questions for some pacifists around the range of action which can be considered nonviolent. The character in this story is arrested while trying to break "the huge plate glass windows of buildings lining the streets of corporate America." Is this nonviolent action? Is this violent action? Where do we draw the line?

Charlotte is now in her early thirties and lives in New York where she was born and raised. After living in the Bay Area for ten years, she has recently "come home again."

She writes, "I feel stories everywhere I look and everywhere I've been. If I had a camera I'd take pictures. If I were a musician I'd play an instrument. Instead, I use my speedy secretary fingers and hit those keys on the typewriter at my job. My stories are the photographs and the music in my mind. I had to start writing them because my friends got tired of hearing me tell them over and over again, and they encouraged me to be the writer I continue trying to become."

While running frantically from the cops on horseback, I had made several attempts to break the huge plate glass windows of the buildings lining the streets of corporate America. My rocks bounced right back toward me. I felt very small and powerless.

It was the late sixties, and my anger at my country's involvement in the Vietnam war had led to my own involvement in anti-war groups and this demonstration. After a confrontation between the city police and members of Youth For Justice, I was arrested along with several other members for rioting. When the cops grabbed me I experienced a certain amount of relief. It was over, I had been caught. I am a small, young white woman. I looked even younger than my eighteen years. For me it was over. Later in the police station I saw them beating a young Black man and one of the white men from the group I was arrested with. I yelled at them to stop. A big burly cop turned, stared at me in disbelief and bellowed, "What's a little girl like you doing in here? Don't tell me you're a commie lover too?" He pushed me into the holding cell as he yelled, "Shut up already, I don't wanna have to do the same to you."

Those of us arrested decided to defend ourselves. I went to court. My knees shook as I looked up at the judge in his black robes. "Your honor, I am not guilty. It is the United States government that is guilty of killing innocent Vietnamese people and using poor and third world Americans as cannon fodder." He decided otherwise, pronounced me guilty as charged, fined me $100 and sentenced me to 30 days in the county prison.

They handcuffed me and took me to the jail in a paddy wagon filled to capacity with other women prisoners—some returning from court dates and others beginning their sentences like me. We sat on the two benches in the paddy wagon deep in our own thoughts. I wondered what the other women were in jail for and worried about the thirty days I was about to spend behind bars. Part of me couldn't believe I was sitting handcuffed in a paddy wagon on my way to jail. It was like another movie in my life with me in the lead role. I cursed myself for not being a faster runner, for having gotten caught. Then I remembered it was only thirty days. That the end, at least, was in sight. Suddenly the paddy wagon came to a screeching halt, and we were all thrown forward landing on top of one another. Each time we would get ourselves re-seated, it happened again. We could hear the driver and the prison guard laughing in response to our cries and curses after these sudden stops.

The paddy wagon pulled into the basement entrance of the prison. From there we were ordered to walk along the right hand wall and not step over the yellow line painted on the floor about three feet from the wall. It reminded me of my junior high school. There, the painted line had been in the middle of the floor to keep the traffic going in the same direction; under no circumstances were the students allowed to cross it, even if their next class was directly across the hall. Things felt painfully familiar. In the basement of the prison I could hear the echoes of the prison life. I heard the men prisoners shouting messages from one cell to another. "Yo, Carlos! Your homeboy Tito was brought in last night. They gave him sixty days for possession man. He's strung out real bad. Hanging over the toilet throwing up all night. Got the shakes today. He's real fucked up." I could also hear the sounds of all the dishes and the prison's laundry being washed in large industrial machines by the inmates. No one talked softly; everyone shouted in order to be heard above the din. When I was handed a scratchy blanket, a tin plate, a spoon and a stiff yellow uniform, I became aware of the goose bumps on my arms, realizing for the first time that it was cold in the prison and that I felt frightened and very much alone. I wasn't so much afraid of the other prisoners. I had been raised by my socialist parents to believe that the prison gates needed to be opened before we could all be free. It was the guards, the matrons and the warden I feared.

When I had spoken to my father on the phone before the trial, he told me he was sorry but he didn't have the money for my bail. He was still trying to raise it and I should hang on. Things had been really tight that winter. He was on unemployment, unable to do his construction work ouside on the scaffolds in the snow and cold. I told him it was ok, that I'd manage. He said that he wished my mother was still alive. She'd know better how to deal with the lawyers that kept calling. I told him not to worry, that my friends and I would defend ourselves. Then I half listened to his standard lecture about how the United States wasn't ready for revolution. That things had changed drastically since he had been involved in trying to right the wrongs and fight to create his union for the merchant marines during the Depression years. He reminded me once again that all his old cronies had sold out and that mine would too. That in the end I would be left alone while their rich parents bailed them all out. He wished I had stayed in school and made something of my life. And look at the mess I was in now! Where was this all going to get me, he wanted to know.

From the basement we were herded onto the elevator. We were not allowed to turn and face the door. We had to remain staring at the back of the elevator until it arrived on the 6th and top floor where the women were incarcerated. All the other floors were for the male prisoners. When I got off the elevator I was confronted with prison bars in whichever direction I looked. As I watched the elevator door close behind me, I realized it would be the last solid door I'd see for awhile and that for the next thirty days all the doors in my life would be controlled by someone else.

The matrons came and brought our group of fifteen women to the infirmary. There we waited while each was given a quick but thorough internal examination to search for contraband. I had enough trouble getting a tampax in—I couldn't imagine it being a place to store pills, heroin or marijuana wrapped in plastic baggies. The thrust of the cold metal speculum into my vagina by a hostile matron made me realize the search was another part of the punishment for our supposed crimes.

After the search, I was taken to my cell. It was six feet by ten feet and contained a single canvas cot that hung from the wall and a combination sink/toilet. Later I would learn of another use for the toilet. When emptied of water it was an excellent telephone to the line of toilets below if they too were dry. It was one of the many forms of inter-jail communication that the inmates had created to maintain some sense of themselves and control of their own lives.

I made my bed, left my cell and went into the dayroom which was the largest area on the cell block where the inmates could congregate. There was a gate of bars separating the dayroom from the row of individual cells. On routine days it was kept open and the inmates had access to the dayroom and each cell until lights out at 9 p.m. This privilege as well as all privileges could be taken away by the matrons at any time for any reason.

As I looked around the dayroom, I realized that I had felt more fear out on the streets trying to aim my rocks at the bank windows and defend myself from the cops than I was feeling right then. In the dayroom I saw over forty women, all ages and mostly Black. Some turned and smiled at me, and already many of my political friends who had also been arrested were sitting with some of the other inmates talking intensely. They were seated at one of the four green-painted, metal picnic tables. The only other thing in the room was an old black and white television which sat on a high shelf and was controlled by the matrons from the other side of the bars. The picnic tables were where the three meals were eaten, the card games were played, the hairstyles were rearranged, the TV was watched and the general hanging out took place. The years of initials and graffiti carved into the table tops made it a very uneven surface; impossible for letter writing and responsible for many shaky coffee cup spills.

I sat at one of these tables and joined my friends. I was introduced to the other inmates at the table. The women were very open to us. They had wanted to know what was going on outside and were very curious about all the white kids they were seeing lately on the TV news running through the streets, throwing rocks at cops and windows. So here we were in the flesh!

Sonia, an older white woman serving time for bank robbery, shook her head in bewilderment and said, "Why you break all the windows and keep running? Shit, you could climb in those stores then and get all kind of good stuff." While my political partners tried to explain our priorities, Sonia's comment sparked some long-forgotten memories of the black-out of 1965. I was doing homework in front of the TV when suddenly all the lights went out. Before long, some of my friends, Pauline, Iris and Joan, called to me through the window. They were downstairs, outside with flashlights. They were going to go through the streets, check out the stores, see what they could get and see what was happening. They wanted me to come along, maybe even to Macy's! But my parents wouldn't let me out of the house. It was candlelight for me and my family that night while my friends roamed the New York City streets looking for treasures. And now I was behind bars, attempting to eat what the prison called dinner. On this night dinner meant lumpy, powdered potatoes, a slab of unidentifiable meat and overboiled green beans whose color now resembled the institutional green walls and bars of the prison.

It was then that I first heard the knocks on the metal venting in the dayroom. They were from the male prisoners on the floors below. Depending on how many and in what rhythmic pattern, one of the inmates would return the coded knock and then go back to the cells to answer the call. If the woman who was being signaled wasn't around, the other women would shout through the cell block to let her know that "her man" was on the phone for her.

After a woman knocked back her code, she'd pick out the cell that was above the one the caller was in—one floor, sometimes as many as three floors below. Laying down some blankets on the hard, cold, concrete ground, she'd get comfortable and speak into the sides of the vents where the sheet metal met at an angle and there was just enough space to feel a small draft. These telephone calls would sometimes go on for hours. Some callers were just friends, others became "lovers" through these vents. Many of the women had more than one "lover" and would use made up names and personalities depending on who was calling. They'd put one guy on hold and run to another cell to talk with someone else.

It was through these same vents that the guards would fumigate for roaches by blowing the spray from the basement up to the cells. Sometimes the warden would forget to evacuate the inmates before the exterminator's arrival. During the first week of my sentence, the clouds came through the vents and quickly filled the cell block and day room. My coughs mingled with the other inmates' until the matrons finally escorted us to a safe area.

That's when I first met Rita. Some of us were seated around a table after the air had cleared. Rita came over and joined us. She started telling us the latest update on her murder trial. "I'm sitting next to a murderer!" I thought to myself with amazement. And I didn't even feel afraid. How could I? She reminded me so much of Pauline, a friend I had grown up with. They both had rich chocolate brown skin and dark almond eyes. Their faces were open and aware. I kept expecting Rita to put her thumb in her mouth at any moment, just like Pauline would have. Even as a teen-ager Pauline had managed to slip her thumb in and out in the midst of conversations with both kids and adults. I found myself staring at Rita's hands to see if her thumb was permanently flat as Pauline's had become after years of constant sucking. I never did find out; I got distracted by the track marks and the craters in her arms from the once abscessed needle punctures. Rita must have had quite a habit at one time.

And Rita had a similarly intense sense of humor that I remembered sharing with Pauline as a child. With Pauline we'd both be on the floor laughing until we cried, and sometimes we'd lose complete control and pee in our pants. Rita was very funny, entertaining and fast and accurate with her wit. I laughed so hard that I would feel tears running down my face as I clutched my stomach begging her to stop making me laugh.

Right away Rita started in with her jokes—"Hey what's the sound pussy hair makes before it hits the ground?" She had an audience laughing hysterically without even hearing the punchline. She had a way about her which created a stage, lighting and curtains just by her presence. When Rita spoke, her whole body was involved. She stood in front of about ten inmates moving every part of herself to emphasize her words. She said it again, her head weaving in the air, "Hey, I said what's the sound" and now her pelvis rotated as she continued, "pussy hair makes" then she stomped her feet for the finale, "when it hits the ground?" Nobody knew the answer and Rita's friends begged her to let us all know. "Yeah, Rita, tell us before we have to find out what's the sound *you* make when *you* hit the ground." "Ok, ok," Rita said as she prepared to demonstrate the answer. "The sound pussy hair makes before it hits the ground is—PITOO," and Rita spat on the floor to make it clearer what the sound was and where the pubic hair had been before it hit the ground.

The reactions to Rita's joke varied. I laughed along with some, while others took a while to get the punch line with the help of Cynthia. Cynthia was a small and powerful Black woman in for forgery. She said playfully to Rita, "Girl, don't be coming round here with your nasty mouth. Not everyone's tasted pussy and furthermore, not everyone wants to neither. I know I don't. But hey, if anybody here wants to, I hear Louise is getting out of the hole soon." Rita immediately came to Louise's defense in her absence. "Cynthia, you know Louise ain't no call girl and you ain't no pimp neither. Anyway she's still crying over Michelle since she got out on bail. I doubt if she'll be interested in anybody else for a long while. And she ain't no playgirl besides—you know she's serious and it has to be love."

I thought about Louise and her love that night. I wondered if I felt as clear as Cynthia seemed to about wanting no part of it. I never got to meet Louise. By the time my sentence was over, she still hadn't been released from the hole where they had put her for talking back to a matron.

One night, Rita arranged with a sympathetic matron to be locked up in the cell with the clearest sounding vents. It was going to be a big night for her and Raymond. She had finally gotten a glimpse of him after two months of phone calls. Through the dayroom window she had been able to see him in the yard, six floors below, as he emptied the trash. My cell was directly across from the one Rita had chosen for the night. After the matron made her evening rounds, Rita carefully set up her blanket and pillow. Soundproofing being what it was, we all heard everything without even trying. Rita stretched out on the blanket and put her ear to the cold metal. Soon Raymond's voice would travel up the three floors and her body would be warm again. Rita told him how much she loved him, and they began to describe the pleasures they would bestow on one another if only they could. Rita placed her hand between her legs and did for herself what Raymond said he would have done. Her passionate moaning filled the jail cells. Rita was making love for all of us.

I lay in my bed under the scratchy blanket watching the snow fall through the bars in the far off window. I listened to Rita and could only imagine what Raymond was saying and doing.

During this ritual I felt such a mixture of feelings—embarrassed, respectful and, finally, turned on.

Rita had been in jail long enough to have several different phone callers. She had lovers, friends from her old neighborhood and her crime partners to keep her busy most every night over the vents or through the toilets.

One of Rita's callers was her old friend Sweet Life. He told her that he wanted to meet one of the anti-war demonstrators. The five of us left in the jail met and decided I would be the initial contact. I was a little nervous the night of our first call. Since it seemed that most of the "relationships" over the vents were sexual, I was afraid Rita's friend Sweet Life would have the same expectations of me. My awareness of my own sexuality had just started emerging a year before. I still felt shy enough about the sounds, smells and tastes of it all in private to even imagine having a public showing like Rita's of the night before. I had definite plans of keeping it on a purely intellectual level.

Our knock was three short and two long. He rang and I went to the cell Rita had arranged for me. Sweet Life informed me that he wanted to have political dialogue with our group through me and that this was the extent of his intentions. When I replied that I thought that was "right on," he was delighted and asked me to say it again. Seems he never had heard a white girl talk that way. He was in jail for armed robbery and had been awaiting trial for over a year and was expecting to serve up to ten years. He knew the life of the jail very well; he'd been there before a number of times. He liked the Black Panthers, had considered joining, and was against the war in Vietnam. Sweet Life wanted us to talk every evening after the news and discuss what we had seen. Whenever I'd say "right on" or "power to the people," which I said alot in those days, he'd laugh with pleasure and ask me to say it again. Sometimes he'd call just to hear me say it.

We shared our life experiences—comparing the New York housing projects I had been raised in to the slums of Chicago where he had grown up. "Our cockroaches in Chicago, they can fly!" Sweet Life exclaimed with a mixture of awe and disgust. I let him know about the New York roaches that could do the backstroke when you tried to drown them in the kitchen sink. He knew about the puddles of urine in the hallways of housing projects. I told him how I first learned to jump as a child, not with a rope, but by having to get from my building's entrance all the way to my apartment door without wetting my feet in those daily puddles. Sweet Life said, in his deep and gravelly voice, "I hear you. I once had me a job as a porter. I had to mop up those puddles. Sometimes they felt like lakes, and, what's worse, they never ended. I didn't last too long. All that mopping and the piss would be there again the next day. There just wasn't any point to it. You know what I mean?" Yeah, I knew what he meant, and he knew what I meant when I explained to him how exciting it was for me to get away from all that when I went to a fancy college on loans and scholarships. And he also thought that maybe he knew what I meant when I said I couldn't deal with all the rich kids at that college so I left and went back home for awhile, back to all those puddles. But he challenged me and said maybe I gave up too soon. "Fuck those rich kids," he said. "You coulda learned just like them. I can tell you're smart. Just the way you talk. Using all them big words. Knowing what's going down in the world. So what if they knew even bigger words and had fancier clothes? You *care* about the world, about *more* than just yourself. They're the stupid ones, they're the ones who won't have anything or anyone when things come down. And we'll all be rich then and I ain't talking about having money; I'm talking about us all having each other and, like King said, having a dream!"

One night I was in the middle of a meeting with my friends, and he knocked as usual. I told him I was meeting and couldn't talk. He was really angry and continued knocking for me most of the evening. He finally called Rita, and she told me Sweets was pissed off and wanted me to return his calls. When my meeting was over I called him back. He laid this heavy rap on me about how I had to answer when *he* called, and who did I think I was anyway? Well, I hit the roof and told him a thing or two about my priorities, and how I didn't have to come when anybody called me unless it was a person in uniform, and what was power to the people all about anyway? He calmed down and said I was right; it was just that he looked forward to our talks and was disappointed when I wasn't there. So we resumed our nightly discussions with the stipulation that he understand I couldn't always be there.

We argued about how soon the revolution would happen in this country. He thought it would be quite a while, and I was positive it was only a matter of months. As the last days of my one month sentence were coming around, Sweet Life got news from his lawyer that he might get off sooner than he had expected. His conversation turned to all that he'd do when he got out. He told me that one of the things he missed most was door knobs. We laughed about that one for days. He wanted us to meet when he got out. He knew just the restaurant he wanted to take me to—soft music, candlelight and wine. I told Sweets to hold on there. Sounded to me like he was getting into expectations we already talked about not having. He told me he couldn't help it. He had fallen in love with me. He made a point of saying he was in love with my mind, that he had never asked me what I looked like and didn't even want to know. He loved my thoughts and ideas. He just wanted us to be together and he wanted to hear me say "right on," and "power to the people," for the rest of his life.

I told him that I wasn't planning to be spending my time going to candlelit restaurants, that my life was dedicated to the revolution. I told him I'd write to him when I got out and try to keep him up on what was going on out there. He was glad I wanted to change the world and glad I'd maintain contact, but he was convinced that when we met at that restaurant he'd turn my head around, and I'd relax a little and see things his way.

Finally the day came for my release. I said "right on" and "power to the people" to Sweet Life through the vents for the last time.

We wrote to each other for a few months. I even broke down and sent him my photograph. Then I wound up in a different jail, and jail-to-jail communication is not allowed. The revolution was fast approaching; I was really busy with the preparations. I wasn't living in any one place nor did I want the authorities to know of my whereabouts—so I never got back in touch with Sweet Life.

Years later, when things calmed down and it was apparent that the revolution in America was not just around the corner, I ran into an old friend from those days. He had spent six months in the same jail. We talked about the prison, the horrible conditions and the humanity the prisoners managed to maintain despite the hardships inflicted upon them. Out of curiosity I asked him if he had ever met Sweet Life.

Seems that everyone knew Sweet Life. My friend even knew about my phone calls and the letters that came later. Sweet Life was well-respected and trusted by all the other inmates. He had been disappointed when my letters stopped coming. His trial had finally come up and he had been sentenced to the maximum of ten years.

Timidly, I asked my friend what Sweet Life looked like. He told me he was a big man, a man who had been around. I had already known about the scar across his cheek from the knife fight during his childhood. During our many hours of talking I had been given a blow by blow description of that fight. But I hadn't known, until my friend told me, that Sweet Life was well over sixty years old.

It all became clearer to me then why Sweet Life had had a vision of a future that included so much more patience than mine. All the time we had spent talking through the vents, he had tried to teach me that all my dreams would take lots of work and especially time. It all came together for me now; Sweet Life had truly been around.

Marder

A young woman is arrested at the Pentagon after committing civil disobedience at the end of the year-long Continental Walk for Disarmament and Social Justice in 1976.

Donna Landerman
Breaking the Racism Barrier: White Anti-Racism Work

Feminists have been in the forefront of combatting violence against women—addressing rape, wife battery, incest, pornography—aspects of violence largely overlooked by the male-led peace movement. While this movement has not consciously identified itself as a nonviolent one, it has consistently employed the best of nonviolent spirit and tactics in fighting patriarchy's brutal oppression. It has utilized positive and constructive energy and encouraged those actions which demonstrate women's courage and ingenuity and actions which return energy to women. Such life-enhancing actions have served to strengthen women's concern for each other while they have undermined the patriarchal system.

Feminists organized to fight rape have, since the late 1970s, begun to address another form of violence—the violence of racism. This essay on fighting racism illustrates the work being done by feminists to root out the racism within the feminist anti-rape movement. In their eagerness to place rape in the context of sexism (as opposed to the traditional view that rape is an act of abnormal or sick men), the feminist anti-rape movement, until recently, tended to ignore how issues of race and class enter into the picture. White feminist theory has too often failed, for example, to deal with various historic realities—most notably the myth of the Black rapist which was used to justify the lynching of more than ten thousand Blacks after the Civil War. Rape crisis centers have largely been staffed and used by white women, and Black and Puerto Rican women have been disregarded or lumped under the common heading "minority."

This essay, by Donna Landerman, is part of a larger work prepared for the Sexual Assault Crisis Service (SACS) in Hartford, Connecticut. Since the Fall of 1976 SACS has concentrated on changing from "an organization dominated by and designed to meet the needs of white, mostly middle class, women to one in which Black, Puerto Rican and white women share decision-making and in which the needs of all of these groups are met."

Donna, a white feminist, initiated and was active in SACS' effort to become a multi-cultural/racial and anti-racist organization. She has worked with the Crisis Service since 1975 and was a founder of Neighborhood Women Against Rape, a local rape-prevention and self-defense group. She currently works with the Connecticut Citizen Action Group. Donna wishes to acknowledge the many Puerto Rican, Black and white co-workers, volunteers and friends at the Sexual Assault Crisis Service who helped her formulate the ideas presented here.

Anti-Racism Work: Why Bother?

In some ways it may seem unnecessary to address the question of why white women involved in feminist anti-rape work or other feminist organizations should bother to confront our personal racism and the institutional racism of our organizations. Most of us on a superficial level at least, are "against" racism. We know that it is "bad" and think it should end. Unfortunately, this is not usually sufficient motivation for whites to actually do something about racism. It is essential for white women who take leadership roles in combatting racism in white feminist organizations to understand more specifically why we choose to do this. If we are going to motivate other white women in feminist organizations to join in this struggle, we must be prepared to explain why anti-racist work is important to white women. Also, combatting racism is hard work. It is crucial to be clear why we are doing it so that we can keep ourselves going during inevitable periods of frustration.

Racism Defines Rape

From both an ideological and practical point of view, it is essential for the anti-rape movement to investigate racism and incorporate an anti-racist perspective because racism in major ways both causes and defines rape. If we are to successfully aid women who have been raped, prevent rape, and eventually eliminate rape, it is necessary to understand and attack rape in all its forms and at all its roots. Racism and cultural and class oppression are some of those roots of rape, and lead rape to take different forms in the lives of women of various races, cultures and classes.

Rape has been used forcefully against Black people — men and women — in a way that reinforces their oppression and makes Black women's experience of rape unique. For example, from the years of slavery until today, white men have used the power to sexually assault Black women with little or no repercussion. In a study of three thousand rape convictions in eleven Southern states between 1945 and 1965, results showed that a Black man who had raped a white woman was eighteen times more likely to be executed than a white man who had raped a white or Black woman. As was noted by the National Commission on the Causes and Prevention of Violence, ". . . White males have long had nearly institutionalized access to Negro women. . . ."[1] The sexual abuse of female slaves by white masters is well documented, as is the lynching of Black men for trumped up charges of rape of white women.[2] These kinds of conditions create dramatic differences between Black and white women's experiences and reactions to rape.

For Puerto Rican women, their experience with white male power has been to a great extent defined by the colonial presence of the United States on the island of Puerto Rico. The concept among male colonizers that rape, like in warfare in general, is just a part of the "spoils" is documented.[3] Perhaps the most recent example of the United States military system supporting sexual abuse of "non-white" women is the case of Vietnam. Soldiers were taught that the Vietnamese were an inferior race. It was a short step after that to convince them that raping Vietnamese women was acceptable. The U.S. military systematically encouraged the rape of Vietnamese women.[4] For Puerto Ricans, the experience of colonial oppression, in addition to their general experience of cultural oppression in this society and the unique characteristics of Puerto Rican culture itself, make the Puerto Rican woman's experience of rape different from that of white or Black women.[5]

There are also certain factors that Third World people share that influence their experience of rape. For example, the discriminatory treatment of Third World men, both historically and presently, in criminal justice institutions influences Third World women's attitudes toward reporting rapes by men of their race or culture to the police. In addition, Black and Puerto Rican victims of assault risk facing racial and cultural discrimination by the police, hospitals, and other service organizations when they turn for help. This has an impact on their attitudes towards putting themselves through these institutions when they have been sexually assaulted. White-dominated rape crisis centers that do not take this reality into account in their police and hospital-related policies and programs, again make the mistake of creating programs that ignore the needs of Third World women.

Our Outreach Project research with Black and Puerto Rican women indicates that it is common for Black and Puerto Rican people to see the oppression of Third World men as a major force leading to their violence against women. When Black and Puerto Rican women were asked why they thought men raped, one common response was that Third World men take out the powerlessness and frustration they feel because of the oppression they experience on those weaker than themselves—Third World women. In addition, Third World women and men share a common experience as racially oppressed that binds them together in a way that is foreign to white men and women. When dealing with an issue such as rape, which confronts the oppression of women by men, such dynamics are crucial factors. They have a major impact on how different groups of women, with unique experiences in relationship to different groups of men, see and respond to rape.

Programs developed by white women generally have not taken into account the oppression of Third World men or the racist history of rape, but have only considered men as rapists and sexist oppressors. We have resisted understanding that Black and Puerto Rican women have at least as much common oppression to bind them together with Black and Puerto Rican men as they do with white women. Our programs, in order to be anti-racist, relevant and fully important to Third World women, must take this reality into account.

Race, Culture, Class and Sexual Oppression are Interrelated

Closely related to racial and cultural oppression is class oppression. Black and Puerto Rican women in the U.S. are at the bottom of the socio-economic scale. Class status affects women's experience of rape. For example, relying on public transportation because they cannot afford a car, poor women are more vulnerable to attack. Public transportation is often irregular and has limited routes and schedules; use of public transportation generally requires walking and/or waiting. The combination of poor transportation, and higher likelihood of late-night shifts (that women with more economic resources can afford to refuse) makes poor women even more vulnerable to assault. Also, because of their tight economic situation, poor women are less able to change jobs; therefore, they cannot respond by leaving when they face situations of sexual harassment or assault at work. Poor women lack economic resources that middle and upper class women have, and therefore have less power to avoid, escape or respond to these dangerous situations. A middle or upper class woman can more easily move to a new apartment if she is threatened, buy a car to avoid the possibility of attack while walking or waiting for a bus, or leave a job where an employer is sexually harassing her. For a poor woman, these options are not so readily available.

In addition, for poor women who are constantly faced with survival issues such as how to feed the children, pay the rent and get decent health care, rape may not appear to be the same priority issue it is to middle class women. It may be as devastating an experience, but they may not have the luxury to focus time or energy on feelings about assault. For poor Third World women, facing all the effects of racism and cultural oppression on top of poverty, this is intensified. Anti-rape programs that wish to effectively combat rape in the lives of poor, Black and Puerto Rican women must take these realities into account.

Once white feminists begin to see the differences between Third World and white women's experience of rape, we begin to see that race, class, and cultural oppression—as well as sexual oppression—are woven together in a tight system that keeps Third World people and women without the power to control their lives. For example, Third World women are more likely to be poor and poor women have fewer resources to protect themselves from sexual oppression such as rape. It is essential for white feminists to recognize the inter-relatedness. Without seeing our struggle against sexual oppression intimately bound to struggles against racism, classism, and cultural oppression, we will continue to alienate Third World (and poor) women from feminist struggles.

If white feminists are not able to get past our narrow white-mindedness, we will continue to design programs that do not meet the needs and interests of Third World women and do not attract them to join the anti-rape movement. By building our organizations's programs and policies on white centered perspectives that ignore the realities and needs of Third World women, we institutionalize racism and cultural oppression into the organization.

Until white feminists begin to confront and change the racist aspect of our work and make struggling against racism a priority, it is unlikely that Third World women will choose to work with us. If however, we hope to create an anti-rape movement—and a Women's Movement—that is truly effective and broad enough to attack the problem in its complexity, it must be made up of and have the combined power of women from all races, cultures, and classes.

Karen Lindsey
Women & the Draft

The following, with minor changes, is the text of a speech given by Karen at the anti-draft rally on September 15, 1979, in Boston. Karen effectively addresses both those liberal men who are in favor of drafting women and those conservative gents who grow faint at the thought.

Since this speech was given, the climate in the U.S. has changed only slightly. In June of 1980 the Supreme Court decided to go with the conservative gents and thus made what Karen might call the right decision for all the wrong reasons.

Karen is a writer and activist. She has written two books of poetry, Falling Off the Roof *and* A Company of Queens *and a nonfiction book,* Friends As Family *(Beacon). Karen is a member of WORD, Women Opposed to Registration and the Draft and has been on the board of PUMA, Prostitutes Union of Massachusetts. She is also involved in feminist spirituality.*

Karen has a brother who died of cancer in September 1981, she writes, "as a result of being exposed to Agent Orange in Vietnam."

My faith in our President has been restored. He has done nothing whatever about the ERA, and he fired Bella Abzug for daring to suggest that under his administration women were suffering economic hardship. I was beginning to doubt that he really cared about equal rights for women. Now, he has proven me wrong. Equal pay, equal voice in government—these he may not care about. But when it comes to equal forced labor, suddenly he's our champion once again.

Somehow, though, I don't think he's going to get too many feminists to go along with him. War is a patriarchal game, and we're tired of obeying patriarchies. Any effort to bring back the draft will inevitably bring up the question of a draft for women. I think it's important that feminists refuse to be blackmailed into supporting any version of the draft.

To the liberals' challenge, "If they draft men, why not draft women?" there's really only one answer—it's *not* okay to draft men. And no, it isn't okay to draft women, and no we don't owe anything to the government, let alone collusion in as patriarchal and misogynist an institution as the draft, whether or not they give us an ERA.

On the other hand, I think we can discount all the hand-wringing gallantries of the conservatives who can't bear to think of women getting killed in a war. I doubt, really, that any draft would actually send women into combat duty—not because of their concern for our lives, but because of their concern for *their* lives. No male supremacist culture can afford to have a population of young women trained to respond to provocation with violence. Women are harassed every day verbally, physically, sexually by men, and I don't think the government will risk training us to fight back with force. No, *we'll* be drafted into so-called "peaceful" work—typing, nursing, or, in the liberals' "alternative" schemes, into doing useful civilian work in hospitals, etc.

On the surface, this can sound deceptively benign. Why *not* have young women doing decent work for society for a few years? In the first place, because the horror of forced labor isn't in the nature of the work, but in the fact that it *is* forced: slavery is slavery, whatever the masters have the slaves doing.

And secondly, there is a terrible irony in the idea of drafting women. We've paid our dues. The stuff they're talking about is the work women have been drafted into doing for men for centuries—and not for any two or four year time limit, either. If we ever owed that kind of work to society, we've paid what we owed already, a thousand times over. Now, in the name of our "liberation," they're asking us to collaborate in expanding that draft yet a step further.

But let's not kid ourselves. The draft isn't, ultimately, about emptying bedpans; it's not about civilian work. The draft is about war. The draft is about providing a ready force of soldiers to go out and kill at a moment's notice. And no feminist—no woman who cares about the welfare of other women—can support that. Whatever else it is, war is a patriarchal institution, and *every* war is a war against women. Because women are the mothers of the men who fight and die in war, certainly. But also—and our government would love for us to forget this—because women are the *victims* of war, whether or not we are soldiers, whether or not we are trained to fight. The reward that is built into every war that has ever been fought—the prize that every soldier has a right to, and that many, many soldiers claim—is the right to rape and kill the women who belong to the enemy. In *Against Our Will* Susan Brownmiller quotes a Marine sergeant's description of a Vietnam gang rape which concludes: "They raped the girl, and then the last man to make love to her shot her in the head."

Such "lovemaking" is the right of every soldier in every war men have fought. It's easy to forget this, living in a country on whose soil no war has been fought for over a century. But if we really care about sisterhood, about fighting the destruction of patriarchy universally, we *must* remember it. And we can't allow ourselves to be used as workers in innocuous jobs so some man can be freed to go and kill our people. I'm not saying that every soldier rapes and kills women, but every soldier is permitted to—even, I suspect, encouraged to—and the social restrictions that work to mitigate male violence in civilian life, weak enough in themselves, are entirely absent in war.

The institution that men officially call war is an escalation of the war against women that patriarchy has been waging for thousands of years, the war that began when man first assumed ownership over women and our bodies. The notion that women should support this in the name of "equal rights" is an obscenity.

At the same time, it's important that we, and not men, define the terms of our participation in the anti-draft movement. Fifteen years ago, ten years ago, our role in the anti-draft movement and indeed in the left as a whole, was epitomized in the words of a woman who, like many of us, has grown considerably in the decade since: We were to be "the girls who said yes to the boys who said no to the draft."

That "yes," of course, was many things besides sexual—we were the leafletters, the typists, the coffee-makers, the comforters, the girl-Fridays, and very frequently, the token honchos who "thought like a man." Since then there has grown up a movement that I believe is the most profoundly radical social change movement in history: the women's liberation movement. We who are in this movement can, and I believe at times should, work in alliance with men fighting against oppression, but as allies, not as servants and not as tokens either.

As allies, we can, and will, refuse to continue any alliance in which we are not treated with absolute respect, with absolute dignity. We're not the girls who say yes to the boys who say no to the draft anymore. We're the women who say no to the draft—no to drafting women, no to drafting men, no to perpetuating the institutions that have sanctified rape and murder and violence against us for too many, many centuries.

As a feminist, as a woman who has been raised to believe there's something shameful in being over 30, I've fought every impulse in myself to regret growing older. But right now, with the government trying to co-opt my movement into providing more human ammunition for more Vietnams, I could wish myself fifteen years younger. I wouldn't mind the privilege of being among the first women to burn their draft cards.

Diana J. M. Davies/Insight

Women arrested for civil disobedience at a Stop-the-Draft Week demonstration in New York City (December 4, 1967) listen to the news on a radio smuggled into the "Tombs" jail.

Helen Michalowski
The Army Will Make a "Man" Out of You

By piecing together fragments from men's stories about basic training and combat, Helen, who grew up on Air Force bases, the daughter of an enlisted man, has created a powerful collage depicting the male experience of the military. Women, she believes, must hear the story told by male voices in order to better fight to end violence against women, violence against the earth. Helen writes, "It is important to listen well to these men who have been through it—and made it back. All romantic and dramatic notions of glory, pride and power associated with war must be dispelled as we enter a renewed era of war-making. Hopefully, a better understanding of the military processes which desensitize and brutalize men will encourage us to prevent the damage all around and to bridge the gulf threatening to widen between women and men."

Helen co-edited Power of the People: Active Nonviolence In the U.S. *(Peace Press, 1977). This photographic history book is included in the annotated bibliography at the back of this anthology. A staff member of War Resisters League/West in San Francisco from July 1977 through March 1981, she coordinated the Feminism and Nonviolence Program and organized resistance to the return of the draft. She is still active with WRL and now earns her living as an editor and secretary.*

Male children are set up to be soldiers. The military takes the attitudes and behaviors already developed in young males and hones them to a fine edge. The attitudes include being emotionally closed, preferring power over pleasure, and feeling superior to women. The behaviors include domination, aggression, and physical violence to oneself and to others.

The military prefers to work on young men who are still unsure of their individual identity and place in the world. (Today the work force in the military is more than half under the age of 24. The median age for teamsters is 38.4, longshoremen and stevedores 44.8 years, policemen 36 years and firemen 38 years. From *Enlisted Times*, Oct. 79, p. 14) In basic training young men are isolated from everyone but people like themselves where they are totally under the control of drill sergeants who conduct a not so subtle form of brainwashing.

Steve Hassna, Army Drill Sergeant:

There's Joe Trainee doing what Joe does best—being dumb. And it's not the man's fault. But it is such a shock to his—to his whole being. You take that man, and you totally strip him, and then you make him like a big ball of clay, and you take and you make him a soldier. Whether he wants to be a soldier or not, you make him a soldier.

...They taught me in drill sergeant's [school], get the psychological advantage off the top. Remain on top; remain the aggressor. Keep the man in a state of confusion at all times, if you want to deal with him in that way, but do not let him get his thing together so he can retaliate in any way, you know what I mean? If in doubt, attack.

...I was gruff—I was gruff to the point where I was letting you know *I am in command.* You might as well strike anything in your mind, any feeling, that you are going to do anything but what I tell you. *(Smith)*

Victor DeMattei, Army Paratrooper:

Basic training encourages woman-hating (as does the whole military experience), but the way it does it is more complex than women sometimes suppose. The purpose of basic training is to dehumanize a male to the point where he will kill on command and obey his superiors automatically. To do that he has to be divorced from his natural instincts which are essentially nonviolent. I have never met anyone (unless he was poisoned by somebody's propaganda) who had a burning urge to go out and kill a total stranger.

So how does the army get you to do this? First you are harassed and brutalized to the point of utter exhaustion. Your individuality is taken away, i.e., same haircuts, same uniforms, only marching in formation. Everyone is punished for one man's "failure," etc. You never have enough sleep or enough to eat. All the time the drill instructors are hammering via songs and snide remarks that your girl is off with "Jody." Jody is the mythical male civilian or 4F who is absconding with "your" girl, who by implication is naturally just waiting to leave with Jody.

After three weeks of this, you're ready to kill anybody. Keep in mind there is no contact with the outside world. The only reality you see is what the drill instructors let you see. I used to lie on my bunk at night and say my name to myself to make sure I existed. *(Letter to Helen Michalowski, December 1978)*

In basic training, the man is made an object, dehumanized, subjugated. The system starts to break down when people are seen as people.

Robert McLain, Marine:

Talk to anybody who was going through Marine Corps boot camp. . . the dehumanizing process is just hard to describe. I wish somebody had a record of suicides that go on at these places. . . [and] the beatings that go on daily. Boys are turned not into men, but beasts—beasts that will fight and destroy at a moment's notice, without any regard to what they are fighting or why they are fighting, but just fight. I have seen men fight each other over a drink of water when there was plenty for both of them. *(Lifton)*

Steve Hassna:

. . . I hated that thing of embarrassing a man in front of 40 people. Basic training is such a dehumanizing process to begin with that when you stand there and dehumanize a person in front of his peers, that he's got to sleep with, and in the same building, that's hard. They lose respect for the man.

. . . But I don't like dying. And killing. It's very weird because I started realizing again, thousands and thousands of men, 18, 19, 20, 22-years-old—I'm thinking, Jesus Christ, man, they're gonna kill every swinging dick in the country! You know, there won't be a male American over 25 left standing. I can't—it just—it got to be bodies. I started to get personal with them. Instead of looking at them as Joe Trainee and that was it, I was looking at them as McNulty and Peterson and Nema and Hill and the other thousand that I can't remember. Well, when you do that. . . it don't set too well. Now it sets even worse because it's taken me seven years to get to the point where I can look back on that and realize—you know, I trained troops. I was a staff sergeant, E-6, with the hat, who trained troops for a year. And probably half of them are dead. And I'll never know. *(Smith)*

The military is a blatant hierarchy. Power and privilege correspond directly with one's rank, but feelings of superiority are encouraged throughout. Especially those men in less desirable, more hazardous assignments are encouraged to feel superior. Inevitably, someone has to be on the bottom. Somebody has to be the scapegoat, the enemy.

Ernie "Skip" Boitano, 9th Division Army:

...The military has this thing where if your platoon sergeant gets down on you and you don't have any kind of karma, something going for you to get him off your back, then all of a sudden the platoon leader's down on you, and if the platoon leader and the platoon sergeant start making you the kicking boy of the platoon, then all of a sudden the CO's [commanding officer] down on you. All he hears about you is bad. And the next thing you know, you're up for an article 15 and then you're up for a battalion article 15 because the colonel's heard a lot of bad things about you. He sees you goofing off and he catches you. You don't necessarily have to be doing anything anybody else wouldn't be doing, but because everybody kind of knows who you are negatively, you're it. It keeps building on top of that. It just starts with one person with a little bit of power to get down on you. He can bend someone else's ear and say, "Hey, look at this clown." It may even be that the whole platoon starts working on him. They want to get in tight with the sergeant or they want to feather their cap. So they're all working on this one poor guy. Once these people get down on you, it's downhill from there. There's no getting out from under it...Maybe that's something about people...I know guys who tried. They went to the field all the time. They did everything they could and it never got any better. It was like somebody got picked out and they put a sign around your neck and from then on everybody just let them have it. Any time they had trouble, that person got it. *(Smith)*

During basic training, the man's insecurity about his own sexuality is manipulated so as to link sexuality with aggression and violence.

Unnamed soldier:

...I [was] very stirred, patriotically [and thought] that I someday was going to have to, might have to, do this...That I would get my chance...I remember questioning myself... saying this may all be a pile of crap...this stuff about patriotism and yet because of this indecision...the confusion within myself, I said...I don't think I'll ever be able to live with myself unless I confront this, unless I find out, because if I [do not] I'll always wonder whether I was afraid to do it...I had the whole question of whether I was a man or not...whether I was a coward. *(Lifton)*

Wayne Eisenhart, Marine:

One of the most destructive facets of bootcamp is the systematic attack on the recruits' sexuality. While in basic training, one is continually addressed as faggot or girl. These labels are usually screamed into the face from a distance of two or three inches by the drill instructor, a most awesome, intimidating figure. During such verbal assaults one is required, under threat of physical violence, to remain utterly passive. A firm degree of psychological control is achieved by compelling men to accept such labels. More importantly, this process is used as a means to threaten the individual's sexual identity. The goals of training are always just out of reach. We would be ordered to run five miles when no one was in shape for more than two or were ordered to do 100 push-ups when they and we both knew we could only do 50. In this manner, one can be made to appear weak or ineffective at any time. At this point, the drill instructor usually screams something in your face like "You can't hack it, you goddamned faggot."

. . . Once the sexual identity was threatened, psychological control achieved, and sexuality linked with military function, it was made clear that the military function was aggression. The primary lesson of boot camp, towards which all behavior was shaped, was to seek dominance. Our mission was always "close with the enemy and destroy him." To fail in this, as in all else, was non-masculine. Aggression and seeking dominance thus was equated with masculinity. Recruits were brutalized, frustrated, and cajoled to a flash point of high tension. Recruits were often stunned by the depths of violence erupting from within. Only on these occasions of violent outbursts did the drill instructor cease his endless litany of "You dirty faggot" and "Can't you hack it, little girls." After a day of continuous harassment, I bit a man on the face during hand-to-hand combat, gashing his eyebrow and cheek. I had lost control. For the first time the drill instructor didn't physically strike me or call me a faggot. He put his arm around me and said that I was a lot more man than he had previously imagined. Similar events occurred during bayonet drill. In several outbursts I utterly savaged men. In one instance, I knocked a man off his feet and rammed a knee into his stomach. Growling and roaring I went for his throat. I was kicked off the man just before I smashed his voice box with my fist. In front of the assembled platoon the DI (drill instructor) gleefully reaffirmed my masculinity. The recruit is encouraged to be effective and to behave violently and aggressively. *(Eisenhart, J. of Humanist Psychology)*

Physical violence against troops is more central to basic training in the Marines than in other branches of the armed forces. All branches associate masculinity with insensitivity, invulnerability and violence—only more subtly.

Wayne Eisenhart, Marine and Counselor:

. . . In [Marine] boot camp, there was a Private Green who had a good deal of difficulty with the rigorous physical regime. He was slender and light complexioned. Private Green was a bright, well-intentioned young man who had volunteered and yet lacked the composite aggressive tendencies thought to comprise manhood. Although not effeminate by civilian standards, he was considered so in boot camp. He was continually harassed and called girl and faggot. We began to accept the stereotyping of him as effeminate, passive, and homosexual.

While in the midst of a particularly grueling run, Private Green began to drop out. The entire platoon was ordered to run circles around him each time he fell out. Two men ran from the formation to attempt to carry him along. His eyes were glazed and there was a white foam all around his mouth. He was beyond exhaustion. He fell again as the entire formation of 80 men continued to run circles around him. Four men ran from the formation and kicked and beat him in an attempt to make him run. He stumbled forward and fell. Again he was pummelled. Finally four men literally carried him on their shoulders as we ran to the base area where we expected to rest. We were then told that, "No goddamned bunch of little girl faggots who can't run seven miles as a unit are going to rest." We were ordered to do strenuous calisthenics. Private Green, the weak, effeminate individual who had caused the additional exercises, was made to lead us without participating. He counted cadence while we sweated. Tension crackled in the air, curses were hurled, and threats made. As we were made to exercise for a full hour, men became so exhausted their stomachs cramped and they vomited. Private Green was made to laugh at us as he counted cadence. The DI looked at Private Green and said, "You're a weak no-good-for-nothing queer." Then turning to the glowering platoon he said, "As long as there are faggots in this outfit who can't hack it, you're all going to suffer." As he turned to go into the duty hut he sneered, "Unless you women get with the program, straighten out the queers, and grow some balls of your own, you best give your soul to God 'cause your ass is mine and so is your mother's on visiting day." With a roar, 60 to 70 enraged men engulfed Private Green, knocking him to the ground, kicking and beating him. He was picked up and passed over the heads of the roaring, densely packed mob. His eyes were wide with terror, the mob beyond reason. Green was tossed and beaten in the air for about five minutes and was then literally hurled onto a concrete wash rack. He sprawled there dazed and bleeding.

Private Green had almost been beaten to death in a carefully orchestrated ritual of exorcism. In him were invested those qualities most antithetical to the military ethos and most threatening to the sexual identity of the individual Marines. Masculinity is affirmed through aggression and completion of the military function. We had been ordered to run around Private Green in order to equate passivity and nonaggression with being a clear and present danger. *(Eisenhart, J. Humanistic Psychology)*

Basic training not only links sexuality with dominance, aggression and violence, it also teaches that the man's very survival depends upon maintaining these attitudes and behaviors. By associating qualities that are stereotypically considered common to women and homosexual men with all that is undesirable and unacceptable in the male recruit, misogyny and homophobia are perpetuated in the military and in society at large. It is understandable that it would take a long time and a lot of work for men to undo the effects of military training as it pertains to their own male self-image and these images of women and gays.

To my knowledge, no studies have been done to establish or refute a connection between military training/experience and violence against women; however, it seems reasonable to suspect such a connection. The purpose of basic training is to prepare men for combat. That experience certainly affects men in their relationships with other people, especially women.

Robert McLain:

. . . When I came back home I was very much anti-war, and yet there was a hostility in me toward other people. . . If someone irritated me, my first impulse was to kill the fucker. . . . I'd catch myself and I'd think of another alternative to deal with whatever the problem was. . . . Today there is still a lot of hate in me—a hatred that makes it difficult to form. . . relationships with anyone. *(Lifton)*

Wayne Eisenhart:

. . . One young veteran I have worked with became completely impotent three years after discharge. Unable to maintain an erection during the last three attempts at intercourse, he was afraid to try again. At this time he purchased a weapon, a pistol, and began brandishing and discharging it. His sexuality was blocked by a frustrated idealized male role which could not tolerate intimacy. The means to affirm manhood was through face to face combat, aggressive behavior, and the seeking of dominance.

. . . [There] is a constant fear of being harmed by someone and a constant elimination of real or fantasized adversaries in order to maintain a feeling of adequacy and security. My personal experience directly validates this. Since I was not exposed to much combat in Vietnam, I can only conclude that this process originated for me in basic training.

Perhaps this can best be articulated if I share some observations concerning my own intrusive imagery. Generally these take the form of daydreams. They consist of brief, very violent eye-gouging, throat-ripping fantasies revealing an underlying hypermasculine ideal. There is usually a woman involved and I am always dominant and inordinately violent in defeating some adversary. These brief images leave me with a feeling of power and supermasculinity. I usually find that my muscles tense during such imagery. . .

As a civilian, one generally attempts to create a more authentic masculine self-image that cannot help but be influenced by the military experience. Constantly in social and sexual relationships I have found myself trying to be "heavy," feeling at times foolishly as if I were a caricature of myself. I have striven constantly to achieve dominance. In the past more so than now, I felt insecure sexually and had a very low tolerance for feeling threatened. Occasional outbursts of violence have shamed and frightened me. This all has cost me dearly in social relationships. *(Eisenhart, J. of Social Issues)*

Robert Lifton, Psychologist who worked with Vietnam veterans:

A number of veterans told how, when brushed by someone on the street—or simply annoyed by something another person had done—they would have an impulse to "throttle" or kill him. And they would directly associate this impulse with patterns of behavior cultivated in Vietnam: with "wasting" whomever passed for the enemy, with the numbing and brutalization underlying that behavior, but also with the rage beneath the numbing. *(Lifton)*

Steve Hassna:

. . . A lot of times I'd wake up in the middle of the night and throw [my wife] out of bed and throw her behind the bunker. And start screaming. She was scared of me. She finally left me. Because I would get to the point where I was so pissed off, I'd tell her, "Don't do it again; don't push me." I didn't want to hurt nobody, but I'd get to the point where I can't relate to people no more and so I just snapped. I was going like this until I realized what it was that sent me to Vietnam, indoctrinated from childbirth, the whole thing, I stopped having these bad dreams. Because I could see it wasn't me that was fucked up, it was my government and my whole society that got me this way. *(Smith)*

Robert Lifton, Psychologist:

Falling in love, or feeling oneself close to that state, could be especially excruciating—an exciting glimpse of a world beyond withdrawal and numbing, but also a terrifying prospect. A typical feeling, when growing fond of a girl [sic] was, "You're getting close—watch out!" The most extreme emotion of this kind expressed was:

"If I'm fucking, and a girl says I love you, then I want to kill her. . . [because] if you get close. . . you get hurt."

. . . It is possible that he and many others continue to associate the nakedness of sex with Vietnam images of grotesque bodily disintegration—as did Guy Sajer, with memories from the German Army experience of World War II: "As soon as I saw naked flesh [in a beginning sexual encounter] I braced myself for a torrent of entrails, remembering countless wartime scenes, with smoking, stinking corpses pouring out their vitals." *(Lifton)*

When people are divided into distinct sex roles, the function of the female is to give birth and nurture, while the function of the male is to kill and die. Powerful cultural myths support the idea that the purpose of the son is to be a blood sacrifice—Jesus sacrificed to God the Father, Isaac to Abraham.

There are some parallels between the oppression of women and men according to sex roles. The media/cultural hype is similar—women love being sex objects and men love getting their heads beaten, whether on a football field or a battlefield. The appeal to virtue is similar. Women sacrifice themselves to serving their family, while men sacrifice themselves to the Armed Service. The cover-up is similar. Until recently no one heard about rape or battered women, and no one ever talked about men who come back from war sound in body but emotionally disabled. And who ever talks about the physically disabled?

One wonders if there is a statistical difference between the incidence of women coming to women's shelters who associate with men having had military or para-military (police) experience and those who associate with men not having had this background. Let's interview women—mothers, sister, lovers—who have had before-and-after basic training relationships with men. What, if any, changes do they notice? Let's also interview women "dependents," particularly military wives. What is their place in the "pecking order"? What kinds of friendships get formed when the family gets transferred every one and a half to four years? Do these women feel isolated? What do they think about the "security" of military life?

Because women have not been in the military in significant numbers until recently, there does not exist a great body of material relating their experience. Let's interview women in the military. Is the training comparable? How do men in the military view and treat women they work with? Women they command? How do women in the military view other military women?

For the last several years women have been recruited to the military in unprecedented numbers; not because the military has any great interest in "equality" for women, but because the male population ages 17-21 has declined by 15%. There is a great and urgent need to deepen and broaden the popular understanding that while women certainly have the right and capability to be soldiers, for women to become like men have been would not be a step toward anyone's liberation.

We have to redefine the word "service" so that it is neither forced nor armed. Rather than women being trained to kill, let men learn to nurture life.

Valerie Miner
Uneasy Borders

This story is about Susan, a pre-feminist woman in 1970, who, with her husband Guy, moves to Canada to protest the violence in Indochina. Author Valerie Miner writes, "There were just as many women as men who did this, but they always get overlooked."

"Uneasy Borders" is part of a novel entitled Movement *published by The Crossing Press in spring, 1982. As the stories progress, Susan will surface to consciousness. In this story we find that Susan is sensitive about the issues involved in the War in Indochina but is not so perceptive about the wars at home. "Both Susan and Guy are naive about Canada and the cultural imperialism they carried with them across the border," Valerie explains. "Clearly their pacifism and their politics face a lot of tests ahead."*

Valerie writes political fiction. As an activist, she is committed to the development of a strong international women's movement. Her novel Blood Sisters *(St. Martins Press, N.Y. and The Women's Press, London, 1981) is about working class Irish women and the IRA. Another novel,* Mirror Images *(The Women's Press, London, 1981) describes the climate of sexual harassment and rape on an American campus.* Movement *concerns the political, spiritual and geographical movement of one woman.*

Valerie is co-author of Tales I Tell My Mother *(South End Press, 1981) and* Her Won Woman *(Macmillan, 1975). Her fiction and journalism have appeared in numerous publications. She also teaches fiction and media in the Field Studies Program at U.C. Berkeley. "Uneasy Borders" was published under the title "Maple Leaf or Beaver" in* Prisma *(Fall, 1980).*

"Will you check the turn-off for Highway 80?" It was the first thing Guy had said for three hours.

"Just past Reno," Susan said. "And from there, let's see, it's about 2,000 miles."

He smiled and turned on the radio.

"By the Time I Get to Phoenix."

Susan watched the dark, bearded man behind the wheel of this van which carried all her belongings—grapefruit crates of clothes and books and the hope of silver coated wedding presents. The van itself was a wedding gift, purchased with a rather grand cheque from Guy's father four years ago. She thought the van suited them perfectly; sensible and unpretentious. She hated cushy sedans reeking of new naugahide and isolated by shock absorbers.

"Doesn't this remind you of a covered wagon?" Susan asked, nervously twisting a curl of her long brown hair.

"Not exactly," Guy said. "I mean, we are wearing seat belts."

"How far do you think we'll get today?" she asked. She didn't say, "What if we can't get across the border?"

"I dunno," he said. "Let's just drive 'til we're tired." He turned up the radio.

"By the Time I Get to Phoenix. . . ."

She didn't really want to talk now, either. She would have a whole life to talk with this taciturn man who was now her husband. Whoever he was. Whomever he would become. "Jesus Christ," her mother had suggested the resemblance soon after she found out Guy was going to be a professor. The image changed to "Rasputin" when Mother saw Guy on KPIX, burning his draft card. Susan, herself, had always thought Guy looked like Peter Yarrow on the cover of "Album 1700." How could she have known that "The Great Mandella" would let them off at a strange border?

She wanted to be with Guy. She loved Guy's commitment and intelligence. She enjoyed being part of his family. They argued about theatre and read *The Economist*. They were interested in her work. They asked about propaganda and objectivity and literary journalism. Not that her own mother wasn't interested. She had always wanted Susan to be happy. She waited on tables in dingy restaurants for twenty years so her daughter could be happy in America. Susan appreciated that her family were good, hardworking people. But they never understood her wanting to go to college, never asked questions about her writing. Maybe she was a little ashamed of their grammar and their bowling trophies. Yes, she was ashamed of being ashamed. And eventually her mother approved of Guy Thompson, approved of her marrying up, although she didn't want her moving away. Certainly not moving as far as Canada. Somehow all of Susan's shame and guilt and regret about their separation got lost in those arguments about Vietnam, Laos and Cambodia. But there had been no choice, no choice about the war.

Susan wanted to stop the van and ask "What if we don't get

in?'' Instead, she kept her silence and watched the asphalt hem into brown Nevada hills. The border guards weren't allowed to inquire about the draft; all the selective service counselors had said so. Still, gossip was that some guys got turned away. What if they couldn't get in at Windsor? Should they try Sarnia? Would they hide out in the north Michigan woods? Susan and Guy had carefully discussed the leaving. They were reconciled about not being able to return to the States. But what if they had nowhere to go? She refused to think about it.

She thought, instead, about last night's conversation with her mother.

''It's against the law,'' her mother said.

''Mother, we've been through this before.''

''You're breaking the law, both of you.''

''Is it a good law? Is it a good war?''

''Why can't you get out of it legally, like your brother Bill?''

''You know that we've tried for eighteen months to get out of it. As for Bill—Bill does ballistics research. That's the same as fighting.''

''Better that Guy go to jail, like Joan Baez' husband.''

''Mother, you're not honestly suggesting that.''

''And what about your job? You're going to leave all that, chasing off to Canada with some man?''

''Well, this is interesting. Since when have you found my career more sacred? Besides, it was a mutual decision. We're both resisting.''

Silence. Patience, Susan reminded herself. It was important that this conversation end well.

''Mother?''

''Yes?''

''When you left Scotland to come to the States, it was your choice.''

''That was entirely different. It was money. I left so I could make a living somewhere. But you, you've got a college education. You could have a nice home here. Listen,'' she spoke more slowly and softly now, ''every country has its problems.''

''Mom, phone calls from Canada are going to be expensive. Why don't we make the best of this?''

''Of course dear, you're right. Remember I love you. Remember. . .''

Susan stared out the van window at the endless road ahead. And she thought about how Guy's parents were such a contrast as they sat around the family breakfast table this morning.

Guy and Susan had risen wordlessly and slipped on the

matching brown and beige terrytowel robes his parents had given them.

Dr. Thompson was sitting at the oak table, slowly rotating a crystal glass of orange juice. Mrs. Thompson called from the kitchen, "Perhaps you should go and wake them, darling?"

"No, no need," laughed Guy. "We wouldn't want to be late for. . ."

His father looked up expectantly, like a schoolmaster waiting for the wrong answer.

"For, for the future," stumbled Guy.

"Precisely," said Dr. Thompson.

Mrs. Thompson nodded briskly to her husband and smiled to her children, "Sleep well, sweet ones?"

"Just fine, thank you," Susan sang and followed her into the kitchen while Guy took the seat next to his father.

The coffee had started to perk. Eggs lay out on the stainless steel counter. Room temperature by now. Ready to be boiled. White against coldwater steel. Susan had never cooked in Mrs. Thompson's kitchen. She had never done anything except wash the dishes. She didn't even dry them because she couldn't tell where all the fancy plates belonged. Susan picked up the eggs one by one with a slotted spoon, submerging them in the hot waves. From the oven, bearclaw pastries sweated sweetly. Mrs. Thompson had been saving them in the fridge since Tuesday. Just as Susan reckoned the eggs were ready, Mrs. Thompson reached in front of her, switched off the gas and placed them in four china egg cups at the end of a silver tray. Susan carried them into the dining room with acolytic care.

Usually the oak breakfast table was spread with green pages from the *Chronicle.* This morning it was bare, save for two crystal glasses of orange juice slowly rotating in their watermarks and the $50 bill which lay between them.

"Be sensible for once, Guy. Your mother and I just want to feel that you're eating properly on your trip north."

("He always makes it sound like a polar bear expedition," Guy would say.)

"Thanks, Dad, but we're both old enough to take care of each other." Last night they had worried together about making it to the end of the month. Guy looked at Susan nervously.

Dr. Thompson flushed. He always bore anger with florid Victorian dignity. "If you can't accept a little help at a time like this, I don't know what's happened to the concept of family."

Susan picked up the $50 and put it on the tray. "It's very kind of you," she said and bent down to kiss her father-in-law.

"That's a girl," said Dr. Thompson.

Such a polite, distracted breakfast, the kind of meal you have with fellow travellers—everyone caught up in their own thoughts, random references to mileage and time of arrival. No mention of departure. After an hour there was no more silence left. Since they had packed the van the previous evening, they only had to load their suitcases now.

And so it ended quietly, without any of the strain or recrimination or tears of the last twelve months. They drove down Fenwick and past the yellow adobe house with the sleek Irish Setter. She reflected numbly that Guy's mother hadn't cried. A tear escaped down his nose, dripping from his moustache like sweat. He asked her to check that they had all the maps.

It was a 2,500 mile waiting room. She read him *Newsweek* and *Ramparts* and *The Making of a Counterculture* as they rode the rainy highways between hashbrowns and scrambled eggs and double cheeseburgers.

"By the Time I Get to Phoenix" was top of the charts in every small town radio station.

NBC Monitor analyzed President Nixon. (*President* Nixon. That still seemed unreal to her.)

CBS repeated instant news. Instant news.

For miles before and after Salt Lake City they heard engagements, marriages, items for barter, prayers of the day.

"By the Time I Get to Phoenix. . . ."

They were cutting right across the country without being there. Rain, asphalt, gas station Coke machines, vacant winter-rate motels, rain, asphalt.

"Shall I read the business section?" she asked.

"I dunno," he said. "What's it about?"

Silence.

"Guy?"

"Yeah, hon?"

"What are you thinking about, dear?"

"An article on Spider Monkeys in the *Journal of Primatologists*, February issue."

"Swell."

"What?"

"Isn't that fucker ever going to get to Phoenix?"

"What?"

"Damn radio," she switched it off. "Inane."

He nodded absently and turned on Instant News, adding, "Maybe in Canada the songs will be in French, and we won't be able to understand them."

She didn't say, "What if we don't get in."

Last summer there had been no barriers. On their pup tent trip around North America, they had looped back and forth from Plattsburg to Montreal to Rochester to Toronto to Detroit to Calgary to Seattle. A trial journey. If they could survive in a pup tent, they could survive exile. At that time, Canada was one romantic option. They were still negotiating with the draft board, medical school, Oxford, the Navy Reserve. Canada seemed like the land of the possible. Everything was possible until December when only the Navy Reserve and Canada were left. They chose Canada. She knew they were right, of course. Of course, as long as they got in.

So this year they celebrated his birthday at the Sleepy Hollow Motel in Iowa City. They didn't feel like dining out. She sneaked the Coleman stove into their room and re-heated the pea soup. They ate silently, stretched out on the coral chenille bedspread watching *Marcus Welby, M.D.*

"I'm going to miss Robert Young," she sighed.

"What kind of shit is that?" he said. "Talk about reactionary values."

"Oh, I don't know. Remember *Father Knows Best?* Kathy, Bud, Betty. There was always a sense of fairness."

He grimaced as he often did, enjoying her optimism but baffled about how it could be so thoroughly misplaced.

"The Andersons," she continued. "The kind of nice, stable family everybody wants. And remember Franco, the Italian gardener?"

"Yeah, I remember. A thoroughly racist role."

"My, weren't you perceptive at ten years old?"

"Silly to argue," he said. "Anyway, you'll be able to watch Robert Young in Canada. They get all the Buffalo stations."

"Cultural imperialism," she agreed sardonically. But this reassured her. And she was glad Guy didn't want to make love but just to hang on. She would feel better the next day when they saw Hank and Sara in Ann Arbor.

It would be good to have friends living that close to Canada. They could all go camping in Northern Ontario together. So much clean, green space. Sometimes she thought of Canada as a huge National Park. Maybe they could all meet for weekends in Montreal. Not that she wanted to huddle with Americans. She had heard of these "Amex communities," full of heavy "political people." She always felt nervous around political people. Not tough enough. They were so suspicious that they made her feel like she really was a CIA agent. She was a war protestor, not a radical. Even her own family agreed after the Cambodian invasion (well, for them, it had been after Kent State) that the War was wretched. To her, Canada was the only reasonable choice. And now, having made that choice, she and Guy were traitors, idealists or good political people depending on who was lecturing or interviewing them.

"Do you feel political?" she asked the next morning in Illinois.

"I feel tired," he answered. "Why don't you read the book review section?"

Hank and Sara's apartment might have been astral-projected from Berkeley—with the same peeling rattan chairs, the same odor of cat pee in the yellow rug. After their famous chili and some good Colombian dope, they were all back on Euclid Avenue.

"Medical school is a drag so far," said Hank. "Two of my ancient professors look like founding members of the AMA."

"You don't have to say that for me," returned Guy. "I'm glad you got a draft deferment. And I'm just as glad I didn't get into med school. Come on now, it's cool, isn't it?"

"Aw, I don't know. But I have met some good people in the Vietnam Aid Committee."

"Some good political people?" asked Susan.

He nodded solemnly and pulled out a white booklet. "Here it is, *Manual For Draft Age Immigrants To Canada*. Everyone is using it. I mean it's been good for some people passing through."

Susan was touched and very frightened. This was like a refugee visa. It reminded her of the job permit which Mother kept under the gloves in her top bureau drawer. Thin blue paper and black ink, "culinary worker." She remembered Rosa Kaburi, her fourth grade friend from Hungary, who had told her about the name tags on their wrists and how they were inspected for lice by the immigration officer. But this was Canada, she reminded herself. You didn't even need a passport to enter.

Sara sat forward, "Actually, we've been talking a lot about our connection in all of this. I mean, of course the phone is tapped. But you should feel there's a way to contact us if you need help. Maybe a code word. Maybe 'maple leaf' or 'beaver.' "

"Or 'help,' " laughed Susan. "We'll be the safe ones."

They spent the evening counting up immigration credits—Susan spoke French and had relatives in Canada; he had more years in university.

"Kind of classist, isn't it?" asked Guy.

"Every country has its problems," said Hank.

"I have five more points than you," said Susan.

"Doesn't count," said Sara. "A wife goes through on her husband's points."

Irritated, Susan thought about this new women's lib business and resolved to do some reading. She wondered, dopily, what Guy would do if she became a raving feminist.

Hank picked up the booklet and ripped off the cover. "Don't let them see it when they search you at the border. Stick it inside one of your chemistry texts or somewhere."

The dope wore off quickly. Guy shaved his beard. Disguises were prepared in rote timelessness. Susan ironed her shirtwaist dress and set her hair. Once these chores were done, the evening lost shape. They crawled into the sleeping bags and read Hank's and Sara's new *Newsweek* before falling asleep.

The next morning, Susan jiggled out of the sleeping bag and walked over to the picture window. Grey. The fog outside the third floor window overlooking Pauline Street was as colorless as the apartment walls. Susan reheated the coffee and found some more bearclaw pastries. Were bearclaws Californian? Was she more Californian or American? Could she be a Canadian? Canada was just over the bridge. Just across the border. Only a few miles away. Canada, land of the free. No reason to believe in Canada. ("What an idealist," her brother Bill had said. "What are the choices?" Susan had said.) So now it was to be Canada. A country big enough to believe in. Yes, she did believe they would be admitted.

"Breakfast, sir?" she said, setting a tray on the floor, next to where he lay, still cosy under the down.

"Feels more like Extreme Unction," he said.

"Good code word."

They laughed, as easily as if they were back in Berkeley.

Detroit was the classic exit. She recalled headlines from the '66 riots. She remembered that unmailed thank you note to Aunt Martha and Uncle Cardiologist who sent them an American flag for their wedding from Grosse Pointe. (Mother insisted it wasn't a joke.) The ride up Michigan Avenue was horrific. Every white man looked like he was about to duck into a telephone booth and emerge in a klan hood. The Blacks frightened her like no one in Oakland had scared her for years. Her racism? Their hostility? They drove past Bertram's Department Store where Aunt Martha had bought that pinafore when Susan was eight. (Susan's mother had inhaled sharply when she saw the pink and grey box. Bertram's was a *very* fine store. Aunt Martha always sent things from very fine stores. Mother might have sent more pink and grey boxes herself, if she hadn't married a feckless sailor and moved to California.) Grey, humid Detroit heat. Petulant showers and then sudden sun evaporating everything. What if they didn't get in? Just get out of Detroit. Love it or leave it. Just get out.

"Shit, Susan, this is the tunnel. I told you we wanted the bridge. Everyone says the bridge is an easier crossing."

"No, they say it's quicker, but the guards at the tunnel are easier."

"Hell, Susan, don't you remember what Hank said about the deserter from Georgia? Shit, Susan."

Her voice was blocked with tears.

"Just tell me the way to the bridge," he barked. "I'm the one who's driving the van. I'm the one who's resisting the damn draft."

"Oh, I see," she turned to him, glared at him, raising her voice. "And I suppose I'm just along for the ride?"

He rubbed the back of his hand along her cheek and kept his eyes on the traffic ahead. "I'm sorry hon. It's our decision. Let's not get *at* each other. It'll be over in an hour. We'll be in Canada. Maple leaf or beaver," he tried to laugh. Then he lowered his voice to soothing. "We'll be OK in Canada."

She didn't say, "If we get in." She said, "It looks as if the Ambassador Bridge is just about ten blocks from here."

When they passed the US border guards, she wanted to wave or give them the finger, but their escape was too tenuous. A small sign in the middle of the bridge said, "Welcome to Canada. Bienvenue au Canada." Before she noticed it, they had pulled up to the Canadian border guard.

"Good afternoon," he said. "What is the purpose of your visit."

Guy's face grew pale. She looked for reassurance in his familiar features, and all she could see was his pale.

"My wife and I would like to apply for landed immigrancy."

("My wife and I," she thought. They had married for this charade. "Immigrancy." Ellis Island. Her mother and Rosa Kaburi. New World. But no one would muck up their name here. Not a nice High Anglo name like Thompson. She knew what she was doing when she took that name.)

"Eh, what was that? Could you speak up, please?"

Those were the right words. She knew they were the right words. What kind of game was this fellow running?

"OK," the guard said finally. "Go to the green building over there after you've filled out these forms."

"Out," Canadian, "out." He hadn't smiled.

"My wife and I would like to immigrate to Canada."

"Did you bring your gear with you?" Another foreign official. Never before had she thought of Canadians as so foreign.

"Gear?" Guy asked.

"Furniture," barked the official, "pots, pans, baby carriage."

"Oh, my parents are sending up that stuff," said Guy, who was always good at charades. "We do have a few things in the car."

Susan wondered what they would think when they saw the sleeping bags, typewriters, guitars. Hippies? Actually, it was true that Guy's mother insisted on sending up the mahogany bedroom set once they got settled.

"Draft dodger?" the guard asked casually.

"In fact," Guy answered cooly, "I'm a teaching assistant in primatology at the University of Toronto."

"I'm the draft dodger," she joked, feeling the vomit rise in her throat with the forced laughter.

The guard smiled and nodded to the door with a grey mesh window.

"Don't have nothing to do with me anyway. *He'll* see you in a minute." He returned to their forms to make sure they had left no white spaces.

"What about the *Manual?*" she whispered.

Guy looked confused. Or was it annoyed? Maybe he was signalling her to shut up. But the question was important in case the van was searched. She leaned over and whispered, "Did you put it in the chemistry book?"

"You were the one who had it last," he said between his teeth and then turned back to a travel brochure. "Did you know that Nova Scotia is the only region outside Scotland to have a registered tartan?"

Her stomach turned. She rummaged for a Tums in her purse. There, bunched with the birth certificates and marriage license, was the *Manual.* Did they search purses?

"Mr. and Mrs. Thompson?"

They followed another guard into a small, spare room. Guy didn't have to repeat so much this time. Maybe the acoustics were better. Maybe he was learning Canadian. The officer asked them questions which they had already answered on the application.

"And you, Mrs. Thompson, what do you do?"

She paused for a moment, as if listening for her mother-in-law

(Will the *real* Mrs. Thompson please speak up) and then she answered, "I'm a teacher." The words came too easily. She dreaded hearing them. It had taken her a year to feel able to say "writer," when people inquired. "Teacher" was just what she wasn't going to be her whole life. However, they needed teachers in Canada, in places like Baffin Island. She would do anything to get them in.

He checked their diplomas, licenses and bank books. Pedigrees seemed to be in order. That was all for now. No questions about why they wanted to immigrate. No speeches about the Great National Park or the three party system or the ethnic mosaic. He had *no* more questions.

"If you'll wait here, I'll be right back with an answer for you."

When he closed the door, she looked at Guy for the first time since they entered the room.

"Your purse," he said.

Her purse lay open on her lap to the *Manual For Draft Age Immigrants To Canada.*

He squeezed her hand. "Don't worry," he said.

She didn't have the strength to squeeze back. She just wanted to throw up. Of course good immigrants don't throw up. The guard might think she had typhoid or something. She stared at the grey mesh window.

"That's it, Mr. and Mrs. Thompson."

The immigration officer was handing something to Guy.

"That's it," Guy said, louder, to her.

The man had his hand on Guy's shoulder, "Bloody awful war."

Toronto. Two hundred miles. The road signs had crowns on them. "Welcome to Canada. Bievenue au Canada."

She turned on CBC to distract them from Windsor.

"War Measures Act. . . ."

The city seemed to mirror Detroit through foul Lake Michigan. And the water looked just as dead from this side.

". . .War Measures Act. Prime Minister Trudeau said in a press conference in Ottawa this afternoon that the decree of martial law will be in effect all over the country. Primary surveillance will take place in Quebec. In Montreal so far, thirteen people suspected of knowing about the Pierre La Porte kidnapping have been taken to jail. The CBC has received no official communiques from the FLQ. Martial law is. . . ."

"Find some music, will you?" said Guy.

"In French?" she asked.

Ann Davidon
Macho* Obstacles to Peace

In this essay, Ann Davidon discusses the "macho mental barrier" which posits coercive force or cowardice as the only two choices, and says that this thinking must be exorcised if we are to survive. She suggests that nonviolent resistance is not only the most effective and humane form of struggle but the most courageous as well.

Ann has had articles, essays, book reviews, stories and poems published in a variety of magazines including Harper's, McCall's, The Nation, The New Republic, The Progressive, Redbook, *and* Win. *She contributed a chapter to the book* Witness of the Berrigans *(Doubleday, 1971).*

In the early '70s she helped start a women's center in Haverford, Pennsylvania and has been a part of women's support groups since that time. Ann has lived a total of about six years in Europe and the Middle East and has worked for AFSC, WILPF, SANE and the American Committee on Africa. Her plays have been produced on stage and radio in New York, Pennsylvania and Denmark.

One of the main attitudes that prevents people from sitting down to solve their problems together in a peaceful and reasonable way is the fear that they will be considered weak, compromising, and unmanly. Such people (and a bit of this *machismo* exists in most of us) would rather have a show of force, bellow and brandish fists, swords, guns or missiles than appear to be giving in to the opponent. I do not focus on this overworked *macho* concept simply because I am a woman and that's what women talk about these days, but because it's a traditional mind-set whose time has come to be exorcised if we are all to survive.

The other side of the macho coin is fear of violence or threats of force. This fear can turn blustering heroes into cowards who betray themselves and others, compromise and sell out basic principles, and become themselves enslaved. In other words, a person who believes in the efficacy of force against others is one who also accepts its efficacy against him/herself; it is a two-edged sword.

In myth and history, though replete with gore, there is recognition of a higher kind of bravery, a courage which is not sex-linked. The hero and heroine who do *not* give in to superior force or threats, or who show mercy despite their own superior force, are recognized as more courageous and admirable than those who rely entirely on brute force. The conflict perhaps is more accurately stated in terms of enlightened long-range self-interest—survival of the species—as opposed to immediate short-range self-interest.

Women are often considered to be the bearers of personal morality who must appeal to man's finer nature. Man the "brute" is understood to be morally compromising, but physically responsible for the larger immediate struggles in the world—the practical, hard-nosed arenas of politics, business and war, and the intellectual calculations accompanying these. The idea of being morally weak is frequently coupled with being physically strong, while the survival of the species and therefore the sometimes self-sacrificing demands of that vision are more identified with the so-called weaker sex.

How all this applies to foreign and domestic struggles today should be fairly clear. What got the United States out of Vietnam was partly the moral recognition forced on our government by the peace movement and the Vietnamese people that we were bestial, cowardly and wrong in that situation. There was also the practical consideration, that a full application of brute force could wipe out Vietnam only at the expense of alienating vast numbers of Americans perhaps to the point of civil war, and would probably arouse the moral indignation as well as the brute force of the other major powers.

When we withdrew from Vietnam we did it only after our government inflicted gratuitous, brutal bombings on the Vietnamese—followed by a great display of moral concern, grotesquely distorted through our disastrous airlifts of orphans and refugees. Then our planes bombed Cambodia, killing more people than we saved in the grandiose attempt to rescue the Mayaguez crew whose safety was already fairly well assured by other means. Another case of macho morality: "We had to destroy them in order to save them."

In the whole Indochina tragedy, our government succeeded in displaying both sides of the macho reality—brute force *and* cowardice—but very little of the bravery and courage with which they presume it to be identified. (I speak of the government, not of individual soldiers.)

But all that is history. Those who believe that power comes from the barrel of a gun are still dominant in both the so-called communist and capitalist worlds. And they are right in one respect: people *give* guns that power because they don't want to be killed, and are willing to do a lot of cowardly blustering or brutal acts they believe necessary in order not to be killed. Thus, all the major powers, and minor ones too, arm to the teeth in order to show each other they are strong and manly and are not going to let the other powers walk all over them. And this, of course, causes the other powers to arm further to show they won't. . .etc., etc.

Adding to the momentum of this spiraling and ultimately self-defeating reasoning are very important temporary factors such as profits for arms manufacturers and jobs for their employees (regardless of the fact that more jobs could be created by non-destructive industry).

If the profit motive is not a major factor in the more or less socialist countries, then the macho factor fills in: they, too, do not want to appear "weak;" they don't want to be caught lagging behind capitalist countries in anything. They want to defend their efforts or what they see as being in their interest, just as the U.S. government wants to defend capitalist interests. And buried somewhere within both sides are some genuine and human concerns for economic justice or personal liberty, both of which can only be trampled and eventually destroyed as all sides continue to arm.

How do we get out of this endless spiral, other than ending it in one big blast, as we are increasingly likely to do? We can start, of course, with ourselves—getting our own heads cleared. As intellectuals, liberals, and leftists are frequently considered softheaded, ideological dupes and bleeding-heart idealists, they often try to show how tough and pragmatic they are by identifying with the military aspects of liberation and revolutionary movements.

Many women, I might add, tend to do the same thing in their own process of liberation, talking tough, taking karate and extolling revolutionary women with guns. This, or course, then reinforces the opponents's conveniently contradictory view of advocates of social change as brutal and totalitarian.

Nonviolent Resistance

But it is possible to share and support these "revolutionary" aims for independence or for a more just and equitable society without accepting the notion that power comes through the barrel of a gun. People who want quick change and strong vents for their feelings are justifiably fearful of the supine and supposedly "feminine" stance of passive acceptance and endurance. They are so brainwashed by the identification of bravery with the traditional macho stance of dominance by brute force, that they apparently cannot conceive of strength through rational persuasion and through nonviolent resistance. They see the choice as either total capitulation or total conquest.

Like mirror images of their opponents, they hasten to assure you that they are *not* pacifists, and that though they don't advocate violence they are ready to use it on behalf of the powerless. This usually means that they do very little except mouth revolutionary rhetoric, or possibly even run guns, while those whose violent struggles they support are the ones who get killed.

Yet out of both belief and necessity, groups without apparent power have been effectively using nonviolent resistance throughout history. Strikes, non-cooperation, boycotts, sit-ins, tax rebellions and resistance—all these are tools of the so-called powerless. This use of methods, different from the militarily powerful, has made nonviolent resistance seem to be a tactic only of the "weak," of the unarmed against the armed. It is also often considered effective only if the armed and powerful are fairly "decent" people susceptible to a nonviolent, rational or humane appeal.

Yet the more brutal a regime, the more brutally a regime would respond, obviously, to violent resistance—and the less likely that violent resistance could in fact be organized. And even the most brutal regime tends to *justify* its violence on the basis of violent opposition, real or potential. Such regimes can deal savagely with nonviolent resistance too—any resistance carries risks—but the *non*violent resister maintains the possibility of (1) de-brutalizing the oppressor, and (2) not brutalizing him/herself.

Though nonviolent resistance has never been consistently used in any external or national struggle, not even in India's, it has always been present, and it may be the philosophy and tactic which is the most effective as well as the most humane and courageous form of struggle. Blacks, women and others who have frequently felt compelled to use this tactic may not have used it by choice, but when they have done so they have often found it not only effective but even ennobling. Yet, nobility is considered a luxury of the leisure class, not the powerless.

It is clearly the powerless, and not those in power, who want and need more control over their (our) lives, and will therefore press for change. I presume we do not want this shift of power to be just another turning over of the dungheap, but a more equitable sharing of power and resources with stability dependent, not on arms, but on people's consent and satisfaction.

Certainly there will always be conflicts of interest in society: a nonviolent activist's aim is not a dead society, but a lively, free, fulfilling one. Just as a family exists with tensions and conflicts, but usually without killing, so can nations. The aim is not to eliminate all differences but to create a psychological climate that accepts struggle for greater equity and a balance of self-interest through imaginative explorations, dialogue and, if necessary, through nonviolent resistance rather than through destructive, dead-end macho reflexes.

Many former peace activists have now gone into personal pursuits and private solutions, but many are remaining in the public struggle and in the long-standing peace groups. These peace groups are combining efforts to resist the ever-expanding militarism of our government which inevitably increases militarism everywhere through fear, arms sales, nuclear proliferation, etc.

If we can break through the macho mental barrier, we may be one giant step closer to demilitarizing our society and decreasing inflation and unemployment through shifting resources to useful production, thus strengthening our real security.

Ultimately, perhaps, we can convert the Pentagon into the national hospital once projected for this structure—or into a transnational mental health center for retired generals suffering from machismo withdrawal.

*Since writing this essay I have been told that "macho" is regarded by some as "classist" and "racist." The "classist" charge puzzles me, since the concept of male domination cuts across all classes and cultures. As to "racism," the fact that the "macho" image which developed in Latin cultures (among others) has come to symbolize male domination, as Latin-root languages have spread, does not mean this image is innate to any "race" or ethnic group any more than the English adoption of the very descriptive word "chutzpah" means this word is racist and applies to Jews. It seems to me that these and other words used within various cultures to describe certain kinds of behavior have been adopted by other groups because they convey a nuance that their language may lack. "He-man" could be substituted for "macho" (would "he-man" then be regarded as a racist term defining all Anglos?) but I think it lacks the more poetic and universal force of the word "macho." In any case, the use of the term is my responsibility, not the editor's.

Linda Hogan
Daughters, I Love You

The poems of Linda Hogan (Chickasaw) express the anguish of women around the world as we struggle to sustain life being destroyed by nuclear arms and nuclear power. She writes, "I hold to the traditional Indian views on language, that words have power, that words become entities. When I write I keep in mind that it is a form of power and salvation that is for the planet. If it is good and enters the world, perhaps it will counteract the destruction that seems to be getting so close to us. I think of language and poems, even fiction, as prayers and small ceremonies."

Linda won the Five Civilized Tribes Playwriting Award for A Piece of Moon *and is guest editor of* Frontiers *Native American Women's issue. The following poems will be in a monograph,* Daughters, I Love You *(Loretto Heights Center for Research on Women. Loretto Heights College, Denver). Linda is also the author of* Calling Myself Home *(Greenfield Review Press) and* The Diary of Amanda McFadden.

Her own introduction to the poems says it all.

Over 50 years ago, many distinguished scientists and military men gathered in Los Alamos, New Mexico to design and develop the first atomic bomb. A few years later the bomb was detonated in Alamagordo. The results astounded everyone, including the developers of the weapon. Soldiers who witnessed the blast saw bones through their own flesh. Many miles from the site of the explosion a blind woman witnessed the only light she ever saw. Oppenheimer, one of the primary originators of the bomb, quoted from the *Bhagavid Gita:* "I am become death, the destroyer of worlds."

Destroyer of worlds. The lessons of Hiroshima and Nagasaki go unnoticed as governments continue to develop nuclear arms and nuclear power.

Uranium mining and milling, mostly on tribal lands, has resulted in high incidences of lung cancer, spontaneous early abortion and physical mutations in children and adults. The history of nuclear energy has been a long record of accidents, radioactive contamination and explosions. The history of the bomb has proven to be one of suffering and destruction, with the future potential for annihilation of all life.

From Hiroshima to Three Mile Island there has been a violation of the spirit of earth and of feminine energy. Many people have come to believe that our planet is at the end of its life cycle but there are great numbers of women now directing their energies into transformation and resurrection. They are exerting great influence. Native women on this continent have long been struggling against the genocide accompanying nuclear development. In the past few years this struggle has been taken up by men and women in all parts of the world. Navajo women fighting uranium mining and milling have received international attention.

Primarily it is women who are involved in the struggle to sustain and maintain life, women who have understood the political and white male dynamics of ambition and who have experienced the effects of that power. Women are developing strategies for survival, are reviving their ancient healing powers and old earth consciousness. Women are speaking and struggling toward rebirth for the life of the planet and the children. These poems are a part of that change and transformation. Out of destruction comes light and hope, the beginning of a new life cycle.

These poems are dedicated to the Navajo women who have been struggling for their lives and safety against the multi-national corporations. They are dedicated to Sister Rosalie Bertell, M.D., whose words reached me at the Black Hills Alliance International Survival Gathering. She said, "Everywhere I go, women are grieving the death of the species. You can either turn it around or help it to die."

These poems are dedicated to gentle women throughout the world who have been mourning the initiation of the death process into the life of the planet.

These poems are dedicated to my Lakota daughters and the children of all women.

Daybreak

Daybreak
My daughter sitting at the table,
strong arms,
my face in her eyes
staring at her innocence
of what is dark
her fear at night of nothing
we have created
light as a weapon against.
Dust floats
small prisms
red
blue
in her hair.
Light in her eyes, fireworks,
the smell of powder on her
is lilac
scenting narrow arms, thigh
The cobalt light of her eyes
where yesterday a colt's thin legs
walked in a field
of energy.
Matter is transformed.
Her innocence is my guilt.
In her dark eyes
the children of Hiroshima
are screaming
and her skin is
their skin
falling off.
How quickly we could vanish,
your skin nothing.
How soft

you disappear confused
daughter
daughters
I love you.

Black Hills Survival Gathering, 1980

Bodies on fire
the monks in orange cloth
sing morning into light.

Men wake on the hill.
Dry grass blows from their hair.
B52's blow over their heads
leaving a cross on the ground.
Air returns to itself and silence.

Rainclouds are disappearing
with fractures of light in the distance.
Fierce gases forming,
the sky bending
where people arrive
on dusty roads that change
matter to energy.

My husband wakes.
My daughter wakes.

Quiet morning, she stands
in a pail of water
naked, reflecting light
and this man I love,
with kind hands
he washes her slim hips,
narrow shoulders, splashes
the skin containing
wind and fragile fire,
the pulse in her wrist.

My other daughter wakes
to comb warm sun across her hair.
While I make coffee I tell her
this is the land of her ancestors,
blood and heart.
Does her hair become a mane
blowing in the electric breeze,
her eyes dilate and darken?

The sun rises on all of them
in the center of light
hills that have no boundary,
the child named Thunder Horse,
the child named Dawn Protector
and the man
whose name would mean home in Navajo.

At ground zero
in the center of light we stand.
Bombs are buried beneath us,
destruction flies overhead.
We are waking
in the expanding light
the sulphur-colored grass.

A red horse standing on a distant ridge
looks like one burned
over Hiroshima,
silent, head hanging in sickness.
But look
she raises her head
and surges toward the bluing sky.

Radiant morning.
The dark tunnels inside us carry life.
Red.
Blue.
The children's dark hair against my breast.
On the burning hills
in flaring orange cloth
men are singing and drumming
Heartbeat.

X-Ray of My Daughter

Beneath growing breasts
the heart's filament and gauze.
White scaffolds of bone
bridge the dark water of nothing
doctors have power to see inside.

They have power

in the shining dark machines,
the silence they force on mothers
who sorrow for the internal stitches
and seams of children.

Her ribs are small wings.
Why is it her still hand
reminds me of war again,
of the five-fingered piece of land
with bare trees and carbon silhouettes,
women brushing their hair on walls.

The humming plane
that dropped such destruction,
Enola Gay,
was named for the pilot's mother.
She weeps in her pillow at night
nightmares of children
lost to power.

This is what lies between us and death,
a hospital door, light
crawling through the keyhole
that touches a tired woman.
She folds paper into white birds.
They fly
over the vast landscape of madness,
passing through the black and white
revelations of bone.

Idaho Falls, 1961

site of a reactor accident, termed a small atomic steam explosion, killing three employees.

Dark fields, dark sky.
Wires carry light to children
resting their heads
against the breast's rhythm.

Light comes
from the distant mystery
inside a lead silo.
A young man opens a switch on power.
Street lamps wake up
the first light
splitting fields where papers blow.

Eyeglasses are flying
in terrible light.
The young man is flying.
Impaled, he is losing
his head to the darkness.
The gentle pale arch of a foot
disappears.

Luminous man,
lampshade of skin,
dark instruments
in his pocket
fall out.

A woman is walking
on soft feet,
the early road to the barn.
Warm light of animals
standing, holy, in straw

turn their heads to her.
Her ear to the breathing cow
listens.

Day is breaking
through doors.
Earth has made another revolution.
New worlds burn
in dark places.
The deaths of men arrive
blazing through narrow wires
birds touch and leave.

Disappearances

Whatever love or hate we hold,
bridges collapse
that joined land to land
like passion between bodies.
Street lamps vanish.
The old horse I love,
in the shadows of trees
it will lie down
too quickly.
Nobody is at fault.

I remember how the Japanese women
turned to go home
and were lost
in the disappearances
that touched their innocent lives
as easily as they touched small teacups
rattling away
on shelves.

These are the lessons of old women
whose eyes are entire cities,
iron dark lattice work
they saw and became.
In their eyes
there is silence,
red ash and stormclouds.
The quiet surprise of space
carrying the familiar shape of what it held.

This moment the world continues.
I pour coffee into a cup my sister made
and count blessings, two daughters
sleeping with open mouths
full of moonlight that ages them one day
through open windows
childhood is leaving.

Outside it is the color of Arizona.
Wide landscape of morning
Where people walk, red light,
like the silent old woman
who rode beside me
long ago to the Indian hospital in Chinle.
She never spoke
but her eyes were full

with the loss of children
brothers and sisters
with the certain knowledge
that it is a good thing to be alive
and safe
and loving every small thing
every step we take on earth.

Prayer for Men and Children

Men sleep
with loose hands that by day are fists
holding fear.
Men sleep and women are awake
because some men are dreaming
cobalt blue, the slowest death
carried by wind
and pure rain looking innocent.
Grandmothers feel this in their bones.
Aunts weep for no good reason.
Mothers guard windows of sand-blown houses
where men and children sleep.

This is a prayer that enters a house
and touches a lantern to light.
For the sleeping men and gentle work
of women. Their hands wash dishes in pans

silent as breath.
They touch water
and dream out the window
toward lost voices of children.
At the window bottles have changed violet.
Pale linen is blowing on the lines.

This is a prayer to save the soft gray dresses
of evening, blowing suddenly off the lines
of their bodies. To save the eyes
that watched flowers on wallpaper
ignite like a thousand suns.
A fire wind. A prayer against heat
that burns dark roses from shirts into skin
because fire passes first through the dark.
Newspapers held casually
write a day's history
across the sleepless faces of women.

Burning, another world enters
through the shadows of bodies
flashed on walls,
the dark wedges between blue fingers
that were praying for sleeping men and children.

Connie Salamone
The Prevalence of the Natural Law Within Women: Women & Animal Rights

Part of the violence which surrounds/engulfs our lives is the violence done to the earth and that committed against the animals. The animal and plant lives that are intrinsically linked to our own are being destroyed. Sometimes we grieve this; sometimes we participate in it; often we forget it, because the images of destruction are so commonplace: birds caught in oil spills and washed onto the beaches; rabbits used to test cosmetics, their sensitive eyes held open and washed with burning chemicals; chickens packed five or six to a cage and kept under artificial light for their entire, miserable lifetimes; young calves kept immobile in narrow pens, deprived of light, essential food elements, contact with other calves or their mothers, deliberately made anemic so that they'll become the tenderest veal chops served in high priced restaurants.

Just as it is not possible to lay claim to a nonviolent life while ignoring or cooperating with a militaristic or racist institution, neither is it possible to be genuinely nonviolent while ignoring the violence done to the myriad varieties of life with which we share this planet.

Connie Salamone, a radical vegetarian eco-feminist, laments the health-nut, navel-gazing preoccupation of many vegetarians and urges feminists to endorse vegetarianism as a political statement. She believes women are, by nature, sustainers and preservers of life, though we compromise our "nature" daily and conform to the expectations of the patriarchy. In addition to refusing to "eat dead animals," Connie hopes women will begin to boycott hunting, rodeos, zoos, circuses, fur coats, and vivisection atrocities as an act of "ahimsa" (nonviolence).

Connie has been a vegetarian activist for over a decade. By 1974 she had travelled across the US and to Europe to bring her plea of including an interspecies solidarity into the emerging feminist manifestoes. A frequent speaker and workshop leader, Connie has authored dozens of papers and booklets, has established a resource library in her Brooklyn, NY apartment and is continually building an archive of slides and pictures on animal oppression.

Connie is also a Fine Arts and yoga teacher and a runner, and in August, 1981, she ran the Women's International Marathon in Ottawa, protesting the sponsor, Avon, which does massive laboratory testing.

Women's Intimacy With Other Animals

Rising from the mud, warm ooze, millennia old, slips from her head and parts at her breasts, and parts again below her belly, runs down her legs and returns to the ground below. She understands this motion, the primordial cycles. An active creator in Nature, she knows she must be of it and with it in order to maintain the species' young through another cosmic cycle. Not that she is virtuous in that she is female; she just is as she is. She has the genetic mechanics and suppressed knowledge of simple animal ecology and Natural Hygiene, (the real science of Nature) impressed within the ingrams of her brain, just as she has the surging of the moon-drawn tides circulating within her blood. The Natural Law is not a "man-made" human law, but one of cause and effect, cause and event, the observed phenomena of the power of Nature that must be abided by in order to fit into Nature's correlations.

When she observes the trickery played out in culture on her healthy vegetarian body—and on the land, the thrashing waters, the bountiful plant life, and the observing animals—she cries out. She knows that at the root of her contemporary inquiry into the destruction and domination of internal spaces (all bodies) and external spaces (all places) is a primitive rage.

Modern women, when left alone to devise a recall of ancient survival, know that they can heal, regenerate, live in tune with the seasons and appreciate the bursting force of life that rises in other forms without the empirical need to control it, dissect it, eliminate it.

> *I love this bird, when I see the arc of her flight, I fly with her, enter her with my mind, leave myself, die for an instant, live in the body of this bird whom I cannot live without, as part of the body of the bird will enter my daughter's body, because I know I am made from this earth, as my mother's hands were made from this earth... all that I know speaks to me through this earth and I long to tell you, you who are earth too, and listen* as we speak to each other of what we know: the light is in us. *(Susan Griffin,* Woman and Nature, *Harper Colophon Books, 1979)*

At the heart of this is not the girl-child "sentiment" that she is identified with and known for, but her unrelenting support and protection of the Natural Law, the intuitive law that all organisms must submit to and not be above, nor bend. It is the aesthetic of untampered biological law, not the artificial aesthetic of male science.

Women know and understand, more easily than men do, the workings of animal communities, animal nations balancing out one another. It is not surprising that the "leading authorities" in his science[1] of animal behaviorism are women: Jane Goodall, chimpanzees; Diane Fossey, gorillas; Thelma Rowell, baboons; Phyllis Jay, monkeys. Brigid Brophy, vegetarian aesthete and author, says of these observations, "Biology certainly offers us no pretext for treating our own species as absolute and all the rest as slaves. Since the discovery of evolution, biology has been making it plain that the frontiers between the species are flexible, that we and other animals have ancestors in common, and that we indeed are animals."

In the last century, Agnes Ryan, feminist author from New England, asked, "Is it possible for a healthy human race to be fathered by violence. . .in war or in the slaughterhouse. . .and mothered by slaves, innocent and parasitic?" Ninteenth Century writer Louisa May Alcott was influenced by her father's vegetarian commune, and passion moved her hand to write, "Vegetable diet and sweet repose. Animal food and nightmare. Pluck your body from the orchard; do not snatch it from the shamble. Without flesh diet there could be no bloodshedding war." Isadora Duncan, the American dancer/choreographer, had compassion in her heart when she said, "Who loves this terrible thing called War? Probably the meat-eaters, having killed, feel the need to kill. . .The butcher with his bloody apron incites bloodshed, murder. . ."

Carol Adams, in her essay, "The Inedible Complex," (*Second Wave,* 1976) wrote, "I am convinced that there is an evolution from becoming a feminist to incorporating vegetarianism into one's life. Perhaps this is why many feminists who still eat meat react defensively and emotionally to those of us who don't. They know either intuitively or consciously that meat-eating is a relic, a remnant, a tie-in with the patriarchal culture we are trying to exorcize. . .Feminists who assert their autonomy and become vegetarian are reversing the objectification/fragmentation/consumption process which enables the oppression of women and animals." Leakey, the anthropologist, notes in his monumental study, *Origins,* that "sexism is roughly inversely proportional to vegetarianism." To many of the feminist animal activists, it is disappointing to realize that the emerging analysis of animal oppression has not broadened feminist criteria. Feminist philosophy is still stuck in the socialist mire, and animals are still seen in the milieu of the environmental cause in general. In "Screwing Mother Earth," Rosemary Radford Ruether wrote, "Women must see that there can be no liberation for them and no ecological solution on bourgeois reformist grounds. They must unite the demands of the women's movement with those of the ecological movement."

Male Misuse of Other Animals and Women

In 1386, the judge of Falaise, France, judiciously condemned and punished a sow pig and her young to be mutilated in the leg and head and afterwards to be hanged in the public square dressed in man's clothes, for accidently killing a child. In the Middle Ages, women of "old truths" were mutilated and killed in like manner. It is interesting to note that their closest animal friends, the dog and cat, were murdered along with them. Woman was a "lover of the devil" and her animals were considered the devil incarnate. Men fear the dark and unfathomable places that animals and women are thought to possess. Men maim and shame woman's closest kind, the children and the animals, with their mysteries and innate knowledge.

The direct fact is this: how men treat the domesticated and indigenous animals is exactly how they will treat the women who surround them. Elizabeth Fisher, in *Women's Creations,* (Anchor Press/Doubleday) 1979, notes, "Direct or indirect as the connection may be, the parallelism between sadomasochistic practices and selective animal breeding is found in widely separated areas of human settlement." In her unique chapter on "War, Sex and Animals," she stresses that oppressive relationships between animals and humans give rise to the accumulative values that encourage raiding, raping, and general warlike traits. "The invention of horseback riding with a 'mounting mentality,' castration, the lasso, saddle and stirrup, was bound to change the patterns of sexual relationships, cruelty, mutilation and sacrifice."

Eco-feminist, Carol Adams notes, "Acts of aggression against animals are on the same continuum. As one man in defense of hunters explained: 'What would all these rabbit hunters be doing if they weren't letting off all of this steam? I'll tell you what they would be doing. They'd be drinking and carousing and beating their wives.'"

In 1975, Peter Singer's book, *Animal Liberation,* brought a flood, even a revolt, of consciousness to the academy in this country. He opens his first chapter with, "Animal Liberation may sound more like a parody of other liberation movements than a serious objective. The idea of the rights of animals actually was once used to parody the case for women's rights." He went on to say that when Mary Wollstonecraft published her *Vindication of the Rights of Woman* in 1792, her views were widely regarded as absurd. Before long, "Vindication of the Rights of Brutes" appeared which tried to make the point that if women had rights then animals did too. The purpose of this being that rights for both animals and women was an absurdity.

Men no longer own and count in limited quantities their possessions; the forests, the oceans, the prairies, the cattle, women and children. What men do today is allow their developed and collective "sciences"—animal behaviorism, ethnology—and environmental "studies" to act as proxies for their governments in order to determine the state and condition of animals everywhere. Leading British animal rights lecturer, Maureen Duffy, makes this point: "Human pride which had had its glorious role of King-making stripped of it, hurried to reclothe itself in gray but serviceable scientific dress."

Woman is appalled, when she awakes to her inner sense of natural healing, that men could conceive to innoculate the tiny arms of children with the pus of a farm animal to "protect" them from ill-health; that the secrets of human well-being could be had by forcing a helpless, innocent animal into paralytic submission and induced sickness, and then that this sickness is put into our bodies to develop an anti-body; that man could know her better by ripping open her female animal counterpart with the zeal of a shaman; and that the fetus of a monkey could become a scientific tool.

These were not the same secrets that women had passed on down through the ages on how to keep an organism at its optimum in balance with Nature. The power of men's deceitful "knowledge" came through the 19th Century discipline of experimental medicine where the "art" of vivisection was just beginning to gain credibility. This cruel art "sacrificed" the living animals for his search of how "Nature works."

Women's Betrayal of Animals

The male phenomena of organic reconstruction of biological life helps to subterfuge, in woman's eye, the very facts of Nature where she was once the source of that knowledge; the healer, the midwife. She now gives birth against gravity and the other animal mothers moan for her. These wise mothers know that she knows another lost way to work with Nature. She has forgotten her own animal form, perfumed as she is in whale oil, costumed in another's skin and fur. To make forlorned animal stares disappear, she makes them non-existent as men do to animals that challenge them; she eats, hunts and vivisects them, with him.

She has been and still is, a killer of other life in the shadows of his traditions; a self-styled "Queen" in his "animal kingdom," a speciesist consort with her brother. Following the man out of the semi-tropical forests, following the hunt after glacial squalor, the female human being lost her potent seasonal reproductive cycle. She succumbed to eating other chattel of which her own kind (women) was just a part in his eyes. Here she could join him in the arrogant killing of animals. In *Surfacing,* Margaret Atwood refers to hunters, saying, "If they didn't kill birds and fish they would have killed us. The animals die that we may live, they are substitute people...and we eat them, out of cans or otherwise; we are the eaters of death...."

Was woman, gentle aged guardian of the smaller creatures, really a Diana, the huntress, of the classical (male) mythology? Squalling life, animal and human, announces itself at our mercy. Woman, protector of barnyard animals, knows that small lives can be throttled to death in her bare, knarled hands the same way that men in the countryside have drowned and murdered the unwelcomed she-child dropped from her egg. Squalling life, animal and human, announces itself at our mercy. Has she taught her children well enough with whispers of little heresies against his order of things, the grace to give life to a toad: "don't cut it up!" Does she have the will to spare life walking aside of the fly that is grounded? Do her young know that trees, the forests, have "standing," legal rights under his repentative law? The animals acquire their protection, not from his love of them, but from his desire to recycle them back into compartmentalized pockets of existence for his available use. Their rights simply reflect his need. Who separated the animal from its natural dignity? Was it woman who first dressed a cat as a doll or a monkey as a child? Why has she continued to feed on more animal flesh, the hunter home from the kill? Why has she given the hunter warm hand-knitted clothes from animal fur and fiber, and listened to his stories of unnecessary gore—with the children within earshot, her earlier whispers still ringing true in their ears?

Ecological Animal Oppression

Let us look at the ecological disaster of hunting, scientific research, urban domestication of the "pet" species and at the intricate biological chain that intertwines all living phenomena.

The Land: Hundreds of animals have become endangered or extinct because of herding and ranch raising; the Dodo Bird, wild pigs, and the Tasmanian Wolf that preyed on domesticated sheep. We poison the Black Footed Ferret and the Prairie Dog who compete for the grasslands of the plains' ranches. We kill off the Pronghorned Sheep, enemies of the cattle industry, as we do the Grizzly Bear in Montana. Coyotes eat cyanide pellets. Man's herds eat up the Prairies until none are left, leaving only the vast wastelands of potential deserts. Eaten directly as meat are the endangered Kangaroo, the Chinese Barking Deer, the River Otter, the Newfoundland Seal, the bear, the elk, the reindeer.

The Sea: Certain species of sea creatures are endangered due to overfishing and ocean hunting. Tuna swim beneath dolphins; consequently the Spotted, Spinner, and Common Dolphin drown in the nets of the Tuna fishermen. Since 1940, the total number of Great Whales has fallen from 1.5 million to 500,000, though this whale feeds only a mere one percent of the Japanese people who hunt it. The rest of its great body goes to feed Mink on factory farms in Russia. Other outdated uses of whale are lipstick, dog food, and lubricant for warfare artillery. The grand old sea turtles, whose flesh and eggs are consumed as a delicacy, are also close to extinction.

The Air: The living beings here fare little better in their struggle to survive. In Alaska, a bounty was paid on Bald Eagles because they were considered damaging to the Salmon industry. In Montana, the Golden Eagle was an authorized kill for the sake of the livestock and ranching interests. In 1975, over one million Blackbirds were left dead of exposure after the Army sprayed them with Tergitol, a chemical that removes the protective oils from their wings. The government was pressured into this killing by local farmers and feedlot operators who claimed that the birds were eating grain laid out for hogs and cattle. These birds roosted in pine forests that the Army had grown; if they had never planted this non-indigenous grove of trees, the birds would never have found their way there!

The general biosphere: The Gir Forest in India, the northern brushlands of East Africa, the prairies of America all have been laid barren due to farming and animal husbandry. The Amazon

Jungle, providing one fifth of the world's oxygen supply, is being reduced to ranchlands and oil wells. Consider your love of water, then think upon its prostitution: it's used in irrigating crops for animal feed as drinking water for "livestock," to clean the slaughterhouses, and for the preparation, packaging and refrigeration of meat. 2500 gallons of water are needed to supply a meat-eater's food for one day as opposed to the 300 gallons needed to provide for a vegetarian's diet. It takes 100,000 gallons of water just to "produce" one milking cow!

Other atrocities: An estimated 80 million animals are shocked, burned, deprived, poisoned, and otherwise abused in needless research experiments. Cosmetic firms test every new product by force-feeding face powder to animals until their internal organs rupture, applying burning chemicals to animals' eyes, or smearing irritating lotions to skin that has been scraped raw. This is done most often with no painkiller. These tests are known as the Lethal Dose-50 and the Draize test. Feminists who still wear makeup would be in tune with their principles to boycott companies such as Avon and Revlon and buy products that are not tested on animals.

Nearly 15 million dogs and cats are abandoned and killed each year for lack of responsible guardians and inadequate spay and neuter clinics. An unbelievable 12,500 living healthy beings called "pets" are put to death per hour because their natural place on Earth has long been claimed by humans, instead of being shared. In *The Violent Sex*, Laurel Holiday says, ". . . the root of the problem is in our blithely taking power over the lives and deaths of other creatures, whose suffering is in no way necessary for our survival."

Female Work: Animal's Conditions

The dominant force behind the development of humane education (especially that for children) is the compassionate female mind, the mother-self, the nurturer. Occasionally, it is sarcastically noted that a majority of the women involved in "animal work" have no children, and that their preoccupation with "helpless animals" is a proxy for child-rearing. Whatever the conclusion, it is not coincidental that the first urban humane societies for the prevention of cruelty to animals had broad moral and benevolent bases. Inner-city child abuse detection was pioneered under these same societies. Until the 1930s, child abuse and animal cruelty were seen as one investigative problem.

Although women may cast the false image as animal welfare

dowagers, they are still basically just running the clubs ("kindness clubs" for children, animal clubs for adults), putting out tables for the perpetual "Be Kind to Animals Week," keeping the subtle torch of humanity passively burning. All this, while the power of the immediate disposition of animals lies with the men in their legislature. It is the men who still decide if we will resume the killing of a whale, allow the Army Corps of Engineers to build a pipeline across the migration path of moose, or build a bridge or dam on the only home of an endangered snail.

As altruistic as humane education aspires to, it continues to carry with it a tricky double standard as to the nature of how animals are to be involved with human civilization. First, it is believed that animals are here on Earth to serve us for food, clothing, transportation, amusement. Second, it is believed that animals are innocent playthings, anthropomorphic friends, or mystical creatures to be worshipped. Neither image serves the animals who are, after all, just other nations of beings, autonomous unto themselves. Classic humaneness[2] has deteriorated in the last century under the weight of Scientific Humanism and political reform principles.

In the mid 19th century, women the likes of Frances Cobbe in England and Netta Ivory in Scotland began lifelong rallies against the escalation of confined cruelty being done in the name of his science. Female saints can really be found, not in his churches, but in her own fiercely run societies. The late 19th century produced Anna Kingsford, the fore-runner of today's activist, a feminist, mystic, vegetarian (when it was unheard of), suffragist, and medical doctor. She was primarily known for her exposes of the torture of animals in medicine which she observed first hand. Her thesis, *The Perfect Way*, was based on ethical and physiological vegetarianism. She left the English women's movement saying, "These women are deluded because they cannot see that the universal peace is impossible to a carnivorous race," and died of pneumonia because she refused to wear the skin of an animal on her feet!

About this time, women who were mobile through their class found a new arena for charity to air their social discontent in the founding of thousands of small humane groups. This mode of activism was accepted, while religion, politics, economics, business, and law were considered men's concerns. In 1869, Caroline Earl White founded the Women's Penn. Society for the Prevention of Cruelty to Animals. She championed bird preservation before the advent of the Audubon Society, and helped to secure protection for Atlantic Shore birds. She advocated laws against pigeon shoots and foxhunts, and founded the *Journal of Zoophily*. She was typical of many women who needed an outlet to express a deeper underlying concern about the world at large.

Perhaps because the English had such an enormous opportunity in the last century to spread their particular mentality of cruelty to animals via the empire, they had an opportunity to advance the cause of animals as well! It could be said that the Animal Rights Movement is about ten years old in its modern sense, and that England was the spawning ground. On one end are the old conservative societies that occasionally give rise to timely issues. Beauty Without Cruelty was founded by Lady Muriel Dowding, a woman whose associations bridge from the 100 year old National Anti-vivisection Society. The BWC works on keeping animal products, such as whale oil, civit, musk, out of cosmetics and finding alternatives to animal testing. Jean Pink, founder of Animal Aid in 1977, has set up hundreds of demonstrations and candlelight marches in order to focus on the issues of animal research and factory farming. She has written, "The masculine aspect of consciousness has been allowed to rule for too long. It has brought about a world where violence, terror and sorrow go hand in hand. We call for a redress of the balance. We ask that the voice of feeling and compassion be allowed to speak. In the present world man has created a hell for the animals as a result of the demand for cheap food, constant supplies of drugs, and playthings like new cosmetics and shiny paints."

Margaret Heard is the co-founder of the Animal Rights Association and the editor of *Action for Psychic Ecology*. This is a unique magazine whose purpose is to "promote awareness and action to oppose abuses against Nature and to disseminate New Age ideals relating to ecology, spiritual healing, animal welfare and social justice." The small group of women in this circle write about, "the re-emergence of the female principle both in material and in spiritual life; they believe in the way of vegetarianism leading to veganism, the sensitivity to plants and the communication with Nature. Atrocities to animals, and the pollution of the planet both physically and psychically, are intolerable situations that need action now."

English women have been in the forefront in going to jail to promote anti-hunting sentiments in the public. Sue Hough and Valerie Waters from the well established Hunt Saboteurs Association were among the first to be incarcerated. Civil disobedience is the byword of the Animal Liberation Front that had confiscated records of animal researchers and laboratory animals themselves. There are even groups that have their own sophisticated underwater equipment to disrupt the work of those that kill the sea animals.

In Canada, the climate is similar. Marlene Larkin and Merlyn Andrews of Toronto have chained themselves to various structures in protest of the annual seal hunts in Labrador. Harriet Schliefer, founder of the Animal Liberation Collective in Montreal, is an Eco-feminist, pro-solar advocate of civil disobedience.

In the USA, women have been prolific on the emerging synthesis that the interrelationship of life with all life determines the quality of life. As a species of rare flower or tiny fly or fish dies away, the homocentric human is impoverished because of it. Every compassionate action sets up a vibration in the universe that touches another. A woman tending her field and caring for the little indigenous animals will affect another woman in another century in the same place. The second woman uses the same gentle hand of the first, but the animals are now the sick and lame horses of a regiment and the peaceful land has now turned battlefield. Male history creates the illusion that during the war women are nowhere to be seen, but women and children in all wars have tended and treated the animal slaves. American women founded the Red Star Animal Relief for wounded war animals in WWI and put out a booklet on the care of dying animals on the open ranges, dying of exposure, thirst and starvation.

Hundreds of individual American women stand out for their work. Helen Jones, Alice Harrington, and Eleanor Seiling all founded national organizations, the latter architected a turning point bill, the Research Modernization Act now in Congress. CEASE (Coalition to End Animal Suffering in Experiments) in Boston and PETA (People for the Ethical Treatment of Animals) in Washington DC are women dominated. In 1979, Patti Kane fought a landmark case at a NYC college, in asserting her right not to dissect animals in labs. In the West, Velma Johnston (Wild Horse Anne) whose organization WHOA (Wild Horses of America), has brought relief to the wild horses on the Plains. Hope Sawyer Buyunihci has an animal refuge (as many women do) for beaver. She writes and illustrates books on the vegetarian lifestyle. Laura Bellos of SPARE (Sympathetic People for Animal Rights on Earth) in New York, works with audio-visual shows. She says, "Animals are capable of feeling pain and fear, and they also live intricate social lives. Animals have families of their own to love and protect, and they have distinctive roles to play in maintaining the ecological balance within their habitats." The trend in these new groups that are cropping up all over the country is "rights" oriented. Petition drives and marches for animal causes linked to all the other causes are emerging into the sleepy public eye. In Bertram, TX the Women's Organic Farm and Sanctuary took shape in the middle of cattle country. Dozens of women's community farms that refuse to enslave animals for food or product are springing up all over.

What can a woman do? She can become a vegetarian. She can restructure her consciousness raising to a deeper level so as to be interspecies.[3] She can legislate for animal concerns and she can exercise civil disobedience, sabotage the machinery and artifacts that kill animal life and the eco-system in general. Finally, she can look to the animal beings for lessons in biological efficiency and humility.

Diana J. M. Davies/Insight

Women of the United Farm Workers sing at a rally.

Priscilla Prutzman

Assertiveness, Nonviolence and Feminism

Where do we look to find the skills we need to function on a day-to-day basis in that middle ground between dish rag passivity and double-fisted aggression? Priscilla suggests that feminist advocates of nonviolence would do well to consider the conflict resolution skills taught in the Assertiveness Awareness courses. Assertiveness, she says, is a tool of nonviolence and provides a way to communicate honestly without having to sacrifice one's dignity or infringe on another's rights. Here she shares her classroom exercises and the insight gained in group lessons.

In addition to teaching Assertiveness Awareness, Priscilla is a facilitator with the Children's Creative Response to Conflict Program and has co-authored The Friendly Classroom for a Small Planet. *A resident of New Paltz, New York, Priscilla is also a puppeteer and is interested in relaxation techniques, gardening, biking and simple living. She does videotaping and has a part-time job in the audio-visual department of the New School for Social Research in New York City where she earned her M.A. Priscilla thanks Kay Reynolds who assisted with this article.*

Recently I was invited to teach courses in Assertiveness Awareness at a local community college. I have worked for years in the area of nonviolence and children, and before that did nonviolence training on many different levels. When I explained that I was skilled in conflict resolution and communication but had never taught Assertiveness Awareness, the reply was : "Oh, it's all the same thing!" So I got the job.

One of my friends was bewildered. "First you teach nonviolence," she said, "and then you teach assertiveness. How can you go from one extreme to the other?" Her confusion was not surprising. People frequently equate nonviolence with passivity or weakness, while the words "assertiveness" and "aggressiveness" are thought to be interchangeable.

Responsible assertiveness assumes a potential for good in each person, just as does nonviolence. It also encourages people to share feelings openly and honestly. It aims at meeting people's needs without risking harm or infringing on the rights of others. Most importantly, responsible assertiveness and nonviolence involve communication without the sacrifice of dignity or self-respect. Responsible assertiveness is nonviolent. Effective nonviolence is practiced from strength, not weakness, and, far from being passive, nonviolence demands the inner strength to take risks, to be open to others, to establish a give and take with the other person's point of view.

The women who came to the Assertiveness Awareness courses were in transition. They were looking for help to fulfill the media image of who they should be. Some were going back to school, hoping to find employment. Others had recently gotten a divorce. Some had been housewives all their lives and were looking for their first jobs. A few younger women felt trapped in dead end jobs.

The biggest concern of the women in these courses was lack of self-confidence. The reasons they gave for not being assertive were: fear of not being accepted, lack of communication skills, fear of appearing stupid, fear of hurting someone's feelings or losing a friend.

Passive/Aggressive/Assertive

The Assertiveness Awareness course is based on looking extensively at what is meant by being "passive," "aggressive" or "assertive." We asked various questions about these terms, for example—when you think of male/female sex role stereotypes, what associations come to mind in relation to these three terms?

When we brainstormed "aggressive male," words such as "confident" were offered, but when "aggressive" was applied to women, the word "bitchy" was one association. Below is a chart showing the results of this exercise:

MALE

Passive	**Aggressive**	**Assertive**
Weak	Strong	Strong
Namby Pamby	Masculine	Fair
Feminine	Successful	
Powerless	Confident	

FEMALE

Passive	**Aggressive**	**Assertive**
Sweet	Bitchy	Strong
Feminine	Loud	
Gentle	Cold	
Ladylike		
Soft		
Good		

Frequently, women in this course had the pattern of saying "yes" and accepting everything along the way, but then would lose their temper over a minor incident. We discussed how, by examining body language and voice levels, it is possible to recognize these cues before anger builds to a point of explosion. In one exercise we roleplayed a scenario where a boss continually asked a woman to go for coffee although it was not part of her job description. Members of the group were asked to walk around as if they were feeling passive in the situation. Then they were asked to "freeze" and to observe their own and others' body language. The participants came up with the following descriptions:

shoulders down
head slumped forward
eyes looking down
feet shuffling

They were then asked to react to the same scenario aggressively. The body language was then described as:

leaning forward
clenched fists
shaking index finger at another person
muscles tensed
face distorted
hands on hips

Finally the participants were asked to react to the same scenario assertively. Their body language was then described as:

standing up straight
not leaning toward or away from another person

relaxed muscles
looking straight ahead
eye contact
some smiles
no facial distortion

In another activity called the "voice walk," people were asked to talk randomly about anything, first in a passive way. Then we listed words describing the voice quality as: quiet, reserved, slow, nervous, hesitant or stuttering, and use of incomplete sentences. Next, people were asked to talk aggressively. Voice quality was described as being loud, fast, high-pitched, and shrill. Thirdly, people were asked to talk in an assertive manner. We noted that we had spoken in confident and well-modulated tones (appropriate volume to the room) at a relaxed pace.

By examining both the body language and the voice quality, women were made aware of their feelings so that they could handle them immediately. They could then avoid feelings building up into an angry, aggressive explosion.

In another brainstorm session the students listed the following problems:

being repeatedly asked by the boss to go for coffee
returning merchandise at a store
having a friend borrow something and return it broken
saying "no" to solicitors (Girl Scouts selling cookies)
confronting someone who butts into the front of the line at movies
contronting a person who doesn't help after agreeing to
confronting "you must come over for dinner"—it never happens
saying "your smoking is bothering me"
saying no to an invitation or party gathering
saying no when someone is asking for help
saying no to a daughter
borrowing clothes
being uncomfortable when people are talking about a person in a negative way
telling someone assertively you don't agree with their actions
responding to someone who is late for an appointment

Our goal was to look at as many of these problems as we could and to come up with ways of acting assertively. One of the activities used in this area was Quick Decision Making. In pairs, the participants were asked to think of solutions to one problem. The solutions were then shared with the whole group and discussed in terms of whether or not they were assertive responses. One of the conflicts used was being able to say "no" to a Girl Scout selling cookies. The real problem in this scenario is that you don't want the cookies, but you feel guilty about turning down the Girl Scouts. The assertive response involves knowing what you want (to not buy the cookies), feeling you have a right to that (and therefore you don't feel guilty) and saying no in a way that is polite and supportive to the Girl Scout. All of these elements were discussed after people came up with their quick decision responses.

Another technique was to break into groups of three and roleplay a passive, aggressive and assertive response to a particular conflict, in order to understand the differences between these responses. For example, if a person asks to borrow your car, the passive response is to hang your head, shuffle your feet, and finally give in and agree—even though you don't want to lend the car. In the aggressive response, you yell "no," are impolite, and shout in anger. In the assertive response, you would state your feelings, be polite and sympathetic to the other person, but reaffirm that you do not want to lend the car.

Another technique and probably the most important one, was that of actually practicing assertive responses. For instance, one of the scenarios roleplayed was sending back an unsatisfactory dish in a restaurant, for example a steak ordered rare which came well done. The natural tendency of many people would be to accept the steak, but the assertive response would be to politely tell the waiter that you ordered the steak rare and ask that he take back the well done steak and give you the one you ordered. If the waiter responds with hostility, the assertive response is to repeat the statement politely, and to do this in a quiet tone to avoid embarassing or offending other people.

Roleplaying was done with several variations including having individuals replay a scenario until they achieved an appropriate assertive response; reversing the roles in order to experience the other person's point of view; and using video playback to look objectively at a conflict from both sides and discuss more effective ways of responding assertively.

Affirmation

The most important need of the students in the Assertiveness

Awareness courses was to have an improved sense of self-worth. This was one of the most significant results of the class. People did leave feeling more positive about themselves.

Activities which stressed affirmation included several "News and Goods" in which people told something "new and good" that had happened to them recently. After a while, this became easier for everyone to do. It was important for the students to become comfortable saying positive things.

We also did an exercise called "Gift Giving." In this, the students paired up and each chose an imaginary gift for the other based on what they had learned about their partner. "Affirmation Sheets" were made for each student to take home, which listed their positive qualities and the contributions they had made to the group. We also tried to encourage people to get up and talk, which was good practice for them.

I enjoyed organizing and teaching this "Assertiveness Awareness" course. It presented assertive behavior in a positive atmosphere. It provided a good balance between nonviolence, assertiveness and feminism, and it afforded an ongoing support system for women in transition, a necessary element in the feminist movement.

JEB

Around the world "Take Back the Night" demonstrators demand an end to the violence against women.

Pat James
Physical Resistance to Attack: The Pacifist's Dilemma, The Feminist's Hope

In this essay, as in Pam McAllister's which follows and complements it, Pat James, a self-defense instructor, addresses the complications, contradictions and concerns of a woman serious about self-defense but reluctant to betray her nonviolent feminist sensibility. Pat writes, "This is certainly the most difficult issue related to self-defense that I have encountered. I will begin teaching three self-defense classes in a few weeks and my approach will certainly be informed by the thinking and reading I've done over the summer in preparation for this article. I have always sensed my own ambivalence about the use of physical force to resist attack and about the idea of passive resistance, and I must admit I'm squarely in the middle of the conflicts with no resolution in sight except for a present commitment to studying and teaching and questioning."

Supplementing the following essay is Pat's essay "Do It Yourself Self-Defense" which appeared in Fight Back! Feminist Resistance to Male Violence *edited by Delacoste and Newman (Cleis Press, 1981). In that essay Pat suggests sixteen exercises designed to empower us and enhance our ability to resist attack. At the end of that essay, Pat records several stories of women's successful handling of a tough situation, including a real prize-winner about a woman with two children in a broken-down car who was confronted by a man with a gun late one night on the New Jersey Turnpike. When the man ordered the woman to let him in the car, the woman looked him in the eye and, like an angry mother, commanded, "You put that gun away, get in your car, and push me to the service area, AND I MEAN RIGHT NOW!" And he did!*

Pat brings her experience as an attack-survivor and her years on the staff of Women Organized Against Rape to the writing of the following essay. She is currently the coordinator of the Women's School in Philadelphia, and a member of the staff of Women's Alliance for Job Equity (WAJE).

I signed up for my first self-defense class less than a year after surviving a nearly fatal attack a few yards from my front door. During that year my feelings had wavered between panic and rage. I never went out alone after dark, rarely went out alone at all. My life was controlled by fear and a sense of powerlessness.

The all-women self-defense class was taught by a husband and wife team, black belts in karate. The woman split her time in class between tending their infant daughter and suffering whatever humiliation her husband chose to inflict. The man taught only skills necessary to maim or kill an attacker. We were ridiculed for suggesting ways to disable an attacker without killing or hurting him. We didn't discuss prevention.

I was one of many who dropped out of the class early, feeling scared, powerless, weak and stupid—much as I had after being attacked. The class offered no mediation between my terror and the violence encouraged by the teacher. I was being taught to become my attacker: a damaged frightened and angry victim of the patriarchy trying to find, in violence, solutions to fear and anger.

Eight years later I joined the staff of Women Organized Against Rape (WOAR) of Philadelphia. The daily work of counseling countless survivors of assault reopened me to the emotional pain and the fear from my own attack. Soon I joined the self-defense class they offered. The class became a refuge two days a week where I could clear my mind of everything but training, and where I could work out physically the overwhelming pain and anger I felt. I left feeling more able to take care of myself each time. I had little idea that studying and eventually teaching self-defense would become a way of life for me, but I knew then that it was central to my ability to cope with the work I had chosen, and with the feelings about my own assault.

I learned that self-defense is much more than the use of physical force demonstrated by my first teacher. Self-defense is self-love. For women it often means replacing lifelong patterns of powerlessness and dependence with strength and confidence. It is a life-affirming process of empowering our selves and our bodies to live safely, to retain control over our bodies and our environments. For many, the empowerment process begins in anger.

Transforming Anger and Unlearning Powerlessness

> *The one anger is healthy, concentrates all one's energies; the other leaves one trembling, because it is murderous. . . Our task, of course, is to transmute the anger that is affliction into the anger that is determination to bring about change. I think, in fact, that one could give that as a definition of revolution. (Barbara Deming, "On Anger," re-*

print from Liberation, *Nov. 1971.)*

It is a lie to suffer abuse and to be silent. The lie hurts both the victim who is consumed by the anger turned inward and the abuser who justifies his contempt for his victim with her passivity. The silence hurts men who dismiss individual women's rage as personal not "political," and it hurts other women who are isolated in their anger.

Many women fear anger and often confuse it with actual violence. We have been taught that being angry is"unfeminine" and when we bear witness to our anger we transform ourselves. Our anger becomes an incredible source of power in self-defense. "I live in fear," is a statement of powerlessness. "I am angry that I live in fear," is a call to revolution. A woman's power is usually *not* thought to be her self-confidence, assertiveness or physical skill. Instead, her power is traditionally found in manipulation, cajoling, pleading, even in using her body to bargain for what she wants. By employing these tactics she is not using her own power but trying to redirect that of another person, usually a man. She must out-maneuver him at his own game. But it is still *his* game. And it doesn't work for self-defense. An attacker wants his victims to plead, to try to bargain from a position of powerlessness that he imposes and controls.

At the WOAR self-defense class, I became aware of how traditional male-defined notions of femininity contributed to my (and all women's) vulnerability to attack. One passage from Marge Piercy's *Small Changes* describes women's learned posture of powerlessness:

> *Wanda made them aware of how they moved, how they rested, how they occupied space. She demonstrated how men sat and how women sat on the subway, on benches. Men expanded into available space... They dominated space expansively.*
>
> *"Women condensed. Women crossed their legs by putting one leg over the other and along side. Women kept their elbows to their sides, taking up as little space as possible.*

Those attributes of standard femininity—passivity, gentleness, sexiness, dependence, incompetence, weakness and the rest—are the price for women's survival in an androcentric, white, male-dominated society. We are taught to trade personal and physical power and independence for protection. We are not taught that this protection is unreliable. All women don't have men around to take care of them; those women who depend on men can't be with them 24 hours a day; and many women are victimized by the men they had looked to for protection. The recent upsurge in attacks on lesbians in San Francisco and other cities shows that women who have chosen independence from men are *especially* targeted for attack by our so-called "protectors."

For some women, passive "feminine" behavior is necessary for survival. An extreme example is the group of black South African women who recently had immigrated to Philadelphia, and were participating in a rape prevention workshop. For them, lowered eyes, soft voices, deferential behavior had meant more than just getting by; it had meant survival in a culture that legally enforces sexism and racism with violence. For many women, however, it is internalized oppression that perpetuates those traditional values about femininity and thus our vulnerability to attack. I often ask women in my rape prevention workshops to make two lists—one of adjectives that mean "feminine," the other of adjectives for the word "victim." It's frightening how many of the same words appear on both lists: passive, weak, sexy, incompetent, dependent, stupid, helpless, quiet, trusting.

The lists reflect the women's sense of their own victimization and powerlessness and their contempt for that victimization. That contempt fuels a blame-the-victim attitude by both men and women. Ironically, women are "blamed" for assault because of something "improper" about dress or behavior (perhaps being "too feminine, too sexy"), not because we do not act powerfully. Women are expected to fight back, but are not expected to learn the skills to fight back. We are then accused of secretly enjoying assault when we do not resist physically.

The contempt implied by the two lists has another, more subtle aspect as well: many women do not value themselves and thus do not believe they are worth defending. They may believe in their worth to their children, lovers, employers, but they do not value themselves *to themselves.* They do not have an intrinsic sense that their lives are important and worth preserving. We have been socialized to live *for* others and to be protected *by* others. Consequently, women are over-awed by the mystique of male strength and aggressiveness to the extent that we feel hopeless about fighting back. One of my self-defense students told her husband that she was taking an exercise class because he ridiculed her for wanting to study self-defense. "Any man who wants to rape any woman is going to do it, no matter how much she fights back," he told her. It's tragic how his ego was much more invested in men's ability to rape women than in his wife's safety. Incidentally, though this woman was quite shy and reticent, she was incredibly strong and well-coordinated, and I have no doubts about her ability to take care of herself in most situations.

Unlearning powerlessness means taking our anger seriously and harnessing it in our own defense. It means redefining "femininity" to reflect positive values about ourselves, and internalizing those values so that we see ourselves as individuals worth defending. It means becoming confident in our power as women, instead of being simply afraid of male power, and it means learning new ways of carrying ourselves to demonstrate that confidence.

Claiming Power

"This culture of manipulated passivity, nourishing violence at its core, has every stake in opposing women actively laying claim to our own lives." (Adrienne Rich, *On Lies, Secrets and Silence: Selected Prose 1966-1978;* Norton, 1979.)

"A pacifist feminist's first obligation is to end her complicity in the violence of sexism." (Jane Meyerding, "Feminism and Pacifism: Doing It Our Way" *Out and About,* March 1978.)

The man who attacked me seemed to appear out of nowhere. Suddenly he was there on my street while I was walking my dog, and he wanted to talk. He was standing too close for my comfort so I sidled away. I smiled because I didn't want him to be insulted or think I was afraid. I *was* afraid. He grabbed the back of my neck and kissed me harshly. I pulled away and said, *still smiling,* "Hey man, I'm not into this. Let's just talk, okay?" His answer was to smash his mouth on mine again. I bit his tongue until I could taste his blood, but then suddenly I was afraid of hurting him. He threw me to the ground and strangled me until I lost consciousness. When I came to, he was gone.

I review the incident again and again. I was afraid and did not act with an effective response to that fear. I couldn't believe, until it was too late, that I was being threatened. I didn't want to be rude or hurt his feelings. I didn't want to hurt him. I was too embarrassed to scream and draw attention to myself, and when he began to choke me I lost that option. I panicked and was unable to put up any effective physical resistance. I was so humiliated by the level of my compliance in the attack that I couldn't face reporting it to the police. To this day, I still wonder how many more women...? I do not blame myself for being attacked, but I do take responsibility for the parts of my victimization that might not have happened if I had behaved differently.

In the WOAR self-defense class, our teacher made us use our voices to shout, scream, give orders. We roleplayed common street situations to practice making eye contact and using strong body language. A common roleplay was of being approached by a man asking "What time is it?" Responses varied: looking away and ignoring the man; smiling, consulting a watch and answering him; getting involved in a conversation and even answering dozens of personal questions; saying "time for you to buzz off;" and kicking him in the groin. Most of the responses demonstrated either intimidation or hostility, but almost all of them showed the woman being out of control of the situation. It was hard at first to realize that we could be firm and commanding and polite at the same time; that we could say "It's about eleven o'clock," using a firm tone of voice and direct eye contact and taking a centered, powerful stance. We could act without being either apologetic and vulnerable, or hostile and responsible for escalating the potential for violence.

During the class I mentally replayed my attack, spotting many places where I could have landed a punch or kick or thrown him to the ground and escaped. It was much more difficult to realize that probably I had the opportunity to prevent the attack in the first place, but that at that time I was just as incapable of defending myself verbally as I was physically. One doesn't suddenly become assertive and verbally powerful in the face of an attack any more than one becomes physically skilled if a lifetime of socialization has mitigated against it.

The Women's Movement has made incredible efforts to erase the myth of the guilty victim, but we have not gone far enough to teach women that, even though we are not to blame for rape, we are responsible for ending "our complicity" in the violence of sexism by becoming more assertive, by relinquishing our dependence on men, by developing our own sources of power and support, and by becoming physically able to defend ourselves.

The Dilemma of Physical Resistance and Nonviolence

"Not only are the myths about rape forms of social control, but the myths about how to avoid rape are forms of social control." (Pauline Bart, *off our backs*, Feb. 1981.)

"We often hear about the necessity of persons overcoming their aggressiveness in order to be non-violent. This is a peculiarly androcentric (male oriented) position because women are not trained to be aggressive. On the contrary, training is in passivity which prevents us from taking action to overcome injustice that is directed against us. In order for women to effectively practice non-violence, and non-violent rape resistance, we need to learn some aggressiveness." (Mary Crane, "Rape Avoidance and Resistance: A Non-Violent Approach," *WIN*, April 26, 1979.)

I believe that women should learn physical skills to resist attacks and that we should learn how and when to decide that these skills are necessary and appropriate. The question for pacifists is, when does self-defense stop being nonviolent? While it is fairly clear that verbal resistance is nonviolent self-defense, it is not clear that throwing an attacker to the ground or poking his eyes are also nonviolent.

My dictionary, *The American College*, Random House, 1963, includes this definition of violence: "an unjust, unwarranted, immoderate or uncontrolled use of force or power." In my tri-weekly training sessions, I punch and kick and wrestle with other students and with my teacher. I suppose it looks violent; it is *very* physical and generally it is also fun, great exercise, and educational. It does not *feel* violent, regardless of whether I'm on the giving or receiving end of a sparring session. It is not competitive. We are not out to beat each other, but to become better practitioners of an art, and to learn self-defense. The most serious injury in my dojo (gym) was a broken toe several years ago due to an improperly placed kick.

My physical strength has increased enormously over the past few years, and so has my confidence in my self and my body. I have learned in my self-defense training that I can withstand kicks and punches and falls, without injury, that at one time I believed might kill me. There is pain, and I respect it, work with it, overcome it and become stronger. Techniques that hurt a year ago now feel comfortable. I have become more resilient. I have become a better and faster decision-maker in crises and my instinct to detect and avoid potential danger has improved as well. As a direct result of my training I am a less violent person.

Before I became involved in self-defense training I saw self-defense as an either-or situation: if attacked, either fight like crazy or give in. Training has made me aware of the countless options anyone has to avoid attack, to defuse violence, to incapacitate an attacker and escape. I have learned to apologize to men who spit on me to deflect further violence, and I have learned to make the decision to use physical force when other options fail.

Common sense as well as nonviolent principle dictate that an aggressive physical response to threat is the last choice for self-defense. Any physical response by the victim is likely to be perceived as violence by the attacker, and the defender should use the least amount of force necessary to stop the attack. Talking assertively, yelling and screaming, making eye contact and using strong body language may be enough force. Or it may not be enough, and physical resistance will be necessary to end the attack.

The main reason for choosing physical resistance in a physical attack is that it is most likely to work. Recent studies of women who had been assaulted, conducted by Pauline Bart, a sociologist at the University of Illinois Medical Center, and Jeannie MacIntyre of the University of Maryland, show that passive resistance "often doesn't work and can lose valuable time for women." The researchers report that the more quickly a woman responds with physical force, the less likely she will be raped, and that early recognition of danger is the single most important factor in preventing or deflecting an attack. Finally, Bart and MacIntyre said that women who successsfully avoided rape generally used a combination of strategies (i.e. screaming, talking, running) as well as physical resistance.

Self-defense, which is the practical application of martial arts techniques for protection, doesn't require superior size or strength to be effective, nor does it require years of training. A good six to eight week self-defense class can teach many of the basic skills needed to deflect an attack, incapacitate an attacker, or escape, as well as how to fall and receive blows without sustaining injuries. The class should also work on decision-making in roleplayed situations so students have an opportunity to practice assessing threat, danger and violence, and choosing an appropriate and effective response.

(A word of warning: as noted in the opening of this essay, some self-defense teachers and practitioners are in it for the violence, and many martial arts dojos actively discriminate against women by refusing to teach us the full array of maneuvers, by treating us like second-class students, or by brutalizing us as part of the teaching. In addition, martial arts and self-defense are not the same thing.)

Many feminist and anti-rape organizations have not dealt with the issue of the offender, usually for the good reason that their resources are already incredibly strained by the needs of survivors of assault. Most rape crisis centers rely heavily upon volunteers in order to stay open and manage to accomplish a great deal on minute budgets. Ultimately, however, changing the conditions that allow rape to continue will mean changing the conditions which compel men to rape, as well as those conditions that cast women as victims, as "the weaker sex."

Several recent studies have indicated that a high percentage of men who rape were physically and sexually abused as children. To this day our society has few resources for any child who is sexually abused, and male children in particular are unlikely to find the help and protection they deserve. Male rape victims are disbelieved and ridiculed by family, friends, police and the courts—many of the same people and institutions who have learned understanding and sympathy for female victims. In this way, the violence of sexism is damaging to men and boys as well as to women and girls.

It is women who will end rape—by rejecting stereotypes and embracing life-affirming self-images; by depending upon ourselves and each other for protection; by changing the conditions of our lives, and by working to change the conditions in men's lives that nourish a rapist culture.

I'm still afraid, and I'm still angry that there is a basis for the fear, but neither fear nor anger controls my life anymore. The belief that someday self-defense could be a relic of our savage past informs my ironic decision to continue to study and teach self-defense.

Pam McAllister
Tentative Steps Toward Nonviolent Self-Defense

Pam, this anthology's editor, is trying to build the foundation for a strategy/theory of self-defense which will be accessible to a wide variety of women and which will offer greater flexibility than either the old notion of passive resistance or the current strategies which rely on physical defense training, mace or guns. In the process, she has begun to see the common sense and radical implications of nonviolence both as a tactic and as a way of life. While space does not allow the discussion of any specific nonviolent self-defense ideas, Pam shares the hunches, insights and feelings which, like beacons, are guiding her way in this search. She urges us to join her in reexamining our current prejudices about strength and in pushing the boundaries of our imaginations concerning self-defense.

Pam's work on violence against women and women as survivors has appeared in Fight Back! Feminist Resistance to Male Violence *edited by Delacoste and Newman (Cleis Press, 1981),* Heresies #6: Issue on Women and Violence *(1978),* Maenad: A Women's Literary Journal *(1981),* Sinister Wisdom *(1980),* Win *(1979). She has written about women's issues for numerous other periodicals including the* Ladies' Home Journal *and coedited the anthology* The Bedside, Bathtub, and Armchair Companion to Agatha Christie *(Ungar, 1979).*

She currently coordinates a book synopsis newsletter for Manhattan's Womanbooks bookstore, a project which she finds deeply satisfying. In spite of her strictly rural background, or perhaps because of it, Pam lives as peacefully and passionately as she can in Brooklyn, New York with a piano, books, plants and a little cat-companion, Emily.

The advantage of projecting an image of invulnerability and fearlessness has long been understood and advocated by women trained in the martial arts. They claim that the primary benefit of training is the development of a centered, confident frame of mind and an attitude of strength. This not only prepares them to cope with potential threats but often deters the threats to begin with.

In accord with this, I suspect it is the attitude of committed resistance, not the technique itself, which usually makes a self-defense action effective. The reason physical combat techniques may work in a given situation is not necessarily because they are superior to the attacker's skills, (though this may be true), but because the intended victim's fearlessness is unexpected.

An attacker seeks and expects to find the power to humiliate and manipulate his victim. He welcomes his victim's fear as powerlessness which will magnify by contrast his own strength. But if we would dare to challenge his most basic assumption, refuse to relinquish a non-threatened perspective, the attacker would be at least momentarily stunned if not entirely thrown off balance. He would be deprived of a predictable confrontation and the premise of his advantage; his "script" would be up for grabs. By refusing the attacker's script, there's a chance that the intended victim would be able to transform the situation from the cut and dried, automatic confrontation script to an open-ended process of interaction where nothing would be pre-defined.

One friend, upon hearing that I'm working out ideas about nonviolent self-defense, quipped, "What do you recommend—prayer?" I don't think it's as hopeless or mysterious as all that.

I am concerned that the range of self-defense options we are likely to consider has been unnecessarily limited to martial arts training and that physical methods of defense have been made to seem easy to use and accessible to all women in all situations. Once, I was surrounded by a gang of young toughs in Prospect Park. The maneuvers I had learned in an eight-week self-defense class were of little use in helping me out of that situation. I had to use lots of fearless fast talk and a good imagination, and indeed, after a verbal struggle, I did get out of that very bad situation. When one tactic didn't work, I subtly shifted to another. What I learned from this is that we cannot afford to limit our tactical self-defense knowledge nor to lock ourselves into the attacker's area of strength—physical combat. It is necessary that we explore other ways in which we might counter the attacker's script with our own, maintaining as much fearlessness and flexibility as possible in each situation.

Clinging to *Our* Truth

A nonviolent self-defense strategy would be more than noncooperation. It is not just that we would refuse to be a part of the attacker's script (by refusing to play the part of the frightened victim) but also that we would hold tenaciously to our own script, not just physically, but intellectually, emotionally, politically, morally and spiritually. Gandhi's term for nonviolence was "satyagraha" which means "clinging to the truth." If we dared to refuse the attacker's coercive, power-hungry script and held fearlessly to our own, we would be, in effect, clinging to the truth. Our truth is that it is not appropriate to be violated or to violate, that coercion and threat are undesirable modes of interaction. We neither value nor rely on violence such as the attacker uses, and we do not recognize power or authority which stems from violence.

Our truth is complicated. Part of the truth we need to speak is the truth of our rage at the stupidity and brutality to which we are endlessly subjected. Once, in a conversation, Barbara Deming told me of the time she and some other women had been leafletting in front of a movie theater which was showing a "Snuff" film, trying to persuade potential viewers not to support this brutal pornography. She stopped one young man and began to explain to him that in this film a woman was disemboweled for the sexual pleasure of a man. As she talked to the young man she was appalled to see that his face displayed a queer smile, a sneer: he was enjoying the thought of this. She felt intense revulsion, but she continued to talk to him, and then she saw another face take the place of the one she had just seen. This face was horrified at the disemboweling—and perhaps, too, at the fact that he had just been enjoying the thought of it. Barbara said that she told herself at that moment: "I must never forget that men can take pleasure in our torture. I must never forget, either, that the very same men can feel dismay at this; and we can require them to act out of the one feeling rather than the other—if we ourselves can find our equilibrium as we hold the two faces of the truth in mind."

In addition to rage then, part of the truth is that we demand something better than the easy violence to which the attacker resorts. And this, for me, is the hard part of the concept. I come to this reluctantly, as an angry, outraged feminist and not as a disciplined peace activist or seasoned pacifist. It grates on me, this insistence on human worth—our own and the rapist's, as though our lives were somehow linked. It is easier for me to tell the truth of my anger and despair than believe in and demand change from the attacker.

When I was very little I had a vivid, instructive dream in which I was kidnapped and taken to a greasy kitchen. There, a "bad man" threatened to hurt me with a paring knife. I held out my hand and offered to be his friend, believing whole-heartedly that this would make him change. "See," I smiled sweetly, "there's no need for you to hurt me." But just as I said this, he grabbed my hand and peeled the skin off my palm. I remember my blood dripping onto the greasy floor and my absolute shock that goodwill had not protected me.

I know now, more than I could ever have known then, the truth of that nightmare. I can read it every day in the papers, and on hot summer nights when the windows are open, I can hear the screams of my neighbor in the next building being beaten by her husband.

I am one who sees too easily the senseless suffering that engulfs our lives when beauty and happiness are torn from us by threats of war, assault, poverty, hunger, humiliation and other unnecessary inflictions of human cruelty. Yet I understand that it is my passion for life which makes me so alert to its distortions. And what is this passion but a recognition that this world is as much mine as it is the destroyers'. I must continue to demand a world of life-valuing people, not in some post-revolutionary lifetime alone, but today as I walk down the street.

I initially understood nonviolence to be a tactic alone, a way of undermining the physical advantage of the assailant in an attack situation by throwing him psychologically off balance. I believed that tactical nonviolence could provide superior defense skills which would be workable and adaptable by most women. I was inspired by examples of nonviolent strategies used successfully by power-deprived groups of people against weapon-laden oppressors and began to translate these experiences into possible strategies to be applied by women who are usually at a physical disadvantage in confrontations with men.

But in my search for a nonviolent self-defense strategy I seem to have swallowed a strange cake which transforms the familiar into the extraordinary, and have grown like Alice with one arm out the window of a too small house. Now it seems that the tradition of nonviolence can offer not just a workable self-defense tactic but a way of life, because truly I am defending myself every minute I live and breathe in this patriarchal world. What I want, and what I think a nonviolent stance can provide both in confrontations with power-hungry militarists and in the more immediately threatening encounters with power-hungry rapists, is a way to protect my political and spiritual self while I defend my body, a way to say the *whole,* unfragmented truth—that I will not let my life be used to sanction the reliance on violence: I refuse to be a victim *and* I refuse to endorse violence by resorting to it. Nonviolence as a way of life includes a self-defense posture which gives me a way to cling to the whole truth, a way to be consistent about the world I am struggling to create, a way to protect my full, sweet woman's body without having to compromise what I hold most basic and precious about my life when I'm not in an attack situation.

Leah Fritz
Abortion: A Woman's Right to Live

The agonizing debate over abortion which is currently rending the fabric of women's right to autonomy, health and survival rages not only in the United States institutions but within the peace movement as well. Some women and men, who would otherwise align themselves with progressive causes, argue that the value of life, even unborn life, is absolute.

Leah Fritz, author of Thinking Like a Woman *and* Dreamers & Dealers: An Intimate Appraisal of the Women's Movement, *directly addresses the predominantly male-led nonviolent movement coming from the Catholic Left and articulately argues that more violence results by the denial of abortion.*

Offering some background to her essay, Leah wrote: "As a pacifist and a feminist I am shocked by the joining of educated humanitarians like Daniel Berrigan with right-wing factions who disguise a callousness toward women behind the euphemism 'Right-to-Life.'

"To thousands of women of all faiths, recourse to abortion is an act of responsibility. In the context of the real world, abortion is a life-saving procedure most often resorted to by mothers of living children who must limit the size of their families in order to provide for them. But there are many other valid life-sustaining and life-enhancing reasons to end an unwanted pregnancy—chief among them that the woman involved does not want to be pregnant. The random accident of union between sperm and egg often occurs under unholy conditions, namely rape, incest, and seduction. What piety demands the bringing to fruition of every devil's homunculus?

"It is insufferable for men whose brothers are responsible for all but the smallest fraction of violent crimes—both public and private—to presume to dictate morality to women. It is categorically immoral for men to play on the conditioned selflessness of women by urging them to give greater consideration to the "viability" of embryos than to their own valuable lives and futures. This is seduction and betrayal of mythical proportions.

"No amount of showy martyrdom in opposition to mere governmental imperialism abroad will affect the universal change of consciousness which the Gospel of Love requires to make peace on earth a reality. I am profoundly convinced that, while the realization of present feminist aspirations may not inevitably bring world peace, there is no chance for peace until women are fully empowered to determine

the uses of their own bodies, minds, and souls, and that men can call themselves pacifists only when they have resigned all physical, social, economic and moral control over women.

"As Florynce Kennedy once put it, 'If men became pregnant, abortion would be a sacrament.' In this spirit I wrote the following essay."

The question surrounding abortion is not whether it is a good or a fine thing to have. It is whether abortions should remain legal. To help decide, I will reminisce with you about what things were like before the right to choose abortion was the law of the land.

I'll start off soft.

There was the fiction we all read. The young woman who ruined a man's life by trapping him into marriage because she became pregnant. She waited breathlessly to see if he would decide to do the "honorable thing." He was an artist or a scientist with his whole life before him, or he was a politician, already married. She, of course, did not have her whole life before her. That was understood.

A Place in the Sun. Oh how we pitied Montgomery Clift, in that movie of the fifties, caught between the allure of rich, glamorous, virginal Elizabeth Taylor and the momentary madness that could have forced him into the arms of poor, lumpy Shelley Winters forever! Of course he drowned her. What else could he do? Marriage to her would have *ruined his future*.

The idea that a woman might have an independent future—that she had the right to plan her own life, above and beyond and perhaps including marriage and the family, just like a man; that she could rise in the world on her own two feet, not on her back—did not exist on a large scale until legal, safe abortions became a reality as back-up for iffy birth-control devices. Before that, a woman had no future or present of her own—and if she knew what was good for her, she avoided having a *past*. For men rose and women fell.

A man was expected to enjoy sex from an early age without consequences, whether or not he married. Commercial facilities were provided for him, and although not usually legal, only the prostitute was subject to arrest. A middle-class man postponed marriage until he had established a career. Acknowledging "illegitimate" children was an option for him. However young she was, the full onus of responsibility and guilt fell upon the "unwed mother."

A woman tried to get married as young as possible, not for any sexual pleasure she knew about nor because she necessarily looked forward to having children (which might happen too often, be painful, and even cause her own death), but because the longer she remained single, the less likely she was to make a good "match"—meaning a man with money and position. Before thirty, she was over the hill. After thirty, he began to climb. With their parents' blessings, girls in their teens were wed to men in their forties. For "protection." Have the latter-day moralists forgotten this?

I'll get louder.

It is rumored that some 10,000 women (and their 10,000 foetuses and all the children they might want to have in the future) used to die annually in illegal abortions. Most of these women were married. Some were unmarried kids. Some had been raped. No small number by their own fathers, step-fathers, brothers, and uncles. Some simply fell in love and believed... oh, how we used to believe! Some had no sex education at all, not at home, not at school (except for on-the-job training). Some were prostitutes, kidnapped or drugged or sweet-talked into the life.

Some (exceptionally) had real lives before them, just like men, that would be ruined by early parental responsibility. Some (daringly) had planned to be writers, doctors, artists, politicians...just like men. Some (wickedly) had affairs ouside of marriage, just like men. Some were menopausal, their children grown, grandchildren on the way. Some were tired. Some simply never wanted to be pregnant or have children, but birth-control methods failed them. Some were Roman Catholic—many were Roman Catholic—and their husbands wouldn't allow them to use birth control, even after six or seven children. Some, of every denomination, of every race and class, had husbands who beat them every time they got pregnant, and beat their children, too. Some had husbands who strayed.

Some were afraid of the pain of giving birth or of dying in the delivery room. (Yes, that still happens.) Some were afraid to give the baby up, not knowing to whom, and acted on an animal instinct to kill what cannot be protected. Some were simply scared to tell their folks, because papa might beat them to death.

Some were utterly frivolous. Just like men.

In a short-story class I took after my own children (the ones I wanted more than anything to have, the ones born years after my own abortion saved me to be a good mother when I was ready) were born, a young Black woman who had struggled for years to be the first college graduate in her family wrote about two abortions she had performed on herself—one by coat-hanger, one by a poisonous pill. Fortunately, she had landed in the hospital in time to save her life. She is still single, voluntarily childless, and a full professor. Would it be blasphemy to praise the Lord?

Legal abortion is not about killing foetuses. It's about saving women's lives. It's about making it possible for women to look forward to futures they, themselves, choose; about saving the children they already have, or might want to have later. Especially, though, it means putting a real decision about whether or not—and if so, when—to assume full responsibility over the life of another into the hands which will carry the burden. It's saying "I trust you" to women as the ultimate authorities they should be over procreation.

One more story out of the past: a religious friend of mind was married to a man equally devout, and they had four children. The man was one of those periodic drunkards who had trouble earning a living, and occasionally beat her, and twice threatened her life. She and her children lived in fear, and from hand to mouth.

Once when he threatened her she called a policeman and he said since her husband had only threatened, he couldn't be arrested. Then she called a priest and he said since there really wasn't anything he could do, he didn't want to embarrass the family in front of the neighbors by turning up at their door. Then she called a psychiatrist, and he said she should urge her husband to make an appointment with him, the next day. She locked herself in a room with her four children. They waited out the night until his drunken rage passed.

One day over coffee she said to me, "I think I'm pregnant again, and if I am, I'm going to have an abortion if it kills me. The church wants me to have children, but will it feed them?

I didn't see her for some time and don't know if her diagnosis was correct, and if so, what she did about it. But I ran into her ten years later, when her children had grown enough so that she could take a full-time job and leave her husband. She still only had four children. I don't know how many pregnancies she had been forced to endure in the interim, how many she was brave and sensible enough to terminate, all secretly, all illegally, all in shame and fear and dread.

Mother Mary, what did You say when she came to You, only You, to confess? Did Your tears fall? Did You say that the fact that she still lived, still protected, nurtured, and supported the children she had was a miracle? Did You say that she behaved with honor? Did You bless her?

How did You feel when nine million witches were burned in Your holy name? How did You feel when ten thousand pregnant women a year were butchered in illegal abortions in the name of Your morality?

Gentle Jesus, are women's lives and futures what we are to render unto Caesar?

JEB

Women's Liberation Zap Action Brigade, April 23, 1981, interrupts the one-sided Senate Sub-Committee hearings on the "Human Life Statute," an anti-abortion bill designed to establish fetal personhood.

Rachel Bedard
Re-entering Complexity

From her journey into lesbian separatism to her astonished discovery that she loved a man, Rachel found support for her transition in the community of nonviolent feminists. Still valuing her time as a separatist, Rachel now greets the complexity involved in a heterosexual feminist identity. She writes, "I have never been so terrified to write about my life. The letter itself explains why. There has been a great deal of pain and uncertainty about abandoning separatism for a different expression of feminism. There has also been negative feedback. I have had nightmare after nightmare writing this. And thank you for giving me the chance to have them! I have known for a couple of years that this whole experience needed out, but I never had the incentive to pull it writhing and resisting into the light of day. Now maybe I can go on to something else."

Rachel is a medical and nursing books editor at J.B. Lippincott Company in Philadelphia. She lived in a comunity of nonviolent social change activists (the Life Center of Movement for a New Society) from 1973 until 1979 and was active in outreach and feminist collectives. She is currently in a Dream Analysis Group of Life Center women.

Dear Pam,

Thanks for your request to write something for an anthology on "the revolutionary connection" between feminism and nonviolence. I've been reading and rereading the list of suggestions you offered. I don't know that any of them really grabs me. I've written about communities till I'm blue in the face and about old patriarchal families' faults as well. I've been enraged by the pervasiveness of sexism and have gotten further and further into a position of not wanting anything to do with men, whom I used to call those "life-sucking inadequates."

I got *so* far into that stance once that I decided just to cut off from men "for good." That lasted about 18 months, but those months were very informative. Subtly, I began to shift my hopes and needs onto the women who were close to me and who were also angry feminists. *We* understood, *we* were justified in our thinking. Therefore, I reasoned, *we* would give me everything I wanted.

I suffered some of my most illuminating disappointments in the heart of radical feminism. I kept expecting that my basic needs (not having been met at various moments in my childhood) would now be simply and fully satiated. I craved encouragement? Well, surely my lover would be the Toklas to my Gertrude Stein and would suffer anything for the privilege of typing my manuscripts. I wanted support financially? She would build me a tower and furnish it in solitude and leather for me to work in. Was it attention I needed? Well, soon now (magically) women would read and love my stories and knock at the door for more. Basically, I came to believe that men couldn't understand any of my reality and women, *because* they were women, should understand it all.

In the article you sent me, Barbara Ehrenreich says that, on the way to socialist feminism, "'theory' became a method of evading any contradictions or tensions."[1] For me, feminist theorizing, during this period of separatism, was just that. I believed passionately in women's cause—I still do—but I used my rage as a shield against contradiction. I coped with the guilt I felt in ending a troubled marriage by claiming that the oppression of women was the original oppression, and by insisting that men work out their feelings with other men. I held male friends at arm's length and attached myself to the woman with whom I'd made this mental odyssey who was just as militant as myself.

I moved into a separatist house with tremendous expectations of feminist support and nurturance. But within weeks we were divided over everything from dinner hour to cats to who owned which soap in the bathroom. We expected too much of one another, and what we had envisioned as at least a two-year community very soon began to break up. Likewise, the relationship with my woman friend was showing signs of wear when she returned to her home country that winter.

We corresponded, and she suggested I join her in New Zealand and travel west across Indonesia, the Near East and Europe with her. The idea allowed me to build a castle of hope on the very shaky ground of our relationship. I willed her to fall madly in love with me.

Willing it made no difference when I joined her in New Zealand. She felt ambivalent about my presence and held me steadily away, but she was my only support, so I kept hoping. I joined the lesbian feminist community whose language and literature were stridently anti-men. I could feel included in their rage when they chastised revisionist women, but when they blasted "imperialist Americans" I felt helplessly shut out. Blanket judgment seemed unjust to me. It made me see that condemning people because of their birth and indoctrination was a way of side-stepping the issue. It was easier not to communicate; the lines were clearer, simpler. But without communication, nothing changed. "Imperialist" was a statement of fear, not of power.

In the midst of this confusion I found a friend, a man. His interests lay chiefly in not harming. A week in a butchery had made him a vegetarian. Since then, he'd been working toward a nonexploitative diet, concentrating more and more on what he could raise himself and what fell naturally from tree or vine. While the lesbian contingent screamed at "fuckin' wankers" (the New Zealand version of "pricks") he meditated and fixed his food and shared ideas about how to live, how to heat with solar and thermal power, how not to disturb the land, birds, animals, plants.

Who did the most harm or good? I don't know. Marching at an abortion rally in Wellington, the capital, gave me a sense of the worldwide struggle to make woman legally and rightfully her own boss. But Mick gave me something else: acceptance. He didn't ask. He didn't take. He *was* and he allowed me to *be*. He effortlessly and unintentionally shattered my image of man-as-enemy.

Such an image can never be nonviolent, and although I hold feminism dear to my heart, I can no longer suggest that we women innately or by conditioning "have it all" over men. Some of the people who have taught me the most—about how to reach behind the mask and touch the human heart—are men. The person who has best been able to step through *my* masks and help me to face my contradictions is also a man. And isn't that nonviolence—that looking-through to the heart, that belief in the other's goodness and courage?

Here is the crux of my dilemma. I find myself, by my own past definition, "in complicity" with men and "betraying all women" because I am in a committed relationship with a man. ("Your marriage was made in heaven," says a male friend of mine. "Well, maybe," I respond, "but it is worked out here on earth!")

I would not trade my experience as a separatist for nirvana. It was a challenging and exciting time, and it was good for me to push past all my limits. Once I knew that I (not some man) was determining the course of my life, that there are no simple solutions, and that women, too, have *human* problems, I could begin to move back to the personal from the political.

Politics had moved me further than my feelings could, in the long run, support: beyond the ties of flesh, of class, of nonviolence. To be "true" in the way separatists mean the term was to reject brothers, father, and good male friends; never to think of sharing the growth of a child with a man; to listen with total respect only to people like myself.

And yet, to move away from separatism was terrifying. Hadn't I been enraged that women accompanied by men could walk in relative safety down the street at night, while women-identified-women and any woman alone were in constant danger of being victimized? Hadn't I stressed women's need for space in which to grow unhampered by established (male) ways of thinking? Wasn't I now at fault for feeling a little safer on the street, for considering relationships with men despite what I knew about the patriarchy?

There were women waiting for me to return to the separatist community after I came back from travelling, but I didn't. I joined a mixed household, and after a few months I became close to a gentle, honest, persistent man.

Naturally, word spread. When I leafleted the movie *Windows* (a film that maligns lesbian relationships), I saw a woman who had stayed briefly at my women's house the year before. She didn't seem to recognize me, so I walked up to her and said, "Hi! I'm Rachel; don't you remember me?" She answered, "Yes, I know who you are," and turned away. Hers was not the only rebuff I got from separatist women.

These rebukes only made my transition harder. I already had to fight my own guilt for not being satisfied with an all-women's culture. Now I had to wonder whether I was to be written off or ostracized by friends as well.

This is where my nonviolent feminist friends came in. Some of them are separatists, and many of them looked on my actions with concern. They wanted to know if getting involved with this man was part of a pendulum swing, and if so where I would finally touch down. They cautioned me to move slowly and helped me through two years of self-doubt. ("How *can* I be involved with a man? There must be something wrong with me. It can't be healthy. But I don't want this warmth and sharing to end.") In the end it was clear that the relationship was a good one, and these friends demonstrated support for and belief in me the whole time. They never thought that if I married I'd stop being a feminist, even though *I* worried about it constantly. They could see me more clearly than I saw myself, because they looked at the whole of me, not just at one role.

Sisterhood works in powerful, nurturing ways. So does nonviolence. Sisterhood gives me the courage to reject limitations that are imposed on me because I'm a woman. Nonviolence gives me the patience to understand others and to reach past their masks. Both feminism and nonviolence are strong, and together they can build a force that each alone cannot. Together they can provide a legitimate road into women's-space and, for those who choose, a way back out to the complexities of heterosexuality. Roadblocks of "betrayal" or "complicity" prevent women's space from becoming a solid alternative within nonviolent groups and damage the trust among feminists. They need not exist, because women like myself (and there are many of us) do not abandon feminism; we carry it deep in our hearts.

Thanks again for letting me share with you.

Rachel Bedard

Dorothy Marder

The Bread and Puppet Theatre presents a grim portrayal of women in war at an anti-war rally in support of the Harrisburg 8, April, 1972.

Jay Bird
. . . And Brings Peace

Janine Bell, whose writings "come from and are shared through 'Jay Bird,'" wrote this poem of woman-wisdom and transforming love, out of her own "peace-loving orientation." She writes that her urgings toward creative expression have increased and developed through an evolving spirituality and identification with the supreme life force, and cites as inspiration Ntozake Shange's for colored girls who have considered suicide/when the rainbow is enuf.

Janine, originally from North Carolina, now lives in Virginia with her husband (a musician), where she works in human relations and on issues of fair housing. She is a member of the National Association of Human Rights Workers. In addition to writing poetry, she expresses herself through Afrikan dance, drumming and the visual arts.

Shh . . . a whisper.
Soft sound but
Oh! so clear
She speaks.

Daily rhythms
Stop, listen
Instinctively
To be nurtured;

My Mother.
My Sister.
My Self:
A Divine Woman.

She entered
The universe and
Made it whole:
Spiritual wisdom.

"Damn!" he said,
"Spirit, be gone!
Fulfill only my
violent needs:

Cook and clean,
Don't be seen;
And lie, and love
Me only."

He sleeps.
Truth flows
From his lips,
"Violence masks my
Weakness.
Violence hides and
Creates my shame."

A flicker of light...
A tear? A smile?
She knows and brings
Peace.

Sue Dove Gambill
The Passive Violence of Noninvolvement and Our Work of Accountability

Thirty-eight people heard Kitty Genovese scream. Some lifted their window shades and saw her being stabbed. Not one called the police or offered any sort of assistance. When asked why they hadn't intervened, some witnesses explained they had assumed it was a lover's quarrel. Other witnesses had made other assumptions.

Assumptions let us off the hook. In the supermarket a harried woman slaps a child a couple times. Do we intervene or do we look the other way assuming that the woman is the mother and further assuming that a parent has the right to discipline her own child in the manner she deems necessary?

The experts have given us many explanatory phrases for passive noninvolvement. We hear about "depersonalization" and "the big city syndrome" or "the good German syndrome." Ministers preach about the Good Samaritan and the solid citizens of yore who were afraid to get involved; major networks air reports on the "detached" Americans.

In this essay, Sue Dove Gambill guides our attention to the passive violence of those familiar, awkward situations we face in our every day lives, which, she says, are of special concern to women who must battle with the expectation of passivity. In the women's community, as elsewhere, manipulation and gossip are often the misguided results of our own failure to directly address our concerns and these usually hurt the individuals involved and debilitate the community as a whole. Sue urges us to risk the "work of accountability" and offers conflict resolution skills and mediation as first aid for community conflicts and antidotes for noninvolvement.

Sue works at The Women's Writer's Center in Cazenovia, New York and has had fiction, poetry, and essays published in various magazines and newspapers.

Violence is often defined as physical and psychological assault, an act of aggression by a person or group against another. However there is another more subtle form of violence that emerges when we passively refuse to engage in a situation that asks for our involvement.

With the fierce individualism this society endorses, we've

learned that there are certain wide boundaries in social interactions which we aren't supposed to cross. Therefore, if we are eating dinner in a restaurant and witness two people in an abusive argument, our impulse is not to intervene because "it is not our business." If such abuse takes place in an apartment next door, the boundaries become even stronger because those four walls are considered personal territory. Similar restrictions exist among friends when we talk about our neighbors who are in economic hardship or who abuse alcohol or who are involved in damaging relationships while isolating them from support. We are afraid of "interfering," and this fear creates situations of paralysis and isolation.

As women, we have grown up in a culture that constantly bombards us with messages that fuel our fears: "we are not capable," "we lack strength," "the issues of our lives are not important." Sometimes we choose invisibility rather than risk confronting these barriers and our own insecurities.

Another response to these debilitating messages is that women have often learned to manipulate people and situations in order to have some control. The danger is that the manipulation will move out of the realm of survival (in our relations with those in power) and become part of the dynamics within our own lives. For example, when we know about a difficult situation, like an argument between friends, and we decide not to speak about it directly to them, we can do more damage by indirectly fueling and manipulating the conflict with gossip.[1] It seems much easier to talk to a third party, particularly when we present only our view of the story. A story passed along two or three times begins to distort just like the circle telephone game we played as children. Gossip is a way not to be direct. It can represent fear of conflict and confrontation, be a means to distort reality, be used to play power off against each other, as well as become an excuse for not taking creative responsibility in a situation where it is feasible and necessary to do so. Severe damage to women bonding, the feminist movement and feminist institutions is often initiated by women who will not take the risk of being direct.

My own experiences with indirectness and passive violence have occurred in many different types of groups. The example I use here took place while I was working in a women's studies program. I had been in the position of administrative assistant for one year when the program began to expand and Donna,[2] a new faculty member, was hired. Before her arrival the quality of my work was never questioned; after she began teaching, Donna and the program coordinator, Lucille, called a meeting with me.

Donna charged that I was not doing my work and that I was antagonistic. Lucille didn't seem to offer me support. I felt betrayed and under attack. I felt I was being professionally challenged because of a conflict of personal feelings which had never even been shared with me. The worst part was there existed no previously established avenue to work through the conflict. When I tried to suggest ways for mediation, Donna at first refused my suggestions. Conflict resolution had not been used in that community and so there was a lack of understanding of how to help us effectively struggle through our differences.

By the time we were able to begin mediation there was a buildup of emotionally charged situations. Not only did we have to work through our conflicts, but we had to try to figure out procedures for mediation. Also, gossip among women in the community added to the conflict instead of helping to resolve it. This made our work more difficult, and I never felt completely resolved in the situation. Nine months later I left the job. There were many different reasons for my departure, but among them the most important was that the work environment had changed for me. There was no longer an openness I could trust, and I felt that several women had changed their perceptions of both Donna and me by "taking sides."

The proportions to which this conflict developed were not necessary; the damages to me personally were painful. I have since learned that other women were also affected in adverse ways. The insidious thing about gossip and passive violence is that they constantly multiply upon themselves like cancer.

To break through this violence it is necessary to learn the simple skills useful for working through our differences; those new skills which will facilitate directness, honesty, commitment, collective support, and situations which challenge us to realize our fullest capabilities. Also, we need to develop new perspectives and attitudes because in the U.S., a country built upon the philosophy of competition and free enterprise, disagreement is frequently used as a weapon against a competitor, instead of being an avenue through which to learn and grow.

Mediation: First Aid For Community Conflict

An important realization to build into our lives is that it is okay, even desirable, to be concerned about each other and to involve ourselves in that concern. One way that can be done is through the use of mediation. I have watched and participated in situations when women used mediation to work through conflicts about friendships, land, jealousies, work, etc. In two particular communities with which I am familiar, mediation has been in use for several years, the women have had more and more practice with its use, and it has become an integral part of their communities, making it easier to turn for help and to offer it when it's necessary.

Mediation, basically, involves one or more women facilitating communication between those who are in conflict. The role of a mediator is to help those in conflict be able to speak and listen, to give support, to help bring out all perspectives, and to lessen defenses so communication can begin to open. This creates a situation in which problems are not thrown on the shoulders of an isolated few.

It's not necessary to wait for problems in order to begin learning about its use. If you want to work with mediation and develop the skills of conflict resolution, contact other women in your community to begin exploration. Consider this a first aid course in community involvement. If the group can start trying out new skills in a calm, learning environment, then there will be a base of support and experience to use in those difficult/complex times. (For some people it might be too frightening to try out something new in the middle of a conflict.[3])

In the practice meetings, women can volunteer situations they want to work on in their lives and/or role play a conflict and begin discussing all the different ways in which the group, or individuals, could help the person(s) work through the difficulty. In this way the participants will see what resources and knowledge are already available and which areas need to be developed. In addition to books, other resources in the community include women with experiences in group dynamics, co-counseling, consensus decision-making and crisis intervention.

If mediation had already been an established tool in the women's studies program I described earlier, I think it would have been used more effectively. There still would have been difficult feelings of jealousy, fear, anger, etc. However, by honestly confronting each other face-to-face, within a supportive environment, those feelings can propel us into change instead of stagnation.

What I am talking about is doing the "work of accountability." It is vitally important that we be accountable among ourselves. This is one of the strong, radical and challenging bonds we can build in the midst of a culture that teaches various forms of avoidance: we've been taught to shrug our shoulders, shut our eyes, walk away, be blasé. It isn't an easy task. It requires time, work and commitment to create new ways of working together which break through the passive violence of noninvolvement. It requires moving past the defense of our small personal territory or clique, letting go of the manipulation with which we build our defenses, and opening to challenges which can help our creative involvement in the world.

Dorothy Marder

Women's Pentagon Action (WPA), Nov., 1980

Joan Baez
Message to the Next Civilization

Joan Baez. We all know her name. She's the one in the spotlight and on album covers and inside People *magazine. Her voice, like her face, is that of an old friend, offering comfort, urging action, leading celebration.*

Joan wasn't always a star. As the dark-skinned daughter of a Scottish-American mother and a Mexican-American father, she faced the prejudice and racial slurs that come with her color in the U.S. Becoming a star merely transformed her troubles. Her voice is called clear and sweet by most people, but her politics are called un-American by some because she insists on working for peace and human rights, and she advocates radical nonviolence.

In 1965, with Ira Sandperl, Joan established the Institute for the Study of Nonviolence. Since then she has sung for, marched with, been jailed with and helped organize activists working on civil rights, anti-war, anti-nuke, rights for farm workers, prisoner rights, draft card protests, Amnesty International, gay rights. Like many of us she has participated in candlelight vigils, has gone to jail. Unlike most of us, she has had access to world travel, publicity, and money. In 1979 she formed a group called Humanitas International Human Rights Committee which is dedicated to fighting human rights violations whenever and wherever they occur. Since that time much of her work has focused on the plight of Southeast Asian refugees and Latin American victims of human rights violations.

Dear Gabe:

I thought I would write my "Message to the Next Civilization" in a letter to you. It is partly my love for you which gives me the determination to fight against the most unreasonable odds for a world in which we have eliminated organized violence as a way of "solving" national and international problems. . . because if we don't at least partially accomplish this goal, my vision of the future is too crowded with fear to paint you pictures of it.

I am not such a dreamer, dear Gabe, that I think *all* violence will disappear from the earth and everyone will love one another. I have already told you that I don't give a damn if you choose to fist fight with some kid who has made you angry, or if you play with cap guns, plastic soldiers and little green tanks. That is not the kind of violence I am talking about.

I am talking about the strange phenomena called "war," "defense" and "armed revolution." The strange thing is that there is only one single thing which all "enemies" seem to agree upon: that they should prove their fight is right by killing the guys on the other side. Everyone except a few sane people thinks it is ok to kill the "bad guys." I don't think it is ok to kill *anybody.*

The way governments set things up, they have chosen the young and healthy and lovely, and most often the poor, to do the killing for the older men and women, while they sit safely behind desks and point to areas on maps and make phone calls and say how brave the young people were when they got blown up for their country.

Go and look up *optimist* in your dictionary, Gabe. I am not one. To be an optimist in a world like ours, full of armies and bombs and fear and hatred, is to be a ninny. But we know that people have a good and loving and kind side to them—and I for one will spend the rest of my life trying to organize those qualities in people and do things the way in which Martin Luther King, Jr., and Mahatma Gandhi did them.

Love,

Mom

Dorothy Marder

Joined by scarves, women circle the Pentagon and read the Unity Statement, WPA, 1980.

Excerpts from the Women's Pentagon Action Unity Statement

For two years we have gathered at the Pentagon because we fear for our lives. We still fear for the life of this planet, our Earth, and the life of the children who are our human future. . .

We came to mourn and rage and defy the Pentagon because it is the workplace of the imperial power which threatens us all. Every day while we work, study, love, the colonels and generals who are planning our annihilation walk calmly in and out the doors of its five sides. They have accumulated over 30,000 nuclear bombs at the rate of three to six bombs every day. . .

We are in the hands of men whose power and wealth have separated them from the reality of daily life and from the imagination. We are right to be afraid.

At the same time our cities are in ruins, bankrupt; they suffer the devastation of war. Hospitals are closed, our schools deprived of books and teachers. Our Black and Latino youth are without decent work. They will be forced, drafted to become the cannon fodder for the very power that oppresses them. Whatever help the poor receive is cut or withdrawn to feed the Pentagon which needs about $500,000,000 a day for its murderous health. . .

We women are gathering because life on the precipice is intolerable. . .

We understand all is connectedness. The earth nourishes us as we with our bodies will eventually feed it. Through us, our mothers connected the human past to the human future. We know the life and work of animals and plants in seeding, reseeding and in fact simply inhabiting this planet. . .

With that sense, that ecological right, we oppose the financial connections between the Pentagon and the multinational corporations and banks that the Pentagon serves. . .

We know there is a healthy sensible loving way to live and we intend to live that way in our neighborhoods and our farms in these United States, and among our sisters and brothers in all the countries of the world.

—A collectively written working statement, April, 1982.

CHRONOLOGY

Here is a chronology of events mentioned in this book. It is not meant as a complete chronology of events relating to either feminism or nonviolence, but should serve as an aid in increasing our historical perspective on their interrelation over the last two centuries. Compiled by David Albert

ca 1600 - Iroquois women organize a successful "Lysistrata" action, refusing sex or childbearing until unregulated warfare ceases.

1659 - Mary Dyer hanged on Boston Commons for refusing to renounce Quaker practices.

1792 - Publication of Mary Wollstonecraft's *Vindication of the Rights of Women.*

1830s - Sarah and Angelina Grimké, Quaker daughters of a slave-owner in Charleston, South Carolina, begin a lifetime of speaking out against slavery.

1833 - Lucretia Mott helps organize Philadelphia Female Anti-Slavery Society.

1838 - New England Non-Resistance Society formed.

1838 - First Annual Convention of Anti-Slavery Women meets in Pennsylvania Hall in Philadelphia. With tacit permission of Mayor and police, mob attacks the hall, burning it to the ground.

1848 - Seneca Falls Declaration of the Rights of Women.

1852 - Susan B. Anthony organizes first open women's temperance society.

1853 - New York Women's Rights Convention. Speakers include Sojourner Truth, Lucy Stone, Ernestine Rose, Susan B. Anthony, Charles Burleigh, William Lloyd Garrison, and Lucretia Mott.

ca 1865 - Sojourner Truth successfully sues a streetcar conductor who had refused service to Black passengers.

1872 - Susan B. Anthony and fifteen other women vote illegally in Rochester, New York.

1876 - National Women's Suffrage Association interrupts proceedings of Centennial Celebration of Independence Hall in Philadelphia to present Declaration of the Rights of Women.

1884 - Ida B. Wells, a Black women from Memphis, brings suit against Chesapeake, Ohio and Southwestern Railroad after being thrown off train for refusing to move from a first class coach to a car reserved for Blacks.

1892 - Ida B. Wells initiates anti-lynching campaign among Black people in Memphis, Tennessee.

1893 - Publication of Lois Waisbrooker's novel *A Sex Revolution,* in which men agree to change roles with women for fifty years as a social experiment, the object being to abolish war.

1909 - American Natalie Clifford Barney, one of the first open lesbians in modern times, opens literary salon in Paris.

1912 - Women organize textile mills' strike in Lawrence, Massachusetts, formulate slogan, "We want Bread and Roses too!"

1914 - National Women's Suffrage Association forbids Ida B. Wells to participate in national suffrage demonstration in Washington, D.C. lest she antagonize Southern white women; she ignores prohibition.

1915 - Founding of Women's International League for Peace and Freedom at the Hague, Netherlands. Jane Addams chosen as first President.

1915 - Charlotte Perkins Gilman publishes *Herland,* a feminist utopian novel.

1917 - Jeannette Rankin votes against U.S. entry into World War I.

1923 - Three women - Jesse Wallace Hughan, Tracy Mygatt and Frances Witherspoon - found War Resisters League.

1930 - Mohandas Gandhi leads Dandi Salt March. Sarojini Naidu, a women Indian poet, leads nonviolent "raid" on Dharasala Salt Works, considered the turning point in the Indian Independence struggle.

1930 - Texas Suffragist Jesse Daniel Ames, perceiving the links between racial violence and attitudes toward women, launches a white women's campaign against the lynching of Black men.

1933 - Dorothy Day and Peter Maurin found Catholic Worker movement.

1936 - Margaret Sanger visits Mohandas Gandhi in India.

1938 - Virginia Woolf publishes *Three Guineas.*

1941 - Jeannette Rankin votes against U.S. entry into World War II.

1942 - Congress of Racial Equality (CORE) founded in Chicago.

1947 - First Journey of Reconciliation, sponsored by CORE and the Fellowship of Reconciliation (FOR), is held, designed to test compliance with Supreme Court ruling barring segregation in interstate travel.

1948 - Organizing conference of Peacemakers.

1955 - Rosa Parks refuses to move to the back of the bus, setting off Montgomery (Alabama) Bus Boycott. Dr. Martin Luther King, Jr. emerges as spokesperson for nonviolent action for civil rights.

1956 - Southern Christian Leadership Conference founded.

1958 - Barbara and Earl Reynolds sail their boat the Phoenix into nuclear testing range following a similar action by Albert Bigelow and George Willoughby.

1959 - Four students from North Carolina A. & T. sit in at a Woolworth lunch counter in downtown Greensboro.

1959 - Marj Swann climbs fence at Omaha Missile Base in protest against nuclear policies.

1960 - 1000 Quakers ring Pentagon in vigil for peace. Committee for Nonviolent Action (CNVA) commits civil disobedience against launching of nuclear submarines.

1960 - Martha Tranquilli, a nurse, serves a year in prison for refusing to pay federal war taxes.

1960-61 - CNVA organizes San Francisco-to-Moscow Walk advocating unilateral disarmament.

1961 - Women Strike for Peace begins as a one day strike by "housewives and mothers" against the nuclear arms race.

1961 - "Freedom Rides" take place through the South.

1962 - Cathy Cade and Howard Zinn hold sit-in for voting rights in Georgia legislature.

1962 - Disarmament walks organized from Canada to Mexico.

1962 - Fannie Lou Hamer, a Black sharecropper, attempts to register to vote in Indianola (Sunflower County), Mississippi; is asked to copy and "interpret" the Mississippi constitution.

1963 - Publication of Betty Friedan's *The Feminine Mystique.*

1964 - "Freedom Summer" in Mississippi.

1964 - Black women hold a half-serious, half-joking sit-in protest in Atlanta office of Student Nonviolent Coordinating Committee (SNCC) against their relegation to typing and clerical duties and lack of public leadership roles for Black women.

1966 - Publication of Barbara Deming's *Prison Notes. Revolution and Equilibrium* follows in 1971 and *We Cannot Live Without Our Lives* in 1974.

1968 - Integrated delegation of the Mississippi Freedom Democratic Party, under leadership of Fannie Lou Hamer and others, seated at Democratic National Convention in Chicago.

1969 - Women Against Daddy Warbucks partially destroy draft files at thirteen draft boards in Manhattan.

1970 - Publication of Kate Millett's *Sexual Politics.*

1970 - The Freedom Farm Cooperative, founded by Fannie Lou Hamer, opens to feed 1,500 Black and white people from 40 acres of land.

1971 - Founding of Movement for a New Society (MNS) and the Philadelphia Life Center as model for collective working and living anti-sexist organization committed to nonviolent revolutionary struggle.

1972 - People's Blockades attempt to prevent bomb shipments to Viet Nam.

1975 - Pacific Life Community organized to conduct nonviolent campaign against the Trident submarine, founded in Seattle, Washington, and Vancouver, Canada.

1977 - First National Conference of Women for Racial and Economic Equality.

1978 - Jane Meyerding and Betty Johana commit civil disobedience in the Seattle office of Save Our Moral Ethics, a group working to deny the civil rights of lesbians and gay men.

1979 - Wall Street Action: thousands attempt a human blockade to prevent operation of the New York Stock Exchange in protest against corporate investment in nuclear power and nuclear weapons.

1980 - Spinsters, an affinity group of women-identified-women, spins a symbolic web of color in support of occupation of the Vermont Yankee Nuclear Power Plant.

1980 - Women's Pentagon Action: civil disobedience against the Pentagon, the seat of U.S. military power and a symbol of patriarchal oppression.

1981 - The Women's Liberation Zap Action Brigade interrupts the one-sided Senate Sub-Committee hearings on an anti-abortion bill.

1981 - Second Women's Pentagon Action. Women weave a web around the Pentagon.

FOOTNOTES

Notes: Introduction

1. Barbara Deming, "On Revolution and Equilibrium" in *Revolution and Equilibrium* (New York: Grossman Publishers, 1971), p. 204.

2. Leah Fritz, *Thinking Like a Woman* (Rifton, New York: Win Books, 1975), p. 119.

3. Barbara Deming, "Women's Consciousness" in *We Cannot Live Without Our Lives* (New York: Grossman Publishers, Viking Press, 1974), p. 172.

Notes: Meyerding

1. Recommended reading: Barbara Ehrenreich and Deirdre English, *For Her Own Good: 150 Years of the Experts' Advice to Women* (New York: Anchor Press/Doubleday, 1979).

Notes: Warnock

1. Laura Lederer, ed., *Take Back the Night: Women on Pornography* (New York: William Morrow & Co., 1980).

2. Andrea Dworkin, "Remembering the Witches," *WIN Magazine,* 1975.

3. Susan Griffin, *RAPE: The Power of Consciousness* (New York: Harper & Row, 1979).

4. Taken from Adrienne Rich's article in *Take Back the Night,* ibid.

5. One and a half million children under sixteen are also used annually in commercial sex, including prostitution and pornography, according to the *Los Angeles Times.*

6. Quoted in Marc Feigen Fasteau's, *The Male Machine* (New York: McGraw-Hill, 1974).

7. Hating women

8. Fear or loathing of homosexuality

9. Anne Koedt, Ellen Levine and Anita Rapone, eds. "The Fourth World Manifesto," *Radical Feminism,* (Quadrangle, 1973).

10. I capitalize "Patriarchy" here and elsewhere, not in deferenc‿, but to mock the Patriarchal tradition of self-aggrandizement.

11. Adrienne Rich, *Of Woman Born* (New York: Bantam, 1976).

12. The word "man" comes from the Indo-European base "to think," and is akin to the Latin, "mens," meaning "mind." "Woman," on the other hand, means "womb of man," and "female," "the one who suckles." Make no mistake that the incorporation of the male in these words was ever meant to imply

that women could have wombs, suckle *and* think. No, according to Patriarchy, intellect is the domain of men, and men alone; women are mothers, mere matter, as the Latin root "mater" indicates.

13. I use the term "man" here in its Patriarchally-socialized, rather than biological, sense. Just as it is difficult for whites to reject all the privileges associated with race, it is difficult for men to change their behavior patterns and ways of thinking. Indeed, all too often the former is done without the latter. While there are certainly men who are to be commended for attempting to undo dominating behavior and reject male privileges, it is an infrequent enough occurrence that I still use the term "male" in its socialized form. It has been my experience that men who demand that the exceptions be noted every time are, rather than showing their sensitivity, all too often using the charge as a defense mechanism to deflect substantive feminist criticism thereby actually revealing their need for further consciousness raising.

14. Nina Swaim and Susan Koen, *A Handbook for Women on the Nuclear Mentality* (Norwich, VT: Women Against Nuclear Destruction, 1980).

15. In India, the rite of sutee, or *widow burning,* was openly practiced until banned in 1823. Still the practice continues disguised as "suicide." For further reading, see Mary Daly's *Gyn/Ecology.*

16. See Phyllis Chesler's *Women and Madness.*

Notes: Freeney-Harding

1. *Crusade for Justice: The Autobiography of Ida B. Wells* ed. Alfreda Duster. (Chicago University of Chicago Press, 1970), p. 35-37.

2. James Elbert Cutler, *Lynch Law* (New York: Negro University Press, 1969), p. 229. This is a reprint of 1906 edition.

3. Ida B. Wells, "Lynch Law In All Its Phases," *Our Day,* Vol. II, 1893, p. 335-336, 338. Also see Duster, pp. 49-52.

4. *Ibid.* p. 336.

5. *Ibid.*

6. *Ibid.* p. 338.

7. *Ibid.*

8. Duster, pp. 53-55.

9. Wells, p. 338.

10. *Ibid.* pp. 338-339.

11. *Ibid.* p. 339.

12. *Ibid.* p. 340.

13. Duster, pp. 78-81.

Notes: Hall

1. *A New Public Opinion on Lynching: A Declaration and a Pledge*, Bulletin No. 5, 1935.

2. Minutes, ASWPL, Jan. 13-14, 1936, ASWPL Papers, Atlanta University.

3. W.J. Cash, *The Mind of the South* (NY: Random House, 1941), pp. 116-20.

4. Norfolk (Va.) *Journal & Guide*, Jan. 20, 1934; Jessie Daniel Ames to Miss Doris Loraine, March 5, 1935, ASWPL Papers.

5. Minutes, *op cit.*

Notes: Jay

1. The one-woman play, *Gerty, Gerty Stein is Back, Back, Back* starring Pat Bond, has been performed in many cities in the United States and on some public broadcasting television stations.

2. Radclyffe Hall, *The Well of Loneliness* (New York: Pocket Books, 1974).

3. Marie Lénéru, as quoted in *Adventures de l'Esprit* by Natalie Clifford Barney (New York: Arno Press, 1975), p. 258. All translations are by Karla Jay.

4. Jean Chalon, *Portrait d'une Seductrice* (Paris: Stock, 1976), p. 188.

5. Barney's poetic theories and her attempts to establish a new golden age of Sappho will be examined in a dissertation I am working on, tentatively entitled *The Disciples of the Tenth Muse.*

6. Natalie Clifford Barney, *Pensées de l'Amazone* (Paris: Mercure de France, 1939), p. 31.

7. *Ibid.*, p. 6.

8. One might note that Barney could take it upon herself to live wherever she pleased in part because she had inherited about two and a half million dollars.

9. Barney, *Pensées*, p. 17.

10. Natalie Clifford Barney, *The One Who Is Legion, Or A.D.'s After-Life* (London: Partridge, 1930), p. 126.

11. Laura Dreyfus-Barney, as quoted in the *Los Angeles Record*, April 13, 1925, page 2.

Notes: Kling

1. George Sewell, *The Black Collegian*, May/June, 1978.

2. Phyl Garland, "Builders of a New South," *Ebony Magazine*, August, 1966.

Notes: Evans

1. See Gerda Lerner, *The Grimke Sisters From South Carolina: Pioneers for Women's Rights and Abolition* (New York: Schocken, 1971), 161-62.

2. Confidential interview; Judith Brown to Anne Braden, September 19, 1968, Carl and Anne Braden Papers, Box 82, State Historical Society of Wisconsin.

3. Elizabeth Sutherland, ed., *Letters From Mississippi* (New York: McGraw-Hill Book Company, 1865), 22-23.

4. Quoted in Cleveland Sellers, *The River of No Return: The Autobiography of a Black Militant and the Life and Death of SNCC* (New York: William Morrow, 1973), 39.

5. Interview with Mary King; "Job Description: Mary King, Communications," carbon copy, n.d., Mary King's personal files.

6. Interview with Cathy Cade.

7. Interview with Mimi Feingold, July 16, 1973, San Francisco, California.

8. Interview with Mary King.

9. Len Holt, *The Summer That Didn't End* (New York: William Morrow, 1965), 12; Interview with Vivian Rothstein, July 9, 1973, Chicago, Illinois.

10. Interview with Dorothy Burlage.

11. "News from SCEF" by Anne Braden (typed), April 30, 1962, and "Statement by Diane Nash Bevel" issued April 20, 1962, (Handwritten draft), Carl and Anne Braden Papers, Box 47, State Historical Society of Wisconsin.

12. Interviews with Jean Wiley, July 26, 1973, Washington, D.C.; Gwen Patton, June 20, 1973, Washington, D.C.; Fay Bellamy, June 29, 1973, Atlanta, Georgia.

13. Forman, *Making*, 276; Interview with Mimi Feingold.

14. Interviews with Fay Bellamy; Mary King; Ella Baker, July 31, 1973, New York City; Cathy Cade; Nan Grogan, June 28, 1973, Atlanta, Georgia; Jean Wiley; Betty Garman and Jean Wiley, July 26, 1973, Washington, D.C.

15. "To: Student Nonviolent Coordinating Committee, From: Joni Rabinowitz, Southwest Georgia Project," April 8-21. (1963) Joni Rabinowitz's personal files.

16. This conclusion is inferred from interviews with Fay Bellamy, Gwen Patton, Jean Wiley, and Betty Garman.

17. Interviews with Cathy Cade, Vivian Rothstein, Sue Thrasher, and Nan Grogan.

18. Interview with Staughton Lynd, November 4, 1972, Chicago, Illinois.

19. Interview with Mary King.

20. Interview with Dorothy Burlage.

21. Interview with Jimmy Garret, July 16, 1973, Washington, D.C.

22. Interview with Staughton Lynd; interview with Nan Grogan.

23. Interview with Howard Zinn, August 7, 1973, Boston, Massachusetts; Josephine Carson, *Silent Voices: The Southern Negro Woman Today* (New York: Delacorte Press, 1969); Zinn, *SNCC.*

24. Interview with Dorothy Burlage; Mary King.

25. Casey Hayden and Mary King, "Sex and Caste: A Kind of Memo," *Liberation* (April, 1966), 35-36.

Notes: Bromley

1. *The American Heritage Dictionary,* 1969.

2. August Meier and Elliott Rudwick, *CORE: A Study in the Civil Rights Movement, 1942-1968* (New York: Oxford University Press, 1973).

3. Eleanor Emmons Maccoby and Carol Nagy Jacklin, *Psychology Today,* December, 1974, adapted from *The Psychology of Sex Differences* (Stanford, CA: Stanford University Press, 1974).

4. Evelyn Reed, *Woman's Evolution from Matriarchal Clan to Patriarchal Family* (New York: Pathfinder Press, Inc., 1974).

5. Margaret Mead and James Baldwin, *A Rap on Race* (Philadelphia and New York: J.B. Lippincott Company, 1971).

6. Shelley Douglass, "Nonviolence and Feminism," *Fellowship Magazine,* July-August, 1975.

7. Francis L. Broderick and August Meier, eds., *Negro Protest Thought in the Twentieth Century* (Indianapolis, IN: Bobbs-Merrill, 1965).

8. Larry Gara, *The 1976 Peace Calendar* (New York: War Resisters League, 1976).

9. Hannah Josephson, *Jeannette Rankin* (Indianapolis: Bobbs-Merrill, 1974).

Notes: Bishop

1. See David Dellinger, *More Power Than We Know* (Garden City: Anchor Press, 1975) for an excellent analysis of problems within the anti-war movement of the 1960s.

2. Andrea Dworkin, "Redefining Nonviolence," in *Our Blood: Prophecies and Discourses on Sexual Politics* (New York: Harper & Row, 1976) pp. 66-72.

3. *Ibid.*, p. 72.

4. Pete Seeger, "Rainbow Race and World Of . . ." in *Survival Songbook* © 1970 Sanga Music, Inc.

5. A Mary Daly word. She explains it: "By biophilic I mean life-loving. This term is not in the dictionary, although the term *necrophilic* is there, and is commonly used." *Gyn/Ecology: The Metaethics of Radical Feminism* (Boston: Beacon Press, 1978) p. 10.

6. Naomi Goldenberg, *Changing of the Gods: Feminism and the End of Traditional Religions* (Boston: Beacon Press, 1979)

7. Adrienne Rich, *The Dream of a Common Language* (New York: Norton, 1978) p. 29.

Notes: Patterson

1. Margaret Adams, "The Compassion Trap," published in *Women in Sexist Society: Studies in Power and Powerlessness,* Vivian Gornick & Barbara K. Moran, eds., (New York: Basic Books Inc., 1971), p. 555-575.

Notes: Costello

1. Louis Fischer, *The Essential Gandhi* (New York: Random House, Inc., 1962), p. 201.

2. M.K. Gandhi, *The Story of My Experiments With Truth* (Boston: Beacon, 1968), p. 276.

3. Fischer, p. 246.

4. Gandhi, p. 278.

5. William Shirer, *Gandhi: A Memoir* (New York: Simon and Schuster, 1979), p. 230.

6. Shirer, p. 236.

7. Fischer, p. 318.

8. Shirer, p. 36.

9. M. K. Gandhi, *Young India,* 10 IV, 1930.

Notes: Leghorn

1. U.N. Report, 1980. Unless otherwise noted, future references and statistics are found in *Woman's Worth: Sexual Economics and the World of Women,* Leghorn and Parker (Routledge and Kegan Paul, 1981).

2. Women's Equity Action Fact Sheet, available from: 805 15th St. N.W., Suite 822, Washington, D.C. 20005., February 1982.

3. Jack Anderson, "Corporate 'welfare' clients feel no pinch," syndicated column, April 27, 1982.

4. Women's Supportive Services Newsletter, Claremont, N.H., Jan.-March, 1982.

Notes: Malpede

1. Mary Daly, *Gyn/Ecology: The Metaethics of Radical Feminism* (Boston: Beacon, 1978), p. 215. The book she cites, *A Sexual Study of Men in Power,* is by Sam Janus, Barbara Bess and Carol Saltus (Engelwood Cliffs, NJ: Prentice Hall, 1977).

2. Jane Ellen Harrison, *Prologomena to the Study of Greek Religion* (London: Merlin Press, 1980), p. 71. All the information on the Greek rites of holocaust and pharmakos is taken from this work.

3. Aeschylus, *The Eumenidies,* trans. Paul Roche (New York: Mentor, 1962), p. 190.

4. *Ibid.*, p. 186.

5. Agamemnon committed infanticide when he sacrificed his daughter for, though she was grown, he knew she was his child. Infanticide must have been the worst imaginable crime in matriarchal societies because women's bond with their children was the primary social bond. Under patriarchy, the same children whose actual lives are threatened by the father's ascent to rule over them owe their allegiance to him. The mother is helpless to save children from their father's wrath because the children must turn away from her for the sake of their own (tenuous) survival. The consequent complex of emotional disorders given rise to by this system of betrayal/fear/authority/obedience is the stuff of Western culture which now threatens to destroy us all. The antidote to world-death is the reestablishment of the mother-child bond as the human connection which imparts its values to the rest of the society. In order to be worthy of this, women have to mobilize our strength until we become able to defend our children against all forms of emotional and physical patriarchal deadenings.

Bibliographic Note:

This paper owes an immense debt to the work of many feminist writers and thinkers who have spoken and published before me. In particular: Adrienne Rich, *Of Woman Born;* Mary Daly, *Gyn/Ecology;* Elizabeth Fisher, *Women's Creation.* I would especially like to acknowledge feminist pschotherapist. Dr. Jean Mundy, novelist and critic Erika Duncan, and Dr. Dorothy Dinnerstein, author of *The Mermaid and the Minotaur,* whose conversations are invaluable to me and whose insights find their way into almost everything I write. Susan Griffin's *Pornography and Silence* was published after this paper was written but it deals at length and so eloquently and intelligently with these same concerns I feel I must mention it here.

Notes: Wright

1. Anne Kent Rush, *Moon, Moon* (Random House, 1976), p. 282.

2. This kind of polarizing—which is really just exposing a conflict already there, and in which no one is permanently a "bad guy" but can shift positions at any stage, and where polarization is just one stage in a fluid situation—is very different from the rigid separating and objectifying that too much sunpower produces.

Notes: Rayman

1. Karl Mannheim, *Ideology and Utopia* (New York: Harcourt, Brace and World, 1936), p. 192.

2. Kate Millet, *Sexual Politics* (New York: Doubleday, 1970), p. 28.

3. Marge Piercy, *Woman on the Edge of Time* (New York: Alfred Knopf, 1976), p. 134.

4. Quote from Barbara Taylor's fine article, "Lords of Creation: Marxism, Feminism and 'Utopian Socialism,' " reprinted in *Radical America,* Vol. 14, no. 4, p. 46.

5. Joan Bondurant, *Conquest of Violence* (Berkeley: University of California Press, 1971), p. 30. This book provides an excellent accounting of Gandhian philosophy.

6. Krishnaldi Shridharani, *War Without Violence* (New York: Harcourt, Brace and World, 1939), p. 316.

7. Barbara Deming, "New Women, New Men," in *We Cannot Live Without Our Lives,* Grossman Publishers, NY, 1974, p. 4. This essay is available in pamphlet form from New Society Publishers, 4722 Baltimore Ave., Phila., PA 19143.

8. Bondurant, op. cit., p. 124.

9. Adrienne Rich, *Of Woman Born* (New York: Bantam, 1977), p. 67.

10. My appreciation to Andrea Dworkin, who in her provocative article, "Feminism and the Radical Left," *American Report* (reprint available Box 1001, Palo Alto, California) quotes Virginia Woolf's *Three Guineas* at length.

11. Taylor, op. cit., p. 42.

12. Hayden, op. cit., p. 187.

13. Mary Roodkovsky, "Feminism, Peace and Power," in *Nonviolent Action and Social Change,* editors S. Bruyn and P. Rayman (New York: John Wiley, 1979), p. 265.

14. Taylor, op. cit., p. 41.

15. George Kateb, *Utopia and Its Enemies* (New York: Schocken Books, 1972), p. 122. This work is an invaluable resource for those interested in the philosophical issues concerning utopia.

16. Virginia Woolf, *Three Guineas* (New York: Harcourt Brace Jovanovich, 1966), p. 142.

Notes: Walker

1. Zora Neale Hurston, *Mules and Men* (Indiana U. Press, 1935).

Notes: Landerman

1. Donald J. Mulvhill, et al., "Crimes of Violence," a staff report to the National Commission on the Causes and Prevention of Violence, Washington: U.S. Government Printing Office, Vol II, 1969.

2. Deb Friedman, "Rape, Racism and Reality," *Feminist Alliance Against Rape Newsletter* July/August 1978, P.O. Box 21033, Washington, D.C. 20009 and Davis, "Rape, Racism and the Capitalist Setting" (April, 1978).

3. Susan Brownmiller, *Against Our Will* (New York: Simon and Schuster, 1975).

4. Davis, "Rape, Racism and the Capitalist Setting" (April, 1978) and Brownmiller, *Against Our Will* (1975).

5. See sections on rape in the Black and Puerto Rican communities in Hartford, CT in the final report, "Evaluation of Outreach to Black and Puerto Rican Women," NIMH Grant No. R01 MH 30620, National Center for the Prevention and Control of Rape, 5600 Fishers Lane, Rockville, MD 20857.

Sources: Michalowski

Wayne Eisenhart, "You Can't Hack It Little Girl: A Discussion of the Covert Psychological Agenda of Modern Combat Training," *Journal of Social Issues*, Vol. 31, No. 4, 1975.

Wayne Eisenhart, "Flower of the Dragon: An example of Applied Humanistic Psychology," *Journal of Humanistic Psychology*, Vol. 17, No. 1, Winter 1977.

Robert J. Lifton, *Home From the War: Vietnam Veterans, Neither Victims Nor Executioners* (New York: Simon & Schuster, 1973).

Clark Smith, editor, "The Short-timers: Soldiering in Vietnam," unpublished manuscript.

Notes: Salamone

1. The word "his" is used here to emphasize that we function in a male world.

2. The word "humaneness" is the author's self-made word.

3. "Interspecies," a coined term, is used here to mean that a person's consciousness is raised to the point where justice is broadened to extend beyond the human race.

Notes: Bedard

1. Barbara Ehrenreich: "A Funny Thing Happened On the Way to Socialist Feminism." (*Heresies*, Vol. 3, No. 1, Issue 9, 1980).

Notes: Gambill

1. The dictionary describes gossip as "trifling, often groundless, rumor; idle talk," *(The American Heritage Dictionary)*. But the root of the word in Middle English means close friend; in Old English, kinsman. Many of our foremothers used quilting bees and canning parties as times to exchange information, pass on history, renew their bonds. Was it within this oral tradition that gossip carried the meaning of kinsman and close friend? Is it only in the present day that gossip has come to mean behavior which fosters division and often distortion of the truth? There is a difference between the networking of information so necessary to our survival and rumors that jam up our collective endeavors.

2. The names of women have been changed.

3. There may be times when one or more persons cannot confront a situation head on. They may need more time, different kinds of support, or, for whatever reason, they might not be able to handle what others want them to take on. It's important to be careful not to force a situation against the will of those involved.

Further Reading
Compiled by Pam McAllister

Books specifically on nonviolence are largely written by men and present a decidedly male understanding of nonviolence; that is, they generally fail to address the possibility that the male tradition as warrior or the predominance and nature of patriarchal values play a part in creating and maintaining violence. Yet there is much for us to learn from these books. I recommend reading them with a red pen in hand so that you can write in the margins, fill in the holes you'll find right at the heart of their work.

A true understanding of the spirit of feminism and nonviolence can best be gotten from reading about the lives of a variety of women, whether those women ever uttered the words "nonviolence" or "feminism" or marched in an anti-war parade. So much of women's literature and life-stories incorporates an organic nonviolent sensibility and provides us with examples of ways to exert life-affirming pressure on oppressive institutions.

This is not a comprehensive bibliography, but a list of books I've found thought-provoking as a student of feminism and nonviolence. They are grouped by theme or genre and loosely arranged in recommended reading order.

Feminism/Nonviolence

- **Three Guineas** by Virginia Woolf (New York: Harcourt Brace Jovanovich, 1938, 1966) . . . *Woolf's witty, scathing look at the prevention of war and the connections between patriarchal values and militarism.*
- **We Cannot Live Without Our Lives** by Barbara Deming (New York: Grossman Publishers, 1974) . . . *the book most often excerpted in feminist/pacifist works . . . here Deming struggles with women's anger, racial inequality, her oppression as a lesbian, and militarism. The essay, "New Men, New Women: Some Notes on Nonviolence" is probably the best single explanation of the concept of nonviolent struggle. If I could recommend only one book, this would be it.*

Also by Deming: • **Prison Notes** (Boston: Beacon Press, 1966) . . . *a journal from the month Deming and 35 other civil-rights peace activists were locked in the Albany city jail, Georgia, 1964 . . . very much about love, courage, resistance, transformation, and the power of nonviolence.*

- **Revolution and Equilibrium** (New York: Grossman Publishers, 1971) . . . *a collection of essays and talks offered as studies of nonviolent action, not in the abstract, but in the context of actual confrontation . . . the title essay is essential to any study of nonviolence.*
- **Remembering Who We Are** (Florida: Pagoda Publications, 1981) . . . *a collection of dialogues including a reply to lawyer Arthur Kinoy in "Love Has Been Exploited Labor."*

- **Our Blood: Prophecies and Discourses on Sexual Politics** by Andrea Dworkin (New York: Harper & Row, 1976) . . . *essays and speeches including the much quoted "Redefining Nonviolence" . . . Dworkin shows patriarchy to be a sexual police state in which women are meant to learn physical and spiritual submission.*
- **Thinking Like a Woman** by Leah Fritz, with afterword by Barbara Deming (Rifton, New York: WIN Books, 1975) . . . *gutsy, insightful Fritz offers essays written over a ten year period of great changes in her life and thinking.*
- **Ain't No Where We Can Run: Handbook for Women on the Nuclear Mentality** by Susan Koen and Nina Swaim (Norwich, Vermont: WAND, 1980) . . . *carefully detailed arguments to defeat pro-nuclear reasoning . . . the authors identify an imbalance in male and female energy and resulting overload of male-defined power as the primary cause of nuclear mentality.*
- **Loaded Questions: Women in the Military** edited by W. Chapkis (Amsterdam, Transnational Institute, 1981) . . . *essays on the ambivalences feminists face regarding women in military service, addressing, for example, the differences between women in liberation armies and those in armies used to repress liberation struggles.*
- **Valiant Friend: The Life of Lucretia Mott** by Margaret Hope Bacon (New York: Walker and Company, 1980) . . . *the story of a radical reformer, Quaker, pacifist, anti-slavery leader and feminist born in 1793.*
- **Lela Secor: A Diary in Letters 1915–1922,** edited by Barbara Moench Florence, foreword by Eleanor Flexner (New York: Burt Frankline & Company, Inc., 1978) . . . *a collection of life-filled letters from a feminist, journalist, peace activist from the World War I era.*

- **From Parlor to Prison: Five American Suffragists Talk About Their Lives** edited and with an introduction by Sherna Gluck (New York: Vintage Books, 1976) . . . *five women tell what it was like to be suffragists in the movement's rank and file.*
- **Moving the Mountain: Women Working for Social Change** by Ellen Cantarow with Susan Gushee O'Malley and Sharon Hartoman Strom (Old Westbury, New York: The Feminist Press, 1980) . . . *oral history which documents how people "behind the scenes" build mass movements for social change.*

Nonviolence

- **The Power of the People: Active Nonviolence in the United States,** edited and produced by Robert Cooney and Helen Michalowski (Culver City, California: The Peace Press, Inc. 1977) . . . *portraits of peace activists, movements, organizations and actions.*
- **Gandhi: A Memoir** by William L. Shirer (New York: Touchstone Books, Simon and Schuster, 1979) . . . *India and Gandhi come alive in these anecdotes which reveal the magic of Gandhi's aura as well as his political inconsistencies and other failings.*
- **Gandhi On Non-Violence** edited by Thomas Merton (New York: New Directions Publishing Corp., 1965) . . . *selections taken from Gandhi's* **Non-Violence in Peace and War** *with Merton's clarifying comments.*
- **Conquest of Violence: The Gandhian Philosophy of Conflict** by Joan Bondurant (Berkeley: University of California Press, 1969) . . . *spells out the central ideas of Gandhi's political thought.*
- **The Politics of Nonviolent Action** by Gene Sharp (Boston: Porter Sargent Publishers, 1973) . . . *a three volume work on the theory, strategies and analysis of nonviolent action.* **Part Two, The Methods of Nonviolent Action: Political Jiu-Jitsu,** *offers almost two hundred examples of different kinds of nonviolent strategies.*
- **Nonviolence in America: A Documentary History** edited by Staughton Lynd (New York: Bobs-Merrill Company, Inc., 1966) . . . *a collection of primary sources—from William Penn to Barbara Deming.*
- **The Quiet Battle: Writings on the Theory and Practice of Non-Violent Resistance** edited by Mulford Q. Sibley (New York: Anchor Books, Doubleday, 1963) . . . *case studies in nonviolent resistance from modern day U.S. as well as from*

colonial Pennsylvania, India, ancient Rome, South Africa, Hungary, Norway . . . however, out of 27 contributions, only one is by a woman.

- **Selma, Lord, Selma: Girlhood Memories of the Civil-Rights Days,** by Sheyann Webb and Rachel West Nelson as told to Frank Sikora (New York: Morrow, 1980) . . . *two young Black women share their unique memories of the events surrounding "Bloody Sunday" and the Selma-to-Montgomery march with poignant anecdotes about Martin Luther King.*
- **Safe Passage On City Streets** by Dorothy T. Samuel (Nashville: Parthenon Press, 1975) . . . *inner confidence, good-will and conflict resolution skills are proposed as alternatives to locked doors and hand guns, illustrated by numerous anecdotes.*

Feminism

- **Feminism: The Essential Historical Writings** edited and with an introduction and commentaries by Miriam Schneir (New York: Vintage Books, 1972) . . . *the best of 150 years of writings on women's struggle for freedom . . . a good basic text.*
- **The Underside of History: A View of Women Through Time** by Elise Boulding (Colorado: Westview Press, 1976) . . . *a macrohistory of women in which militarism is treated as pathology.*
- **Rape: The Power of Consciousness** by Susan Griffin (New York: Harper & Row, 1979) . . . *the best book I know on the rape mentality, these powerful essays are both exposé and poetry.*

  Also by Griffin: • **Woman and Nature: The Roaring Inside Her** (New York: Harper & Row, 1978) . . . *patriarchal thought, distorted, fragmented, "objective," is exposed and true knowledge restored in this healing work.*
- **Diving Deep and Surfacing: Women Writers On Spiritual Quest** by Carol P. Christ (Boston: Beacon, 1980) . . . *Christ analyzes works by Kate Chopin, Margaret Atwood, Doris Lessing, Adrienne Rich and Ntozake Shange which give voice to women's search for spiritual renewal while the traditionally sacred texts exclude women.*
- **Mother Wit: A Feminist Guide to Psychic Development** by Diane Mariechild (Trumansburg, New York: Crossing Press, 1981) . . . *a political awareness of feminism and nonviolence informs this collection of meditations, rituals, and exercises for healing, spiritual growth and psychic awareness.*

- **The Politics of Women's Spirituality: Essays On the Rise of Spiritual Power Within the Feminist Movement** edited by Charlene Spretnak, (New York: Doubleday Anchor, 1982) *. . . arranged in three parts: "Discovering a History of Power," "Manifesting Personal Power," and "Transforming the Political."*
- **This Bridge Called My Back: Writings by Radical Women of Color** edited by Cherrie Moraga and Gloria Anzaldua, foreword by Toni Cade Bambara (Watertown, Massachusetts: Persephone Press, 1981) . . . *prose, poetry, personal narrative and analysis covering issues of class struggle, racism in the women's movement, homophobia.*
- **Take Back the Night: Women on Pornography** edited by Laura Lederer with afterword by Adrienne Rich (New York: William Morrow and Co., Inc., 1980) . . . *proposes that the $4 billion pornography industry in the United States is about violence against women.*

Poetry and Fiction

- **For Earthly Survival** by Ellen Bass (Santa Cruz, California: Moving Parts Press, 1980) . . . *these poems express the deep anguish of a mother whose joy and love for her baby mingle with agony at the threat of nuclear destruction.*
- **Meridian** (a novel) by Alice Walker (New York: Harcourt Brace Jovanovich, 1976) . . . *a young Black woman holds to her belief in nonviolent resistance even as the Civil Rights Movement gives way to the spirit of violent revolution, and through her struggle we are confronted with the dilemma of how to change the patterns of society without destroying what is good in it.*
- **The Wanderground: Stories of the Hill Women** by Sally Miller Gearhart (Watertown, Massachusetts: Persephone Press, 1978) . . . *Mother Earth has revolted: men's cars, machines, penises no longer function outside the highly technological, computerized cities . . . women have fled to the hills where they struggle to live in harmony with nature and each other.*
- **Woman On the Edge of Time** by Marge Piercy (New York: Fawcett, 1976) . . . *a utopia seen through the eyes of a late 20th century female Hispanic patient in a mental institution . . . the good future is one in which women and men share work and love and nurturing responsibilities.*

- **Herland** by Charlotte Perkins Gilman (New York: Pantheon Books, 1979) . . . *written in 1915, Herland presents an all-woman utopia in which "home" and "wife" as well as the devil, damnation and a personalized god are all eliminated and denounced.*
- **The Kin of Ata Are Waiting For You** by Dorothy Bryant (New York: Moon Books, co-published by Random House, 1971) . . . *describes a highly ritualized utopia where social and inner harmony is pursued according to the dictates of each person's dreams.*
- **Happy Birthday, Wanda June** (a play) by Kurt Vonnegut Jr. (New York: Dell Publishing Co., Inc., 1970) . . . *this rather zany play makes some good points about masculinity and war.*

Bibliographies

- **Readings on Feminism and Nonviolence** compiled by Vicki Rovere (War Resisters League, also printed in WIN, March 9, 1978) . . . *especially good for the pamphlets and articles suggested.*
- **A Bibliography on Nonviolent Action** by Lynne Shivers (Philadelphia, Movement for a New Society) . . . *highlights basic texts on nonviolence with concise synopses.*
- **81 Women Leaders in Nonviolence** (based on the research of James Bould and students at Scripps College, Claremont, California. Distributed by War Resisters League/West, San Francisco, CA) . . . *a list of women who have worked for nonviolent social change.*
- **Women In America: A Guide to Books, 1963–1975, With an Appendix on Books Published 1976–1979** by Barbara Haber (U. of Illinois, 1981) . . . *annotations of 650 books about American women beginning with the publication of Friedan's* The Feminine Mystique, *in 1963.*
- **Disarmament and Masculinity** by John Stoltenberg (Palo Alto, California: Frog in the Well, 1978) . . . *an outline guide and bibliography for studying the connection between sexual violence and war.*

INDEX

D

E

F

This index is the work of the Twin Oaks Indexing Collective. Twin Oaks is an egalitarian, nonviolent, utopian community located in Virginia.